Future's Theory

FUTURE'S THEORY

The Future's Theory series showcases original works on the secretive, emergent, and multiple worlds to come. These include visionary reflections on eventual or hypothetical futures that will irreversibly transform society, culture, technology, ecology, literature, philosophy, art, political movements, information pathways, biogenetics, architecture, media, and design.

Each volume searches after the most far-reaching implications and conceptual territories of the next epochs: artificial intelligence and virtual reality, surveillance regimes and megacities, speed and migration, digital knowledge and machinic power, image-worlds and object-worlds, utopia and dystopia, the human and the inhuman.

Ultimately, by placing renowned thinkers at the forefront of this multidimensional constellation of futuristic themes, simultaneously confronting the limitless challenges and possibilities of the beyond, Future's Theory offers rare speculative insight into those forces and events that are changing our paradigms for all time to come - a looking-glass into the outer boundaries of the unknown.

Editorial Board: Arshin Adib-Moghaddam, Nandita Biswas Mellamphy, Una Chung, Cymene Howe, Amy Ireland, Ed Keller, Nora Khan, Bogna Konior, Carla Leitão, Anna Longo, Dejan Lukic, Michael Marder, Dan Mellamphy, Thomas Mical, Reza Negarestani, Laura Tripaldi

Other titles in the series:

Spectral Futures, edited by Bernd Herzogenrath

Future's Theory

Philosophies from the Worlds to Come

**Edited by
Jason Bahbak Mohaghegh**

BLOOMSBURY ACADEMIC
LONDON • NEW YORK • OXFORD • NEW DELHI • SYDNEY

BLOOMSBURY ACADEMIC

Bloomsbury Publishing Plc, 50 Bedford Square, London, WC1B 3DP, UK
Bloomsbury Publishing Inc, 1359 Broadway, New York, NY 10018, USA
Bloomsbury Publishing Ireland, 29 Earlsfort Terrace, Dublin 2, D02 AY28, Ireland

BLOOMSBURY, BLOOMSBURY ACADEMIC and the Diana logo are trademarks of Bloomsbury Publishing Plc

First published in Great Britain 2026

Copyright © Jason Bahbak Mohaghegh, and Contributors, 2026

Jason Bahbak Mohaghegh has asserted his right under the Copyright, Designs and Patents Act, 1988, to be identified as Editor of this work.

Series design by Charlotte Willow Retief
Cover image © Marcus Cramer / Unsplash

All rights reserved. No part of this publication may be: i) reproduced or transmitted in any form, electronic or mechanical, including photocopying, recording or by means of any information storage or retrieval system without prior permission in writing from the publishers; or ii) used or reproduced in any way for the training, development or operation of artificial intelligence (AI) technologies, including generative AI technologies. The rights holders expressly reserve this publication from the text and data mining exception as per Article 4(3) of the Digital Single Market Directive (EU) 2019/790.

Bloomsbury Publishing Plc does not have any control over, or responsibility for, any third-party websites referred to or in this book. All internet addresses given in this book were correct at the time of going to press. The author and publisher regret any inconvenience caused if addresses have changed or sites have ceased to exist, but can accept no responsibility for any such changes.

A catalogue record for this book is available from the British Library.

A catalog record for this book is available from the Library of Congress.

ISBN: HB: 978-1-3504-2104-2
PB: 978-1-3504-2103-5
ePDF: 978-1-3504-2105-9
eBook: 978-1-3504-2106-6

Series: Future's Theory

Typeset by Deanta Global Publishing Services, Chennai, India
Printed and bound in Great Britain

For product safety related questions contact productsafety@bloomsbury.com.

To find out more about our authors and books visit www.bloomsbury.com and sign up for our newsletters.

Contents

Prologue: Enter Future Jason Mohaghegh viii

Part I Seven Prophecies of the Future 1

Chapter 1.0 Chimera 4

Chapter 2.0 Cipher 24

Chapter 3.0 Temple 44

Chapter 4.0 Reign 62

Chapter 5.0 Oracle 82

Chapter 6.0 Surface 99

Chapter 7.0 Idol 116

Part II Future Labs 141

Chapter 1.0 Future Time Lab: Concepts: Speed, Memory, Death *Ed Keller* 144

Chapter 2.0 Future Space Lab: Concepts: Atmosphere, Dimension, The Infinite *Jason Bahbak Mohaghegh* 152

Chapter 3.0 Future Movement Lab: Concepts: Wandering, Migration, the Border *Una Chung and Will Scarlett* 166

Chapter 4.0 Future Body Lab: Concepts: Sensation, Metamorphosis, Desire *Laura Tripaldi and Dana Dawud* 184

Chapter 5.0 Future Image Lab *Concepts: The Vital, the Visionary, the Artwork Dejan Lukic* 197

Chapter 6.0 Future Illusion: Concepts: Dream, Hallucination, Simulation *Nora N. Khan* 211

Chapter 7.0 Future Cosmos Lab: Concepts: Nature, Animality, The Geoscape *Damon Quasravie and Zahra Bonari* 217

Chapter 8.0 Future Thought Lab: Concepts: Consciousness, Perception, Imagination *Dan Mellamphy* 235

Chapter 9.0 Future Machine Lab: Concepts: The Digital, the Cybernetic, the Artificia *Nandita Biswas Mellamphy* 257

Chapter 10.0 Future Power Lab: Concepts: Struggle, Spectacle, Utopia *Arshin Adib-Moghaddam* 277

Chapter 11.0 Future Fashion Lab: Concepts: Appearance, Touch, Materiality *Ghazal Zamani and Jason Mohaghegh* 296

Chapter 12.0 Future Virtual: Concepts: Immersion, Escape, Hyper-Reality *Ali Eslami* 306

Chapter 13.0 Future Violence Lab: Concepts: Decay, Terror, Poison *Reza Negarestani* 315

Chapter 14.0 Future Mysticism Lab: Concepts: Ritual, Sacrifice, Eternity *Andrea Cetrulo* 317

Chapter 15.0 Future Prophecy Lab: Concepts: Speculation, Question, Return *Anna Longo* 322

Chapter 16.0 Future X Lab: Concepts: ? *Federico Nieto, Sasha Shestakova, Anna Engelhardt* 332

Chapter 17.0 Non-Future Lab: Concepts: Threat, Disappearance, Destruction *Danna Albanyan, Sahej Rahal, Damon Quasravie, Asad Khan* 343

Part III Future Library 359

Chapter 1.0 The Cosmological Archive 360
Ed Keller, Nora Khan, Carla Leitão, Jason Mohaghegh, Sahej Rahal, Will Scarlett

Epilogue: Exit Future: Author: Bogna Konior 391

Notes 392
List of Contributors 417
Index 422

Prologue
Enter Future

Jason Mohaghegh

What does it mean to study the unknown, the secretive, and the not-yet-arrived? How does one begin speaking in the enigmatic tongues of the unforeseeable, or execute that rarest imaginative challenge of being three steps ahead of reality? There is, first and foremost, a question of how even to cross, invade, or set foot (password: enter future).

Here we find notes from the eventual, the potential, the imminent, and the unstoppable. This alter-anthology is an endeavor toward visionary thought in an age of disquiet, led by those tempted to explore the most cutting-edge questions facing our next-world horizons. These include captivating shifts in societies, cultures, technologies, ecologies, political formations, information pathways, biogenetics, art and architecture, media and design, film, literature, and philosophical circles. Such a future compendium can therefore be many things:

- A pseudo-oracle—one of double-sided impressions, accurate or misleading prophecies that mark the irreversible (point of no return) or the impossible (never to happen).

- A pseudo-laboratory—one with its own fractal constellation of figures and thematic dimensions stored like liquids in countless vials or tubes (time, space, movement, body, image, illusion, mind, power, machine, the non-future . . .).

- A pseudo-looking glass—one that stares telescopically into prototypes that will change things for all time to come (speed, migration, utopia/dystopia, the cosmological, the holographic, the inhuman).

- A pseudo-library—one that houses all the hypothetical books of a universe, including those not yet written and those never to be written (its own invisibly proliferating archive).

All futures are impostors, one might say. Therefore, the logic of the "pseudo" alone (born of suspicion and pretending) must guide our authors here: that nothing is as it seems, and everything means something else.

[*Note to the Reader*: There are literally thousands of figures, texts, artworks, relics, and events mentioned throughout the coming pages, though the authors here have deliberately chosen to suspend the practice of academic citation and assume a different method (closer to an echo chamber). Instead, you will find in the Endnotes an aerial mosaic of leads and allusions to search at will, an index branching in every direction to form its own tunnel system or control room. These links are meant to be walked like tightropes (to send one somewhere).]

Seven Prophecies of the Future, CityX, Venice Biennale 2021 (Design by Asad Khan).

PART I

Seven Prophecies of the Future

The Seven Prophecies of the Future series was designed as a special program of far-seeing encounters combining images, narratives, and experimental philosophy. Each live-recorded installment between two figures would revolve around one of seven conceptual passwords: Chimera, Cipher, Temple, Reign, Oracle, Surface, and Idol.

In every prophetic episode, speakers were asked to present (1) one obscure myth, fable, legend, fairy tale, or superstition; (2) one aesthetic work from the contemporary realms of visual art, architecture, design, installation, music, dance, theater, cinema, or virtual reality; (3) one emergent phenomenon (innovation, device, object, movement, event) that might allow us to peer into some strange futurity.

These seven episodes were captured as part of the Future Studies Program's exhibition for the Venice Biennale 2021 and transcribed hereafter in seven chapters [moderated by Andrea Cetrulo].

1.0 Chimera

2.0 Cipher

3.0 Temple

4.0 Reign

5.0 Oracle

6.0 Surface

7.0 Idol

PROPHECY 1.0

Chimera

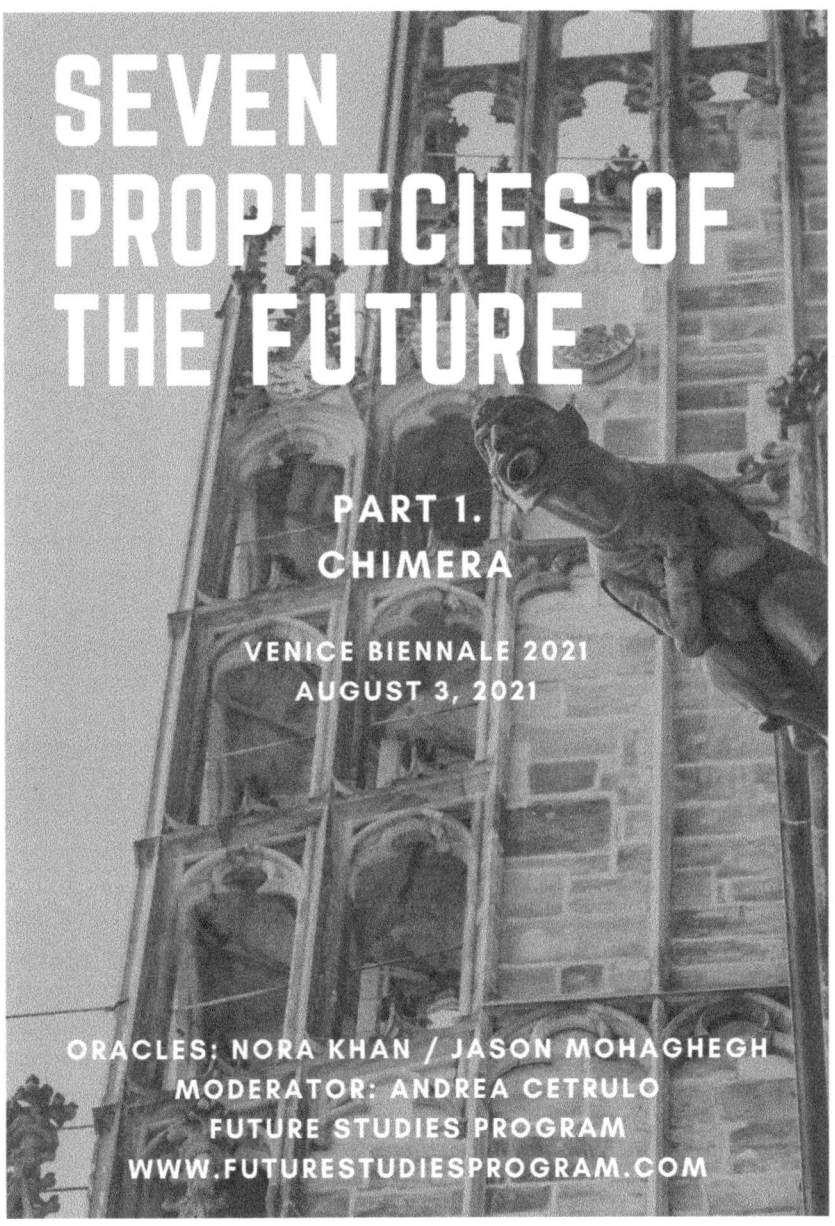

Part 1. Seven Prophecies of the Future (Chimera). *Source*: Artist: kirill_makes_pics.

Chapter 1.0
Chimera

Oracles: Nora Khan, Jason Bahbak Mohaghegh
Guide: Andrea Cetrulo

Andrea Cetrulo: Welcome to Seven Prophecies of the Future, a futuristic series that will take you on an interdisciplinary or transdisciplinary journey of discovery. Each episode will invite two guests who will act as oracles and reveal a secret password to enter a realm filled with poetic images and intriguing phenomena. All oracles are part of a wider divinatory, speculative endeavor—the Future Studies Program—and will be sharing their premonitory visions of the future on the occasion of the Venice Biennale 2021 (Italian Digital Pavilion). We will guide you through corridors that lead us to these oracles of futurity.

In this episode, we will enter the dimension of the hybrid, the monstrous, the non-binary, the seemingly impossible. Password: Chimera. Traditionally, the chimera has been conceived as an individual composed of cells with different embryonic origins that can adopt myriad forms and have diverse, often divergent, connotations. An impossibility or a potential? Today we will expand this notion to other dominions. Theorist, storyteller, and professor of world literature and philosophy Jason Mohaghegh, and writer of fiction and non-fiction focusing on emergent technologies Nora Khan—it is my pleasure and welcome. Each of you will now introduce us to three images that illustrate prophetically what future implications can be found through a particular myth, artistic image, and current phenomenon related to the chimera. Let us start with your myth of choice.

I. Myth—Djinn; Minotaur, Sphinx

Nora Khan: The first chimeras I submit under *Myth* are the djinn. *Djinn* are figures known across the pre-Islamic and Islamic world as spirits; as spirits close to humans, oblique to humans, seeming like humans, who mirror us. And, for many, for my family growing up, they are ever cryptic. In Bangladesh, they are sometimes considered representative of a kind of dark magic. They are a kind of psychological interruption, a bogeyman that you internalize. They live in toilets; they live in wet places, and they hang outside your windows watching you as you go to sleep.

Appealing to djinn, in my experience, or speaking too excitedly of them, was understood to be taboo. They represented a whole other parallel world of near human-like beings. I heard a glut of stories growing up about djinn trying to take folks off the right path, as they were often evoked as a kind of moral prompt: for one to either display religious texts more prominently or to pray evil out of a person (and other drastic moves). Day to day, they were conjured in conversation as a way to terrify you back onto the right path, being scrupulous with each of your decisions.

While barely visible, they can manifest in animal form or human form, or as fire—they are born of smokeless fire. They are a chimerical mix sometimes of animal, human, and fire. They linger in empty parts of the house; they are in the deserted places. And they are real markers of the tiny moral fears that rule the quotidian: to be clean, to say your prayers, to be careful when going out at night, or to not go out at night at all.

Let us consider some images by the Iranian artist Morehshin Allahyari from a series called *She Who Sees the Unknown*. It is a beautiful VR work on djinns from personal memories of the artist, and from her grandmother and her mother, rooted in bathhouses in Iran where djinns were spoken of as lurking in the corners. While Morehshin was making this piece, we together shared a few neuroscientific studies that describe and theorize djinn as manifestations of psychic, collective trauma. Djinn, sleep demons, sleep paralysis figures are other forms in this menagerie. Among the Hmong refugees in the United States, beginning in the 1970s, there was an epidemic of nocturnal deaths—sleep deaths—in which a figure would appear to the sleeper at night and scare them to death. This horrifying phenomenon was later studied and understood as a possible result of the psychic wake of genocide.

And so, for my part, knowing many who grew up in Bangladesh, hearing these kinds of stories, it was not all that hard to imagine the cultural roots of djinn as being rooted in the real. Statistically, women are more likely to believe in djinn's existence, and in possessions by djinn; this can be tied to or concurrent with anxiety, depression, and other mental health issues.

There are many beautiful figurations of djinn we can find in religious texts, but the image that I associate with djinn is this: the partially open window at dusk. I remember my mother sweeping through the house, closing all the windows, saying small prayers under her breath so they would not come in. Djinn are chimerical beings that appear right on the edge of consciousness, right at the open window ledge. A partial human being, about to enter your space.

They are a perfect psychological chimera; they morph and shift with the anxieties and fears of any given moment in a culture. They roam at free will; they shatter a firm notion of the human. They cause mental and emotional harm; they mirror a host of social and personal ailments. Perhaps most importantly for this theme, they are partially known. They linger, partly defined, in one's most intimate spaces and in one's mind.

At last, I think of djinn as intriguing for this conversation as a kind of way to speak on what is not spoken of directly—gender and class violence, the hard-to-capture "outcomes" of war and exile, which are usually the cause of significant mass health issues. But they manifest in day-to-day conversation, in spoken whispers and utterances as a figure that is barely known. A partial way of knowing the world, its changes, and its traumatic turmoil, a stand-in for memories and experiences that are impossible to process at once or look at directly.

> **Andrea Cetrulo:** That is fascinating, Nora. And Jason, what do you have for us as a myth? Your myth of choice?
>
> **Jason Mohaghegh:** If the challenge is for us to explore how the chimera allows us to imagine the future—with chimera generally meaning an unlikely or impossible creature that fuses different species in a dazzling genetic mixture—then immediately we realize that we are in a realm of blurring, confusion, entrancement, and fear. Chimeras are elegant, yet they are also vicious; they possess a profound philosophical consciousness, yet they also consume humans alive and whole, breaking the bones of unfortunate travelers in their jaws. And this paradox of their existential makeup—at once refined and brutal—is what makes them unstoppable.

The two mythic prototypes that I wanted to display are those of the Minotaur (a half-bull, half-man) and the Sphinx (half lion, half-woman or sometimes man), precisely because they use opposing trajectories and semblances to arrive at the same fatalistic outcome. The spatial zone of the Minotaur is that of the labyrinth, which actually embodies a prison or death chamber whose ever-multiplying aisles find him walking or hunting in agonized paces. The aesthetics of the Minotaur is that of rugged beastliness, his horned appearance inspiring repulsion and flight from all who behold him, with the screams of so-called innocent people echoing in his ears. The effects of the Minotaur are pain and rage: the first because his very currency is that of laceration, mutilation, and trampling; the second because his destiny accelerates him to states of frenzy, carnage, and blackout oblivion. The technique of the Minotaur is that of following pure instinct: this emanates from his dominant animality and hunger—note that hunger is a far smoother concept than desire, as it has none of the psychoanalytic layers that impede us—which leads him to the event of the perpetual chase. He stalks beneath elaborate columns; he breathes heavily and relentlessly; he haunts dreams, becoming the iconic representation of monstrosity and destructive force for entire civilizations.

On the other side, we have the Sphinx. The Sphinx is an ambiguous and immense creature whose spatial theater is that of the gateway, as she sits on an elevated pedestal testing all who dare to enter certain cities or pyramids; in this sense, her lethal form and the gesture of her ritualistic questioning together form both the key and lock for outsiders to make passage within. The aesthetics of the Sphinx is that of enchantment; she is alluring, hypnotic, irresistible, and otherworldly; her winged lioness appearance is itself a gravitational energy of seduction (interestingly, her name in ancient Egyptian etymology means "living image"). The effects of the Sphinx are enigma and secrecy, and her technique is that of diabolical obscurity, which means she devises these little music boxes of the riddle that entrap and condemn whoever encounters them in states of bewilderment and futile searching. And then she feasts upon them; when the mind fails, the body feeds, turning human ignorance into her banquet. For centuries, then, and across myriad cultures, she becomes the emblem of the radical unknown; she is an omen at the limits of thought, and she reminds us that we pay a mortal price for our lack of answers.

With all this established, these mythic figures share many rare traits infused in them by virtue of their chimeric origins. First, both are guardians who stand at thresholds in ambush, one the protector of the maze of a mad king and the other the protector of sacred monuments. Second, both are figures of intense solitude, one wandering the endless stone hallways of his house alone and the other left stranded in a resting isolated position on the desert sands. Third, both are agents of terrifying proportions and merciless potential; they impose punishing ends upon those who cross their awful paths. Fourth, the Minotaur and the Sphinx, like almost all chimeras, are synonymous with power, and power defined specifically here as a will to devour, for the ancient definition of catastrophe is just this: that which makes one inseparable from itself, like those petrified victims of volcanoes that we have seen suspended for all time in the flow of lava, ash, and debris that envelops them. So here too, then, chimerical power is represented as that which drags the other into its own folds (encapsulation), or more precisely into the depths of the stomach. Lastly, for all of its ferocity, the chimera is also a figure of the most extreme vulnerability: they are prone to masochistic occasions and a drive to self-annihilation. This is why, when the Argentinian writer Jorge Luis Borges writes the story of the Minotaur, he envisions him actually as a delicate, tormented outcast who ultimately surrenders himself to the blade of the hero because he wishes to die; and similarly, when interpreters explain why the legends of the Sphinx all end with her hurling herself down from her rock and shattering her skeleton below, some say that it is because she fell in love with Oedipus and therefore sacrificially shared with him the answer to her riddle, cheating for him, while others say she simply grew tired of the interminable procession and despair of her practice, as a holder of puzzles, and she decided to take her own life to be released from her duty. Both these mythic outcomes bear some resonance for the futures awaiting us all.

Jinn building a wall for Dhul-Qarnayn to protect the civilized peoples from the barbarians Gog and Magog, sixteenth century, Chester Beatty Library, Dublin.

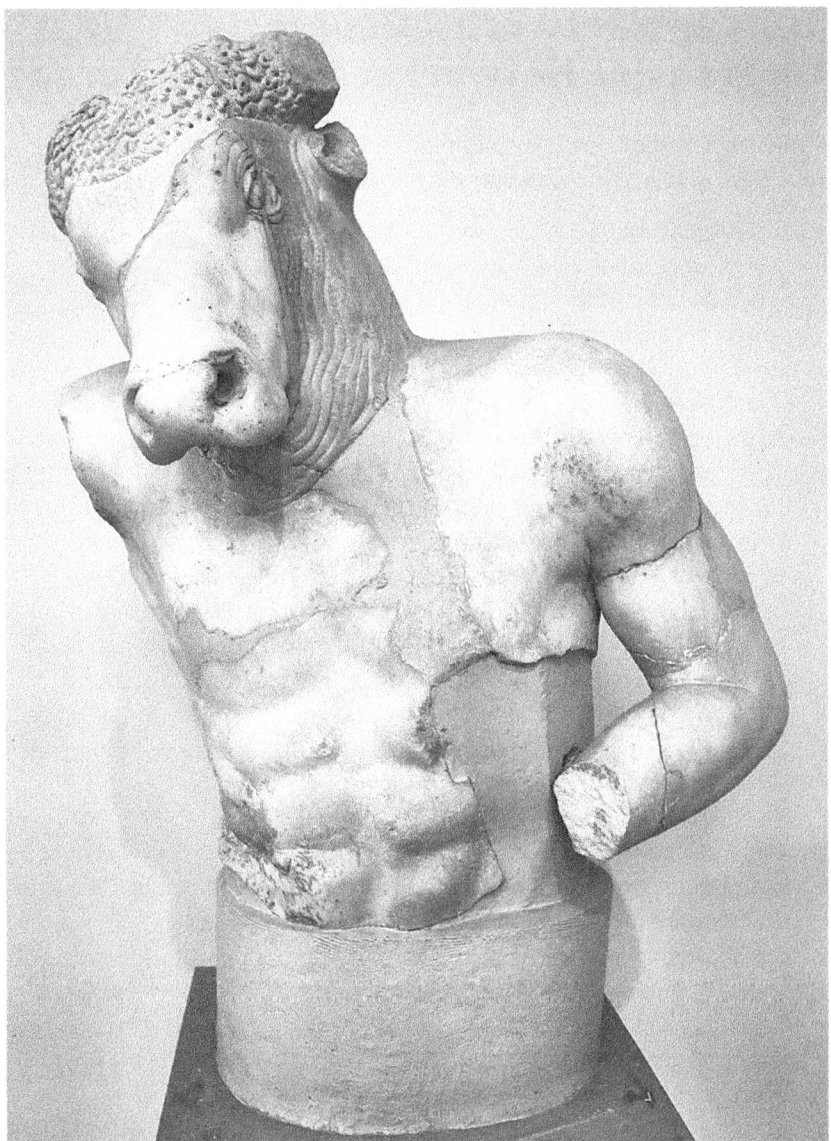

Statue of the Minotaur [Wikimedia, Author/Contributor: George E. Koronaios]. Pentelic marble. Found in Athens, near St. Demetrios Katephoris in Plaka. Roman copy of an early Classical statue by Myron. Accession Number: 1664. National Archaeological Museum of Athens. Athens, Greece.

II. Image/Artwork—Generative Adversarial Networks; Hanging Torsos

Andrea Cetrulo: Now let us move on to the artistic image. Nora, can you share what you have chosen and tell us why?

Nora Khan: I chose, for this section, chimeras of images spit up by GANs (Generative Adversarial Networks). I was looking at the work of Casey Reas (in this particular case, in collaboration with Jan St. Werner). I think of Casey within the vast field of art made with artificial intelligence, with algorithms, with machine learning, drawing on and creating from handcrafted lovingly created datasets—as a standout. He is using the chimerical aspects of generative adversarial networks, GANs, as material in his artistic practice. (As an aside, I am working on a book on the stakes of AI art, and their uniquely chimerical aspects, and keep running into this unique difficulty in capturing what we see as the outputs of these algorithms without a new set of terms.) There has been a great deal written about the potential for AI tools, for machine learning for art—but a majority of the critical descriptions of the images that come out usually focus on "the dream of the machines," or the "product of a collective hallucination," and in some sense the aesthetic is so easily slotted within the suggested imagery of dreams, or what one might imagine a machine dreaming could look like.

But what I think is even more compelling about these images, as I would love to argue in this short bit, is that they have a chimerical kind of logic. When we understand these images as representative of an algorithm in the process of learning, they can be better understood as a capture of a hybrid space—an image that at first seems to be emerging from nowhere, and with inspection, an image that can be placed within a vaguely recognizable aesthetic of a set of symbols, myths, suggestive themes, and figures that we can pin to the film or art the model was trained on.

Further, we are "looking at" a very clear mathematical process—the products of a process in which a trained discriminator algorithm and generator algorithm learn about a set of data, in the case of these images, images from the films of certain directors, like Ingmar Bergman or Alfred Hitchcock. One might understand these images as more than just a machine dreaming. They are captures of growing pattern recognition in process, a neural network "learning" as intended. With effort and analysis, the images might even say something new about Bergman or Hitchcock. A GAN trained on images from *Persona* might start offering up, if we think of the film, types of split faces and fused faces, the ways that Anna, the nurse, and Liv, the stage actress, merge, the famous patterns of Bergman's style, merging their faces, their selves, together throughout the film. We might start to think of the film *Persona*, in terms of its inherent patterns, symbols, and depictions of fusion—and the GAN images, offering a chimerical space of new access to a well-known film through its non-visual world, its negative space, using its still images at a scale and speed that would be impossible for us to achieve without computation. Perhaps, as some artists and critics claim, GANs could help us see film, photography, the canon, anew. This weird seeing through mathematical process is a chimerical relationship.

I see continuity between the psychological figure of the ancient djinn and these future-leaning images. We have always lived comfortably with partial ways of knowing the world. When I try to apply a strict art-historical analysis to these images, I also see human-like figures, partly of the network, partly coming into form, pulled out of a third space. The efforts to capture and name what we are seeing in the depths of AI images are chimerical in nature. The chimera here exists in language; the chimera resists, even defies, the critical language we have and exposes its inadequacies. We are moved to move with the technological subject and the aesthetic chimera presented to us by this or that GAN. Our subject, our precious place as a viewer, is destabilized, and we must move with the figures that are moving before us. What this means for visual criticism is the next stage of chimerical transformation.

Andrea Cetrulo: Thank you Nora. And, Jason, what has captivated you? If you can please share it with us.

Jason Mohaghegh: The artistic figure who I selected to continue unraveling this thread is the South African woman artist Nandipha Mntambo, whose exhibitions over the past years have shown an increasing fascination with the aura of the chimera. From the titles of her exhibitions alone—*Warriors*, *Metamorphoses*, and *The Snake You Left Inside Me*—one can easily uncover these themes of self-transfiguring entities. Her earliest work already displayed a transfixed gaze on the chimera in the form of hanging torsos draped in cowhide that left convoluted the boundaries between the human and the inhuman, the beautiful and the grotesque. Moreover, she describes the material process of shaping these floating silhouettes in an almost excruciating way, stating: "My journey begins with the process of sorting through piles of salted cowhide for the perfect one. In the past I've had the hides tanned for me, but this time I purchased a home tanning kit comprising various different chemicals. Unfortunately, the instructions in the kit didn't adequately prepare me for the next step: power tooling my way through thick layers of fat which need to be removed—a thoroughly nauseating process! After this the hide has to soak in a chemical bath for a week. I then stretch it over my mould—a combination of casts taken from my own body and the limbs of store mannequins, joined together using cretestone and resin. I have to really pull, stretch and nail down the hide so that it takes on the desired shape."[1] So, we see here a procedure that binds the most visceral natural realms—flesh, sinew, muscle, hair, skin, blood—with the realms of the unnatural or artistic artificiality—fabrication, sewing, sculpture.

But these installations also open up several further sub-conceptual chambers related to the chimera: the first is that these body-casts are arranged in rows of almost militant alignment, giving them the sense of being a kind of violent armor, the shape of a legion or squadron, though they are hollowed of their absent wearers (no hero, soldier, fighter, or champion); nevertheless, they are remnants of an age of war.

Second, they are garments that demand hybridity, much like those ancient tribal warriors who would dress in feathers or fanged skulls of the animal before battle; these fighters often devised intricate choreographies that imitated various creatures (wolves, panthers, bears) or adorned their eyes with cosmetic shadows that would allow them to channel the talents of the wild being (their speed, brute strength, or poisonousness). Some tattooed their bodies with scorpions or made prayers to whatever totemic animal spirit in the hopes of opening a vicarious channel of sorts for a short while during the state of emergency that is war. Note that this ritual practice requires a principle of becoming chimera, in that their performative dancing or howling was meant to fling them into an experiential (not literal or metaphoric) transmutation.

Third, it's an intriguing detail that the artist Nandipha Mntambo initially studied to become a forensic pathologist (a field linked to the study of causes of death in a post-mortem body), and so it might also be the case that the chimera must be perceived as a pathological category whose secrets could only be disclosed by forensic formulations, like one image where several hanging chests begin spilling into elongated, tangled roots that get lost in their own twists and turns.

Fourth, like many chimeric versions, the artist's work plays at disturbing the fine lines of androgyny (her *Minotaurus* statue places a feminine spin on the classically virile masculine narrative); but beyond erasing the man-woman divide, she demonstrates a covert chimerical format: that it is only through creative assemblage (mixing particles, segments, and definitions) that one can achieve a state of dissembling (the deceptive concealment of intentions), their complex constellations allowing one to build figures that hide themselves in plain sight.

Finally, it is in Mntambo's latest installation titled *The Snake You Left Inside Me* that she begins tracing the mythic outline and possibilities of Echidna (literally meaning "she-viper," also known as the "mother of monsters," half-beautiful woman and half-hideous huge serpent) who has genealogical links to all teratological offspring including Medusa. Here the artist fashions an incarnation where a silken gown gradually spins into a long, coiling tail—thus the separate fragments of woman and snake are woven into an almost liquid current of intimidation and wonderment. This leads to the final premise of the chimera here: mystification. A perfect amalgamation that retains its disorienting influence—its perplexity, horror, and mysterious implications—even when illuminated. Somehow the closer one comes to it, the more unfathomable it becomes.

III. Phenomenon—Virtual Influencers; Immortality Labs

Andrea Cetrulo: Now Nora, could you follow this up with an emergent phenomenon related to the concept of chimera that has captured your attention?

Nora Khan: I appreciate this exchange. Taking the material Jason presents, watching it transmute it into the next offering. This example speaks to the ideas in Nandipha Mntambo's work and develops it along other, new paths. For an emergent phenomenon: perhaps not immediately, emergent but *she* has evolved in the last four to five years. I chose the chameleon pop icon, the figure of Lil' Miquela. Lil' Miquela is someone that I interviewed about four years ago. She is a virtual influencer who, at that point, had been around for about three years. She is a professional avatar; materially speaking, she is a series of digital paintings on Instagram of a very uncanny teenager who has incredible social justice savvy—a critical studies PhD mixed with incredible style, slouchy, off the runway and deconstructed. The kind of controversy and fandom that she attracts is unbelievable. If you go to any post on her Instagram and read the comments underneath, you can find debates over whether she is human or AI, what does it mean for an AI to feel, and what would it mean for her to actually be in our world, and whether she actually is, in our world. In many ways she is real: she makes $12 million a year; she has an agent through CAA; she is friends with celebrities who appear on her Instagram all the time; she is on billboards everywhere.

She is, for now, a fascinating figure to mine; every day she shares her vulnerabilities, her fears, written in very tidy captions, carefully composed by a team. She has chart-topping singles. For many teens and young adults, she feels like a friend. There are ongoing, raging debates about her morphing ethnicity, her commitments, and her authenticity.

Back then, I was quite struck by how she changed from day to day. Her skin tone would shift; her moods would shift; her style would shift; she would be cutting out posters for Black Lives Matter protests and the next day she would be wearing Prada without a political sentiment in sight. Currently, she is hawking NFTs. She has great writers. You find yourself sucked in immediately and maybe a bit infuriated by her shifting with the day's trends. Lil' Miquela is unusually a virtual figure who has lasted, who figures an algorithmic imagination, by definition chimerical, which we develop in relation to her, to engage with her. We all have professional avatars; we have our figures on Instagram, on Twitter, our professional selves, our real selves—whichever self that may be. I have a student at RISD who describes this as the year of coming out of isolation, after a year of engaging with each other's professional avatars, our faces carefully arranged on Zoom—the multiple digital ambassadors that we live through. Any "authentic self" is an amalgam of all these shifting selves. Lil' Miquela marks a chimerical imagination, the imagination needed to move with her shifts, conflating modes of racial ambiguity, different tactics of oblique appropriation and conflicting social commitments: one day she is committed to capitalism and then she is committed to socialism the next, to techno-utopianism one day but then a critique of technology a few hours later.

Highly provocative, if silly, is the fury that she engenders, which is rooted in the contradictions that her digital self seems to hold. This fury seems to refuse that we are chimerical, contradictory, and complex, changing from moment to moment. That she changes from day to day feels, to those she enrages, like a betrayal, in a flat paradigm in which digital utterances should suggest some fixed sentiments we hold in our hearts.

Wendy Chun, in her new book, speaks eloquently of the effort to authenticate ourselves through all these shifting selves. Being user authenticated has not made, as she argues, the internet any safer: anonymity is not protection. Chimerical shifts are the norm; we confront people who shift in their presentation, rhetoric, and style all the time. These avatars are a bit like djinns, like the half-dreams of GANs, yet another entry in this space where we live with figures we barely trust from day to day. Instead of trying to lock down Lil' Miquela's identity, we shift with her switches, and must understand the shifting performance. There is a delicious challenge in mediating between all these shifting presentations, utterances made and retracted overnight, a moving logic that moves us.

    Andrea Cetrulo: Very intriguing. We will talk more about this later. But before, Jason, what can you tell us about your emerging phenomenon and why we should be paying attention to it?

    Jason Mohaghegh: The phenomenon that strikes me as having chimerical consequences is the gradual rise of immortality labs across the world.

Of course, narratives of immortal beings are not limited to the modern age or to the future: The ancient Babylonians, Egyptians, Persians, Greeks, Chinese, and Aztecs all had their depictions of undying gods, though this did not necessarily mean that such immortal entities were without suffering. Indeed, many of them could be wounded, disfigured, imprisoned, starved, mutilated, or occasionally killed—though they all possessed some power of regeneration, resurrection, or return. These legends of divine immortality of course then translated down to their other celestial counterparts—angels, spirits, and even certain prophets or saints—who remained eternal either in some transcendent faraway sphere or by being embedded in nature (as deities of rivers, mountains, or wind) or as night constellations.

Nevertheless, immortality was not a right given exclusively to the benevolent pantheons, for evil creatures could also win this indestructibility and thereby escape the vanishing touch of time. While some East Asian traditions believed that the cruel dragon species derived immortalizing force from its relation to fire, Middle Eastern folklore spoke of other races (like the *ifrit*) who could grant wishes of enduring life, while still other African, Caribbean, and indigenous cultures would tell fables of sorcerers whose malice or ingenuity had stolen them thousands of years beyond their destiny. Still, what we call demons in ancient terms are obviously the prime example of this accursed immortality, having the same permanence as gods or guardian angels, and we notice to this day that so many characterizations of the monster in our horror genres—the vampire, the werewolf, the mummy, the zombie, the ghost—hold this immortal gift despite being depraved or even soulless.

Moving onward, there also arose countless mythologies about certain spaces that could extend immortality: secret caves where people could sleep for centuries unchanged, remote island hideaways where aging becomes irrelevant, ethereal gardens that had the same properties as paradise, or fountains of youth that with one droplet of their water could cure all afflictions and transfer endlessness to their recipient. Intriguingly, there is a covert history of those conquerors, explorers, or mad adventurers who went in search of such sacred and miraculous sites of immortality, many of whom never returned.

Even more specifically, there emerged narratives surrounding particular rare objects—talismans, rings, gemstones, enchanted mirrors, preserved animal organs, blood, holy grails, or magic lamps—that, if found through courage, theft, violence, or pure luck, would forever protect their newfound owner from the reaper's knife.

But what does immortality mean now, and how does the futuristic search for immortal possibilities borrow from or alter older paradigms? Are we not equally consumed by the chase for the interminable and the unfading, or has this dream perhaps even accelerated to a new obsessive register? This is the essence of the immortality labs, all of which have chimerical repercussions.

First, it was in the 1950s and 1960s that scientists began experimenting with cryonics or cryogenic freezing, where corpses right after clinical death would be stored in low-temperature chambers in the hopes of someday being thawed out and reanimated from their ice states and cured of whatever physical limitations caused their demise. This technology, although gaining in popularity, is often considered controversial and pseudoscientific since it requires a leap of faith that future medical advancements will be able to reawaken the brain's neural networks without severe damage, and also that we can later heal diseases that are presently incurable in our own time.

Our second example is digital cloning, holograms, or even cyborg replicas of the dead. In the first instance, massive archives of information are provided to an artificial intelligence program that then analyzes the data to reproduce the personality of the dead individual with remarkable accuracy and complex detail, even being able to spontaneously answer new questions and react to new situations by logically expanding the identity patterns of their original source. This would be a kind of holographic immortality. In the second instance, the old science fiction paranoia over clones suddenly crossed a real-life threshold when the Russian corporation Promobot invented the world's first humanoid android, which can be designed to resemble any human being and which provides simulated companionship to those who have lost loved ones, although their ultimate aims are to inject these robotic imitations (that can nevertheless act autonomously in some key respects) into every conceivable industry (including education, entertainment, and even government). This would mark an age of electronic immortality.

Still further, there are other elaborate strategies in today's technological discourse, especially those pertaining to the promise of downloaded consciousness. More precisely, this relies on the advent of a digital capturing of the individual's thoughts, memories, conditioning, and fantasies to transmit these components of our being like data particles or computed information capable of being seamlessly implanted in new systems (whether that means an actual new physical body or in the more abstract virtual environment). Imagine the consequences of a human whose entire mental existence can be resuscitated limitlessly by virtue of being contained in a portable storage device that allows signals and interfaces to bring us back to the restart position. Would this not start to resemble those video games in which the player has infinite lives to spare, and what might the effects on society, culture, and self be when the game never concludes? Might this culminate in an excessive sense of exhaustion, nihilistic meaninglessness, or absurd repetition?

Lastly, while we could mention companies that now convert dead family members into decorative objects, concentrating their ashes into diamonds that can be worn as jewelry, let us turn to the more serious debate at this point in human history surrounding what has been titled the "immortality threshold." This refers to a singular crossroads at which genetic engineering, nanotechnology, and other medical advancements escalate to such a degree that they can postpone or eliminate death altogether. Are we gradually reaching this bizarre stage of accomplishment or unnatural mutation? There are several potential answers, each of which hangs in the balance of a different technique of perpetuation: whereas some laboratories are currently researching gene editing in the hopes of preemptively eradicating disease from the DNA substrata, other facilities are studying the secrets of cellular regeneration and other physiological solutions in order to achieve super-longevity. For instance, Google's Calico Lab (which stands for California Life Company) has a team of physicians who, behind closed doors and in confidential, high-security buildings, are developing biotechnology that might allow them to manipulate reverse-aging and stop neurodegeneration. To do this, they are studying a rare species of jellyfish (among other entities) that appears never to die, at least not by natural causes, and to inject such capacities into human genetics. This event, if ever to transpire, would effectively constitute the gateway across the immortality threshold, but it is also an absolute chimera threshold as well: for all of these diverse methods previously discussed imply that we must become interchangeable with ice, machine, avatar, algorithm, or sea creature.

IV. Questions

Andrea Cetrulo: Having traversed these six examples of the chimera, let us proceed with a first question then. As you are both inaugurating oracles of this series, I would like to ask you: What would a prophetic attitude entail? It seems quite evident that imagining alternative futures or even pasts is a difficult task when we are caught up in narratives of the present. So, how could you say that fictions or storytelling of non-binary or contradictory chimeras might help us depart from conventional narratives of the future?

Jason Mohaghegh: I think that the supreme task in contemplating a prophetic imagination in its futural aspect might be to distance ourselves from any of its metaphysical associations and instead go back to what it means to think in terms of trajectories and arcs. Great archers know that, when one is trying to strike a moving target, one must aim ahead of its spotted location. You cannot aim straight at it, and so this requires all kinds of calculations: intuitive ones, experiential ones, the reading of air drafts, the reading of climates, atmospheres, and elevations, which are neither instinctual, because they have a circumstantial reality, nor are they rational, since the pure mind in a vacuum proves useless. But what that also demands is an understanding that the future can fail. Yes, the future can fall apart, and with it the concept of destiny suddenly holds no absolute determinism. There are often rivaling destinies, multiple destinies, missed destinies or lost destinies, defective destinies, gambling destinies; and so there is no guarantee that just because one is endowed with some fatalistic prophecy that one will indeed make it to that culminative moment. You know, Fate also competes with its younger sister, Luck, and luck has its say in the game, has its share of our existence as well—not to mention the Will and a thousand other contestants that are vying for their place in the arena. Along those lines, I remember once reading a great East European writer, Ruxandra Cesereanu, who has an untranslated work about fugitives who make incredible prison-breaks, and the first thing that must happen for them to succeed is the realization that the odds are against them: the improbability of the venture, and the likelihood of being caught. If one proceeds with a heavy air of confidence or delusion of grandeur, then one will not survive because it hinders the ability to become versatile and resilient at the time of escape.

Nora Khan: I return, always, to *The Carrier Bag Theory of Fiction* which has sustained so many writers and artists at this moment: a short sharp essay by Ursula K. Le Guin in which she reads prophecies of scientific advancement and technological advancement, the dream of power, the hero's journey. It is a four-page warning shot, a plea for the desperate need for new stories—both of failure, Jason, as you just described, and of alternate ways of knowing and alternate ways of explaining the story of the world. In any technological era, alongside a dream of perfect explainability, be it perfect AI explainability, there also comes a rise in mystification and mysticism. And so, I was compelled, Jason, in your lab, by this description of how we have depended on other entities throughout history.

We can think of this menagerie of human-like beings or humanoid beings—as representative modes that we have invented, modes of partial knowing. My hope for future prophecies is to have space for acknowledgment of how the partially human, and these ways of partial knowing, have been vital for our psychological evolution. Whether it is animist studies or thinking about spirits or thinking about AI, these figures are stand-ins for our own ability to evolve steps behind rapidly evolving fields, psychological scaffolding for reading and making sense of massive trends beyond our cognitive reach. They are scrying screens for heady computational leaps, for obscene technological leaps; we have new djinn-like myths for the algorithmic. Our trust or mistrust of new avatars with our voices, of virtual beings who will speak sense to us, of mythic future AI: these are all part of this continuum. My fear of djinns coming in through the window as a child is now my wariness of animate AI selves that are partial zombified representations of parts of people's instincts accumulated over ten years, twenty years. We are evolving our methods for technological explainability *alongside* these necessary ways of partial knowing. Ways of partial knowing and explaining—fumbling to explainable states—are essential to stories of a future and to our collective cognitive evolution.

> **Andrea Cetrulo:** Yes, I guess that already *partially* answers what I asked and was going to ask now that is related to the chimeras and all the examples you presented. They integrate elements of the real and the unreal and leave us wondering about the natural versus the artificial, the real versus the unreal, the machine versus the human intellect. So it is a modern ethical debate where the natural has often morally triumphed over the artificial. But I was wondering if you have anything to add about this debate, and if you think it is worth even thinking of them as dissociated anyway, as in the case of AI-generated personae which are programmed by algorithms but also by our own personalities and thus mirror many aspects of our desires, tastes, and possibly flaws.
>
> **Jason Mohaghegh:** If she wishes, Nora, as the author of the Future Illusion Lab, should feel free to take the first step here.
>
> **Nora Khan:** I'll try. We have used artifice to make sense of and distill the world, from cave paintings, from the first flint on stone. My favorite "__ is a technology" anecdote is about the "discovery" and creation of synthetic blue paint needed to capture the heavens and the divine in ancient paintings. Artifice has always been a way for us to make sense of and process the world, and further, create mnemonic storage systems; whether the technology was writing, printing, or machine learning, there is a continuum. Pop, flat phenomena like Lil' Miquela, are intriguing for the fear, anxiety, confusion that she engenders, cluing us into an expectation that the digital or the artificial remain on its side of a binary: a clean gap between the real and the artificial.

And yet we have created elaborate external mnemonic architectures and needed artifice to create time, language, and concepts to navigate the world. Thought experiments—like decoding the funny, bizarre creations of neural networks, what they cough up—requires a blurry critical language where I can best think about the future we are creating. This space of hybrid imagination requires embracing shifting logics. Algorithms update and models teach themselves, and we are already well-trained to move with shifting digital landscapes.

As I move toward the future, I sense my thinking becoming less fixed. I am less interested in a singular theory or master argument than in inhabiting many arguments that move with the fluctuating nature of technological development, and in doing so at a faster pace, with more accuracy in concepts and terms, which is a challenge for criticism, philosophy, and theory. How do you move with a subject that has no respect for your paradigms or your rules whatsoever? I think that is something that we might become better trained to do.

Andrea Cetrulo: Jason, your impressions?

Jason Mohaghegh: I agree with essentially everything Nora just articulated, though here I would only intensify the stakes in a way that leads us to a war-stance. As philosophers and thinkers, whatever that means, sometimes we must choose. And so, I side with Nora's lab—the Future Illusion Lab; I side with illusion over the real, to the point of the latter's extinction, and I admire those who become figures of sabotage, those who use writing as a chance to steal realities back into illusion. Not just to uphold this recently popularized, important idea called "hyperstition" whereby imaginary states are transfused into realities like self-fulfilling prophecies but also the reverse arc of a magic touch that can dissolve reality regimes back into the realm of the waking dream, the paranormal, the supernatural, the fabled, and the shadow. Still, for this we may need to reacquire an older practice that belonged to mystics and storytellers: that of speaking through whispers, rumors, allegories, gestures, or lies even. Lies that nevertheless remain vitalistic in the sense that they are not intended sadistically to drain power, dominate, or coerce—but rather to enchant a disenchanted world.

Andrea Cetrulo: A very beautiful way of finishing this part but, before we go, I would like to give some final continuity to this conversation by summoning two future oracles and having you ask them each a specific question. This answer will be revealed in the next chapter of this Seven Prophecies of the Future sequence where the password will be Cipher. Nora, what would you ask our next oracle?

Nora Khan: I would summon Amy Ireland as our next oracle and ask her: In a moment when every aspect of our lived existence is mediated and decided by ciphers that we don't necessarily write or have little access to by design, which are the ciphers, by the technological priesthood, that we truly even need to decode, and which ciphers can and need to stay disguised?

Andrea Cetrulo: Excellent, that will be relayed. Now, Jason, you can ask a question to the other oracle.

Jason Mohaghegh: I would summon Ed Keller forward as the next oracle and ask him: If the etymology of the word cipher, which comes from the Arabic *sifr* (meaning "zero"), is to be taken seriously, then what is the relationship between future and the experience of the zero-degree?

PROPHECY 2.0

Cipher

Part II. Seven Prophecies of the Future (Cipher). *Source*: Matrix, Code (Pixabay, 2014).

Chapter 2.0
Cipher

Oracles: Amy Ireland, Ed Keller
Guide: Andrea Cetrulo

> **Andrea Cetrulo:** Welcome again to Seven Prophecies of the Future, a series that embarks upon a transdisciplinary journey of discovery into the unknown. Each thinker here dares to play the role of oracle, and their vaticinations of the future will guide us through whatever corridors of the times to come. In this chapter, we will enter the dimension of nothing, the experience of zero, the form, the encoded, the secret, the encrypted. Password: Cipher. The word cipher comes from the Arabic *sifr*, a black dot which originated the mathematical notion of zero. It often carries a connotation of that which needs to be deciphered or discovered. I welcome our two Oracles: Amy Ireland, theorist and experimental writer focusing on questions of agency and technology in modernity, and Ed Keller, architect, designer, professor, writer, and musician.

0. Answers

Amy, could you start by answering the question that our oracle from the previous chapter posed to you? Nora Khan asked: In a moment when every aspect of our lived existence is mediated and decided by ciphers that we don't necessarily write or have little access to by design, which are the ciphers, by the technological priesthood, that we truly even need to decode, and which ciphers can and need to stay disguised?

> **Amy Ireland:** I don't think that there is an absolute answer to this kind of question since it is always going to be contextual and decided in the moment because ciphers are like technology: they are two-sided. They

can equally be used for devastating means as well as potentiating, productive, and emancipatory means. So it can be just as important to be able to lock someone out of access to something if you are vulnerable and need to keep them away, as it can be to break through someone else's encryption in order to access something that they are keeping from you, thus depending on the relative positions of power in any given scenario. Moreover, I think it is important to note that, in talking about the temporality of encryption, it is a lot faster to encrypt something than it is to decrypt it. Hence, there will always be a kind of cat-and-mouse game between powers that encrypt and powers that decrypt, such that sometimes the minoritarian powers might be using encryption, but other times they might be needing to use decryption as a resistance strategy. Both are always going to be in play.

Andrea Cetrulo: Is there any example of something that you would say we should be deciphering or should aim at deciphering?

Amy Ireland: Yes, to stray somewhat from an abstract mode, the one thing that I think should be decrypted is the body. It would be awesome to be able to decipher the codes of the body; not just genetics but the endocrine system, the way that it composes the things that we use to tag people and hold them to specific identities—in order to completely unravel that and become more creative with the material instantiations in which we all currently still have to exist. So yes, secrets of the body. I think that tech-speak and the sort of projects that the technological priesthood typically connect to, more often than not, privilege ways of trying to escape matter, the body, and materiality, and try thereby to disappear into a realm of "freedom"—freedom from the flesh. And while I somewhat respect this kind of cyberpunk narrative, I very much remain an advocate for the continuation of materiality, and if technology is going to be used in interesting and productive ways in the future, I think a big part of that is going to be through matter, not mind.

Andrea Cetrulo: That's very interesting because then it would be complementary to any speculation on culture or, as it persists in the body: to actually access biology in different realms that are transdisciplinary, which is what we are striving to do here.

Ed Keller, we will start with the question from our previous oracle of the first episode of Seven Prophecies of the Future, Jason Mohaghegh. He has summoned you as the next oracle, and his question to you is as follows: If the etymology of the word cipher (passcode for this chapter), which comes from the Arabic *sifr* (meaning "zero"), is to be taken seriously, then what is the relationship between the future and the experience of the zero degree?

Ed Keller: This is a very interesting question, and to approach it I think we could situate the idea of cipher against the concept of noise within the discipline of encryption. A cipher is an encoded block of information, and if it's perfectly encrypted, a cipher would be indistinguishable from noise: thus, the most perfect encryption is just seemingly noise. So, from one point of view, we see only noise, or we perceive or decode only noise, but, from the right position in space and time, decrypted, the cipher is readable—it is decoded. This makes me wonder about the concept of zero, then: from the wrong point of view, perfect encryption as noise has a kind of kinship with zero. Zero means an absence: an absence of information, an absence of everything, no information; but pure noise isn't actually zero; pure noise is a kind of presence, it's got a character, it's got a texture. In fact, from many points of view—mathematical points of view, encryption points of view—pure noise is very valuable, so it's not zero either. And there's maybe almost a messianic aspect to this if we recall Walter Benjamin writing about this task of the translator: he implies in that essay that the most perfect, divine text would be universally, automatically translatable; there would be no need for translation of the divine word. There's also an interesting counter-read of that point which Benjamin makes right at the end of this essay: that the divine word would be somehow untranslatable, never translated properly into any language. So that is one take on this, a response to Jason's question or prompt; still, another would be to say: to experience zero subjectively might be the equivalent of non-being. And that's also very different from noise, as it would be the cessation of all subjective perception. So maybe an overwhelming flow of information through an individual—whether a human, animal, or ecosystem—would be noise. But objective zero is harder to grasp for us. Zero as it sits in a number, say 2021, is a placeholder for a non-zero block of time; it's a non-zero time-space in our world. Objective zero isn't that; objective zero is non-being. So I wonder how we can situate this idea in relationship to the etymology of cipher. The absence of everything? Perhaps even the absence of god-like beings, minds, entities.

I. Myth—Book of the Law; Book of Kells

Andrea Cetrulo: This leads us to our first example based around futurity and the cipher, and I would invite Amy to share her mythic example of the cipher.

Amy Ireland: I am going to talk about something that happened in Cairo, Egypt, on the 8th, 9th, and 10th of April in 1904. Now the status of this event as a myth is maybe a little ambiguous: there are those who will retell this story as if it were a concrete historical occurrence and those who will understand it as an ingenious work of self-mythologization. But either way, it shares two key traits with tales that are commonly understood as myths: one, it involves the realm of the supernatural; and two, it serves as the basis for communicating a specific worldview. It also, much in keeping with the project of the Seven Prophecies, functions as a prophetic work. So, my first example for "Cipher" is the cipher of the *Book of the Law*, otherwise known as *Liber AL vel Legis* or *Liber 418* for reasons that I will explain shortly, and one can search to find images of any of the most studied pages from the original manuscript.

The *Book of the Law* is the central text of the doctrine of Thelema, an esoteric sect developed and promoted throughout Britain, Europe, and the United States in the early twentieth century by the magician Aleister Crowley. According to Crowley's own account of the events that took place in Cairo, he and his wife Rose were traveling through Egypt on their honeymoon, where they had organized to stay in the king's chamber of the Great Pyramid of Giza. It was here, on the 16th of March in 1904, that Crowley conducted a ritual that concluded with Rose falling into a trance and saying to her husband over and over again, "They're waiting for you." Now Crowley was curious about this strange message, so a few nights later, Rose once again agreed to go into a trance while her husband invoked Thoth, the god of knowledge, to find out more. And to his surprise, his wife, who wasn't at all versed in Egyptology or magic, explained that the Egyptian deity Horus was the one who was waiting for him. And when she was asked to answer a series of questions about Horus—questions that Crowley knew his wife wouldn't be able to respond to on her own—she answered every single one of them correctly. She also explained that her interlocutor, Horus's messenger, was an entity named Aiwass. Aiwass spoke through Rose several more times before eventually giving Crowley the instructions that would produce the *Book of the Law*.

Between noon and 1:00 p.m. on three consecutive days, Crowley was to enter the temple and record, through automatic writing, everything that he heard there. Crowley obeyed, and from April 8th to April 10th, he diligently transcribed the three chapters of the book. He writes in his recollections later: "The Voice of Aiwass came apparently from over my left shoulder, from the furthest corner of the room. It seemed to echo itself in my physical heart in a very strange manner, hard to describe . . . I had a strong impression that the speaker was actually in the corner where he seemed to be, in a body of 'fine matter,' transparent as a veil of gauze, or a cloud of incense-smoke . . . Aiwass was an 'angel' such as I had often seen in visions . . . " Although the book is written in plain English, Crowley, reflecting on the work much later, maintained that the text was encrypted with a cipher that he was unaware of at the time of the transcription, for he "could not have prepared so complex a set of numerical and literary puzzles" himself, and that, even after more than a decade of study by himself and by his followers, the true meaning of Aiwass's message was only just starting to be revealed for what it was. He wrote in the introduction to the *Book of the Law* that Aiwass must have done this in order to prove not only its reality in the eyes of the skeptics but also its superior knowledge and power, such that the prophecy concerning the fate of humankind that was being delivered by the book would have to be taken seriously. So the cipher of the *Book of the Law*, while hiding an extra layer of information in plain sight in the text, available ultimately only to adepts of Thelema, thus has a validating function: it operates both as a guarantee of divinatory authenticity and of the text's strange manner of reception, since Crowley maintained that it wasn't until later on that he even understood that the message was encrypted.

Ciphers also temporalize information—they impose a delay that's equivalent to the time of decryption or deciphering. And this delay is increased in conditions where the existence of the cipher itself is something that needs to be discovered. Much of the cipher of the *Book of the Law* is related to the hermetic tradition of Kabbalah and in particular the method of calculating the numerical values of words known as gematria. In fact, Crowley would later begin referring to the *Book of the Law* as *Liber 418*, having determined that 418 was the number corresponding to Aiwass, and also the magical formula of the new Aeon that the book prophesized; "Abracadabra" is the other word that corresponds to 418. Much effort has been poured into the task of deciphering the text. At the top of one page, it states that there are mysteries hidden in the "chance shape of the letters and their position [in relation] to one another," and because of this, people have drawn grids across copies of the official manuscript, counted how many letters there are of a particular kind in each line, looked at strange artifacts embedded in the paper itself, and engaged in all kinds of wild stuff. It was precisely because of the suspicion that the answer was hidden in the layout of the words on the page that Crowley also determined that images of the original manuscript were to be published in print editions of the book.

Curiously, the exoteric *Book of the Law* also demands of its readers the creation of a novel gematria for the new Aeon that's prophesied within its pages, stating in the underlined sections: "Thou shalt obtain the order and value of the English Alphabet; thou shalt find new symbols to attribute them unto." This has led to the invention of new ciphers, some of which have then been applied retroactively to the text itself, folding further temporal twists and turns into the otherwise more straightforward delay of the original cipher.

Finally, the cipher of the *Book of the Law* can be understood as taking part in a much broader culture of mystical or divine writing; a tradition that understands madness as a kind of inspiration, and to quote Crowley himself on this: "Salvation, whatever salvation may mean, is not to be obtained on any reasonable terms. Reason is an impasse, reason is damnation; only madness, divine madness, offers an issue. The law of the Lord Chancellor will not serve; the law-giver may be an epileptic camel-driver like Mohammed, a megalomaniac provincial upstart like Napoleon, or even an exile, three-parts learned, one-part crazy, an attic-dweller in Soho, like Karl Marx. There is only one thing in common among such persons; they are all mad, that is, inspired."[1]

Andrea Cetrulo: Now we can jump to Ed's choice of images to illustrate a mythic prophecy based on the notion of cipher.

Ed Keller: I was interested in a very classic reference: the *Book of Kells*, as an example of the cipher of divinity, where the concept of divinity would be formally and steganographically embedded in an image. There is a very famous plate from the *Book of Kells*, the Chi Rho plate. The book itself is an illustrated manuscript in Latin; it has some of the Gospels from the New Testament and yet, in its particular design, we can see the intricacies of geometry functioning partly as a vector for the expression of divinity, or a human conception of divinity; human creativity in the face of certain social constructs and socio-political frameworks. The proliferation of ornament in this image and in the *Book of Kells* in general is an expression of an aesthetic encounter with the infinite, and at the same time, these forms emerge in the way that Henri Focillon discusses in his book *The Life of Forms in Art*: they emerge because of an internal vital force that they themselves have, and Focillon's argument here is fascinating because it almost compares to the Deleuzian notion of the machinic phylum; it's an animate way of looking at base matter, physico-chemical systems, weather systems, stone material systems, cultural production; these forms are alive, they evolve, they make themselves. I would like to read a quote from Focillon because it's incredibly beautiful, where he first meditates on form and then specifically talks about the *Book of Kells*. First, he says, speaking about form: "Can form, then, be nothing more than a void? Is it only a cipher, wandering through space, forever in pursuit of a number that forever flees from it? By no means. Form has a meaning, but it is a meaning entirely its own; a personal and specific value . . . [it] has a significance, and form is open to interpretation. An architectural mass, a relationship of tones, a painter's touch, an engraved line exist and possess value primarily in and of themselves. Their physiognomic quality may closely resemble that of nature but it must not be confused with nature." So, there stands the problem of cultural production, the cipher as an encoding of cultural beliefs, yet at the same time, an internal logic that drives form. And then he goes on specifically to note this example from the Book of Kells:

> By copying the coils of snakes, sympathetic magic invented the interlace. The medical origin of this sign cannot be doubted, a trace of it persists among the symbolic attributes of Asclepius. But the sign itself becomes form, and in the world of forms it gives rise to a whole series of shapes that subsequently bear no relationship whatsoever to their origin. The interlace, for instance, lends itself to innumerable variations in the decoration of the architectural monuments of certain East Christian sects: it may weave various shapes into single, indissoluble ornaments, it may submit to syntheses that artfully conceal the relationship of their component parts; or, it may evoke from that genius for analysis so typical of Islam the construction and isolation of completely stylized patterns. In Ireland, the interlace appears as a transitory, but endlessly renewed meditation on a chaotic universe that deep within itself clasps and conceals the debris or the seeds of humankind.[2]

This is where the cipher functions; it "clasps and conceals the debris or the seeds of humankind" such that this mythic cipher is an operation that encodes and casts forward in time a series of (sociopolitical) constructs. To return to Focillon: "The interlace twines round and round the old iconography, and devours it. It creates a picture of the world that has nothing in common with the world, and an art of thinking that has nothing in common with thought." And so, it's important to observe here that the cipher is a compression-decompression algorithm, but what we need to pay attention to is what it's compressing and what it's decompressing. It's not only compressing socio-political beliefs and religious beliefs and casting them forward into the future; it also has a life of its own and a logic of its own in terms of what it can capture and what it casts forward: the formal principles.

Andrea Cetrulo: I was wondering in this presentation how you previously introduced the idea of noise, and now you are speaking in a way about animism when you mentioned minerals and everything having (in this world) a life of its own, plus the idea of translation, all of which resonates with Michel Serres, who I know has influenced your thinking.

Ed Keller: I will switch to the contemporary cipher soon, but on the way there, we do find a perfect connection to Michel Serres in our shared fascination with the balance between noise and formal systems as the natural world constructs them. And so, when he speaks of the relationship between the concept of thermodynamics that we hold from physics, mathematics, and information theory, and the way that matter itself organizes, looking at an example like the silver crystal, which is a crystal deposited out of solution catalyzed by an electrical flow, we see the intelligence of matter itself and the way it reacts to gradients in the kind of atmosphere around it (in this case, a liquid atmosphere that is heavily saturated with silver). And so, I would draw a comparison between the way that matter can self-organize given certain kinds of energy flows or information flows and the way that Focillon talks about the *Book of Kells* in how the ornamentation and the life of forms themselves have organized. Here, in both cases, we would be looking for some sort of animate principle and also for the rule sets that make it possible for noise to reverse entropy and generate form (whether its material form or its life form).

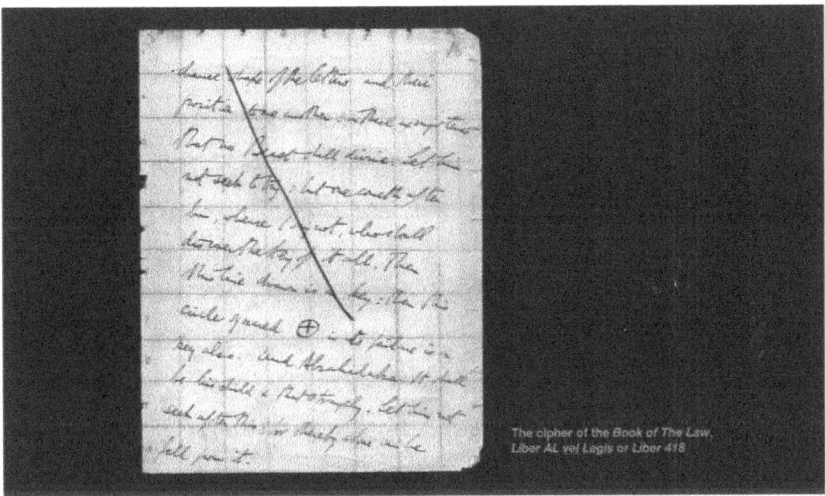

Aleister Crowley, *The Book of the Law*. 1904, *Source*: The mysterious "grid" page of Liber AL's manuscript, "for in the chance shape of the letters and their position to one another: in these are mysteries that no Beast shall divine. . . . Then this line drawn is a key: then this circle squared in its failure is a key also. And Abrahadabra."

The Book of Kells, Folio 34r, Chi Rho page.

II. Image/Artwork—Crypto-Art; Annihilation

>**Andrea Cetrulo:** Amazing. So, let us move now to the artistic image. Can our first oracle share a piece by a contemporary artist who you feel has generated some representation/manifestation of the concept of the cipher?
>
>**Amy Ireland:** My second example is a work from 2020 by pioneering crypto-artist Rhea Myers called the *Hash Gematria*. It shares a lineage with the cipher of the *Book of the Law* insofar as both draw on gematria or the calculation of numerical values of words, but Myers uses gematria in a wholly new way. While traditional gematria assigns numbers to letters and then adds the letters of a word together to find the value of that word, paying special attention to words that share the same values, Myers uses modern cryptographic hash algorithms to generate the hashes of her words and then searches for collisions in the numerical sequences of the prefixes of the 64-character hexadecimal strings used to encode the much longer and more complex sequences. While traditional gematria capitalizes on the lack of scarcity or uniqueness of possible word values, Myers's hash gematria works against this principle, since cryptographic hash functions are designed specifically to produce scarcity synthetically. It is because of this quality that hashes are an indispensable part of the modern security infrastructure. They are used to validate passwords, authenticate data, and they are used for proof of work systems in blockchains. The same hash algorithm will always generate the same hash from the same input, which is why they can be used to authenticate data. However, an incremental change in the input data will yield a wildly different hashed output that has absolutely no correlation with the previous hashed output, which makes the process basically irreversible.

While it is incredibly easy to encrypt a piece of information, such as the word "cipher," by hashing it, it is impossible by design to reverse engineer a hash in order to find out what in it remains encrypted. It is this feature that distinguishes cryptographic hash functions from more traditional ciphers for which the property of reversibility is integral. Cryptographic hashes are also designed to be unique—gematria, on the other hand, exploits coincidences. Since hashes are long, complex, unwieldy strings of numbers, they are made more tractable and readable for us humans by their representation as hexadecimal strings, with each two hex digits encoding one 8-bit byte of the original hash. And Myers uses this to get around the problems of uniqueness and irreversibility by focusing the zone of coincidence on the "prefix," or the first few characters of the hexadecimal sequence that encodes the much longer hash sequence in the same way that software systems like Git or Docker do. So, while for Crowley, using gematria as a means of deciphering the messages hidden in the *Book of the Law* functions in the modality of revelation, Myers sees her much more modern method as one of construction. She writes that the connections she finds are "useful irritants, spurs to the generation of actual structure that would otherwise not occur."[3] As an artwork, the hash gematria isn't an object or an image but a piece of executable code. Thus, its status as an artwork is kind of unorthodox, even iconoclastic; it doesn't represent anything; it does something—it immediately puts something into action or into being. The image on the screen thereby shows what the program looks like when you run it.

I have given it the word "cipher" as an input. The arrows on the left show the names of the hash algorithms being used, while the arrows on the right show the hex strings that are encoding the hashes, and the program is searching for collisions in the first sequence of digits, which have been underlined. So here we are seeing four-digit or two-byte numerical channels or resonances appearing between the word "cipher" and "commie," "emasculatory," "producibleness," "rougher," and "stonemasonry." This is using the BLAKE2 hash algorithm. I wonder if that last one is a weird message from the Masons—who knows? The same goes again for "intractable" and "overdazed" but using the MD4 algorithm. And at an even higher level of coincidence, you have "disapprobative" with a five-digit or two-and-a-half-byte length collision; a token of displeasure, perhaps, from the old gods.

> **Andrea Cetrulo:** That's certainly astonishing, Amy; I had never heard of this before.
>
> **Amy Ireland:** Rhea's work is amazing—I encourage people to check out her book, *Proof of Work*. She is one of the original crypto-artists, having created one of the first NFTs—which she made in 2014, and which just sold at Sotheby's for some huge amount of Ether. Someone who keeps a very low profile yet is very worthy of mention.
>
> **Andrea Cetrulo:** Now Ed, could you please share your second selection of an artistic work?
>
> **Ed Keller:** For the contemporary example, I wanted to switch focus to the film *Annihilation*, Alex Garland's adaptation of Jeff VanderMeer's novel. In this contemporary cipher, we see a science fiction reading of multiple ecological gestures and cognitive architectures. Multiple ciphers interlaced across each other and operating. Amy Ireland has

written about this in one of her texts, when she says that "Decay sets in unnervingly quickly in Area X,"—the place where the novel and the film play out. She further writes that "compasses and watches are ineffectual, gravity is fractious, radio waves, light waves, genetic information partake in an opaque commerce under a strange logic of transversal refraction, cause-effect relations are indecipherable if they even apply at all," and Garland's film adaptation of the novel was a very interesting kind of cross-adaptation in that it also merges themes from J.G. Ballard's *Crystal World*. It actually takes character names directly from Ballard's novel and deploys them into VanderMeer's setting. I felt that one of the things it does is meditate on a profound gesture between the human and the non-human through a cinematic-narrative engagement, and its contemporaneity stems from its dealing with the question of how to frame a gestural ecology (to use Nandita Biswas Mellamphy's concept of ecology and gestural notation). What does it mean when humans merge with the radically non-human? And this is something that has been historically dealt with for thousands of years—in the mythological fable, Daphne is pursued by Apollo, and she is rescued by her father, the river god, through transformation into a laurel tree. She passes from one real to another, as Focillon says, so this deep-time mythic relationship between the human and the non-human is something that today we have to take on much more substantially as we find ecologies decaying, falling apart; as we see—as Ballard would have put it—time itself looping back on itself, as we see the potential creation of artificial intelligence which attains nearly godlike proportions. And so, I think that one of the other things that is particularly valuable from this film, Garland's *Annihilation*, is that it shows a shedding of the human diagram, but it nonetheless preserves some dignity, the form of life that Focillon and other thinkers like Giorgio Agamben are interested in, which all of us share; all of us human, non-human, ecological, animal, and plant life. Thus, there is this excerpt from the film:

[Tessa Thompson as Josie Radek]: "It will be in all of us. It was so strange hearing . . . Shepard's voice in the mouth of that creature last night. I think as she was dying part of her mind became part of the creature that was killing her. Imagine dying frightened and in pain and having that as the only part of you which survives. I wouldn't like that at all."

So we see that she is already becoming Daphne, and Henri Focillon talks about Daphne in the following quote: "Held against the wind, spread out and separated like a frond, they—her hands—urged her on to an understanding of fluids, they provided her with numerous and delicately sensitive surfaces for knowledge of atmosphere and of water. 'My hands, in metamorphosis, experience even those translucent currents which have no substance, and which the eye does not see'." And so, as Daphne's hands become tree branches, nonetheless Daphne is in contact with something that is a cipher, from the human—and a cipher, in the case of *Annihilation*, even from the normal ecosystems because in the science fiction narrative of the film, animal DNA is hybridizing with human and plant DNA, the Shimmer—Area X is a zone, as Amy Ireland points out, that becomes a place where things are refracted through each other. And the fascinating thing for me about ciphers here would be how they can sometimes connect with each other and decode each other . . . but sometimes they cannot.

III. Phenomenon—Memory Parlors; Feedback/Feedforward Loops

Andrea Cetrulo: This takes us directly to our last question for the oracle: Can you tell us about your chosen emerging phenomenon linking the cipher to futurity and why we should be paying attention to it?

Amy Ireland: After talking about two ciphers, I wanted to take an abrupt about-face here and consider a speculative vision from hardcore cyberpunk writer Pat Cadigan's novel *Fools*, which may or may not be named for the zero card in the tarot—of what happens in the total absence of ciphers or encryption. One could look at the cover for the French translation of the novel, which is visually arresting but also because the translated title is truly interesting—it's not called *Fools* in French but rather *Mise En Abyme*. Hence the term *Mise En Abyme* literally means to put into an abyss, and it describes a mirroring effect. If you directly hold a mirror up to another mirror with no mediation, no interference, no encryption, no interruption, or anything to break the feedback of the signal, you get something that looks like the cover.

Fools tells the story of Marceline, who is a memory junkie. She buys the memories of famous people or people with more interesting and satisfying lives than hers, and she has them jacked into her brain at a kind of back alley black market service known as a "memory parlor" through an interface in her eye sockets, and she experiences these memories as if they are her own. She also toys with something called a "personality overlay"; in Marceline's world, if you get sick of who you are, you can buy another personality or sometimes steal one and have it superimposed over your own so that you effectively merge your mind, personality, memories, intelligence, and so on, with those of someone else.

Professional method actors use personality overlays as part of their job, literally becoming their characters for the duration of a particular role. I have only given a brief summary of some of the ideas in the novel, but Cadigan pursues the potential of this technology in multiple directions. It is important to note that we obviously have nascent versions of mind-machine interfaces being developed today, with things like Elon Musk's "Neural Lace" on the horizon. However, it is also possible in Cadigan's world to go, not mind-to-machine, but mind-to-mind, directly with another person. So instead of buying a record of someone else's experience—their memories, or a copy of their personality—you are directly plunged into the depths of their psyche, with no sensory mediation, censorship, or ability to withhold or protect yourself from information that you don't want to share or know. Its singularity and intensity are all derived from the absolute lack of encryption—since there is no encryption, there is no temporal delay, no time to adjust to or assimilate the information to which you are exposed. And this experience is so intimate in *Fools* that not even lifelong partners choose to do it. To cite a passage from the book that describes the experience:

> He was slow to manifest, he kept putting some obscuring element between us—a waterfall, a fog bank, a dark pane of glass—but he would have had to have been in much better shape to maintain such a thing within the system. Like the unforgiving light in a dressing room, being mind-to-mind showed no mercy. Actually, it wasn't so bad, it gave me time to get accustomed to what I was going to see. An environment was forming around us, something vague and semi-dark like the inside of a cave or a grotto. There was no sign of anyone else besides us. Dark patches in the space around us began to swirl lazily, like oil floating on the surface of water, as if a relaxation exercise had leaked through. Except it wasn't completely abstract. Here and there, there were hints of pictures, faces mostly, but they didn't last long enough to identify. She was right, so they said suddenly, it is more intimate than a married couple should be; than lovers should be; than we ever should be. There hadn't even been the time for second thoughts. When you're mind-to-mind in this inner system, the speed of thought makes the speed of light look like snail's pace. Perhaps if there had been time to reconsider my nobler instinct might have won out. But I hadn't had that option, and neither had he.[4]

Consequently, Cadigan's main interest in the book, as in many of her novels, is the way that technology exposes the fragility of personal identity. And, in this scene, one of the characters discovers that they are, in fact, a member of the "Brain Police," deeply undercover, so much so that they themselves aren't even aware of their true mission. So, Cadigan's story, it turns out, is quite literally about "killing the cop inside your head." I suppose I will leave things here—in the supreme ambivalence of pondering what it might mean to remove encryption from the world entirely.

> **Andrea Cetrulo:** It might be highly undesirable, though there really is no discontinuity between the myth and the future as we see it now. It adopts different forms and becomes transfigured, and it is placed in different contexts, but it is the same thing.

Ed, could we now jump to your choice of a current phenomenon? Please tell us a little bit about something that has captured your imagination or attention these days, an emergent option related to the cipher and futurity, of course.

> **Ed Keller:** My emergent phenomenon—it is very old, but also very current—is that of feedback and feedforward loops. We can see a beautiful example of this in the way that rivers explore a river basin over tens of thousands or even hundreds of thousands of years. In the famous US Army Corps drawings of the Mississippi River meanders, we see the oxbows forming, we see the cutoffs; each of the colors shows a different layering across thousands and thousands of years, and we see that the planet itself is indexically thinking; material systems bundle together different temporalities, and this allows for feedback and feedforward. The Earth has these registers of what you could call, using Michael Witmore's term, "massive addressability." Massive addressability allows certain parts of a system to communicate with other parts or to be connected to another moment in time, another moment in space. And yet, they are also blind to each other because, if one thinks of the way that water moves the sand in the earth, gravity is a universal force which constrains the water to a basin, flow is something which drives the system across the basin, and ecosystems are produced by the flow across the basin. Sometimes they are in direct communication with each other and sometimes they are ciphers for each other. Humans have tried to handle this problem; we have created closed worlds, isolated ecosystems like the biosphere project—we imagine doing this in space. We have seen the problems of closed worlds, such as the image from Saint-Exupery's *Little Prince* where he talks about a planet overrun by a system, in this case the baobab trees: "Now there were some terrible seeds on the planet that was the home of the little prince; and these were the seeds of the baobab. The soil of that planet was infested with them. A baobab is something you will never, never be able to get rid of if you attend to it too late. It spreads over the entire planet. It bores clear through it with its roots. And if the planet is too small, and the baobabs are too many, they split it in pieces . . . "[5] And so, the idea of an isolated

world or an isolated system with feedback loops and feedforward loops that can overrun the system, is what we are dealing with. Of course, *The Little Prince* is a children's story; it is an allegory about a young human in space with trees, a beautiful image—and it is a cautionary tale that asks what happens if we do not model our networks well. What happens if we misunderstand the feedback loops and the feedforward loops? This is what happens when we misunderstand them, if we look to the image of the bird from Chris Jordan's "Midway" photographs. Someone designed a plastic bottle cap, someone designed a lighter, it was eaten by an albatross, and it killed the bird. The designer of the plastic bottle cap, the designer of the BIC lighter, never thought an albatross would eat them. Nonetheless, the plastic and the design were capable of futuring—it fed forward, it connected another system to which it was a cipher, but only a partial cipher; of course, the bird did not have a light flaming in its belly, but it was killed by this plastic debris nonetheless. Hence the ciphering of the feedback and the feedforward loops is what proves crucial to us right now, and of course across history it has always been crucial to us, but it is ever more crucial to us as we start to leave our planet.

If we think about the arcs of ecosystems: the hundreds of thousands of years, the millions of years of partial ciphering, and the places where a value is generated. Aldo Leopold talked about this in 1949 in *Sand County Almanac*. Leopold said:

> The geese of the world . . . each March they stake their lives on [an] essential truth. In the beginning there was only the unity of the Ice Sheet. Then followed the unity of the March thaw, and the northward hegira of the international geese. Every March since the Pleistocene, the geese have honked unity from China Sea to Siberian Steppe, from Euphrates to Volga, from Nile to Murmansk, from Lincolnshire to Spitsborgon. Every March since the Pleistocene, the geese have honked unity from Currituck to Labrador, Matamuskeet to Ungava, Horseshoe Lake to Hudson's Bay, Avery Island to Baffin Land, Panhandle to Mackenzie, Sacramento to Yukon. By this international commerce of geese, the waste corn of Illinois is carried through the clouds to the Arctic tundras, there to combine with the waste sunlight of a nightless June to grow goslings for all the lands between. And in this annual barter of food for light, and winter warmth for summer solitude, the whole continent receives as net profit a wild poem dropped from the murky skies upon the muds of March.[6]

So, a cipher once again: Who is there, one hundred thousand years ago, to hear the geese honking and dropping their wild poems? Other animals, the ecosystem heard, but barely registered it. Nonetheless, the geese have been doing this for hundreds of thousands of years, and they have slowly been changing the face of the Earth. Thus, the question of how the cipher becomes deciphered; by ecological gestures as a sort of grammatology [to adopt Nandita Biswas Mellamphy's concept around the gesture]—in an incredibly beautiful fashion that demonstrates the critical place of the gesture. And this is where it would tie back to the mythic and Focillon's notion of the gesture. Or we could jump forward in a fantastical way to *The Little Prince*, through a beautiful baby's book adaptation of *The Little Prince*. Deixar o meu planeta. Je quitte ma planète. So, will out-of-control feedback loops, will the breakdown of the cipher lead us to want to flee the planet? We have already begun fleeing the planet, so I suppose what we need to do is see if our departure will be as poetic as Saint-Exupery's *Little Prince*, who was a cipher not just for the author but for all of us with cosmopolitical aspirations. Or will we see this kind of culmination of the breakdown of the cipher as we are poised on the edge of a potentially superhuman intelligence? Some have called this a hard takeoff looming in our future with artificial general intelligence; whether it's created by us as humans in fast forward accelerated feedback loops and feedforward loops with our planet, where ciphers break down and some run amok—out of control—or by an interaction with a non-human intelligence as Kubrick and Clarke have shown us in *2001: A Space Odyssey*. This is the kind of contemporary problem of feedback and feedforward that I see us facing: where one decoding of the cipher would lead us to a fairly benevolent conclusion of a neutral hard takeoff.

IV. Questions

Andrea Cetrulo: Now, Amy, to finalize and also to give some last continuity to this conversation, I will invite you to summon one of our oracles from the following episode and ask them a question related to their passcode, which is "Temple".

Amy Ireland: I wanted to summon Carla Leitão. It is commonly known historically that, in periods of great upheaval and innovation and foment, religious groups effloresce and blossom, and I think it is interesting that in the West we have this narrative of technological civilization being connected to secularism. Still, perhaps we are starting to hit the end of the kind of disenchantment of the world that this signaled originally, to come out on the other side into a re-enchantment. So, I wanted to challenge my oracle to invent or imagine a sect, creed, order, cult, or church based on some kind of contemporary—developing or future—technology.

Andrea Cetrulo: And, Ed: Who would you like to summon, and what is your question?

Ed Keller: I would summon Dan Mellamphy, and I would ask him: "If we dig deep—very, very deep—perhaps towards the center of the earth, or far out into time—what foundations might we find, what most primitive algorithms might govern and constitute the rules that form the temples we have seen across history, and also the temples we might build today? What forms of societies, politics, biology, love and mind would these temples make possible?"

PROPHECY 3.0

Temple

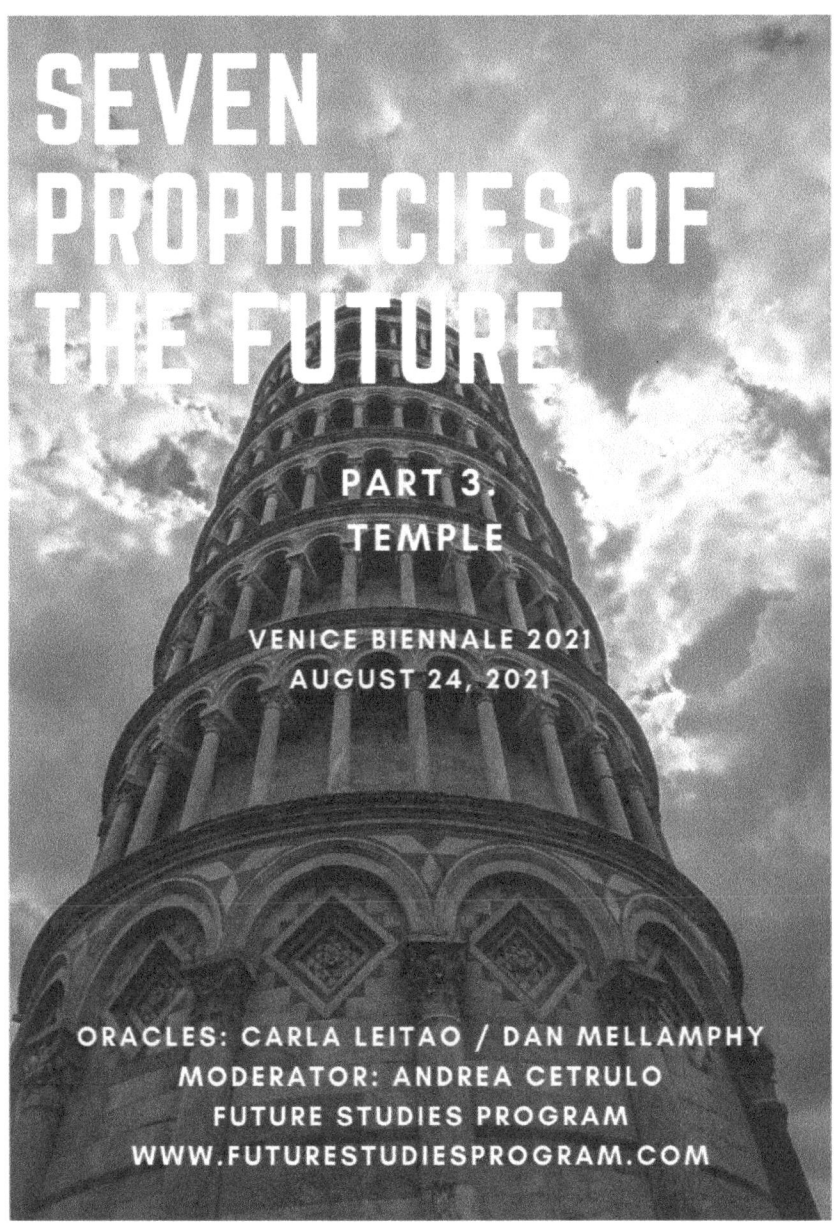

Part 1. Seven Prophecies of the Future (Temple). *Source*: Artist: Francesco Ungaro, "Concrete Structure Under White Sky" (2017).

Chapter 3.0
Temple

Oracles: Carla Leitão, Dan Mellamphy.
Guide: Andrea Cetrulo

Andrea Cetrulo: In this third episode, we will enter the domain of architecture, of worship and the sacred. Password: Temple. Temple is defined as a building used to or for the worship of a god or gods in some religions, but what kind of deities can be found in futuristic temples, and what sort of worshiper will build these structures of the future? To answer this and more, we have invited two oracles of futurity: Carla Leitão and Dan Mellamphy, both builders of real and imaginary temples.

0. Answers

Welcome to you both, and I would like us to start this session by relaying the questions from our oracles of the previous episode of Seven Prophecies of the Future. Starting with Carla, Amy Ireland has extended more of a challenge than a question: "It is commonly known historically that, in periods of great upheaval and innovation and foment, religious groups effloresce and blossom, and I think it is interesting that in the West we have this narrative of technological civilization being connected to secularism. And I think that we are starting to hit the end of the kind of disenchantment of the world that this signaled originally, to come out the other side into a re-enchantment. So, I wanted to challenge my oracle to invent or imagine a sect, creed, order, cult, or church based on some kind of contemporary—developing or future—technology."

Carla Leitão: Many religions imprint the belief in magic contiguity or continuity between humans and each other or humans and something else. Or the belief that what humans wish for others could come true—like a curse or a blessing—a belief that one's behavior can influence theirs and someone else's life. We observe a "break in belief"—or hypocrisy—by a member/practitioner of a religion when they seem to not be carrying this belief through; that is, making a maximum effort to abide by that criterion such that their behavior changes theirs and someone else's future. So, a technology would have to be truly radical and therefore magical—a real definition of technology; it would have to be something like a drug, a brain redo, or a more effective and absolute form of hypnotism. Something beyond the already very radical idea of telepathic control proposed by Alfred Bester in his novel *The Stars My Destination*, whereby humans have advanced levels of empathy because they can live in each other's minds. This technology, which we might use for some new religion, would have to be a new way to truly see energy and matter—following Einstein's view of matter as just another form of energy—and to understand how that would change our ideas and imagination about priority and hierarchy. Our following of routines to celebrate this state of things would have to be the absolute opposite of a dogma, but as well potentially imply a non-focus, a non-interest, in a past cultural history. I bring this up as we face a cultural moment—a globalized pandemic—where we have grown so close to each other on Earth that any future we have demands that we get our stuff together in that very radical way.

Andrea Cetrulo: Thank you, Carla; this somehow brings us back to the previous episode, where we encountered examples of futurity and mind reading. For now, I am going to welcome Dan and relay Ed Keller's question: "If we dig deep—very, very deep—perhaps towards the center of the earth, or far out into time—what foundations might we find, what most primitive algorithms might govern and constitute the rules that form the temples we have seen across history, and also the temples we might build today? What forms of societies, politics, biology, love and mind would these temples make possible?"

Dan Mellamphy: *Demons*—*djinn*, *"genies"*—have shown (i.e., *demon*strated), throughout the various fabulous tales that have come down to us over the ages, that when one is "summoned" one should always be very aware (and wary) of "who" has summoned us, and—to sum up a djinnialogical mode of operation—try to fold the requests and/or questions of the summoner back onto the *quester*, the *questioner*, the *requester* (in sum, on "the summoner"). In this case, summoned as I am by Ed Keller, I should say (first off) that the man climbs *mountains*—climbs *hill-sides*, *rock-faces*, Sisyphean *boulders*, what-have-you—and hence has a keen sense of the vertiginous relation between great heights and great depths; what's more, if you read through his collected writings you will find that his penchant for scaling cliff-sides translates itself into a consistent "collected works" working and wording out of "SCALABILITY," since he tends to explore issues from the most *micro*scopic to the most *macro*scopic scale in his essays—and from the most profoundly *chthonic* to the loftiest levels of the macro-*cosmic*. Hence HE HIMSELF is probably best suited (in both his flesh suit and mind tux) to answering the question he has posed. . . . Taking a cue from Cronenberg Junior's horror movie *Possessor*, I could simply don the Ed personam—the Kellerian hypokeimenon—and VENTRILOQUIZE! . . . heck, I could lift any passage at random . . . say, for instance, the opening lines of his contribution to Leper Creativity, where he writes of "the fraught relationship between the sun and the earth within a broader, cosmologically-scaled economy of excess and consumption, of overlapping layers of time where futures and pasts are enabled or erased": "What is the manner by which humans can position themselves in relation to this magnificent, excessive [enabling and] erasing machine?"—*What is the manner by which* ("what primitive algorithms might govern and constitute") *the rules that form the various positions and dispositions, the various perspectives/perspectival frameworks, the architectural arrangements and assemblages, that enable-and/or-erase "takes" on the world—"takes" on, or "ways of contemplating," the world?* . . . This is a question that questions the very conditions of the CONTEMPLUM: the "temple" in/through/out-of-which all "forms of society, politics, biology, [etc.] are made possible" (here, hear, I've remixed a *lot* of Ed Keller—leprously lopping off lines from his Punctum Books *Cyclonopedia*nalysis and futural *Summoning-Question*).

To switch from a *demonic* to a perhaps-more-*angelic* approach, let me answer the call (this Cthulhu-like "summons") with part of the book I was translating at the time of the *Cyclonopedia*-Conference: namely, Simondon's elaboration of his assemblage theory *On the Mode of Existence of Technical Objects* and "Religio-Technological" Subjects. What Ed calls "the primitive algorithms"—indeed "the *foundations*"—"that govern and constitute," Simondon calls "the primitive, indeed 'magical', schema" that "maps" or "lays-out" the world through a set of "key [contemplative, perspectival] points." In his treatise *On the Mode of Existence*, Simondon's basic hypothesis, in his own words, "consists in supposing the existence of a primitive mode of man's relation to the world—which is the *'magical'* mode"; "from an internal rupture of this relation arise two simultaneous and opposite phases, the TECHNICAL phase and the RELIGIOUS phase. 'Technicity' is the mobilization of the figural functions, the extraction of the key-points of man's relation to the world. 'Religiosity', on the contrary, refers to a respect for and the perspective of ground functions. . . . 'Æsthetics' preserves the nostalgia of man's primitive relation to the world: it is a neutrality between the opposing phases—but its concrete character as 'constructor of objects' limits its power of mediation, for 'the æsthetic object' loses its neutrality, and consequently its power of mediation, by seeking to become either 'functional' or 'sacred'." "According to this general hypothesis," he continues,

> We suppose that the primitive mode of existence of man in the world corresponds to a primitive union—prior to any split—of *subjectivity* and *objectivity*. The first structuration, corresponding to the appearance of a "figure" and a "ground" in this mode of existence, is the one that gives rise to the "magical" universe. The "magical" universe is structured according to the most primitive and meaningful of organizations: that of the reticulation of the world into "privileged places" and "privileged moments". A privileged "place"—a place that has a "power"—is one *that summarizes and contains* the force of a compact mass of reality: it *summarizes and governs* it, as a high-land governs and dominates a low-land (the elevated peak is the lord of the mountain, just as the most impenetrable pan of the woods is where all its reality resides). The "magical world" is thus made of a network of "places" and "things" that have power [*magh:* the root of the word *magic*] and that are "bound" to other things and other places that also have a power. This path, this enclosure, this *temenos*, contains all the "force" of the land: the "key-point" of the "reality" and "spontaneity" of things.

The "temple," here hear, can be taken as one such *temenos*, as one such "high-point" qua "key-point," or what Ed himself might call a bouldering/mountaining hand-or-foot-hold. It is a place that allows us to grasp—to hold and behold—the larger picture, if you will: the whole complex of things (*objects* and *subjects*—or, in the more primal/primary/primitive case, prior to the stark division of objects and subjects).

I. Myth—The Egyptian Temple, The Hindu Temple, and The Ray-Cat

Andrea Cetrulo: Thank you so much, Dan. There is a lot to unpack there, though I believe your answer to this question does not stop here; it will be complemented by the first example of this oracular session, which is the myth.

Dan Mellamphy: Yes . . . The roots of the word "temple" are uncertain (that-is-to-say contested), but the three dominant hypotheses — the contested A, B, and C threads — are A, that it derives from the Greek *temenos*, designating a section of land *cut-or-marked-off* from the rest — a "sacred enclosure" (a "sacred space") *set-aside* from other more mundane locations; B that it stems from the Latin *tempus*, meaning "time," and demarcates an alternative "time" or "time-out" marked or set out for contemplation, for contemplative practice; and C, that it comes from the Proto-Indo-European *templom*, meaning "to stretch-out or extend." The word "temple" in French — *temple* — resounds of the second thread (each thread, as a thread, extending the third one, which actually IS a thread stretched-out or stretched-over space and/or time) . . . that-is-to-say, *temple* in French resounds of a "time" ("*un temps*") or a "climatological condition" ("*le temps*" — *peut-être* "*la tempête*," *peut-être aussi* "*la température*"): in this case a time or temporal condition SET-ASIDE FROM THE REST: the condition of a "time out" or an "out-of-time" that is within (with and in) the very definition and delimitation of "the temple." "The temple" thus enfolds *time:* it is, itself, "*un temps plié*": a "folded" and "enfolded" *time* — and *place*, of course; a "folded" and "enfolded" *time and place*, or set-aside "spacetime." This folding, this enfolding, accords with all three hypothesized etymologies (A, B, and C). . . . I have a lot to say about folds — from the fact that this is what the body does (what bodies *do*), or that this is key to self-consciousness and self-reflection (indeed, *all explication* and *every complication — every complex notion — we have* and have ever come up with) — to a whole host of other physical, metaphysical, and downright pataphysical considerations . . . but rather than get all Leibnizian or Deleuzian (or again, *Jarry*esque) about it, I figured I should stay grounded in and on "the temple" itself and remain in this way a kind of *templar* (perhaps even a bit of a devilish or dæmonic temp*liar* — who knows?).

Speaking of lying: that which lies at the root of the temple is utterly and/or unutterably interesting, and definitely worth folding into this particular rant or thieves' cant (by which I mean Jargonesque Academese or para-academic discoursing). I'll mention two things — give two examples — with respect to this, referring first to the Hindu temple (for instance, the temple of Meenakshi in Madurai, near the southern tip of India) and second to the Egyptian temple (for instance, the temple of Luxor — ancient Thebes — in the middle of Egypt, along the banks of the Nile). Actually, I will reverse these: referring first to the Egyptian temple and then to the Hindu temple.

Ok . . . One of the interesting things about the building of Egyptian Temples is the so-called "seed stone" that is literally "planted" at the outset (the beginning) of construction: this is a stone taken from the walls of an earlier temple that has fulfilled its calendrical-astrological (that-is-to-say temporal) purpose and been dismantled. This is an example of the temple as a *"temps plié"* or a "folded time" since here the "previous" time (the previous temple) is folded into and enfolded by the new one. The new temple is *founded on* and *grows out of* the old through a kind of lithographic gene-splicing (even the hieroglyph-marked face of the older stone section is taken into account with respect to the newfound/ foundational position or countenance, since it is always planted "face downward" so that its text can grow in and as the direction of roots and thus "root" the new building). Other stones from the significant and symbolically chosen old temple often get placed at various points—various joints and junctures—in the newly built temple, appearing at what might be perceived as "odd" parts of its hieroglyph-covered walls (why go to the trouble of incorporating these "odd" bits and pieces into the new temple if they are not somehow significant, if they did not somehow carry elements of the old temple into the new?). Many examples of these can be found in the three-volume study of Luxor published in 1957 as Le Temple de L'Homme: Apet-du-Sud à Lougsor—a three-volume study that makes reference to (and extends in the direction of Egypt) Stella Kramrisch's two-volume study published in 1946 as The Hindu Temple. Both studies, however, refer to the Hindu architectural principle of the VASTUPURUSHAMANDALA, which is the "seed," "plan," "base" and "basis" of divinely-and-environmentally- "attuned" architecture—that-is-to-say "architecture" that allows for and folds in (into itself) "this-world"ly/*mundane* and "other-world"ly/*divine* forces and flows. Whereas figures such as Leonardo's *Vitruvian Man* mandala are based on a body with outstretched arms and legs—limbs extended to their maximum range— the "Man"-Form qua *Purusha* of the VASTUPURUSHAMANDALA (or *Vedic Man* rather than *Vitruvian Man*, if you like) is, by contrast, *compact, compacted, confined by* (rather than *configuring*) the mandala or "seed"-form/plan/base/basis as such— it is *un-extended*, in other words, rather than in a state of extension. "Extension" in the Vedic Vision (the VASTUPURUSHAMANDALA) gives rise to "the building" that is *based on* and *grows out from* that basic mandala—a building that stands as an extensive "symbol" of the latter (THE MANDALA ITSELF remains purely intensive). "Extension" in the Vedic Vision takes the form of a *dismemberment*, moreover, following Book Ten of the Rig Veda: as Joseph Rykwert explains in his Dancing Column: On Order in Architecture, "the 19th hymn of the Rig Veda [. . .it's actually the *90th* hymn rather than the *19th*—probably just a typo. . . . Anyhow, the 90th hymn of the Rig Veda] suggests the creation of the cosmos and of society through a sacrificial dismembering of *Purusha*, the first man"—or, quoting Stella Kramrisch, "the *Purusha* SACRIFICES ITSELF INTO EXISTENCE . . . it spends itself in an ever-renewed, ever-proceeding sacrifice by which the universe [and its existents] subsist." Sacrifice (*sacer-facere*): a "making sacred" by division, divestment, dissection. *Purusha*—the "man" in the mandala—as the body out-of-which/out-from-which existent things (objects and subjects) *unfurl*, *unfold*, and *come to be*. *Purusha* BEGINS intact, whole, all-together, and ENDS-UP altogether dispersed, distributed, doled-out and rolled-out as the *map-and-territory/terrain/topos* of the world.

> **Andrea Cetrulo:** Thank you very much, Dan. Now, Carla, what is your mythic example of temple and futurity?
>
> **Carla Leitão:** Dan, thank you very much for that amazing introduction to temples and their etymology, and thank you for talking about Egyptian culture because that allows me to bring some cats into the picture. So, I want to advance a very awkward concept of "Temple" — perhaps less expected from an architect. Contemporarily, in our so-called Western culture, architects are very interested in landscapes, environments, and the way we inhabit spaces and landscapes through information or knowledge. The Ray-Cat project (1984) is an example I would like to bring to this discussion because it was an early biosensor project to read landscapes. The project was that of genetically engineering a domestic cat so that it would change color in the presence of certain radioactive substances. It was the response by French author François Bastide and semiotician Paolo Fabbri to the problem of how to identify the presence of nuclear waste and its invisible storage to discontinuous (in time) generations of civilizations. In the words of Abe van Luik, it was a way of warning civilizations that will happen so far into the future after anyone that any of us ever cared about or will care about has died. The problem of how to create these long-term warning messages was implemented in the last quarter of the twentieth century through the Human Interference Task Force, a group of thinkers around the US Department of Energy and the Bechtel Corporation with the goal of designing a way of preventing humans and/or future cultures inhabiting Earth from unintentionally intruding on radioactive waste isolation areas and being harmed by them.

The Ray-Cat concept stands on the shoulders of other ideas that investigate how to create persistence of memory in human beings across cultures and time. Some of those ideas include the proposal by linguist Thomas Sebeok to create an atomic priesthood: a group or council that would preserve the knowledge of these messages and its own longevity as a panel of experts. In the Ray-Cat project, biology was seen as a mode of entertaining longevity: the cat would continue to breed more biosensing units, and our historically observed persistent cultural proximity to cats promised a continuity of this relationship for some future ahead. These factors entertain the possibility that this quality would not be forgotten — the message/signal embodied by the cat — as well as that it would always be visible (they would always be close to humans). Models and criteria for these long-term warnings evolved to acknowledge relative risks and expectations of recovery ambition for the messages. There were even mandates that explained all that. For instance, with the Environmental Protection Agency (EPA) mandate in the 1990s to create such warnings as part of these storage facilities emerged the real timelines around radioactive decay—hundreds of thousands and millions of years—and the settling of 10,000 years for the possible regulatory mandate for the design of these messages. A time criterion that should apply to both material conservation (preserve signal) as well as messaging/signal performance (understanding of meaning). The Ray-Cat project is an endeavor from the past, the 1980s, that would make use of a technology from the future—a radiation-sensing cat—to communicate with a very deep future: a future you have no idea what it will be, being beyond imaginable scenario design timelines. It is a deep hyper/ultra-ethical project. It relied on both the extreme familiarity—the cat as a pet—and on the unnamed rituals we can foresee of affectionate behavior from both species.

It adds a reliance or belief in the power of stories and rhymes to persist and help humans remember. However, if all cultural short-term transmission (1–2 generations) fails—it relies on a kind of universal language of pure observed consistency (logic, mathematics) to communicate with entities that we have no real capacity to understand/foresee: a biological agent (deeply from the physical ecosystem) changing color consistently across a landscape—a sign of difference, potentially danger.

The Ray-Cat, much like the messaging into space, focuses on a viewpoint or perspective which is extraterrestrial—that is unknown—and to a certain degree omnipresent. It focuses on the ability to communicate trans-culturally and, in that way, find some level of universality in the medium which could translate into universality in the message, which we can imagine has some trans-ethical or ultra-ethical dimension—the project of planetary unity as one that is simultaneously deeply human and non-human: so very sacred. The project is also aware of the tsunami warning stones of Aneyoshi village, some of which are six centuries old, and the often-forgotten nature of their message. Douglas Rushkoff reminds us of the lost art of pattern recognition: as we skip generations, cultural forms rely on newer technological artifacts such as measurements, alarms, and predictions that nevertheless may lack a history of observation and local mapping and marking that accumulated local generational knowledge and may be more foolproof. These constructs are supposed to explain on our behalf when we can no longer distinctly speak, or when we don't know, can't perceive, nor imagine who we are talking to, nor—as in the space messages—whether they exist, or will listen or come. They are comments on what we think are more or less mute landscapes: much like quadri-dimensional facades, they aim to manifest, conjure, make visible, incomprehensible and invisible aspects of the technological magic we have created, which are now unrecognizable to most of us due to their nature and scale.

Main gate of Meenakshi Temple, Madurai [Author: AccessCrawl].

Interoceptor VMAX Card.

II. Image/Artwork—Contortionists; Testbed

Andrea Cetrulo: Thank you, Carla—always a good omen to see cats. And now, Dan, I think we can move on to our second thought-image, which is the artistic sample on which you can proceed to comment.

Dan Mellamphy: Contemporary Contortionism. . . . Not only is the contortionist who can fit his or her body into a tight container a rather mesmerizing three-dimensional example of the compact/compacted VASTUPURUSHAMANDALA, but the very word "contortionist" (from the Latin *contortus*, designating a *"twisting along with"* or a *"folding along the lines of"*) twists-and-folds-itself into-and-onto our thematic *topos*, "the temple" and its *"temps plié."* The contortionist here folds his body into and out-from tight places—spaces where the good-old Vitruvian Body shouldn't fit. In this little video (playing to my left), the yogic contortionist Roman Kricheli unfurls-and-unfolds his arms, legs, and so on, from a compact glass cube. Prior to his unfolding, he looks like the VASTUPURUSHA in its MANDALA. The VASTUPURUSHA, too, is encased/enfolded into a tight square container—in this case (pun intended) as the model for the building or structure that is based upon it (for which it is the *basis*). This relates both to the Hindu temple and to the Egyptian one—even to the extended (rather than unextended) plan of a temple like Luxor, the extended plan of which has three main "folds," three bent "axes," of which I will speak in a moment. First, though: in the video here provided, yogic contortionist Roman Kricheli starts off encased in a square (or rather *cubic*) enclosure—a tight *temenos*, which *holds* him (compactly *encases* him) and "contains" in this way all the "force" (all the "forces") of his body, that is all that emerges from this box (not a "black box" here, but rather an entirely *visible* and *lisible* one—a box the contents of which can clearly be seen or "surveilled"). Through the looking-glass *one can behold the whole thing:* "all that will unfold from there," if you get me. Alright then . . . So, proceeding from the VASTUPURUSHAMANDALA and the encased Kricheli (along with the post-encasement creaking of the Kricheli-Body's bones—of *the whole skeletal structure* as it emerges, uncompacted, from the constraints of that enclosure), let's cast a brief glance at the extended-rather-than-compacted skeletal structure of the Egyptian temple of Luxor, hearkening back to the first image of this presentation (prior to the contortionist-video). Ok then: just as the classic Hindu temple arose and unfolded from a compact and intensive anthropomorphic model, so did the Egyptian temple of Luxor arise and unfold according to an *extended* and instead *uncompacted*—that-is-to-say *stretched* and *drawn-out*—anthropomorphic model, leading the French scholar and symbolist René

Schwaller (following after the work of the Austrian Stella Kramrisch and her studies of the VASTUPURUSHAMANDALA) to call this Theban temple "The Temple of Man": the "Man" here likely being THE IDEALIZED PHARAOH, since the Temple of Luxor is dedicated to the Eternal Rebirth or Rejuvenation of *Kingship* (likely the place where the pharaohs of Egypt were crowned). "The architecture of the Temple of Luxor is, at first glance, disconcerting: from the southern sanctuary to the northern pylons, the axis along which it is set never ceases to deviate. There is scarcely a regular shape in the plan: what seems 'square' is rhomboidal; the inter-columnal spacing increases occasionally in the direction of the sanctuary; moreover, the entire construction was carried-out in several phases"—indeed, the temple construction spanned the reigns of *Amenhotep the Third*, *Tutankhamun*, *Horemheb*, and *Ramses the Second* along three distinct "principle axes." The "disconcerting" contortions and deviations of the temple's successive sections and various inner subsections correspond—according to Schwaller's twelve-year on-site examination— to the various "parts" and "organs" of the human body. "The study of these axes shows that each correspond to a purpose: each axis is a theme that rules the direction of the constructions related to it. In fact, each wall was built in relation to one or another of these axes, with no regard to the obvious disorder that would ensue. Thus we have here a discovery that is extremely important for studying the architecture of the temples and for deciphering the meaning of the pictures and texts traced on their walls." The correspondences to the human body were found to be as follows:

The head is located in *The Sanctuary of The Covered Temple* area, with the oral cavity in the area of *The Barque of Amun*. The clavicles are marked by walls; the chest is located in the first hypostyle of *The Covered Temple* and ends in the temple's platform. The abdomen is represented by the peristyle court and the pubis is located exactly at the door separating the peristyle from *The Colonnade of Amun* (which is dedicated to the femurs—the thighs). The knees are at the site of the gate in front of which stand the two colossi marking the entrance to this colonnade. The tibias are in *The Court of Ramses*, whose legs (tibias) are particularly pronounced. The little toe falls exactly at the northwest angle of the pylon. Any human skeleton—as long as it is harmonious— can be projected onto the plan of the temple and will coincide with it. All the proportions of the skeleton may be checked against the actual measurements of the temple.[1]

Andrea Cetrulo: Carla, would you share an artistic image that has captivated you and that somehow encapsulates our conceptual password, "Temple"?

Carla Leitão: My "now image": "Testbed"—this is the name of a project, a more recent 2017 proposal by Tei Carpenter, Arianna Deanne, and Ashley Kuo for one of those long-term warning-messaging systems I was talking about in the first segment. The Ray-Cat was an early precursor to the same problem. The "Testbed" is a 12,000-foot by 12,000-foot by 9,500-foot "cube" that transforms a nuclear waste storage facility area—the waste isolation pilot plant WIPP—into a climate-engineering experiment-site.[2] Rather than communicating with a warning through monument or obstacle, the project manipulates the geology of the site itself by setting in motion an open-ended assemblage of processes that generate an entangled scientific earthwork composed of agitated hybrid formations neither natural nor human-made. "Testbed" is a very different approach to a previous concept of installing scary spikes across the top of the storage area in Landscape of Thorns in 1992 by Michael Brill and Safdar Abidi. But spikes, much like other scary symbols, can become softened over time and in this case through erosion across deep timelines on pure matter. Testbed, the project, is a radical proposal—it deploys this array of carbon dioxide capturing strategies across the website including *ex situ* mineral sequestration, *in situ* geologic storage, and direct air capture farms to generate this active marker system that passively stores one type of energetic byproduct—carbon dioxide—in the surface, above another, the transuranic waste that is secured below.

By using climate engineering to create a new geology, "Testbed" takes advantage of the site's already compromised condition to encumber it through experimentation, doubling down on this disturbance to ensure that the site will remain undisturbed. Through their continued growth and transformation over time, these new geological forms mark the site as something that is deeply strange and unfamiliar, communicating an otherness by intervening in a fundamental process that is taking place around it. So if "Testbed" is a *monument*, or a *temple*, or a *message*, or a *narrative*, it is so by relying on an identifiable, dynamic image rather than a permanent one. It addresses the permanence and stickiness of message by following natural processes and by exacerbating their expression in ways that become visually, chemically, and environmentally visible, potentially addressing several kinds of sensing intelligence from different perspectives. It communicates a permanent presence by, albeit its blurry borders or limits, revealing a continuing, dynamically changing relationship with everything else around it.

III. Phenomenon—Origami; Interoceptors

Andrea Cetrulo: Excellent. And, finally, I will ask Dan to reveal his last fascination of the day in the form of an emerging phenomenon relating temple to futurity.

Dan Mellamphy: The Japanese word *ori* means "folding" and the Japanese word *kami* means "paper"; hence *ori-kami (ori-gami)* is the art of folding paper (the art of *paper-folding*). "*Technorigami*"—"technical" or "technological" origami, known in Japan as *origami sekkei*—is an "origami design-approach" wherein and whereby novel origami models can be theoretically "plotted-out" before any actual folding occurs. Robert Salazar (a contractor intern at NASA's Jet Propulsion Laboratory) explained the significance of origami in the tech world as follows: "Origami offers the potential to take a very large structure—even a very *vast* structure—and fit it into relatively small spaces, for instance into a small rocket, from which (after launch) it can then 'deploy' back out again," that is, be folded out once again to its actual unfolded operational size. "Folding a large object into a relatively small space is not a simple task. A big challenge in 'origami design' in general is that because all of these folds share a single resource (a single sheet) everything is highly interdependent—so if you change just one feature it has an impact on everything else." . . . According to NASA Jet Propulsion technologist Manan Arya, "Folding an object the size of a baseball-diamond so that it can fit into a rocket is the goal of a NASA project called *Starshade*. Once it opens in space, *Starshade* would allow a space-telescope to better see the planets around bright stars. Seeing an exo-planet next to its parent-star is like trying to 'image' a firefly next to a searchlight—the searchlight being the star. *Starshade* seeks to block-out that starlight so you can 'image' any really faint exo-planet right next to it."

The key principle used in technorigami is "origamic tessellation," which came into being in the 1960s . . . "tessellation" as in covering a surface with "tile"-like patterns ("*tiling*" it, in other words) along the folds of which a two-dimensional shape can be converted—or contorted—into a three-dimensional one. The most famous example of "origamic tessellation" is the so-called "Miura fold," which was developed in the 1970s by Kōryō Miura, a Japanese astrophysicist who worked on solar arrays for the "JAXA satellites" Corporation. Using the "Miura fold," one can fold a piece of paper into a smaller area and then unfold it again IN A SINGLE MOVEMENT. When unfolded, the Miura pattern looks like a mosaïc made of rows of parallelograms. "Miura folds" are an example of what is called "rigid" origami wherein the facets of the Miura origami structure remain flat, and "deflection" only happens along the tessellated folds.

To fold things together here: the word "tessellation" (and the "tessellated") comes to us from the Latin word *tessera* (a *cube*, like Roman Kricheli's glass box or like the six-sided dice Lord Shiva used in his game against Parvati—a game where he gambled away all his attributes, all his extensions, and in doing so replicated the dismemberment of *Purusha*, whose body parts gave rise to the world as we know it).

Andrea Cetrulo: I had never seen this before. Had you, Carla? Did you know about it?

Carla Leitão: As an architect and educator in architecture, I see this level of research quite often: connecting logics of mathematics and geometry to discover form, structure, and space—including forms of nesting spaces such as the example. This kind of work is particularly compelling because, although it is an outcome of mathematics being played out in space, it does feel at times like illusion or magic. Geometry is truly the universal language of reality, connecting culture and biology.

Andrea Cetrulo: Carla, what do you envision as the perfect representation of the future and the temple?

Carla Leitão: To ask one to bring an image of an emergent phenomenon is akin to asking someone to hunt fire and bring its head as evidence. So, I would like to bring an *anti-temple* temple—a "Tower of Babel" of sorts. This is the collective work of several anonymous fake Pokémon card artists who name themselves *The Interoceptors*. *The Interoceptors* believe there is a great babbling entity that one day will connect the perception of the individual human body and mind with the perception of a healthy universal space where they assemble collectively and expand into other dimensions. More than a child's game or a wild card, *The Interoceptor* is a dynamic card that believes its imperfect starting health factor can be modified by continuing to play its same choice of attacks: the "Babble Whipper" which constantly waits three turns to actually play, or the "Backlash Twist" which only adds energy at the cost of five times more damage, including to itself. And this is also known as the "under-the-rug sweep-attack." Like the archetypal "Tower of Babel," it is a construction that clearly did not set out with the perfect plan and dimensions and therefore did not think about foundations. It did not know how it wanted to relate and structure itself with some kind of pre-existing condition: a history, a geology, a set of principles; rather, it was about a spiral of pure levitation, ever upwards, potentially sinking the bottom in and itself through the sheer pressure of matter at the expense of energy—of shifting reliabilities on different soils and of shifting reliabilities on different expertise.

Georges Bataille, in *The Accursed Share*, argues that we should focus on waste—waste in all forms—and not equilibrium. He describes the extravagant waste by societies on temples, pyramids, and cathedrals, along with war or the waste of life in rituals in primitive societies, and he links this need for waste with the accretion of energy which creates a surplus that must be released. The ritual of potlatch, gift-giving, or the construction of extremely luxurious works of architecture is a mode to channel such release within cultural forms. Scenes that we have imagined as our futures talk, in different ways, of ourselves as "past." Donna Haraway imagines our dead human and technological bodies as the shells, the waste of the future—what we have built (printer?) in order to build something else that will no longer work in the future (a printed obsolete concept, idea, or message?)—but which was what we were focused on at the time (email?)—is what really remains in the future: a plastic body of the printer with mixed materials circuits. There is an argument here that we should think of the future in terms of those shells that we build in order to build those other things we think are the important ones. That we shall think really seriously of what we create and leave on the way to creating the things we think we really want. James Lovelock does something similar in terms of its application to intelligence, proposing that something more ethical than us, created by us, can be created to take care of us, nearly positing a future Earth with our survival as part of its stewardship project. Thus, our survival is an important thing to preserve—in some sort of higher temple where we all fit together.

Going back to the original image, then, there are myriad versions of this card game being played right now, all over, online, all with subtle differences between them such that only experts can spot them. One example, for instance, has lost its "V" (big "V") which would give it "V-MAX" force. This is a completely reasonable strategy of game theory: faithful to their fate, *The Interoceptors* believe that if this kind of upward spiraling motion of attacks is great enough, the tower will actually find a footing, so to speak, and settle like a badly turned wedge, floating in the debris of its own creation.

IV. Questions

Andrea Cetrulo: At this point, then, I will ask you to summon two oracles for the following episode and pose them a question related to their conceptual passcode: which will be "Reign."

Carla Leitão and Dan Mellamphy: Yes, we have decided together to read the same question to two different oracles: Arshin Adib-Moghaddam and Nandita Biswas Mellamphy. It is as follows: "In thinking about differences between reign and governance, is there ever a way to imagine a benevolent reigning or governing entity?—and if we could *design* it, so-to-speak, *what would it look like?*"

PROPHECY 4.0

Reign

Part 1. Seven Prophecies of the Future (Reign). *Source*: Artist: Reza Hasannia, "I and Me are Always Too Deep in Conversation" (Tehran, 2018).

Chapter 4.0
Reign

Oracles: Nandita Biswas Mellamphy, Arshin Adib-Moghaddam
Guide: Andrea Cetrulo

Andrea Cetrulo: In this episode, we will enter the domain of power, governance, the will, and the sovereign. Password: Reign. Reign is defined as a period when a particular person, feeling, or quality is very important or has a strong influence. Or, alternatively, when a king or queen reigns, he or she rules a country. Now, today we are going to expand this concept by asking our oracles: who could that queen or king of the future be, and in what domain—secret or public—could she or he reign? As such, I welcome our two oracles of this episode: Nandita Biswas Mellamphy, associate professor of political theory at Western University, who has published several books on Nietzsche, political thought, power, warfare, and governance, and Arshin Adib-Moghaddam, professor of global thought and comparative philosophy at the University of London SOAS, also the author of several books on politics, revolution, surveillance, and post-human warfare specializing in West Asia and North Africa.

0. Answers

Welcome. I will start by relaying the question from our oracles of the previous episode, Carla Leitão and Dan Mellamphy, relating to reign and futurity. They both ask you: "In thinking about differences between reign and governance, is there ever a way to imagine a benevolent reigning or governing entity?—and if we could *design* it, so-to-speak, *what would it look like?*"

Nandita Biswas Mellamphy: What a great—and in many respects, challenging—set of questions. What I will do here, I think, is tease out some very provisional responses. . . . In thinking about the ideas of "reign[s]" and "governance"—and the differences between them—I would say, first of all, that they do indeed overlap quite a bit. A key distinction might be that the word "reign" is typically associated with a *regime* and/or *ruler*: a "head" or "heading" under which everything is yoked. Whereas "governance" does not necessarily have to be capped by a head—that is, it can be "headless," indeed it could be a *mechanism* or *assemblage of mechanisms*. Then again, such differences really do not hold up in the long run. A monarch can reign, but so can an abstract mechanism. So perhaps we should pay attention to the convergences between both of these concepts, these terms which have similar etymologies. "Reign" for instance, comes to us from the Latin word *regnum*, meaning "kingship," "dominion," "rule," "realm," related to the Latin *regere* "to rule," "to direct," "to keep straight" and "to guide," from the Proto-Indo-European root *reg-*, "to move in a straight line." Interestingly, it is related to the Sanskrit word *raj-*, designating a "king" or a "ruler," and the Persian word *rahst*, meaning that which is "right" and "correct," though it is also related to the Greek *oregein*, "to reach or extend," and the Old Irish *rigim*, "to stretch out." Similarly, the word "governance" comes from the Old French *governance*, meaning "government," "rule," "administration" or "conduct." Thus, this is a question having to do with *rule, ruling,* and *rulership*, including and extending to questions of *authority, influence,* and *dominion* . . . questions like *who rules?, over whom?,* and *in whose name?* I think it also involves more subtle questions of *design, organization, scale,* and *relationalities* such as governance in relation to *oneself* or *self-governance*, governance of oneself *in relation to others*, and governance of *collectivities*.

There have been many attempts at imagining ideal rulers and designing optimal regimes of rule (the vast literatures and histories of political ideas in various cultures around the world attest to that). But what is a *utopia* for some always turns out to be a *dystopia* for others. We don't all have the same perspectives, nor do we occupy the same positions and locations. Still, we do have to think about the design of our institutions, our political arrangements and relations, and salutary ways of conducting ourselves so that there is a planet for future generations of humans and non-humans. Whatever else politics is, it is very fundamentally about imagining and designing alternative ways of conducting and governing ourselves.

Arshin Adib-Moghaddam: Nandita did a fantastic job cutting the topic down, so maybe I can focus on the second part—on what type of reign or governance would be benevolent or less oppressive, perhaps, than some of the models that we have currently observed. Power comes into play, of course, when there is a regnum, when there is the sovereign exercising some type of politics on us, so power is important when it comes to reigning, and the more power is aggregated—the bigger it is—the more oppressive it is, because there are hierarchies involved, and they are formalized: it doesn't matter if it's your boss, your professor, or prime minister, or president, there are kinds of rules and formalized ways of power that make it possible for them to exercise it in hierarchical manners. So, were we to look at it from another angle, we would then logically have to say: if we cut power down, into like almost little atoms, miniscule pieces, at that stage it becomes manageable—less oppressive maybe even—and it also allows for more resistance. Thus, that spatial aspect I think is very important: across one spectrum, you have the kind of monopoly on power—aggregated, sturdy, and quite authoritarian—on the other side, you have this little power, if you like. If we could get there, then it would probably translate into what was said: into a society that is less oppressive and more libertarian, or some version of a utopia.

I. Myth—The Ouroboros (Snake/Dragon); The Ghoul

Andrea Cetrulo: Excellent, thank you both for those responses; you will be able to follow up in more detail as we continue with this conversation. And so, I would like to do that by asking Nandita what you have for us in terms of a mythic example of reign?

Nandita Biswas Mellamphy: . . . Just to offer a slight preamble: . . . Despite our being part of the "Seven Prophecies of *the Future*," it turns-out that *the past* in many and most ways proves to be a real treasure trove of sources and inspirations for the task of imagining or reimagining, designing and redesigning, what a beneficial—and equally beneficial to all—polity would *be*. So I am going to take us through four images that will allow me to touch upon several subjects that have interested me for some time now. I will refer to various *cosmologies*, *time-periods*, and *literatures*, but ultimately everything does flow back to the concept of "reign," and specifically to the question of how *cosmos*—which simply means "orderly arrangement"—is to be imagined and designed.

Of course, there are so many different ways of approaching and entering into this weaving of words and worlds, so mine will be rather *random* and *provisional*, and admittedly even *improvisational*, but one thing I did want to provide you is some kind of weird *peripheral*-but-*provocative*—and ultimately perhaps *dark*— vision of these topics. The images that I will discuss are, in turn, somewhat dystopian (i.e., on the "dark side"). The first "mythic image" is less "myth" *per se*, and more a "mythic *symbol*"—one that can be found in many different forms and cultural contexts. The mythic aspect to which I refer in relation to the theme of "reign" is that of the *ouroboros*, as it was called in ancient Greece. The *ouroboros* is depicted as the reign of a *serpent*, or *dragon*, eating its own tail, continually *devouring* itself and being *reborn* from itself (hence the crown on the dragon's head). The *ouroboros* epitomizes the ruling (or principle of) unity of the material and spiritual planes, which revolve in a cosmic cycle of destruction and recreation. The *ouroboros* is the symbol of the *loop* marking both the beginning and the end: the "feedback-loop," so-to-speak, that governs all processes of transformation. The *ouroboros* as an emblem of *cosmos* or "orderly arrangement" seeks to privilege the ouroboric principle which, as I will get to, is really about *transmutation*, both spiritual and material.

The word *ouroboros* comes from the ancient Greek *ouro*, "tail," and *boros*, "devourer." The oldest-known image of the *ouroboros* was found in the tomb of the Egyptian pharaoh Tutankhamun dating back to about the thirteenth century BCE. Generally, for the Egyptians, the symbol expresses cyclical time and constant transformation. Like the recurring seasons, the annual flooding of the sacred Nile, or the journey of the rising and setting sun, the icon of the dragon eating its own tail symbolized the temporal repetition and renewal of cyclical time. Primarily associated with the idea of protective enclosure, the dragon eating its own tail has been conceived of as a divine force functioning at multiple scales: *cosmic*, *planetary*, and *individual*.

In the ancient Indic traditions, the dragon eating its own tail is depicted as supporting both *the foundation* upon which the Earth rests and encapsulating *the heavens*, drawing all beings—*divine*, *human*, and *nonhuman*—into the fold[s] of BECOMING. In the Indic theory of temporal cycles from the epic *Mahabharata*, all of creation is divisible into four great *epochs* or *yugas*; and like the ancient Greek theory of time, the Hindu cycle depicts time as a gradual process of decay that degenerates into a phase of destruction which nonetheless initiates cosmic transformation, renewal, and rebirth. According to the *Mahabharata*, the world is today in the final phase of destruction and the tail-end of its cycle.

In the alchemical traditions of Europe, the *ouroboros* expresses what is called "the action of the dragon"—that-is-to-say, the active or transformative power of poisonous diffusion, symbolized by the cosmic and chaotic dragon eating its own tail and exhaling fire from its nostrils, creating the fiery circuit of *the alchemical ouroboros*: the ouroboric *drakontos*—heraldic hieroglyph of transmutation itself, represented as the transformation of iron or lead into gold. Originally, the dragon was depicted as serpentine, since the blood of a serpent-dragon was said to have acidic and corrosive qualities. In European cartography, the dragon was used as a spatial symbol denoting dangerous or unexplored territories—*hic sunt dracones*: "here be dragons!" In alchemy or proto-chemistry, dragon blood was the symbol for the active property in all red oxy-sulfuric metals, and so it is related to the alchemical phase known as *ios* or "the reddening," which holds the key (it is said) to the secrets of alchemical transformation. The related Latin word *virus* derives from the Sanskrit root *visham* (poison) by way of the Greek *ios*. According to Berthelot's *Collection of Ancient Greek Alchemists* published in 1888, the action of *ios* or poison describes *viral transformation*, or the active property (and transformative power) of poison—which, for example, occurs in the oxidation of metals or when the volatile principle of mercury is harnessed and transformed. Quoting Berthelot here: *"Ios . . . derives from the substance which has lost its corporeality through the action of the dragon."* The "action of the dragon" is therefore to unbind and *to propagate through the operation of unbinding*; it activates dissolution and unbinds the forces of stasis by unleashing venomous agents that cannot be contained or neutralized, but out of which renewal and regeneration spring forth anew. Alchemically, the *ouroboros* is considered a *purifying* glyph. The "tail-devourer" is the symbolization of the endless circle of existence as transformation, as well as a symbol both of the union of opposites, particularly the beginning and the end, as well as the union of all into one.

So what can this image of the dragon eating its own tail tell us about *governance*, *self-governance*, *governance of others*, and *governance of the whole*? Does the *ouroboros* ultimately promise the hope of a common cosmopolitan or unified world that could be the basis of a sustainable political and ethical design for the governance of future generations? Like a kind of cosmic federation of living forms united by the ouroboric principle of transformation? Or rather, does the *ouroboros* portend the opposite: the revelation that there is no one design of unity, no single cosmos but only multiple, divergent worlds? I am not going to answer that question, because it would probably take the whole history of philosophy to do so, but I leave it open-ended.

Andrea Cetrulo: Thank you Nandita—and, Arshin, how would you like to follow up this fantastic example?

Arshin Adib-Moghaddam: In this strange meeting of minds, it seems we actually have a shared passion for creatures that appear sinister and devious. Going back to what Nandita wonderfully set out in the etymology of *regnum* ("to reign"), it also always has to do with size. The monarch or the sovereign rules, and expansion or conquest becomes a part of that. And so, I have brought the figure of the ghoul here who is a giant, a mythical giant, but we will see that this mythical giant actually has an existence of its own in various cultures. We can see him in an image from the *Book of Kings*, the *Shahnameh*, Persian tales of the tenth/eleventh century, all the way until the recent Netflix series *Ghoul* produced in India, alongside various other ghouls roaming and floating around historical eras. Thus, the first set of images speaks to this spatial aspect of our theme, and this is the Ghul in Arabic or Ghoul in English from which the term ghoulish is derived—a whole genre of horror movies can be associated with that.

The Ghoul is a humanoid giant who was born in the Arabic fables compiled in the legendary *Thousand and One Nights* but whose gigantic presence expands to many other cultural territories in a truly trans-spatial format much in the same way as our term "reign" implies. Like Goliath and the empires, the ghoul too is all about size and expansion. Indeed, the word Ghoul is also closely related to an Arabic adjective which means to size up.

In the first session of our series, Nora Khan quite brilliantly introduced the djinn as a mythical creature. The Ghoul is related to the djinn in a more gargantuan sense—so going back to the issue of space, but certainly related. He could also appear as a temptress or at least an enchantress, as certain ghouls have also been identified as a female creature who is sometimes called Mother Ghoul (*Umm Ghulah* in Arabic) or a relational term such as Aunt. She is portrayed in many tales luring hapless characters, who are usually men, into their home where the ghoul devours them.

While we will get to the vulnerabilities of the ghoul in the latter part, I do not want to only portray her or him or it in a negative light: rather, I think there is a lot of compassion one could have for the ghoul as well—the ghoul as the ultimate "other," so to say, of the mythical world and hence also a harbinger of resistance and traumas that he or she or it needs to filter out. And perhaps it is these facets and the adaptability therein that explain why and how the spirit of the ghoul has departed from its original habitat in the Arabic-Persian world and conquered various realms of society throughout the globe.

In another set of images, you can find the ghoul rising throughout the Japanese Manga and Anime genre (Manga being a type of Japanese comics), particularly in the famous Tokyo Ghoul Anime series. Here one detects a female ghoul on one side, a non-gendered ghoul on the other, such that (going back to our spatial definition around the issue of expansion) you have even an expansion of questions of gender as well (appearing both female and non-gendered). So again, space is not only a factor in oppression or hierarchy; it can also be emancipatory, as in this case. But you find the ghoul also in the US television series *Buffy the Vampire Slayer* when Buffy battled with four female ghoul enchantresses—indeed, one of the episodes was actually called "Ghoul Trouble" and was populated with menacing and evil-looking formulations of the creature.

In a more shocking example from a real tragedy, the so-called "Plainfield Ghoul" in 1950s Minnesota refers to Ed Gein—a mentally ill murderer and body snatcher who built furniture out of the remains of corpses which he stole from local graveyards. This is unfortunately a true story, and one can uncover images of the dwelling where he created those sinister furniture pieces out of human bones. In fact, some of the household names of evil characters, like Hannibal Lecter in *The Silence of the Lambs*, were modeled on this individual. Ed Gein himself was also, however villainous and criminal, in many ways a victim of his childhood: his father was a horrible alcoholic, and he had serious mental health issues; therefore, we again do not want to further depict the ghoul (even in its real manifestation) as uniformly evil.

And finally, the ghoul even appears in *Harry Potter* as a rather benevolent, almost cute creature that lives in the attic of 12 Grimmauld Place, which was the ancestral home of the Black family located in the borough of Islington in London. A ghoul task force exists at the Ministry of Magic under the Department for the Regulation and Control of Magical Creatures. So, you have a rather sweet-looking ghoul here, but size still appears to be an issue—namely, the gigantic proportion of the ghoul is certainly one of the main features. And of course, we should not be surprised that the ghoul has such a vivid presence in global culture, as the Swiss psychoanalyst Carl Jung said: "We are living our myths and dreams, sometimes without even knowing it, and we live it as a common human experience." Hence, this is how the ghoul could escape the tales of the *Arabian Nights* and travel as far as J.K. Rowling's *Harry Potter*.

The Ghoul as myth, as reality, is an expression of the collective unconscious. This global travel itinerary expresses core ideas that are part of the human species as a whole. This common origin in the collective unconscious explains why a mythical creature such as the ghoul, which was born in societies at the opposite end of the earth, can be strikingly similar to our own humanoid monsters.

Ouroboros [Encyclopaedia Britannica], Wellcome Library, London, from The Black Book (eighteenth century).

Tokyo Night (2017). Artist: Simon Launay.

II. Image/Artwork—Chinnamasta (Transformation Goddess); Florescencism (Revolutionary Flowers)

Andrea Cetrulo: Thank you; it is great to see how the different oracles and mythical creatures are conversing with each other throughout the episodes. So now, let us transition to the second thought-image. I will ask you, Nandita, to share an artistic work that you think has generated some form of representation or manifestation of the concept of reign.

Nandita Biswas Mellamphy: It is striking how similarly ghoulish our minds are, Arshin, and I am glad you led with that because it now makes my own images, especially in their foolishness, *resound*. The second set of visuals that I would like to present here are those of the Hindu *Chinnamasta*: the first, on the left-hand side, is called "the German Renaissance Chinnamasta" and was produced in 2018 by the artist Rav Zupa. The second is a mid-eighteenth-century Kangra painting of Chinnamasta from India (c. 1800 CE). I wanted to show both because I think you can see that what Zupa has done is take the themes and iconography of the eighteenth-century-paintings of Chinnamasta and repurpose them in a compelling way. I have placed these images side by side to juxtapose them, but also to show their similarities.

Who is *Chinnamasta*?: a Hindu goddess of transformation (again this thematic [ouroborically] *comes back*) . . . She is one of the Wisdom-Goddesses or *Mahavidyas*: one of ten incarnations of the goddess. She is depicted holding her own severed head, which she has just cut off. Known as the self-decapitated goddess, she is recognized as a divine incarnation of *primordial cosmic energy*, or *Shakti*. Stories of her origin vary, but there is one that relates that the goddess *Parvati* was bathing with two attendants who asked the goddess to satisfy their hunger. After putting them off several times, *Parvati* looked all around and then finally cut off her own head; three streams of blood came from her neck and at this point, *Parvati* was transformed into the goddess *Chinnamasta*, whose name literally means "severed head."

In other versions, *Chinnamasta* is portrayed as standing atop a couple who are in the midst of coïtus. The couple is said to be *Rati*, the Goddess of sexual desire, and her husband *Kama*, the God of love. *Chinnamasta* is depicted as a young woman adorned with a garland of skulls and a necklace of bones, like the goddess *Kali*. She wears a serpent as the sacred thread on her naked body, and in the second image, she is covered by lotus flowers and strings of beads. The most gruesome detail, of course, is that she has cut off her head with a sword, holding the sword in one hand and her head in the other. The blood gushing out of her decapitated head sprouts in three jets. The scene is set at the site of a crematorium where death reigns supreme.

What can the image of this goddess who has severed her own head tell us about *governance, self-governance, governance of others, global governance,* and *planetary governance*? . . . These depictions of *Chinnamasta* evoke varying and conflicting aspects of life and death: of self-destruction while nourishing others; of violent death as well as the joys of sexuality and sex; the juxtaposition of destruction and creation, of joy and suffering. These images of *Chinnamasta* combine elements of heroism *(vira)*, terror *(bhayanaka)*, and eroticism *(srungara)* and portray a composite picture of death as intrinsic to the multiplicity of life. *Chinnamasta* in her energetic form shows the power of transformation in action, it is said. And, in this sense, such a headless deity forges a symbol of transformation and transmutation of ontological and material states and scales.

Chinnamasta also epitomizes *liminality*, both *pre-* and *post*-human: the libidinal and overabundant energetic conditions of life and death. She is *multiple* and *terrifyingly inhuman*. She is almost *obscene*, subverting civility, *furious*, presaging doom and destruction, as well as *erotic*, depicting pleasure and sexual release. What George Bataille, referring to *Kali*, called *Chinnamasta*'s "transgression"—her "transgressive nature"—conjoins *the void of death* and *the plenitude of eroticism (life)* in which the profane and homogenous economy of restricted use-value gives way to the sacred heterogeneity of an excess that no system can control and that must be *squandered*, lost without profit, *spent* gloriously and catastrophically. While bloodthirsty and destructive, she is also considered the chaotic Guardian of the Cosmos, her destructive and uncontrollable powers being the necessary precondition for renewal and regeneration. Her presence portends the emergence of War as the presiding paradigm; and Terror *(ghora)* as the primordial affect that powers its circuits: not War and Terror as instruments of Human Power, but the Human as Fuel and Fodder for the transmutation of the Overhuman. In *Chinnamasta*'s FURY, fatality and fertility *collude*, conspiring to commit ontological sabotage. Against and in contrast with a Hegelian schema of *reason, recuperation*, and *recognition*, *Chinnamasta* marks a transgression of *sociality, utility,* and *intentionality;* rather she is *inhuman, irruptive,* and *virulent*—what Nietzsche would have called a Dionysian (rather than Apollonian) mode of becoming. Barbaric, she opens onto the realm of the forbidden beyond the conventional and socially sanctioned, thereby liberating it from the inherited, imposed, and inhibiting categories of "proper" and "improper," "good" and "evil," "polluted" and "pure." *Chinnamasta* embodies becoming *untameable, unassimilable, unanthropomorphizable*. So, these images of *Chinnamasta* conjure and evoke an important but often undiagnosed aspect of our networked future: that the networked condition we are currently in is manifesting itself in more and more furious ways. It is itself becoming more *pack* or *animal-like*—that is, *prehistoric*, *inhuman*, *heterogeneous*, and *multiple*.

Andrea Cetrulo: Thank you, Nandita. Of course, you mentioned Nietzsche, but somehow it also reminded me of Max Stirner's idea of egoism. Now, Arshin, what is your artistic image of choice to illustrate the reign?

Arshin Adib-Moghaddam: To step back from the ghoulish depictions and share something slightly less horror-bound, there is a painting whose origin I will explain in a second, but again first I would like to set out that the reign or *regnum* has to do with space. This is how we started, and then I added that the sovereign also has an imperial outward-looking mentality—like a conquistador's outlook; he or she is a geopolitician, since it is all about a kind of *lebensraum* (habitat, or "life area") as the German theoretician Leopold von Ranke put it. The realm of the sovereign invariably demands territory: it can be physical, mental, and these days increasingly virtual—which I will get to toward the end. Hence, space is important when it comes to reigning, and expansion is a part of that: but for the sovereign, it's always also important to have speed, power complemented by speed. That brings us to this wonderful painting made by Lida Sherafatmand, an incredibly talented Maltese-Iranian artist who paints with flowers—thus, you can see intricate flowers within bigger flowers, and they frame and enunciate everything that she does. The method itself is called Florescencism, for which she composed a manifesto.

In this one particular painting, though, we can see that the phoenix in a central position, a symbol in a kind of personal lexicon, is really flying with such a supersonic velocity that it almost disintegrates, exuding, in this case, the elements of an imagined national identity. There is a romantic part there which speaks to Persian poetry, as you see dervishes whirling around in an allusion to Persian-Turko-Arabic culture, and also revolutionaries, the vanguard that brought about the revolution in 1979, Khomeini the ghoul of the revolution alongside Lenin and Robespierre wrapped in one, and many other aspects of that imagined or mythical national identity. Nevertheless, speed is all-important in this iconography, and the phoenix is meant to represent that kind of speed. For speed has always been the great guerrilla tactic of the hunter and the warrior, as hunting and pursuit are at the heart of revolutions, wars, and combat. Empires were at the top of this hierarchy of speeds—for to reign, to possess territory, to expand, also means to have the best means to scan the world in order to colonize it.

Accordingly, here we have the transition to the virtual world of today: if in the past we were governed by an incredibly alienating, ghoulish colossus or "the machine," as the Iranian intellectual Jalal al-e Ahmad famously named it, then today's data-driven techno-politics are foreshadowing an equally intrusive form of supersonic governmentality that operates invisibly, at astounding velocities, and with borderless immediacy. There are many examples of these weapons of mass control to "reign" us in: for instance, the global biometric data that is collated as part of our health apps, our social media footprint which merges into algorithms that decide our mortgage application, employability, parole, or even our ranking in programs that determine how attractive we are.

III. Phenomenon—The Drone; The Cyborg

Andrea Cetrulo: Thank you very much, Arshin. Now, lastly, I will ask Nandita to share with us an emergent phenomenon or her choice linking reign to futurity and to tell us why it is worth our attention.

Nandita Biswas Mellamphy: Well, I promise that Arshin and I did not plan this ahead of time—but it is amazing how *in sync* our "flow" is today, regarding what Arshin just presented in terms of speed and the phoenix in that beautiful (almost beatific) image that nonetheless still has ghoulish implications, since it very nicely dovetails into my last image. Many may indeed recognize it because the event happened very recently: this is the 1,800 flying drones that formed a globe at the recent Opening Ceremonies of the Tokyo 2020 Olympics. And this image, in many ways, represents the kind of data-driven pursuit that the entire globe is currently undertaking. To the world, this impressive technical feat symbolized the perfect fusion of human ingenuity and non-human technicity representing (presumably) the potentials of future human/non-human collaboration.

Yet, of course, it might be interpreted in other, darker ways. The drone is more than just a current technology: it symbolizes *a future tendency*, and even *an emerging horizon* in which more and more decision-making will be technically driven by machine-to-machine communications and human-computer interfaces. According to Ben Noys, drones inhabit a metaphysical field embodying dreams of transcendence and destruction that have haunted the Western imagination. And I quote Noys here: "The drone finds its destination as the signature device of the contemporary forms of power, our mobile all-seeing eye."[1] Paul Virilio also described the aim of such military forces—what he called "sight machines"—

by suggesting the following: "In a technicians' version of An All-Seeing Divinity, the drive is on for *a general system of illumination that will allow everything to be seen and known, at every moment and in every place.*"² Thus, juxtaposed with the ethereal and godlike flying drones aestheticized by the Tokyo Olympics' opening ceremonies (in which 1,800 flying drones combined to form an aerial globe), the Predators and Reaper drones of drone warfare also incarnate this global and godly vision. Explicitly reflecting on drones, Virilio later comments that "The Eye of God is *everywhere.*"³ The theological resonance here is even noted by drone operators themselves, with one reported as having said, "Sometimes I feel like a God hurling thunderbolts from afar."⁴

It is no coincidence that *the information-surveillance powers now available to police, governments, and third-party security-corporations* are being compared to quasi-futuristic sci-fi scenarios like that of Philip K. Dick's 1956 *Minority Report*, which was turned into a very successful film by Spielberg in 2002, and features a plot in which advanced technologies enable police to predict, identify, and incarcerate people before they actually commit a crime. The cop at the heart of what is called the "Pre-Crime" Unit, John Anderton, is totally on board with this—with the goals of the unit—until he himself becomes a victim of its predictive technologies and is identified as a "Pre-Criminal," eventually going on the run to evade the authorities that are in hot pursuit. The Department of "Pre-Crime" criminalizes people before they have even committed a crime—a truly ethical dilemma based on current legal frameworks of individual rights and responsibilities—by bringing the norms of wartime into the civilian spaces of peacetime. In this way, civilian spaces begin to operate as if they were military battlefields. *The normalization of information-surveillance technologies* has the effect of *militarizing civilian spaces* as the logic of war invades the physical and psychic spaces of civil society on a global scale.

The current global pandemic and the rise of extreme weather caused by climate change have many key international institutions talking about the need for transnational, global, and planetary-level cooperation. Many favor the idea of the "global citizen" and theories of "cosmopolitan citizenship." Notwithstanding the various conceptions of cosmopolitanism in contemporary political, social, and moral philosophies, the standard vision claims that all human beings, regardless of their differences, can and should be regarded as citizens of a single human community or confederation. Standard cosmopolitanisms thus tend to depend on the primacy of the Liberal Enlightenment conception of the human individual endowed with basic human rights and are, as such, grounded in Humanism. At the outset of the twenty-first century, however, widespread engagement with the advanced digital technologies of the Information Age has extended the reign of technologies over human boundaries, beyond just the global to increasingly planetary and post-planetary (as Ed Keller says) or even transhuman scales. As the recent anthology *Critical Posthumanism and Planetary Futures* asks, what kinds of futures await contemporary societies "in this age of the limit condition of the human"?[5]

Transhumanist cosmopolitanists might seek to extend the concept of cosmopolitan citizenship beyond the limits to include non-human life forms—animal, vegetal, mineral, and machinic—which would entail the affirmation of hybrid human/nonhuman interfaces and identities. However, efforts to actualize transhuman cosmopolitanist agendas have demanded the widespread adoption of an impoverishing and instrumentalizing fantasy of technological enlightenment. Post-human post-colonialists would thus criticize the "Prometheanism" of transhuman cosmopolitanist narratives, instead emphasizing their complicity with the inequities and inequalities produced by a hyper-consumptive, hyper-technical form of capitalism.

Drones are the invention of a new kind of war machine that sustains itself in and upon so-called "peace," or more precisely upon the "militarization of peace." These viral agents, these weapons, are *larval operatives*: under cover of peaceful and peacetime activity, they open themselves up to the virulent fog of *larval warfare* that everywhere propagates the force of unbinding—politics, economics, culture, society, all of the curatives of human ingenuity have lost their power to bind; rather, power's main effect today is to obfuscate, corrode, contaminate, unbind and thus potentially alter, modulate, recombine, and perhaps even transmute. The virulence of this larval warfare unleashes the immuno-political responses that attack the State's own body politic within the logistics of peacetime, by fomenting paranoia, pitting citizen against citizen, and unbinding the State's civil institutions and institutionalized values, rendering them fragile, porous, and open to further insurrection. Within the alchemical logic of larval warfare, no visible or transgressive act of war or of terrorism is required for the body politic to begin *cannibalizing itself*: especially when greased by the lube of petrochemical narratives, the biopolitics of the State become subject to the autophagic process of decay unleashed by virulence. In contemporary terms, this might be a good way to understand the rise of the "New Right" and the "Alt-Right," with their focus on "meta-political" strategies that seek to transform the broader landscape of culture outside of established political channels. Even in cases where these movements have taken hold of the levers of government, the aim of political strategy is to *unbind* the body politic. In this scenario, the system is rigged: all ideologies and beliefs can be used as bait for the active propagation of unbinding across various environments. The aim of this kind of move is to unleash the virality of War; to capture the system in order to exploit its weaknesses, to use the system against itself in order to unbind it and return it to a state of nature which—as Hobbes reminds us—is *bellum omnium contra omnes*—a TOTAL WAR OF ALL-AGAINST-ALL. Today, the aim of warfare is not just *territorialization*—that is, to gain political hegemony over physical territory—but increasingly perhaps, to unleash and exploit *deterritorializations* and systemic *insurgencies*.

The logic of contemporary network culture is clearly *viral* and can be understood as a mode of action that follows the specific logic of *contagion* and *repetition*. Memes—a dominant viral form in contemporary network cultures—may be "contagious consumer objects" (as Jussi Parikka warns), but they should also be thought of as poisonous actants with subversive agendas and voracious appetites for the galvanizing effects of decomposition. This is the pestilent power of "the California Ideology," the reigning creed of Silicon Valley, that grows and flourishes in the age of virality—which is also the age of democratic ruin; it is the age of the exploitation of the weaknesses of the democratic body politic by way of democratic rhetoric; it is the age that makes way—as Plato already noted in books 8 and 9 of *The Republic*—for *the tyrant*, for *tyranny*, for *fascism*, which becomes the logical outcome of democratic failure. For Walter Benjamin, fascism obscures and distracts energies that would otherwise be used by the *demos*, the many poor, to revolt against the capitalist system. Instead, fascist virulence both aestheticizes and anesthetizes the *demos*, or to quote Benjamin here: "The masses have a right to changed property relations. Fascism seeks to give them expression while keeping these relations unchanged. The logical outcome of fascism is the aestheticization of political life."[6] Thus, "behind every fascism, there lies a failed revolution." The very parasitical logic of the virus is to unbind the polis—not by killing it immediately, indiscriminately, and once and for all—not by wiping it out; but rather and instead by slowly exploiting its weaknesses, harnessing and transmuting its powers, operating *with* and *in* the prey's economy of survival, *sustaining itself* (once again) by keeping host organisms *in an ongoing state of decay*.

So we see that *today*, *at present*, riding high on the tide of Silicon ideology—in this time period ruled by Human Supremacists, in which *technicity* has rapidly outpaced *the human* itself—the concept of "the *Anthropocene*" is but a harbinger of what could be called "the *Electrocene*" (as I have argued elsewhere): the era of electro-technical connections and transmutations that unleash and electro-technically unbind the polis and its demos, and arguably, "the human" itself. So here "*there be dragons*" for sure, *in all their cyber-fury*; here there be FURIES *come back* with a *vengeance*.

> **Andrea Cetrulo:** Thank you, Nandita. To take further the synchronicity that our oracles are demonstrating today, what can you tell us, Arshin, about an emergent phenomenon in the realm of the "reign"?
>
> **Arshin Adib-Moghaddam:** Once again, there is a lot of fascinating congruence here. For my last saddle of images, one might remember that at the session's outset I tried to rescue the ghoul (and probably

even all evil creatures and human beings) from a one-dimensional depiction as purely evil, and I would try to continue it even in response to the wonderfully detailed analysis of Nandita to look at the other side of the spectrum. We started out with it when we talked about forms of governance that could be benevolent in their reign, but also what can we do to resist? Is there the option to do something about this terribly oppressive world that we have set out thus far?

Starting with our ghoul again, and his or her DNA: first of all, they are a humanoid who could easily transmute in this techno-society of ours into a cyborg. This is just one step away: we already have people like Kevin Warwick with neural interfaces who can control things from their arm and remote areas of the world, so this hybridization that we talked about is already happening; we already have cyborgs, and they are one way or another very much related to our ghoul. So, as a cyborg, the ghoul continues to be like the chimeras of the past: modulated creatures with some human characteristics that merge with biomimetic technology. As such, the ghoul as cyborg, as other, creates an "interregnum"—a space between the two *regnums*—from the present to the future. I remain very interested in that space between, what happens between the reign/*regnum*, and how we can extend that space, since we should consider dwelling in it as far and as often as possible. So here the ghoul correlates to traumas of marginalization that led them to become the ultimate fallen creature. They cleanse themselves by delving into the opportunities that our techno-society affords them. Unlike the tragic and sad creature in Mary Shelley's *Frankenstein*, the future Cyborg Ghoul finds fellow wayfarers, a whole host of bandits and outsiders who show hostility to restrictive social values and arbitrary rule. This interregnum forms the basis for social alliances that are both trans-spatial and transhuman, as the Cyborg Ghoul becomes the déclassé of the future. Hence the ghoul has an opportunity, if you like, and not as the ultimate enemy.

So, I will end with a set of questions building on that alliance with the cyborg ghoul: Is the continued fascination with mythical monsters not also the celebration of deviance as a way of life? Does it not inform the identification with Bohemia, with tribal cultures, the search for the exotic and the irrational, for mystical, hallucinatory, and other modes of seeking to transcend the quotidian, the mundane, the everyday, and the routine (part of what we are doing in this very program)? And does it not inform identification with all kinds of "alternative," "underground," and minority social groups and "deviant" subcultures (deviant of course in quotation marks)? One thing is for sure: for every giant system that attempts to reign us in, there will be an equally powerful ghoul that questions that authority to rule over our lives. As a consequence, the ghoul could be enemy or friend. The choice is still ours.

IV. Questions

Andrea Cetrulo: Excellent. Now, to finalize but also give continuity to this conversation as we do in every episode, I invite you both to summon the oracles for the following encounter and ask them a question related to their conceptual passcode—which, in this case, is somehow self-referential and is "Oracle." They will be answering in the next chapter of Seven Prophecies of the Future.

Nandita Biswas Mellamphy: I am summoning Anna Longo to the following question: What is the value of oracles in an age of quantum AI?

Arshin Adib-Moghaddam: And I would like to summon Dejan Lukic, with my question for him being also very succinct: Who are the ghoul-oracles of our present existence, and what do they do with our bodies and minds?

PROPHECY 5.0

Oracle

Part 1. Seven Prophecies of the Future (Oracle).

Chapter 5.0
Oracle

Oracles: Anna Longo, Dejan Lukic
Guide: Andrea Cetrulo

> **Andrea Cetrulo:** Welcome again to Seven Prophecies of the Future. In this episode, we will enter the domain of prophecy, divination, futurity, the projected, and the real. Passcode: Oracle. Oracle is often defined as a person, such as a priestess, through whom a god was believed to speak, but what shapes can an oracle take and how has the concept itself mutated according to the context in which it was used? To answer this, we have invited Anna Longo, author of the Future Prophecy Lab in the Future Studies Program, who is a philosopher focusing on themes of rationality, fiction, and speculative theory, and Dejan Lukic, professor at the Institute for Doctoral Studies in the Visual Arts with an interest in mysticism, charisma, and enchantment.

0. Answers

Welcome, Anna and Dejan—as usual, I will start the fifth episode by asking you to respond as the oracles that you are. These are the questions that Nandita and Arshin from the previous episode devised for you, and this one is for Anna specifically: "What is the value of oracles in the age of quantum artificial intelligence?"

> **Anna Longo:** Actually, the last section of my presentation is an answer to this question. I will discuss the Matrix Oracle, which is an artificial intelligence program, and it is there that I will precisely try to address

the difference between traditional oracles like the Delphic Pythia and contemporary algorithmic predictive systems.

Andrea Cetrulo: Thank you, Anna. Now, this question goes to Dejan: "Who are the ghoul-oracles of our present existence and what do they do with our bodies and minds?"

Dejan Lukic: This is a tricky question, and I have to modify it slightly in order to answer. As I listened to the question, three things came to my mind: first, that ghouls are connected to evil, cannibalism, anthropophagy in general, traditionally or classically speaking. Now, if I think about ghouls today, I don't think we need to be afraid of any figure of the ghoul itself because what we have to be afraid of is the spirit of the age which has ghoulish affinities or ghoul-like qualities. That is to say, we as a collective are ghoulish; this is why ghouls in the movies and the comic books are seen as concrete figures while we embody the characteristics of ghouls in our own hearts. So, that is one significant thing—the connection to evil and the spirit of the age which is itself ghoulish rather than literal figures.

The other thing that arose from Arshin's question for me is a unique term that he used in his session—"interregnum"—which seemingly interests us both a great deal. Similarly, I was considering that term, and it appears to me that we live inside the interregnum period all the time (which is defined as a period when normal government is suspended between successive regimes), so it is hard to even think about what a normal government today might mean. Instead, what I see is a permanent state of interregnum with shifting intensities—political events rising and falling constantly, just like different wildfires on the planet. Once more, then, I don't see a particular figure of the ghoul: I see a permutation of the characteristics in the society itself. The same is true of the interregnum: I don't see it as an interval but actually as our own continual existence, which we live as a prolonged interval or an infinite interval.

And then the final element is the question of the body and mind, or what kinds of ghosts those might be without bodies and minds, or what they would do: this is hard for me to summon but I would start with my own presupposition that there is no existence without body and mind—of anything—so it is not a question of whether they have bodies and minds but just of what type of body and mind it is. I assume that we are talking about non-human bodies or hybrid bodies or cyber-bodies, but even a human body I would like to see as inhuman: permeated with viruses, all kinds of microorganisms, inhuman ideas, and so on. So, human is a designation that is just a mask, and there are no realities without this body/mind, such that, even when people contemplate life after death, they envision some spiritual body, and even if there is no spiritual body, there is a kind of cosmic consciousness proving that they always exist in some elemental form.

Finally, I just want to agree with Arshin's disposition, which is a positive disposition toward ghouls and the effort to turn them into positive figures. For any creative gesture to occur—politically, artistically—there has to be some kind of contract with the devil, which is to say there has to be some implementation of the molecule of evil. Though I cannot get into the question of what constitutes evil now, I think that following the previous conversation makes sense of this for us—evil as some sort of counter-narrative. And this has always been the case, by the way; this is nothing new or prophetic—artists, writers, philosophers make that contract by refusing to compromise, and it leads them to all sorts of pathways. In any event, that could be called the ghoul-like tendency—this desire for a contract with the devil that leads to uncompromising creativity.

I. Myth—The Sibyl; Socrates and the Delphic Oracle

Andrea Cetrulo: Now I would like us to expand on the concept of oracle by inviting you both to share a mythic representation or manifestation of this concept. Can we start with you, Dejan, and your image of choice?

Dejan Lukic: Before I show the image and enter its technicalities, let me define what I have pulled from the idea of oracle. On a most basic level, the oracle is a person or agency providing prophetic predictions (one should add here: inspired by deities). However, I think that this is more and more irrelevant for us, this element of divine inspiration, though it will continue to resurface in our examples. But this is why I like the term agency more than person—an agent providing prophetic predictions, because the one predicting the future turns into something other than herself—a possessed entity or an impersonal force of mediation. So, while the oracle is an individual traditionally, I would like to point out an alternative perspective whereby, during the act of the oracular event, in the oracular happening, he or she becomes an impersonal channel. By this definition, the oracle appears in all forms of religion from monotheisms to animism to polytheism, even in atheism. Plus, if we take the speeches of revolutionaries, which were predictions of future political systems, we can say that radical leaders in all ages also carry these oracular characteristics.

Moving forward, predicting the future through speech means inscribing it as a reality, which is perhaps the key difference between oracles and non-oracles as regular human beings: that we speak about the future but that this future is not really inscribed; it is only a speculation which may or may not happen (in fact, most of the time it does not happen or it happens because we are referring to something archetypal that other people have said many times before). Thus, the word oracle itself connotes "to speak" in Latin, signifying a particular form of utterance—but what kind of utterance? A rant, a whisper, sometimes accompanied by grunting and inhuman sounds. However, it is important to say that this utterance is not an interpretation—it is not hermeneutical—because the oracles are not seers, not wise women and wise men, but rather voiced portals through which messages of gods are streamed. To put it poetically, we could call them mouthpieces of gods. There is something tragic about this, of course: being enslaved by the divine that speaks through you.

The prime and most famous example is that of the Pythia of Delphi in ancient Greece, who exerted enormous influence on Hellenic culture and was the highest authority in an otherwise male-dominated society (an interesting paradox). In images, we can view the site itself where the Oracle of Delphi operated. The mythology is tied to so-called sibyls or female prophets found in Ancient Greece, Asia Minor (which is today's Turkey), Southern Europe, as well as Libya, Egypt, and other parts of the world around the eighth century BCE. But of course, we could also assume that prehistoric humans already had these prophetic proclivities, for being alive means being oriented toward the future in some sense. Hence, I would speculate that as soon as humans started to utter certain speech patterns, oracular expressions occurred.

Now, I set this historical backdrop to mention how this myth was employed in a most stunning way in a book—a tiny little work of fiction called *The Sibyl* by the Swedish writer Pär Lagerkvist, originally published in 1956 but a largely forgotten text and writer even though he won the Nobel Prize. The book is based on the Delphic prophecies and the sibyls that inhabited them, particularly one priestess or former priestess who is now living in disgrace outside of the town on the mountain above the temple with her son who holds some derangement (it is not clear exactly what he is). We get the sense that he is not human, and later it starts to unfold narratively that this is a son that she had with the god she was serving, and the whole story is her discussion with a cursed wanderer who came to her house to ask her questions. However, she is a retired sibyl, a banished prophetess, and she talks about her experience and her life instead. The beautiful thing here is that the classical myth of the sibyl is slightly disturbed because it deals with her betrayal of the mystical and erotic relations with the god that gave her this oracular proclivity.

Accordingly, I will just mention a couple more things: (1) it is the betrayal of the divine that leads to punishment, though this punishment itself brings a higher power/foresight; (2) the actual place where the oracular proclamations happen is described with incredible detail as a crack in the earth from which vapors are rising. Now, scientists and archaeologists speculate that these gas vapors depicted in literature could have been petrochemicals that intoxicated the person who was sitting above them. In any case, what I find fascinating in the first principle is that her betrayal becomes a micropolitical gesture or form of micro-rebellion, and in the second principle I am drawn to this hyper-reliance on geological phenomena or a micro-environmental fact. And both examples lead us to the present in which gods have receded and whereupon, as I noted at the beginning, the oracular is not truly inspired by the gods anymore. I think the way in which we detect those oracular elements now is in meteorology and weather prediction and speculations of what will happen to the Earth through this knowledge of the climate and the environment.

> **Andrea Cetrulo:** Many thanks, Dejan. Anna, are you ready to share your contribution with us for the mythic example on the Oracle?
>
> **Anna Longo:** I am starting with a quote from Plato's *The Apology of Socrates*, the famous passage where Socrates explains the role that the Delphic oracle played in his life:

Well, one day he actually went to Delphi and asked this question of the god— as I said before, gentlemen, please do not interrupt—what he asked was whether there was anyone wiser than myself. The Pythian priestess replied that there was no one.

When I heard about the oracle's answer, I said to myself, "What is the god saying, and what is his hidden meaning? I am only too conscious that I have no claim to wisdom, great or small; so what can he mean by asserting that I am the wisest man in the world? He cannot be telling a lie; that would not be right for him."[1]

Facing a trial for impiety and for corrupting the youth, Socrates defends himself by explaining that his activity is the fulfillment of the prophecy that the most accredited and respected oracle of the time delivered to him: how could he be guilty if the choices that oriented his life are but the destiny the gods planned for him?

As he refers to the judges, his existence was transformed when a friend of his named Chaerephon went to the Oracle of Delphi and asked the Pythia if there was anyone wiser than Socrates. The prophetess answered that no one holds greater wisdom. Informed by Chaerephon of the response, Socrates felt extremely puzzled: on the one hand, he knew that the Oracle cannot lie, or usually does not lie; yet on the other hand, he felt that he was not the wisest man. He therefore launched his inquiry to find if there was someone wiser than him throughout the world, questioning people around him to test if they were actually something to be defined as wise people. Anytime he met politicians, craftsmen, artists, or any kind of social category, his method showed that there were no wise individuals despite what he thought and what they thought they were. Since he did not find anyone who was wiser than himself, he finally realized that the prophecy was basically correct, but it was so only because human wisdom is not real knowledge; it is nothing with respect to the knowledge of the gods, so no human can be wise since the kind of knowledge we have on Earth is nothing; it has no real value, such that Socrates was only wiser than others in his realization that he was not wise. As a result, people started to hate him because he showed them that they were not as aware as they assumed, whereas young people adored Socrates because of this very gesture and started following him.

And what interests me in this myth is that Socrates' philosophical inquiry originates from a prophecy, and so philosophy itself can be considered the fulfillment of a prophecy. More precisely, philosophy is simultaneously both the fulfillment of a prophecy and prophecy itself.

Accordingly, Socrates claims that, despite being accused of sophistry and manipulation, his activity cannot be compared to any other kind of technique. Philosophy is not practical knowledge since it does not yield any material benefits, but it is a way of achieving a superior kind of wisdom. The knowledge of the Sophist allows him to make predictions that are useful for obtaining success in life. Sophists know people well enough to manipulate them for personal profit. On the contrary, philosophy starts with the recognition of the insignificance of human wisdom, and this very lack opens up the possibility of looking for the truth that only gods know. The signs of this divine form of knowledge are sent by the gods as ambiguous signs, as oracular enigmas to be interpreted. And it is the very activity of deciphering these signs of which philosophy consists. As a consequence, philosophy is, at the same time, the practice triggered by the divine promise of wisdom and the wisdom that corresponds to the same fact of dedicating one's own life to the research of authentic knowledge. Hence, it was the prophecy of the beginning of philosophy that the Oracle announced to Socrates, and Socrates fulfilled it by spending his life trying to understand what authentic or divine knowledge should contain: philosophy is nothing less and nothing more than this never-ending inquiry into its conditions of possibility.

Philosophers, like prophets, are said to be inspired by gods: this means that they look at reality as the effect of a superior destiny, and this destiny is the destiny of the soul. The souls saw real light before incarnation, for in this myth the soul belongs to the realm of ideas and then they fall to Earth: they are embodied and think they know because they can live in the world, but they actually have forgotten real truth. Thus, the destiny of the soul is to read the signs in reality to remember, to recollect, what they saw before incarnation, and in this way regain wings to go back where they belong (toward the unspeakable truth of ideas). So, the philosophical prophecy is one of liberation from the needs of the body and their terrestrial preoccupations and a rediscovery of the light before incarnation through contemplation.

For this reason, as Plato explains in *Phaedrus*, philosophers are like prophets and poets in that they see supernatural truths they cannot tell but produce ambiguous signs. This is, for instance, the role of "myths" in Platonic dialogues. Whenever Plato treads into some very difficult speculative concepts that cannot be explained, one can use myths—a kind of poetic fictional way of addressing a truth that is unspeakable according to logical language (the language of sophistic knowledge). The theory of recollection is such a myth, a story that reveals a deeper destiny, a prophecy the truth of which is the fact of it being told. Like the Oracle, the philosopher is animated by "divine madness," the source of a supernatural inspiration the truth of which can be proven only if it acts as an inspiration for new journeys toward the unknown. I conclude with a beautiful quote from the *Phaedrus*:

> If madness were simply an evil, it would be right, but in fact some of our greatest blessings come from madness, when it is granted to us as a divine gift. For instance, the prophetess at Delphi and the priestesses at Dodona have done Greece a lot of good—not only individuals, but whole communities—in their madness, but little or nothing when they are in their right minds. And if we are to mention the Sibyl and all the others who, when possessed by a god, use prophecy to predict the future and have on numerous occasions pointed a lot of people in the right direction, we would only be lengthening our account with information that was already completely familiar.[2]

II. Image/Artwork—The Sea Monk; Exhalation

Andrea Cetrulo: Excellent, Anna, thank you very much. I think it is also a very relevant introduction to the oracle as it becomes clear how poetic images are so important and closely linked through, in this case, the inauguration of Western philosophy. As we know, Eastern philosophy has an even more extensive tradition of the thought-image relation in that sense—the poetic, direct experience rather than the rational or the ideal. This motions us nicely to the artistic image, and Dejan, what is your case study?

Dejan Lukic: There is an image of a sea monk: it is an Ukiyo-e woodblock print from 1845 by a Japanese artist, Utagawa Kuniyoshi, and it addresses the story of a sea monk called Umibōzu, who is also a spirit in Japanese folklore (who one can see looming prominently in the image itself). The monk is said to capsize the ship of anyone who dares to speak to it; he flips and overturns the boats which to him look like toys. Sometimes he asks a riddle and, if the answer is satisfactory, he lets the ship be. There is something humorous in this image and the figure of the mercurial spirit who does not hide his dislike for people's chatter—in other words, an utterance has to be worthy of the sea, the waves, and the spirit, which I find particularly relevant since we mentioned that the oracle is primarily a form of speech. So, in this regard, the utterance must be like an answer to a riddle, or in other words, it has to be oracular in order to survive the waters.[3]

Andrea Cetrulo: Very intriguing—I had never seen this image before. Anna, please continue for us with your aesthetic example.

Anna Longo: *Exhalation* (by Ted Chiang) is a short story about the record of a scientific experiment that leads to a surprising discovery about the nature of cognition. Here is an opening quote:

But in truth the source of life is a difference in air pressure, the flow of air from spaces where it is thick to those where it is thin. The activity of our brains, the motion of our bodies, the action of every machine we have ever built is driven by the movement of air, the force exerted as differing pressures seek to balance each other out. When the pressure everywhere in the universe is the same, all air will be motionless, and useless; one day we will be surrounded by motionless air and unable to derive any benefit from it. With every movement of my body, I contribute to the equalization of pressure in our universe. With every thought that I have, I hasten the arrival of that fatal equilibrium.[4]

Now, the researcher who is conducting this scientific experiment belongs to a peculiar race of mechanical thinking beings—we do not know who they are, but they resemble strange machinic entities—who inhabit a world, the inner nature of which will be revealed once they arrive at a full understanding of the function of the brain. This protagonist tells the story of his experiment: essentially, he constructed a device to open his own skull and put a sort of microscope behind his open head so he could look inside his mind while he was analyzing the mechanism's condition. So, he was really observing his brain observing himself. And he discovered that there was an exceedingly complex architecture in the brain and that it was built with very tiny, metallic, golden leaves, and memories were inscribed on these leaves. Still, the more astonishing feature was that everything was moving because of fluxes of air moving these leaves. The inscriptions of memories on these golden leaves were basically the edges of little conduits for making the air flow, such that each inscription was the instruction to move the leaves according to these air fluxes. A thought was therefore the result of his movements originating from the connection between thoughts, and any time there was a new thought, there was a re-inscription of the leaves (causing a kind of continual change and animation in the brain).

Once again, the book's protagonist realizes that the brain is a sort of computing machine for redirecting air currents, while thinking itself was the result of the movement of these leaves (with individual thoughts encoded on these moving, golden plates). But then he recognizes that the very condition for thinking is air, and what makes air move is a difference in pressure, such that his world, which was a sort of closed world with a closed sky, like a container, was characterized by a difference in pressure between the low level and the high level. There was this differential in pressure that made air flow from the bottom to the top, and he eventually reasons that, according to the law of entropy, the destiny of the world was to reach equilibrium—that is, to reach the same pressure in the walled container—and that this would be the end of thought, of course. Equalization of pressure was the entropic equilibrium of the world, and this explained why people in the story were thinking slower and slower than ever before, leading him to predict scientifically that it's the end (or very close to the end) because anything we think, any thought we have, is accelerating the process toward equilibrium, entropy, and the end of thought.

While others start trying to find mechanical solutions, only to sense that they are increasing entropy rather than resolving the problem, our protagonist of *Exhalation* has another idea that reveals him to be more an artist than a scientist. His proposition is to write a short story that was meant to be a letter addressed to visitors from another world, speculating that there were other zones whose creatures could create a tunnel to use the air in his world to make it flow to theirs. Still, he also thinks that they could have visited the planet, which is both his prophecy and his hope, and addresses the potential visitor by warning that if they find his people paralyzed, frozen, lifeless, they could read the patterns inscribed in their dead brains to learn the patterns of those who came before. Through this process, they will bring new life to thought, to thinking, a kind of prophetic letter intended to make thinking, to make memories, to make worlds live again in this future.

And so, this is the kind of prophecy that any artist generates while producing an artwork that does not contribute information useful to finding a practical solution or to the exploitation of resources, but which haunts spirits forever. Like ideas which are meant to survive in the minds of other people and haunt them for eternity: an artwork in this sense, like this short story *Exhalation*, is a prophecy about the eternity of the life of an artwork which can survive despite the existential limits of the creator.

Utagawa Kuniyoshi, The Sailor Tokuso and the Sea Monster, showcasing an Umibōzu (1845).

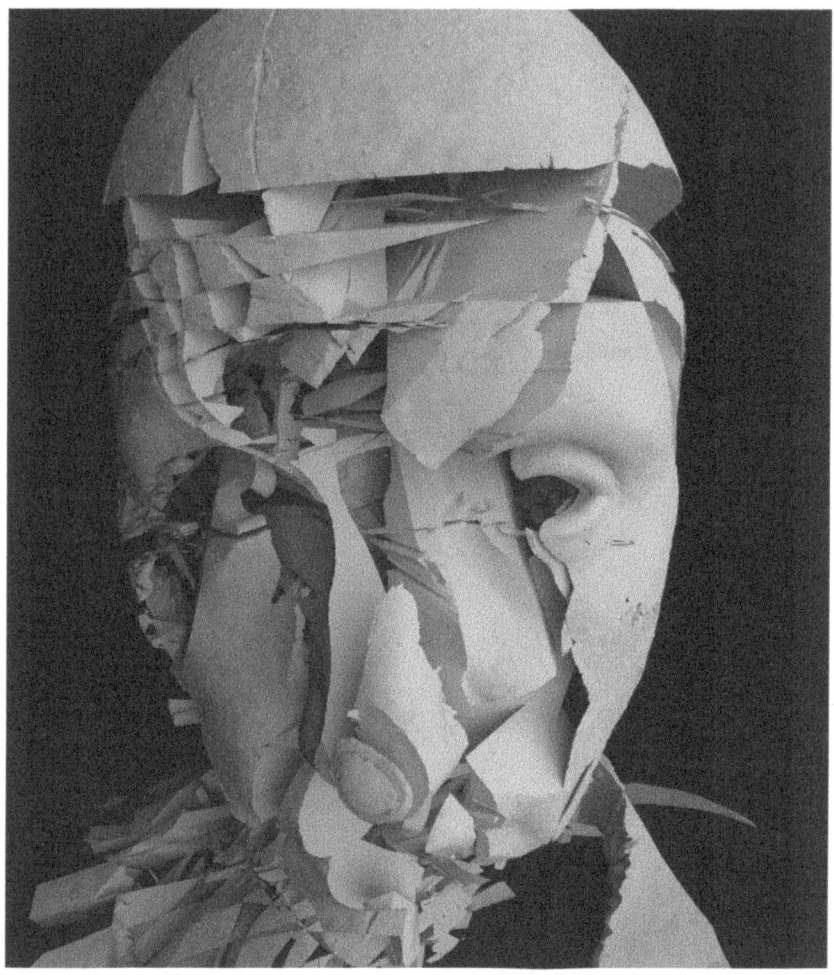

Erick Butler, *Shattered Robot* (2022).

III. Phenomenon—The Spiderweb; The Matrix

Andrea Cetrulo: Thank you, Anna. Now our last example related to the oracle will be centered around an emergent phenomenon that has caught your attention. Dejan, would you share yours first?

Dejan Lukic: The emergent phenomenon that I chose is a spiderweb. There is an image I took months ago on an island in Croatia called Dugi

Otok, an area of which was covered with enormous spiderwebs, these hanging half-bell shapes and just imagine dozens and dozens of them one next to another suspended among this beautiful vegetation on a dry island. So, I started thinking about to what extent a spider could be an oracular creature since it makes these amazing structures.

This particular species is called *Argiope lobata*, and it populates Africa, southern Europe, and Asia. A far better image of these spiders than mine is from Tomás Saraceno—a visual artist from Argentina who has been studying and working with spiders for over a decade. To what end? To raise some form of arachnean consciousness, which is an endeavor I like very much and that Saraceno has successfully tested with all the intricate work that he has done. Arachnean consciousness, one could say, is an extreme sense of otherness. Now, he has countless images, some that remind me of those formations that I saw in nature itself, but he has also made 3D visualizations of the spiderweb in collaboration with scientists encased in the glass boxes that he constructed.[5]

The web itself is a great enigma of bioengineering: it is lighter than air and has unusual elasticity; it is rich in vitamin K, which prevents bleeding. Even though it has existed for a hundred million years, I consider it a novelty since it contains some kind of mysterious purpose that exceeds myth and art. This is perhaps why certain scientists say that the most accurate image of the universe is a spiderweb, and this is also why the artist Tomás Saraceno called the app he developed for smartphones "Arachnomancy," which one can download and use, and advertised it as "An invitation to attune to our sympoetic futures."

>**Andrea Cetrulo:** Thank you, Dejan. Now, Anna, are you ready to walk us through the oracle in the form of an emergent phenomenon?
>
>**Anna Longo:** Of course, my last example is from the movie *The Matrix*, and it involves the character of the Oracle. She appears as an African American woman dressed in green and orange (like Michelangelo's Delphic Sibyl). She famously says things like "you've already made the choice" and "everything that has a beginning has an end," but then also the following obscure insight:

Look, see those birds? At some point a program was written to govern them. A program was written to watch over the trees, and the wind, the sunrise, and sunset. There are programs running all over the place. The ones doing their job, doing what they were meant to do, are invisible. You'd never even know they were here. But the other ones, well, we hear about them all the time . . . Every time you've heard someone say they saw a ghost, or an angel. Every story you've ever heard about vampires, werewolves, or aliens, is the system assimilating some program that's doing something they're not supposed to be doing.

At the outset, there is a reminder of the Delphic Sibyl which is made explicit by the inscription on the door of the Oracle's house in the film: as Neo enters, above the door is written *Temet Nosce* ("Know Thyself") which is the motto carved in the temple in Delphi where the Pythia's ritual occurred. Since the first scene, then, we have this connection between the Delphic oracle and the Matrix oracle, with the difference being that the latter is actually an artificial intelligence program, and I will address the value of a prophecy for today which can be assessed only once the difference is acknowledged (the difference in artificial intelligence predictions). While there are various parallels between the ancient and futuristic oracles, there is also another parallel between Neo and Socrates because Neo does not know who he is and needs the Oracle to orient himself—he is aware of his own ignorance, just as he knows that something does not add up in the reality in which he is living.

However, it is important to make the clear distinction: first, the Matrix oracle is a program, so she is an artificial intelligence. The Matrix oracle can predict people's actions in the same way as predictive algorithms used by platforms like Amazon or Netflix can make predictions about the user's decisions. The Matrix oracle observes the decisions of people connected to the Matrix to understand the preferences that they have and anticipate their behavioral patterns, supposing that they are taken in order to maximize expected utility. This is why the Oracle tells Neo that he has to understand why he has made some choices; she is a rational agent for whom one of the conditions to make efficient decisions is to have a current set of preferences. So, the Oracle is just telling Neo that you are also a rational agent who must know that your decisions are consequences of your preferences. This is the framework in which the Matrix oracle is thinking and working: she makes hypotheses based on observed decisions that allow her to predict that Neo is "The One" based on his previous choices. In this case, it is a pattern of action that is determined by a preference for freedom, though it is important to stress that freedom here is intended as a will to know about the causes of representations. Accordingly, Neo's quest can be said to be a scientific inquiry, meaning that he wants to understand the causes of phenomena. This led him to successfully assess that he is living in a simulation, alongside the rest of humanity.

This inquiry, however, does not lead him to discover that the knowledge he had within the simulation is false since most of the beliefs about the phenomena in the world that he had in the simulation are still valid outside the simulation. The knowledge that one has about the laws of nature, for example: the laws of physics inside the Matrix are the same outside the Matrix—it's not a world with different laws, so most of the beliefs that are true inside the Matrix are also true outside the Matrix. So, most knowledge is valid inside and outside, and he will use this knowledge that he had inside the Matrix to defeat the machines outside the Matrix in a similarly kind of world. Indeed, the world outside the

Matrix is not only governed by the same laws that are valid in virtual reality, the same beliefs, but inside and outside the Matrix there is the same economically oriented competition occurring. The only difference is that rather than fighting for personal success in society, outside the simulation Neo must fight against the machines that are exploiting human bodies. Here, Neo is literally fighting to aid humans in maximizing their expected utility and to share with machines in the exploitation of terrestrial resources rather than being exploited as resources for machinic energies (something that humans are not conscious is happening to them). There is no contradiction, just a new and different kind of knowledge.

No doubt, The Matrix has often been compared to Plato's allegory of the cave: as we know, the allegory presents a set of slaves or prisoners who are chained and facing a wall, and on this wall they see shadows produced by the movements of objects/people passing between the back of the prisoners and a fire. These chained figures who see only the wall think that these projected shadows are real. In this respect, Neo is just unchaining himself by turning his head and seeing that the shadows are produced by objects moved by the machines to manipulate humans, showing others the falsely simulating mechanism of the cave, but then it ends there. On the contrary, in the real Platonic allegory of the cave, there is another phase when the philosopher goes outside and looks at the sun; the light of the sun is too strong, it cannot be looked at, so the senses are inefficient to grasp it, and the soul is left alone to identify itself with this light. In Plato, the philosopher accesses the light of the sun outside the cave, and this is the light of divine madness we were talking about before, and this is the source of a totally different kind of knowledge—of a totally different kind of reality. Thus, while Neo engages himself to allow humans to be freed from the chains of exploitation and to live as free beings in the cave of material reality, the Platonic philosopher aims to free souls from the cave, not only from the chains of illusion but also from the chains of scientific knowledge and phenomenal reality. And, of course, this means to free them not only from exploitation in the world but from the game of exploitation or control of resources.

Consequently, the Matrix oracle orients Neo's decisions in order to achieve peace with the machines, herself being an artificial intelligence program who is basically urging those in the Matrix with preferences for freedom to traverse outside the code for the goal of harmony between humans and machines. And the program has been rebooted many times already, but humanity and the machines were not yet ready for this before, such that Neo's sacrifice and the killing of Mr. Smith (who was duplicating himself like a kind of cancer in the Matrix) bring about not just freedom but the maximization of all sides' utility through compromise.

In conclusion, unlike the Matrix oracle who suggests practical solutions, the Delphic oracle orients the philosopher to look into the sun and to live in conformity with another kind of truth that has nothing to do with the maximization of terrestrial utilities. In Platonic terms, to go back to the source does not mean to access the code as the real cause of perceived reality, nor to achieve a deeper scientific knowledge of phenomenal reality because this reality is the cave; rather, going back to the source means to free the soul from what is believed to be knowledge since scientific knowledge is knowledge of the cave structure rather than of the unknowable origin of any possible contingent reality, of any possible cave. So, while the Matrix Oracle, as an Artificial Intelligence, suggests rational decisions that are meant to maximize utility, the Delphic oracle suggests that these kinds of wise decisions are based on non-necessary beliefs and that the real destiny of the soul is to be unbound from the competition that humans take for reality itself.

IV. Questions

Andrea Cetrulo: In this instance, I have devised a question of my own for the next incoming oracles, Michael Marder and Laura Tripaldi, who will cast us across the conceptual terrain of the "Surface": How do you envision a future in which appearances—superficial or material remnants—are taken seriously and rendered as relevant as the transcendental in our lives, and do you have any examples of fields where this might already be happening in meaningful ways?

PROPHECY 6.0

Surface

Part 1. Seven Prophecies of the Future (Surface). *Source*: Artist: Nathan Anderson (2017).

Chapter 6.0
Surface

Oracles: Michael Marder, Laura Tripaldi
Guide: Andrea Cetrulo

Andrea Cetrulo: Welcome to Seven Prophecies of the Future. In this episode, we will enter the domain of appearance, of textures, the intangible, the microscopic, the mechanical, and the vegetal. Password: Surface. Surfaces are formally defined as the outside part or uppermost layer of something; in geometry, a continuous set of points that has length and breadth but no thickness. It commonly denotes the exterior or upper boundary of an object or body, but in order to expand and challenge the concept of surfaces, we have invited two oracles of futurity: neuroscientist Laura Tripaldi, author of the book *Parallel Minds* published by Urbanomic, and Michael Marder, professor of philosophy with an interest in phenomenology and author of several books on the subjectivity of plants, energy, waste, and dust.

0. Answers

Welcome oracles, Laura and Michael—I would like to start this episode by asking you a question of my own since it seems to me that there is an increasing interest in surfaces reflected in your work, Michael, on the phenomenology of dust, and yours, Laura, on the imbrication between organic and inorganic, our bodies and the materials that surround us. So, this shedding of light on surfaces, toward surfaces, which perhaps takes us nowhere else but to the surface itself seems persuasive to me as an alternative, perhaps, to transcendental views of the world with the insistence on digging or going deep into the core of things.

Hence, my question for both of you would be: How do you envision a future in which appearances—superficial or material remnants—are taken seriously and rendered as relevant as the transcendental in our lives, and do you have any examples of fields where this already might be happening in meaningful ways? Laura, would you like to start?

Laura Tripaldi: Sure, I would say that I fully agree with you that the usual relationship between surface and depth should be or could be reversed. We think of surfaces as mere shells, limiting the existence of objects, which hide their true essence inside the boundary of the surface; however, we never access anything but the surface of things. This is true for human bodies, which define their identities based on the signs that they carry on the surface of their skins, all the way down to fundamental particles in physics, because fundamental particles appear to us as bundles of superficial effects. I believe that science has been showing us that the deeper we dig into reality, the more we discover hidden surfaces rather than solid volumes. I often think about how the atoms that make up matter are essentially composed of empty space and that what we perceive as being full is actually mostly made up of surfaces in reciprocal interaction with each other. In this sense, I believe that dismantling the metaphysics of volumes and favoring what we could define as a surface-oriented ontology could paradoxically guide us to a deeper understanding of the nature of matter and reality, and I see two fields—two practices—in which I believe this new surface-oriented thinking could actually be crucial for the future. The first field is probably the most expected from me, and that is material science and nanotechnology. Nanotechnology encompasses all the techniques of working with matter on the nanometric scale, and I believe that nanotechnology has unveiled the potential of surfaces by creating a space where they actually become more important, more relevant, than volumes. This has allowed nanotechnology to access incredible complexity by working on the same scale as biological life.

The second field or practice in which I believe a surface-oriented thinking would be relevant is the slightly less obvious one of feminist theory or feminist practice. Understanding gender and sexual identities as the result of performative surface effects rather than the results of deeply rooted identities could help us overcome the oppressive aspects of identity politics, as Judith Butler asks as a series of important questions in *Gender Trouble*: "In what language is 'inner space' figured? What kind of figuration is it, and through what figure of the body is it signified? How does a body figure on its surface the very invisibility of its hidden depth?"[1] So, the surface forms critical questions even for the future of feminist theory.

Andrea Cetrulo: Thank you, Laura—and Michael, what is your take on this?

Michael Marder: Thank you for the question, which goes right to the core of my philosophy and its various iterations from the vegetal to my work on energy, dust, and many other things that are broadly guided by the phenomenological perspective. As we know, in phenomenology, appearances are paramount, though it is not only the actual appearances but also the act of appearing that is crucial. Appearances *and* how they emerge (the how of appearing matters) are what phenomenologists pay attention to. So, it is true that, as phenomenologists, we are no longer enthralled with the hidden dimension of depth as the inaccessible realm of metaphysics per se, but appearances themselves do not exhaust everything that is to be said about the surface because "surface" is as much a noun as it is a verb. When dealing with surfaces as things around us, in English at least, there is also the verb "to surface"—signaling how it is that things come up, how it is that they present themselves to our senses: to touch, to vision, to hearing, and to all of the other sensory interfaces that we have with the surfaces of the world, with the myriads of varied surfaces that the world itself is.

Thus, my answer is somewhat ambiguous because (in the history of metaphysics) there is not one single notion of depth and surface that we could apply to the whole range of Western thought. For instance, if you look at ancient Greek thought, depth is equated with materiality—matter is deep and dark and there is no way to access it in and of itself; we need some images, we need some surfaces or appearances to make sense of it, and the appearances that surface, those that float on the surface of the material abyss, are precisely the forms, the images, of the Platonic stratum. So, beneath the seemingly immortal, eternal, and immutable realm of ideas, there is the deep realm of matter which is inaccessible in and of itself—this is Plotinus' take on Plato, to be exact.

But then if we think about the rest of the history of Western theo-ontology, especially with respect to Christianity, we immediately notice that the concept of interiority/depth became subjectivized: it became the deep space of the subject as opposed to matter which is external, out there in the world, acting sort of like a container for the uncontainable. This is the indwelling of God within the finite being, and this is what depth implies in this kind of transformation in Western metaphysics. Hence, there is no one answer precisely because, on the one hand, depth is matter itself, and, on the other hand, depth is the nascent subjectivity of a Christian ilk and the infinity of God that it contains.

Having said that, I absolutely agree that we need to rework, reimagine, and rethink the relation between surface and depth, above all in an applied field where such an effort is perhaps least expected, namely energy. My own philosophizing moved along these lines in my 2017 book *Energy Dreams: Of Actuality*, following the idea that our contemporary practices of energy production are destructive precisely because they are extractive: the idea is that energy is contained in depths: in the deeper strata of the Earth, in the subjects who have knowledge that can be extracted from them, in the value that things contain and that can also be extracted from them, even as we throw away the material shells of those things. So, our practices of energy production are destructive and extractive because we look for energy in the depths of things, and we seemingly need to break through the surface appearances in order to get to that valuable energetic kernel.

From my standpoint, then, alternative energy paradigms are not just predicated on renewable energies but on those cherishing the energy of the surface, the energy that freely circulates on the surfaces and their interfaces that increases insofar as more surfaces unroll in the world, opening up to the other or to others. We can find such a model of energy in plant life, for instance—photosynthesis and the receptivity of the leaf to the solar energy that gives plants a big bulk of their own energy. This is something we can learn from plants, I think, notably a much more surface-oriented and essentially superficial approach to energy allowing it to circulate, receiving it as opposed to wresting it violently from things by way of destroying their surfaces.

I. Myth—The Broken Tablet, Face of God; Arachne's Thread

Andrea Cetrulo: That is a great trajectory, Michael, and it leads us to the expansion of this concept of surface by sharing a mythic representation or manifestation of this concept. We can start with Michael's image.

Michael Marder: I have chosen Rembrandt's painting *Moses Breaking the Tablets of the Law* from 1659. By way of introduction, I would say that every surface is a kind of face, the face that all animate beings and even inanimate objects have. There is, in fact, always more than one face or surface to things (an infinite number, perhaps) in a reality boasting three or more dimensions. Some surfaces hide others from view by virtue of their very self-presentation: by showing themselves, by handing themselves over to sight and to other senses, they withhold something. This *something* is not depth—it is not the deeply buried secret essence of things—but their other surfaces or faces.

In Hebrew, "face" is said and written in the plural, *panim*, "faces." Each face, each surface, is in itself faces—surfaces. So, there is no singular form for face: in the singular, it is already plural, a little bit like God, seeing that one of the words for God, "*Elohim*," which is said also, and quite irreducibly, in the plural in this religion that claims to be the first monotheistic faith. The face of God is faces of gods, "*p'nei Elohim.*" It is (they are) unrepresentable, yet humankind is created in the image of God—that is, in the image of countless divine surfaces and faces. Unrepresentable, not only due to a sacred prohibition but also, and above all, because the representation of some will conceal others from view. A political problem built into theology and ontology . . . In the same sense, nothing is really representable, as even the multidimensional vision of Cubism shows.

So, how should we interpret Jacob's declaration in Gen. 32:30, that he has seen God face-to-face ("*panim-el'-panim*"), yet his life has been preserved? And what is the sense of his brother Esau's exclamation a few verses later, "seeing your face is like seeing the face of God" ("*p'nei Elohim*")? What is the meaning of God "speaking to Moses face to face ('*panim-el'-panim*') as one speaks to a friend" (in Exod. 33:11), so that afterwards the face of Moses shines? Does it not mean that one has become capacious enough to acknowledge and accept innumerable faces and surfaces in the Other, in others, and in oneself, letting these faces and surfaces face out into the world? Does it not imply the flourishing of surfaces that, inexhaustible, are the interfaces between the I and the other? What law is there other than that of the anarchic proliferation of surfaces? In Rembrandt's painting that you have before you, the stony surface of the tablets is dark (the tablets that have the inscription of the law, and it is the face of Moses that irradiates light (just look at the glare from his face on his left sleeve). I will not say more about this image but would urge you to face it and to explore its different semantic, symbolic, and visual surfaces through these brief reflections on the being-surface of surface.

Andrea Cetrulo: Thank you, Michael—and now, Laura, are you ready to share your mythic contribution with us?

Laura Tripaldi: I have chosen to talk about the myth of Arachne from Greek mythology to signify the complexity of the concept of surface. As everyone knows, Arachne was a young woman who was incredibly gifted in the art of weaving. She was so gifted, in fact, that her talent would eventually awaken the anger of the goddess Athena, who disguised herself as an old woman and challenged her to a weaving contest.

Seeing that Arachne's tapestry was much more intricate and beautiful than hers, Athena was so furious that she tore Arachne's tapestry to pieces. Arachne was so desperate that she decided to hang herself from a tree. Athena was moved to pity by the poor Arachne and decided to save her life but, as a punishment nonetheless, she transformed Arachne into a spider. Arachne then metamorphosed into a spider-form, and she would spend the rest of her life weaving her spiderweb.

I find this myth to be particularly illuminating with respect to the concept of surface, as it relates to the idea of the technological interface. By interface, we usually mean the surface where human and technology meet and establish a reciprocal communication. In the case of Arachne, we can see how the fusion of the woman's body and her technological device, the loom, produces a hybrid body that is neither natural nor technological, neither human nor inhuman. I think the most critical point here is asking ourselves why, in the Greek myth, this outcome is presented to us as a curse. I would argue that our material culture is founded on an aversion toward surfaces, in the sense that the surface is the place where our identity is constantly constructed through processes of representation, but also the place where identity is perpetually put into question. In the context of technology, we are used to conceiving of surfaces as passive and smooth substrates, which we try to make increasingly immaterial and increasingly invisible. I would say that the two surfaces we are most familiar with in the context of technology are the mirror, which is the surface that represents ourselves, and the screen, which is the surface that represents the world. Both the mirror and the screen are material bodies, but they create the illusion of disappearing behind the images that they are representing. This apparent invisibility results in a constant forgetting of the materiality of the surface, which is never as passive as we assume it to be. In this regard, I believe that the myth of Arachne proposes an alternative paradigm for our relationship with surfaces, as the technology of weaving (in itself) is based on the idea of the surface as a material space of mutual interaction. The threads of the fabric are entwined in a way that maximizes their surface contact.

The same thing takes place within the silk of the spiderweb since each thread of the spider silk is the result of an enormous number of nanometric components in constant interaction with each other. As I have already stated, the idea of nanotechnology is precisely that of expanding the extension of surfaces to create a network of interacting components. And, in this sense, there is a strong connection between the concept of the surface as an active material space and the future of our relationship with technology. In the case of Arachne, the interface between woman and technology produces a mutual influence, so that not only the human is acting on technology, but technology can retroactively change the meaning of what we assume to be human.

This is particularly evident in the depiction of Arachne that I have selected. This is an engraving made by Gustav Doré in 1868, and it represents the encounter between Arachne and Dante Alighieri as it is described in the 12th canto of Dante's *Purgatorio*. Here, we see Arachne in an intermediate condition where she is no longer fully human but not yet fully animal. This ambiguous and somewhat monstrous state is representative of the interface as the material space where two bodies can be mutually transformed. I believe that we perceive this transformation to be monstrous only as long as we assume that there is such a thing as a human before technology. In reality, it is the surface between human and technology that is precisely the space where our human identity is constructed.

II. Image/Artwork—Chernobyl Photograms; Liquid Orb Droplets and the Minakata Mandala

Andrea Cetrulo: Thank you, Laura. We can *weave* this example into the following one, which is our segment for artistic images, although we are already kind of there with the fantastic Rembrandt and Doré visuals. But this one intrigues me greatly as my own initial question (before this session) about surfaces and their intrinsic value was primarily concerned with art in mind. So, Michael, what is the specific image that you have brought today?

Michael Marder: This image is from Anais Tondeur's *Chernobyl Herbarium*, and it is a specimen of a plant from the exclusion zone of Chernobyl. I will say a few words about the artistic practice that resulted in this image to begin with. Art is the play of surfaces and the interplay of interfaces. It is an activity that allows as many surfaces as possible to emerge in the perceptual and cognitive fields and to encounter (to touch or to brush upon, really) other surfaces, previously unregistered, unthought, and unappreciated. When I say "play," I am not diminishing this essentially superficial activity of art; there is, perhaps, nothing more serious than this play. I would even risk asserting that there is nothing *but* this play and that reality itself is impoverished when the play of surfaces (or the play *with* this play) is regulated in such a way that only a few are allowed to appear, to brush upon, or to touch one another, and our senses or minds.

In the aesthetic practice of contemporary French artist Anais Tondeur, surfaces are paramount. *The Chernobyl Herbarium*, from which this image has been extracted, comprises a series of photograms that were accompanied by textual fragments I composed and published to mark the thirtieth anniversary of the Chernobyl disaster in 2016. The artworks in it are a case in point of Tondeur's commitment to surface. Her technique is based on arranging the irradiated plants from Chernobyl on photosensitive paper, letting them leave a trace (including a trace of radiation), and supplementing these traces with other chemically induced effects. The material support for the artwork meets plants surface-to-surface, receiving their impressions. This exposure repeats the earlier exposure to radiation from the soil of Chernobyl, laced with radioactive isotopes. Through her art, Tondeur allows the surfaces of the world to touch, to communicate, to exchange bits of being itself. The repetition of exposure she enacts breathes with the promise of redemption, without denying the staying power of radiation, without sweeping the problem of environmental contamination, of an environment truly contaminated for centuries or millennia to come, under a beautifully embroidered rug of aesthetics.

Is that not what art has always done, in different forms, styles, genres? Has it not permitted a greater contact among the surfaces of the world, unfurling those surfaces that have been barely noticed, obscure, or altogether nonexistent? Has it not brought them to bear on our senses, so that our vision, hearing, taste, and smell, as well as touch itself, would be altered by these surfaces? However conceptual it becomes, the art of the future will be the art of surfaces— of surfacing (letting or making surface).

> **Laura Tripaldi:** The artwork I have selected is a short video by the Finnish, Berlin-based artist Jenna Sutela, which was shot in collaboration with Mikko Gaestel.[2] Sutela's artwork usually explores concepts such as the boundary between the organic and inorganic, the self-organization of matter, microbial life, and the relationship between matter and language. This particular artwork is structured around three different material elements and conceptual references, which I believe can all support our discussion on the concept of surface in different and interconnected ways.

First and foremost, we see in the video a metallic structure or sculpture. This is a three-dimensional reconstruction of the so-called Minakata Mandala, a drawing made by Japanese naturalist Minakata Kumagusu at the end of the nineteenth century. Minakata was one of the founders of contemporary ecology and believed that all things were interconnected in a kind of network or web. He represented this concept in the form of a diagram, or mandala, composed of many entangled threads. Minakata's drawing was devoid of any center, signifying that the fabric of reality is essentially decentralized, arising spontaneously from the relations between all things, organic and inorganic, living and nonliving.

The second element of Sutela's artwork appears as some kind of liquid metal, possibly mercury. We see several droplets coalescing together to form a larger structure. This is a reference to the movie *Terminator II: Judgement Day*, where we are introduced to an improved model of the first Terminator, T-800. This new model is called T-1000 and, in contrast to its predecessor, it has a completely soft and self-organizing structure that can continuously change its shape. This improved technological model makes the T-1000 essentially indestructible and invincible. The difference between the two Terminator models refers to two different paradigms of material culture: on one side, we have the hard-assembled, rigid structure of old technology, while on the other hand, we have the self-organizing new materials that blur the boundaries between living and nonliving.

Finally, the third element of this artwork is a living organism known as *Physarum polycephalum*, also commonly known as slime mold. Its scientific name, polycephalum, literally means "many-headed." Slime mold is a yellowish organism that belongs to the kingdom of Protista. It has an acellular structure, meaning that instead of being composed of cells, it is composed of free nuclei swimming in a protoplasmic sack, enclosed inside a flexible cellular membrane. Much like the T-1000, *Physarum polycephalum* can change its shape, and its internal, decentralized structure makes it one of the most interesting organisms known to us. Despite appearing incredibly simple, *Physarum polycephalum* has been shown to possess incredible intelligence and problem-solving capacity. Some specimens of slime mold have also been used in new material substrates for alternative forms of computing.

In summary, we have three elements, one from philosophical thinking, one from speculative technology or fiction, and one from nature. I would argue that what these three elements have in common is a shared concept of the surface as the place where complexity takes place. In all three cases, we can see how complex and intelligent structures can emerge from simple elements by building interactive and flexible surfaces. In the Minakata Mandala, the surfaces between the different threads build the foundational network of reality. In the T-1000, the shape-shifting surface overcomes the limitations of traditional technology by self-organizing and adapting to the environment. In *Physarum polycephalum*, the smart, sensing membrane is an intelligent interface that does not simply protect or isolate the organism from its environment but defines its behavior within the outside world.

Gustave Doré, *Arachne* (1861).

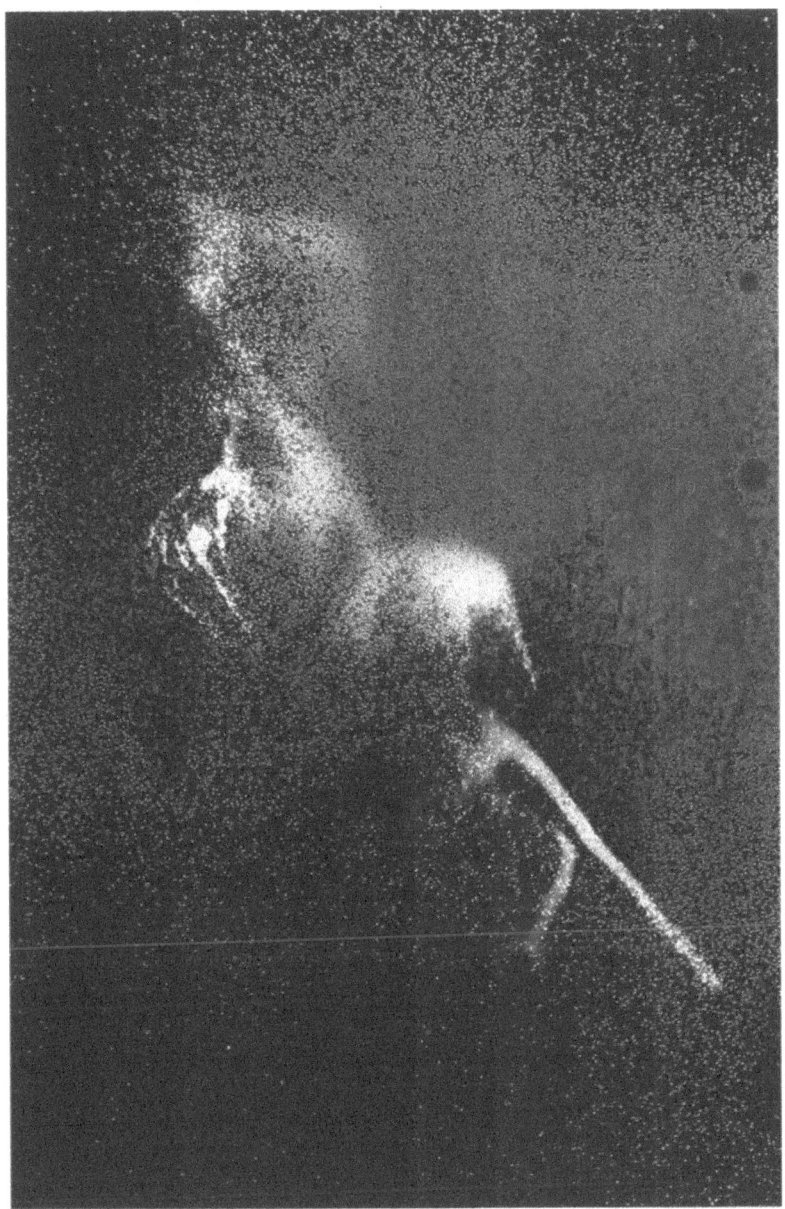

Anais Tondeur, Linum usitatissimum, Exclusion Zone, Chernobyl, Radiation level: 1.7 µSv/h from *The Chernobyl Herbarium* with Michael Marder (Open Humanities Press, 2016).

III. Phenomenon—Electronic Skin; Klein Bottle House

> **Andrea Cetrulo:** Wonderful—and our last examples of surfaces will revolve around an emergent phenomenon of your choice that has caught your attention.
>
> **Laura Tripaldi:** The emergent phenomenon that I have selected is that of so-called "electronic skin" or "e-skin." I think this is one of the most astounding spheres of technology today: the field of wearable technology. Electronic skin is a material device that can be applied to human skin and used as a new kind of interface between human and technology. One of the most promising applications of electronic skins is that they can be used for medical purposes, for instance as a way to "read" physiological parameters of patients in real time, or as prosthetic implants. But they also hold the possibility to change the way we are used to interacting with digital technology by constructing a continuous interface between our skin and our electronic devices, so that we can control them by moving (directly moving our bodies). The sense of touch is one of the most complex senses we possess, but possibly, it is also the most overlooked. Our culture, our metaphysics, and our epistemology are dominated by metaphors of vision, and this shapes the way we approach technology. A great deal of effort has been put into creating technologies of vision and simulating our human sense of sight in robots and artificial organisms, but engineering a robot that can "feel" the world with its own skin would introduce a radical shift in our approach to robotics. Electronic skins could allow us to create robots that feel their surroundings just as we humans do, or even in a radically different and alien way.

I believe that e-skin can help us access at least three different meanings or layers of the concept of surface. At the most material level, the e-skin is usually produced by nanotechnology, meaning that the interactive material structure of these devices is made possible by embedding a multitude of tiny, nanometric elements within a flexible matrix. These elements can self-organize and become functional as a result of decentralized surface interactions, thus highlighting the crucial importance of surfaces in processes of self-organization. As opposed to vertically assembled, hierarchical models of technology, nanotechnology focuses on bottom-up assembly, revealing the intelligence and agency of nonliving matter and technological objects.

Second, the e-skin is a new model for the interface between human and technology as opposed to the model of the screen that I have mentioned earlier. The screen, as a rigid and flat device, appears like a "window" and is always placed at a "safe distance" from its user. As a consequence, our interaction with technological devices is structured around our eyes and hands, while the rest of our bodies are entirely excluded from the interface. E-skin overturns this paradigm and proposes a new approach to interfaces that will be crucial for the future of technology. By extending the human/technology interface to the whole surface of our bodies, e-skin brings technology in much closer proximity to us. This unveils the deep interconnection and mutual transformation between ourselves and our technological devices, and shows that the interface truly is a material and productive space.

Thirdly, electronic skin allows us to reflect on the surface as the space where matter is transmuted into information and information can retroactively influence material structures. By acting as a material space where information on our bodies can be gathered and stored, e-skin reveals both the promises and the dangers of virtualization and technological disembodiment. The surface, being the boundary of the body, is the place where our bodies stop being simple material entities and acquire their linguistic and social meanings. As Donna Haraway said in her essay "Situated Knowledges: The Science Question in Feminism and the Privilege of Partial Perspective": "Bodies as objects of knowledge are material-semiotic generative nodes. Their *boundaries* materialize in social interaction. Boundaries are drawn by mapping practices; 'objects' do not pre-exist as such. Objects are boundary projects. But boundaries shift from within; boundaries are very tricky. What boundaries provisionally contain remains generative, productive of meanings and bodies. Siting (sighting) boundaries is a risky practice."[3] The surface, being the space where meaning is constructed, blurs the boundary between political and technological action, and this is the reason why I feel that speculating on the concept of surface is truly necessary as we step into the future.

Andrea Cetrulo: Thank you, Laura, that is all so alluring—and Michael, we are now ready to share your selection.

Michael Marder: As an example of a contemporary phenomenon, I have selected an architectural work: a Klein Bottle house designed by the firm McBride Charles Ryan. And so, I want us to reflect very briefly on the meaning of architecture in the context of surfaces as opposed to depth. We usually assume that to dwell—to inhabit—is to be inside, to hide within the interiority of a prosthetic shell that architecture creates for human beings. But this is a very specific notion of dwelling that is influenced by our identification with the animal world, with various species of animals who hide in holes in the ground, in tree hollows, in caves or lairs. Plants inhabit the world otherwise, both exposing their leafy surfaces to the sun and the atmosphere and burrowing deep into the earth with their roots. We would do well if we were to learn from plants how to balance the surface and the depth in dwelling, how to be inside out and outside in.

The spatial experience of a habitable structure, where the inside passes into the outside and vice versa, is the Klein Bottle house designed by McBride Charles Ryan in Australia. The Klein Bottle is a non-orientable object, similar to the Moebius strip. (In fact, should you dissect the Klein Bottle, you would obtain the Moebius strip.) Simply put, it is a one-sided surface that, if traveled upon, could be followed back to the point of origin while flipping the traveler upside down. Being in a Klein Bottle is being on a surface that has no boundary where it would abruptly stop, no absolute edge. It is infinite within the finitude of the here-and-now.

I would not claim that the Klein Bottle house is a perfect ecological structure. The reason why I like it, though, is that it realizes the seemingly crazy idea of living in and on the surface, an infinite boundaryless surface that is still attached to the finitude of existence. For too long we have considered our dwellings as containers for our belongings and bodies—boxes into which we can retreat on a daily (and nightly) basis. Now that inhabiting a surface has become possible, the next task is to imagine how to combine the surface of the dwelling with the evolving, growing, decaying, metamorphosing surfaces of the world.

IV. Questions

Andrea Cetrulo: To finalize but also give continuity to this fascinating conversation, I would ask you both to summon a future oracle from the last visionaries of the Seven Prophecies series, either Jason Mohaghegh or Reza Negarestani, and to ask them a lone question. The answer will be revealed in the next episode, for which the password to their prophetic chamber is "Idol."

Laura Tripaldi: Both of you, Reza and Jason, have explored the way in which divinity, as a cultural and human artifact, becomes gradually emancipated from humanity, acquiring autonomy and becoming a self-sustaining force of transformation and change. So, I would like to summon Reza to answer my question. Reza, in *Cyclonopedia* you wrote that "to desertify the earth is to make the earth ready for change in the name of the Divine's monopoly, as opposed to terrestrial idols."[4] I have always thought that this desertification is a way to hide the inevitable materiality of even God himself. In fact, in your work, you have shown very effectively that even divinity is always dependent on a number of material processes. Would you say that the monotheistic God is inherently different from all terrestrial idols, or is it just an idol whose material vessel is always hidden? Is the distinction between Gods and Idols becoming more blurred or more defined as we move toward the future?

Michael Marder: And I have a series of brief questions for Jason: Have one-dimensional images displaced idols in the twenty-first century? Has the difference—however minimal, however spectral—between the idols and the images been erased? Are images our idols, and, if so, how do they fare in the Night?

PROPHECY 7.0

Idol

Part 1. Seven Prophecies of the Future (Idol). *Source*: Artist: Egor Myznick, "Anubis, God of Embalming and Funerals" (2020).

Chapter 7.0
Idol

Oracles: Jason Mohaghegh, Reza Negarestani
Guide: Andrea Cetrulo

Andrea Cetrulo: Welcome to the final episode of the Future Studies Program series: Seven Prophecies of the Future. Before we welcome Jason Bahbak Mohaghegh and Reza Negarestani, our guests of this episode, I would like to make a few remarks as we approach the end of our Seven Prophecies of the Future series. Above all else, our thanks go to the Future Studies Program faculty for allowing us to enter a world of magic, in the etymological sense of the word, meaning of foreign things—the unknown—and that which transforms the world around us and opens new possible avenues to experience reality, and for doing this so graciously from a place of enchantment and fascination through storytelling and honest speculation along the seven episodes that have composed the series (Chimera, Cipher, Temple, Reign, Oracle, Surface, and Idol). Through these encounters, we were able to open a space for alternative narratives to emerge—narratives that don't follow the conventional format of a chronological account of history but rather seek to find the points where events meet and resonate with one another. As the art historian Georges Didi-Huberman puts it: "A historical discourse which is never born but always recommences."[1] It is in this manner that our guests have elegantly addressed the future, bringing groundbreaking observations on futurity without forgetting the legacy of those who have done it before them. Our oracles of the future have summoned all sorts of eclectic phenomena and correspondences: the unknown, the unseen, or simply the overlooked. Monsters, ghosts, artworks, and creatures that transcend human self-representation have made their appearance. We hope that this injection of enthusiasm and original thoughts has somehow quenched the thirst many of us in our contemporary world have for hearing stories that escape the ordinary experience of reality itself. I am Andrea Cetrulo, and it has been a pleasure to guide you toward these chambers.

Tonight, I am joined by the Future Studies Program founder, philosopher Jason Bahbak Mohaghegh, and by fellow Iranian philosopher Reza Negarestani. Their conceptual password: Idol. Welcome, Reza and Jason, to the grand finale that marks the end of the Seven Prophecies of the Future series. Both of you will be our oracles of futurity, leading us to the chamber that holds the figure of *the idol*. I believe tonight we have two teams: the monotheistic team and the idols team. So, let us start with the monotheistic team and its Player One, Reza.

I. Myth—Abraham's Paradox; The Assyrian Idol Curse

Reza Negarestani: The title of my mythic segment here is: "If idols are real, then we should invent a God to smash them." This sounds excessively monotheistic in its nature, but I assure that it is not, and for those of you who have come from Middle Eastern cultures or Muslim societies, you would know that there is a story that every child learns and is exposed to in elementary school. This is the story of Abraham's rebellion against idols—also what is usually called the "paradox of idolatry"—or in the Book of Isaiah, it is called the "paradox of human fingers." This story can even be watched as a cartoon on Friday mornings and is quite simply this: at night Abraham goes to the grand temple of King Nimrod—of the Babylonian Empire, though probably there is a confusion of different ages and kings according to whatever versions—where there are numerous idols of different ranks, different priorities, different statures, and different composures. And, within the temple, there is also the Grand Idol, which epitomizes the bad. So, Abraham wields an ax and he starts to smash the heads of every idol in this temple except for one: the grand one, Baʻal himself. Then he puts the ax around the neck of Baʻal; he exits the temple, sleeps as if nothing has happened, and the following morning the priests come to the temple and notice the complete chaos of someone having sabotaged and broken all the idols except one. Then they start to inquire, and some people say: "Well, we have seen Abraham at this time of night going to the temple, so it must be him." They bring Abraham to the courts, put him under pressure, interrogate him, and Abraham explains: "Look, it cannot be me, since the one who is responsible is the person who noticeably wields the ax. Namely, Ba'al, the grand idol." And then the priests react in outrage: "How can this be? Are you out of your mind? How can a statue essentially smash other statues?" And Abraham responds: "Well, if they are mere statues, then why are you in fact worshiping them—namely, if they are incapable of exerting any sort of power, even the lowliest of human powers, then why are they venerated?" This is also why it's called the paradox of human fingers because Isaiah, in a verse, says that their land is full of idols, their fingers have made these idols from water and dirt, and they think that they have also created them—that they have given them their lands and so forth. So, these are products of monotheism, so to speak from which monotheism begins to basically, kind of, advance against the cult of devotional images.

Now, I want to make this clear, and I know that Jason probably would not like this idea: that any sort of talk about idols (in the original sense of the word) is already coming from a presupposed and established position that has been set either within the ambit of monotheism or within the ambit of enlightenment—that is early enlightenment, philosophy in a grand enlightening sense of Plato. Now we know that for Plato they are *eidolons*, namely appearances, as opposed to the *eidos* which all have divine origin and are called the forms. And the key thing is that you must shatter the appearances, the wall of appearances, in order to get into the nature of forms. And *eidos* is good itself. So, that is one way to see these appearances (*eidolons*), such that even calling them idols in this negative sense that is usually associated with them, or seeing them as many representations, is itself already assuming that there is a unity behind such representations. You are approaching them negatively precisely because you are already beginning with a paradigm that starts from a unity—unity of nature, unity of ideas or forms, or unity of the divine.

This is a Platonic story, although you can see it in monotheism as well, and here I am not talking about Abrahamic monotheism but actually starting with a much older form of monotheism: that of the Aten cults of the Sun-Disk, whereby the pharaoh Akhenaten's heresy created an uproar in traditional Egyptian society for almost twenty years by commanding all records of gods and lesser deities to be expunged. The only things that were being preserved were related to Aten, the picture of Aten, as a sun god usually associated with Ra but not having the anthropomorphic figuration of Ra—rather, it is just a disk of sun emanating rays from itself, and always placed high in the sky above for people to look at in amazement and awe. Sometimes, the most anthropomorphic variations of this disk are that the rays take the shape of hands, but that is as anthropomorphic as it gets. So, this creates a disquiet in Egyptian society and obviously results in a major coup against Akhenaten, a coup against the complete heresy he committed against a sort of proliferation of images upon which Egyptian polytheism thrived. Thus, this unification, this picture of unity behind what Plato would have called the confusion of fluxes, the confusion of passing illusions and images—*eikonos*—is precisely an enduring core of the monotheistic enlightenment. Francis Bacon, for example, proposes his theory of idols as what you might call blind spots that prevent us from seeing the true essence of nature in an enlightened, scientific sense. So, we see that it is an enduring theme: that there is some sort of unity out there behind this mere flux of sensations and representations, a flux that by its very nature is paradoxical, because if we buy into this very idea of flux according to this sort of unity of nature, unity of the one, unity of the forms or ideas, then obviously we are not talking about reality. Indeed, we can no longer even talk about reality anymore: we would be just talking about ourselves projecting onto reality, projecting our mere sensations, dogmas, and opinions onto reality. Why I am saying dogmas here in a negative sense (even though it is a neutral word) precisely is because, if we are immediately living in the benighted universe of sensory fluxes and proliferation of images and representations, then is it possible for any of us to communicate the same representation that we experience of reality to another person, knowing that it would be the same representation, or would it become a completely futile project? Would the very idea of communicating in the deep sense of experience—of interpersonal experience—be hamstrung and rendered almost impossible? No doubt, there are these sorts of concerns that go to the origin of Greek philosophy, to the origin of proto-enlightenment, and effectively into the origin of monotheism itself.

Let us come back to monotheism—for again, the very fact that we are talking about idols implies that we have already adopted a certain sort of monotheist or unitary position, which is why people who actually live with idols (so-called idolatrous groups) do not hold them in the negative sense that we mean. They might have rankings for them—smaller or larger, of lesser or greater influence, deities and demons, and so forth, but that would be the extent of it. It would not comprise any sort of fight against a negative understanding of idols as obstacles or as things that fundamentally proliferate for the sake of proliferation or which ought to be purged, since they are all coming from a kind of background monotheistic position or unitary mindset. Regardless, what I want to focus on today is the nature of monotheism at its core, and the proto-philosophical concerns that have gone to the core of monotheism.

> **Andrea Cetrulo:** Now I think it is time to hear from you, Jason, the member of Team Idol, unless you have been somehow persuaded by Reza's propositions. So, how would you like to start your exploration of the idol, Jason? Go ahead, please.

Jason Mohaghegh: This was an exceptional reflection on Reza's part which clearly establishes both snares and openings to consider, but I still think that we can dodge the bullets of monotheism the way that it is being defined here. To respond to some of the prior points, then: first, it is just an empirical fact that idolatry predates almost every monotheism (thus the idols are not indebted to the epistemology of a single God, at least not for thousands of years); also, key anthropological accounts show that idol cultures in the ancient world allowed for the trading, metamorphosis, abandonment, and distortion of god-types much more easily than monotheistic traditions. You can switch your idols, you can bargain your idols, you can sell your idols, you can desert your idols far more easily than monotheistic orthodoxies allow. They are even physically portable in most instances, which lends them a rotational flexibility in the mind as well, just like there exists a greater versatility in the political structures of barbarian city-states than with later empires: for the barbarian king or queen is only ruler as long as they are visibly prevailing but can be immediately overthrown upon defeat, failure, or corruption because they have no greater metaphorical legitimacy or symbolic structure beyond their practical or instrumental effect in war. The day we go hungry is the day the barbarian leader can be substituted for someone else, and I think that idols follow this model of erratic resiliency as well.

Furthermore, while I appreciated Reza's point about the Abrahamic story, I find it actually vindicates my side to a large extent because this feature that the idols can be shattered by the ax means that they are embedded in the realm of extreme vulnerability, and this instantly makes them far more interesting to me than untouchable or transcendent divinities who cannot bleed, who cannot experience pain, and who cannot be killed. Clenching them to the realm of the body and touch is absolutely crucial to my mind not only at the destructive level (allowing them to be eliminated) but as a fulfillment of Nietzsche's wonderful saying that "I would only believe in a god who could dance." One should take that qualification quite seriously as an invitation to a tangible otherworldliness. Even if one looks at the Biblical tale of Jacob wrestling the angel, it describes his ability to steal the blessing through touch, through the immediate physicality of a grip, just as when our great grandmothers in the ancient world went down to worship their river god they were not praying to some faraway bearded overlord of the river: they were worshiping the river itself—the river *was* the god in that idolatrous realm—which meant that individuals could bathe in their god, could wash clothes in their god, could swim naked in their god, which then also frees potentials for becoming apotheosis. A god whose residue can linger on your skin exudes godlike powers and bestows godlike fortunes. So, I think that notion is worth mentioning as precisely where Abraham's story falls apart: for fragility is power, or at least an alternative type of power than that of a totalitarian oneness. In a similar vein, with a little interpretive trickery we can remember that the Black Stone in the Cube (*al-Ka'ba*) in Mecca around which everyone circumambulates is a piece of meteorite rock that supposedly comes from the time of Adam and Eve, some oval shard that fell to earth in their vicinity. And though believers for centuries have stridden around it as a symbol of monotheistic devotion, the truth is that they cannot pull off the amazing choreographic event of their collective motion, a virtual whirlpool in unison, thousands of entranced legs shifting around a cubed gravitational center, with just an invisible god. They absolutely need the supplemental force of the black stone to consolidate it energetically; nothing happens there without this miraculous stone projectile (which definitionally is a kind of idol). You see, that is where even God needs the idol.

Lastly, I would accept Reza's accusation that if we remain purely in theological or philosophical chambers of reflection, then idolatry might indeed stumble into some of the same traps of monotheistic metaphysics, but then I study other disciplines and methods of expression which challenge this equivalence. Literature, poetry, mysticism, sculpture, theater, dance: here they are entirely irrelevant universes to one another. And I would strongly maintain that there is a massive qualitative difference in the creativity which comes out of idolatry versus monotheism: namely, that the subcultural aesthetics and performative registers that arise from the idol worlds are far superior. Dance, incantation, metamorphic readings, and recitations—things of that nature that can manifest only under the shadow of the idol.

Hence, I want to begin my mythic exploration of the idol through the prism of a single poem. Titled "Tale of the Assyrian Statue," it holds several astounding subliminal messages, one of which is that it narrates an immense passage of time from the perspective of an old Assyrian idol's own consciousness. It is actually written in the sinister voice of the idol itself, which opens a dark level of tonality that we can never find in human expression. Furthermore, its author, the reclusive poet Mahmoud al-Buraikan, was himself someone who rarely ever released his own poetic works, preferring a life of obscurity, such that the few remaining pieces of this Iraqi literary genius come to us as smuggled documents that friends stole from his house and published against his will. So merely by reading the following lines, we are automatically in possession of a forbidden work, and this criminal trespass itself has much to do with the circulatory networks of piracy and trafficking that have always accompanied the world of idols.

Let us look to the three opening verses from "The Tale of the Assyrian Statue," where we find the graven form after thousands of years now placed in a display case in some modern museum.[2] From the first lines alone, where it sits "in a glass room . . . confronting the eyes of men, paralyzing them," we start to understand the intricate nature and strange effects of the idol that differentiate it from archetypal sacred objects and symbols. To begin with, the fact that it is a deserted artifact that comes from a "lost city" is an essential detail, as it reveals the idol as a plaything in the hands of impermanence, indeterminacy, and potential obsolescence. It is not guaranteed an eternal status—neither immemorial (since it was constructed one day in time) nor everlasting (it might not make it to witness the apocalyptic limit of the world); it can be subjected to merciless abandonment. This god of the idol admits that it can fail; this god admits that it can die. Second, it speaks of its "elevation"—though not to some celestial register, only high enough that it can stare directly into the eyes of all followers: the idol is therefore not the invisible God who looks down, but rather the one who casts a paralyzing gaze straight into the pupils of its human subjects. Not the all-seeing remote gaze of the witness, but the knife-and-dagger glare of the expectant, the overseer of high prices who sees right through you, who makes you want to tear out your own eyes from dread, and who demands unbearable tasks in its service. The idol is the manifested god in whose empty sockets we drown and tremble, the full awe of the abyss embodied in a miniature physiology for the ages. Third, the idol speaks of "silence": unlike the traditional deities who hang their authority on the logos, inscribing endless texts and demanding endless regurgitation and nightly prayer words, this rock or metallic figure hangs back in the realms of the unspoken, the unsaid, and the untold. This silence is more gravely intimidating than any commandment or hellfire threat, for it is the signal of radical calmness, inevitability, and the omen. The idol does not need to speak, for the idol has already set in motion the deranged set of events that will lock one in its fatalistic grip. This is the sound of pure terror, what the poet calls the "terror of the ninth century"—not the void of noise but the hush of inescapable measures, one that whispers: *it's already done, already too late*.

In the second verse, we are introduced to the paradoxical riddle that the idol's dominance—written here as the "Master"—emanates from its origination in an "inscrutable moment." This is a telling departure from those gods whose origin stories precede even the origin stories of the cosmos or earth—instead, the idol here confesses openly that they are an artificial item forged at the hands of some random craftsman. Theirs is neither a hallowed nor sacrosanct beginning—rather, it is a whimsical or artisanal emergence in the world of materiality, proportion, and appearances. No depth, only the contorted infinity of the surface found in "halls of stone and clay." So, if the idol is enigmatic, then it is not because it partakes in some game of hide-and-seek between heaven and world; it does not cloak itself in mysterious distances and withhold esoteric answers. Instead, the idol is the true secret: meaning that it is what remains an unstoppable force of secrecy—disorienting, demented, unfathomable—even when existing in full transparency (right in front of you). In fact, it is its awful presence—its immediacy in space, instantaneity in time—which is the source of its mystification.

We open the third verse, then, with a reiteration of the word "terror"—though on this occasion linked to the sacrificial rites of "blood offerings" made by "tribes of the dead." Now we already recall that the idol's constructedness—molded into being by some rogue sculptor—did not diminish its wrath or affective intensity but somehow enhanced it. This is because there is perhaps nothing more disturbing than the idea that the human can reach beyond itself, can summon the inhuman, can fashion unanticipated things which then spill out of their own control and become lost causes or runaway events. But beyond this, the fact that the idol belongs to a tribal populace is a critical facet: for it is therefore not a universal god-type, but one of particularity, exclusivity, and territorial dominion. Weirdly enough, it is these partial gods who should be feared more than the all-encompassing ones, since they demand different currencies of devotion and sacrifice than their omnipotent counterparts. Hence, the "blood offerings" are not metaphorical gestures of loyalty—they are evidence of an actual thirst, a survival instinct and vampiric desiring mechanism at work in the idol. The idol does not require formal spectacles of violence like the ritual slaughtering of lambs; the idol needs to drink blood to stay alive. Thus the incantations of the tribal sorcerers—"cadence of the chant," as the poet says—are not profound metaphysical truths but rather the hunger pangs from the empty stomach and twisting entrails of the idol. And there is also a beautiful geo-poetic suggestion in the fact that its nomadic setting, being moved from landscape to landscape, city to city, sand dune to oasis, affords it the versatility of "being called by many names." Like the blank domino or the wild card in poker, like the skeleton key that opens every room, the idol can shape-shift in a single flicker of movement; it can wear multiple guises and disguises, suit multiple narratives and inhabit divergent cosmologies; it can change allegiances and bring new talismanic gifts or curses to whomever stumbles across its eroded body in the desert and picks it up again. If it is forgotten in time for a while, then this is only so that it can make its eventual return. Only that which disappears can appear again.

II. Image/Artwork—The Earth Spy; The Stratachrome Master

Andrea Cetrulo: Let us take the duel between God and idol into the domain of a single image or artwork. Reza, can you advance a work that testifies to the monotheistic outlook?

Reza Negarestani: Particularly, I want to narrow down my focus to give a rather science-fictional account of what monotheism is. I imagine that those who have read the Strugatsky brothers' *Hard to Be a God* probably know what I mean by a science-fictional account of one God. A Soviet novel from 1964, it is essentially the story of an extremely advanced

Earth civilization that has created simulations all over different planets—simulations of what history could be—and the narrative happens from the perspective of an Earth spy who acts like a watchman (observing without making any interference with this planet). So, this planet and its human civilization have started in a magnificent way, and then the medieval times begin, and he finds himself living in the Dark Ages surrounded by a lot of superstition and religious fanaticism. Suddenly, he starts noticing that something odd is happening in this civilization: namely, that this civilization is not going through the supposed historical progression in a Hegelian sense—meaning that from the medieval era they are skipping all the Enlightenment stuff and are rapidly progressing toward a techno-fascist society. The Enlightenment did not happen; the Industrial Age did not happen; simply a straight line from the Dark Ages to technofascism. Therefore, we return to this earth spy who is looking at these ant-like humans on a different planet—and he cannot interfere, as the Earth Directorate has absolutely disallowed any agents from influencing this history so they can observe how it evolves without any external intervention. But then he realizes that there is too much at stake for the people around him, such that he must interfere as a god (since he is a god technologically from the historical perspective of these people). Thus, we have the title: *Hard to Be a God*. This is a certain kind of story that I am very interested in recreating for monotheism: asking what monotheism would look like to us if we were aliens inhabiting the planet Earth and reporting back to our base about the historical progression of things happening, though not just those events that everyone knows on the planet Earth but how things are transpiring according to our own eyes.

Obviously, the sort of monotheism that we are talking about here has a very twisted beginning and is moving toward ever-twisted ends. It seems that monotheism did a great job at fighting the proliferation of images or appearances, precisely because I think that (and this is a very controversial thesis) the adoration or veneration of polytheism is even worse than the veneration of monotheism. Polytheism has (what one might call) all the negativities of religion, but under the banner of some sort of multitude—multitude for whom? For the rise of religion again under a different guise? At the very least, monotheism is honest about its ulterior motives: we know what monotheism is. As monotheists, we say no to the legion, to the proliferation of idols or appearances.

Monotheism essentially comes with a strategic plan of how to deal with the proliferation of images, namely the problem of religiosity. The problem of the *theós*, or the proliferation of deities, the proliferation of gods, and the proliferation of opportunities for these gods. It is extremely hard to fight idolatry as monotheism understands it. Killing too many birds with one stone just will not work. Then, within polytheism, one still has theism plus a small degree of proliferation of these deities in a constrained way. You need to have a family of resemblance, a web of idols of different sources that are ultimately responsible for it. They have a hierarchy of idols, which is why polytheism essentially works. But under tribal idolatry, everyone can have his or her own garage-made idol, deity, or god; I can invent a religion in my garage, simple as that—or in my tent (unlike polytheism's minor constraints of familial resemblance alongside hierarchization among idols). It is this kind of systematization that goes into the evolution of religion. Thus, while killing too many birds with one stone (idolatry) is impossible, and killing two birds with one stone (polytheism) sounds really great on paper but is usually too good to be true and ultimately does not work, monotheism goes one step further, asking: How about we just kill all of that? Smash all the idols. Stop the proliferation of images by all and any means necessary and bring about the third alternative mode: Killing one bird with a giant boulder (monotheism).

Nevertheless, I would say that, from my science-fictional point of view as an alien agent inhabiting the planet Earth, this is actually not a very interesting reading of monotheism, even if it might be true: instead, everything that we have seen in the modern rise of monotheism has actually given us evidence to believe that this is not an end to monotheism. That monotheism is, in fact, God's death sewage—or rather, God's dead man's sewage. Essentially, it is the only way that religion can uproot itself by basically exposing God as something so detached, so outside of space and time, that there is no use for it. So, we see that through the progression of pure idolatry to polytheism to monotheism, there is a movement toward a certain kind of restriction of anthropomorphization of religious deities or natural forces. Before, it was as if any sort of fluctuation in the fabric of reality or nature could have a name (as demons, so to speak). And then we have that new polytheistic qualification that forces and the representations of them must work in unison, must always balance one another in some sort of titanic battle at the end of time, and that is the reason that we can live in this world (because we could not exist if they were not in some degree of unison). Essentially, they convey the premise that you are living in a world precisely because it is always at the brink of a war that has not happened yet but might arrive from the future. Monotheism takes it one step further by completely annihilating every sort of human attribution or human characterization to the divine: the divine is the very essence of a time—a conception of time that has no edges, meaning that it is a time of futurity, it is no longer the time of the past because past is an edge, because we know the myth of the origin. The myth of origin is not really that important for monotheism: what remains crucial is to establish a God that holds over the future, which can be done by simply turning many gods into one God that is so remote that its name is equivalent to the cipher of the future itself.

Andrea Cetrulo: And now, Jason, what aesthetic would you call forward on behalf of the idol?

Jason Mohaghegh: For a contemporary artistic image that imposes something like the heavy air of idolatry—in all its wonderment and fear—I would look to the elaborate installations of David Spriggs, who has refined his own "stratachrome" practice, wherein he synthesizes multiple painted layered transparencies and metal frameworks to bring about the most spellbinding boxes of cascading light, shape, and color. These rooms have all the mesmerizing sensibilities of a mystery cult, and they command atmospheres resembling something like a trance.[3]

No doubt, when staring at these installations it feels as if an entire world might hang in the balance: we are just not sure which world or whose world. We are not certain to whom these idols might belong, if their estranged owners might crave our good fortune or harm, and if they might return while we are caught stealing glimpses of their antechamber. Let us imagine this hypothetical race for whom such alien idols (indecipherable to us) have palpable, urgent meaning: What might we deduce about those absent foreigners for whom such radiant, glowing works were contrived?

The key perhaps lies in studying the many spatial paradigms that form the full theater of operation here, the first of which is The Altar. Indeed, as one walks in slow counter-clockwise circles around the installation, one gradually realizes that there is an induction principle at work. It is nothing less than an initiation rite, for which the suspended clear-glass strata announce an existence in the last throes of its own ephemerality. Still, altars are typically sites of supplication; they are where we pay tribute yet also where we are allowed to make wishes. But what might one ask of these hanging etherealities?

The second spatial paradigm in play is that of The Capsule: for to tread into this installation room is to immediately feel encased or enveloped in some peculiar way. Moreover, The Capsule gives rise to the sensation of a third spatial category, that of those sensory deprivation tanks where subjects were made to rest horizontally in small pools of water and experience the total void of light-proof and sound-proof environments. But these isolation pods or flotation centers were known to have another active output: namely, they incited vivid hallucinations of luminescence. Are such installations, then, in fact the incandescent figments that arise from our being stranded in the black? Are they the collective projection of insane neuropathological abstractions from within the heart of nothingness, the optical delusions of our oblivion? Is this the meaning of The Capsule: a last flash of astonishment before annihilation sets in?

The fourth spatial paradigm we encounter is that of The Tower, and here we can begin speaking about the fact of the unmistakable immensity of such works. They are forces of inundation; they daunt and overwhelm; they are literally breathtaking. Their monumentality dwarfs our slender torsos that veer in sheer futility around the colossus; their disproportion haunts us, with their elongated limbs, massive heads, or hurricane-like smoke. They thereby bring us into a titanic orbit where their blurred profiles are enough to dethrone us as the epicenters of even our own perception. The installations are more foreboding than shrines: they are the citadels of the usurpers, the abductors, the conquerors who have taken our entire reality hostage (if even for a short while).

The fifth spatial paradigm we unlock is that of The Prism, which definitionally rests upon a certain protocol of refraction, acute angles, and translucence. But prisms also have telescopic and kaleidoscopic potentials; they create their own idiosyncratic spectrums. To what extent, then, do these hovering installations filter the magnificence of a looking glass, but not one that increasingly clarifies but rather one wresting us carefully into the ever more faded and apparitional logic of things? We should note the great paradox in the fact that the master artist behind the curtains takes excruciatingly long periods of time to craft and delicately assemble these installations that themselves do not often last long (their materials are brittle and easily corroded). This is the essence of the apparition who also does not have long in our world, who lives on borrowed time and faces an hourglass countdown for risking even a second of exposure.

Finally, we arrive at the sixth spatial paradigm, which is that of The Mist. The Mist is the kingdom of the silhouette and the intimation—those partial-glance, runaway beings who drift through our peripheral vision and evaporate. Note that such installations can house multiple kinds of beings—from secret society gatherings in one titled Gold to giants astride horses in another titled Regisol (meaning Sun King), to elemental disasters of the whirlwinds, clouds, and cyclones in further installations titled First Wave and Axis of Power. It does not matter whether it is a conspiracy of strangers, a gargantuan rider, or the natural phenomenon of a storm or blood-red vortex: they all come into the mist and then dissolve into thin air. Their subsidence makes these installations something of a reverse inkblot test: never comprehension, only apprehension; instead of interpreting a hazy image that makes an unconscious world of meaning legible, here we stare upon a fog of semblances that brings all watchers crashing toward their own disintegration.

David Spriggs, *First Wave*, Oku-Noto Triennale, Suzu, Japan (2021).

Salvatore Tonnara, "Sonic Reverie: Enigmatic Hooded Musician Conjuring Melodies on Handpan" (Unsplash, 2023).

III. Phenomenon—The Terrorist; The Spirit Army

Andrea Cetrulo: Is there some timely or untimely phenomenon, Reza, where you see the monotheistic trajectory being sketched forward?

Reza Negarestani: Here I would ask a provocative question: Is terrorism the new avant-garde or is it reactionary throughout? Once more, monotheism is virtually an engineering project to make a new abode for a God that truly represents the future, and for whom precisely everything that comes thereafter will be under the reign and sovereignty of this God as well. You see, idols do not have that much power in the original Sumerian or Babylonian renderings; they do not have that much sway over the future, but rather usually exercise or flaunt their powers of the past (for instance, in origin myths like Gilgamesh). But to create a god that is so beastly, so ferocious, that wants to become the God . . . time itself needs to become edgeless time, which I think is the bold move of monotheism. The thing is that monotheism has not taken its ultimate assumptions, or its ultimate engine, to its final conclusions. As a shortcut, we should keep returning to this notion that, when the most dramatic forms of monotheism shine through and reveal to us their undergirding mechanisms, we discover that monotheism absolutely hates traditions, hates the past, and instead manifests its true radical essence as futuristic by nature. Precisely because it does not want us to submit to a god that has come before and has ceased to exist, but to submit to a god that is as unexplorable and open as the idea of the future.

For example, in radical Islamic theology, we see that Allah is often defined by complete disconnection from attributes of temporal-spatial characteristics or qualities. Not to go too Lovecraftian about this, but it is essentially something outside of space and time; that is the kernel of Islamic exotericism, and having that initiation is a preparation for the future in which those who believe in such a God are the people who are going to survive. And this takes us to the propaganda that has circulated since the emergence of Wahhabism and Salafism, whose exact difference forms the division between Al-Qaeda and ISIS. Al-Qaeda is fundamentally traditionalist even though it contains some traces of desert-like monotheism—the desert of God, the non-place of God—but it still abides by certain kinds of traditions and imageries that seem to be idolatrous from the side of Salafism (namely, ISIS). Whereas Wahhabism tries in Saudi Arabia to subtly level the grave of the prophet Muhammad's daughter or other sorts of shrines by natural disasters—for example, there are reports of Saudi Arabia rechanneling underground water flow throughout the city to particular zones where it starts to erode these sacred sites from within, thereby blaming it on nature with no active enmity toward the image—the true radical monotheist, if they want to take the core engine of their hatred against idolatry seriously, on behalf of the god which is the future itself, must actively destroy everything of this proliferation of images. And here is where we see at once that ISIS has characteristics of Marinetti's futurism—and for those who do not know, Marinetti was extremely attracted to this sort of Islamic radicalism as a part of his fascination with Orientalism. There is even this image in the manifesto of Marinetti talking about the futurist boys who chase after death, and they are actually sharing intimate stories about the next age under the lampshades of a mosque on an oriental rock, only then to start running from the mosque and chanting *viva futura* and leaping toward death like lions. That sort of imagery is quite similar to the videos that ISIS uses for propaganda.

I am sure that this has been mentioned before by numerous others who are looking into the art-historical connections between ISIS and the avant-garde. Perhaps they have noticed that Al-Qaeda looks quite outdated by comparison: their videos are badly edited, despite having financial resources, but ISIS is absolutely high-tech. They have this kind of Matrix-style bullet-time technique; they have great montage skills; everything is about speed, about technology, and holy warfare against all idols, and then we receive these images of them swarming museums to shatter the Assyrian or Akkadian status. This is probably why the question is continually going around—Is ISIS the new avant-garde?—though the majority of these essays draw on extremely random connections between the artistic avant-garde and this political movement. Nevertheless, if one really stares into the conceptual dimension of it, I would say that it is not far-fetched: for what is the whole idea of avant-garde? First of all, the word avant-garde is a militaristic term, a French word coming from a very eccentrically Roman and Ottoman word *yeniçeri*, which we know in English as "janissary." Janissary simply means a guerrilla soldier who is at the frontlines of it all. So this completely brings into the open that the avant-garde, in what might be called its ideological side, believes that culture can be militarized and that culture has a militant role. And the same thing holds for ISIS: this group precisely operates, and this is part of that radical monotheistic fight, under the assumption that culture can be militarized (without caring whether such images of them destroying idols create any sort of impression on young people or not). It probably does so as a means of propaganda, which is why they share such images widely, but those who think that these are simply a bunch of tired techno-Muslims or disenfranchised youth with nihilistic tendencies trying to destroy civilization using the technological means of civilization are quite wrong. No, we have to take things from that alien bird's-eye view: that this is what monotheism ultimately is. Monotheism is the creation of the desert, and that desert is a null place with a name: it is called future. I would keep it to this enigmatic ending.

Andrea Cetrulo: Jason, if you would like to elaborate on all of this by sharing your representation of a nearing or prescient phenomenon that would complement the idol's position.

Jason Mohaghegh: The futuristic phenomenon that I will describe is that of a recently excavated, subterranean spirit-army in Xi'an, China, constructed by the first Chinese emperor Qin Shi Huang over two thousand years ago in 210 BC. It is a massive archaeological discovery that unearthed a collection of terracotta statues which span over 600 underground pits and 50 square kilometers, and these statues surround the tomb of the dead emperor who held the megalomaniacal belief that he would require protection from his enemies even in the afterlife. According to historical reports from the period, the task was executed by over 700,000 builders and took over 40 years to complete. But what are we to make of the underground spirit-army that stands watch over this funerary city, a mausoleum of the ancient capital with archers, horsemen, spear-bearers, and chariots of bronze horses in fired clay form?

The first lesson of this ghostly encampment is that the idol does not abide by any life-and-death binary. Rather, the emperor's decision to convene this legion signifies a morbid third existential condition: that of immortal mortality, better known as the undying or the living dead. This takes us into the sphere of monstrosity, that which throws the death-wish or death-drive to an absurd outer edge, where violence cannot cease its cyclical recurrence over and over again. These idols are therefore only seemingly frozen in inanimate states, like those cats once buried alive among the pharaohs to guide them in the afterlife; really, they lie in waiting, with the ultra-animate impetus to stir with a killer's potential whenever the invaders come. The spirit-army confirms a worldview where vengeance is the prime law of all things: here there will always be a pattern of intrusion, violation, and betrayal. We are in an exceptionally shaky terrain where each domain of being hides its own team of cutthroats, traitors, or assassins. Thus, the spirit-army gathers as a preemptive strike against those who would draw first blood; they win retroactive vengeance or punishment on behalf of the half-sleeping emperor. They dispatch with utter precision and mercilessness those who would challenge the throne in any age to come, which in turn gives the idol the status of the immanent enemy.

Now for all their nobility, for all their aesthetic elegance, we must not elide the fact that such a gigantic architectural complex is a testament to the most expansive paranoia that the world has perhaps ever seen. Its sinuous vaults and serpentines, its trenches and treasuries, are the labyrinth of a mad king who envisions downfall around every corner. It is even speculated that the emperor's burial mound, which is insulated by rivers of mercury, might be full of lethal traps for those who traverse its threshold. This is the mindset of doom: in its modern sadistic framework, this leads to the killing fields, prison dungeons, and concentration camps of those utopian ideologies that ran grotesquely across the twentieth century with the intent to impose a paranoiac tyranny of sameness. In its ancient masochistic framework, however, we see paranoia galvanize the rise of an empire of idols (the vitalist coming to life of an entire necropolis beneath the dirt). Furthermore, scholars have observed that each warrior figure has its own unique physiological features, stances, and slightly varying facial expressions: no two idols are identical, leading to a hypothesis that they were perhaps fabricated based on actual living individuals from the time. Hence, lunatic distrust leads to an exalted resurrection principle whereby the idol defenders stay forever poised in the state of war. This is the meaning of the guardian's posture: the one who holds vigil, who keeps watch over the resting soul of the leader, who remains suspended in wakefulness for millennia. Their apparent stillness is a choreography of militant pacing through the halls of the enclosure: they congregate, they glower with hands resting on hilts and belts, and thereby maintain the fortress walls.

And this brings us to the final implication of the spirit-army for our business with the idol: In what ways do they redefine the paradigm of sacrificial force? In what ways are these spectral champions a typology of martyrdom unknown to us thus far? Again we return to the premise of the extreme death-drive that they harbor in their glazed facades: namely, that they are the ones who are willing to remain undead forever in order to perish gloriously for their emperor in a ring of victory and fallenness. Stated otherwise, they are stranded in a looping martyrological instant that permits no afterlife. They are the personification of the dangerous words of an avant-garde filmmaker who once instructed us to "Become immortal, then die."

But how exactly does this example stand for a futural phenomenon? It is because of the bizarre outcome that has now befallen them as the archaeologists expose more layers and gain international acclaim for their discovery. As we speak, several of the life-sized figurines, including their weapons and carriages, have been sent around the world to various museums in a kind of traveling show. Is this displacement from the sovereign's grave to the glass-case world of the gallery and exhibition a disgrace to them? Do they languish and agonize once wrenched from their protective arena? Even more than this, and this is where the futuristic modality comes into play, there are projects being devised to recast the idol-warriors in immersive virtual reality interfaces, 360-degree online tours, and interactive programs that would manipulate their limbs and showcase them in rank-and-file procession. So now they are entering a holographic destiny. And what does it mean when the blade of a warrior-idol is transported to the matrix of digital augmentation? Is this a sad defeat that they are enduring; is the cyber-replicated screen the ultimate battlefield in which they lose once and for all? Or is this a discreet alliance with technology, a counter-siege tactic that will afford them a new kind of violent telepresence? At long last, a way to make them invincible.

Interlude

Andrea Cetrulo: Before we conclude with a final set of oracular questions and answers, I would like to give Reza a chance to respond to any of Jason's previous impressions.

Reza Negarestani: I have just some minimal comments, the first of which is that I completely understand the exchange power at the time of idolatry for the creation of various communities—but you see, even from the same empirical facts, you cannot simply create what you might call a proto-capitalist society. This type of mere exchanging in tribal idolatry or even idolatric civilizations is not enough. There always needs to be a certain kind of monopolization: you can see it in Egypt, where the pharaoh of Egypt as a deity holds a sort of monopolization of all the idols (or as a representation of all the idols themselves). And monotheism just takes what is already there to a different level. Unfortunately, whether we like it or not, you simply cannot generate any version of what you might call a capitalist or proto-capitalist economy without something called scarcity. And monotheism is great at creating fake scarcity: it is the greatest, absolutely, for the monopoly of god by its very existence yields the scarcity upon which the economy will start to thrive. This is Max Weber's intrinsic link between monotheism and capitalism—whereas purely tribal idolatry is what some have called "the collectibles," the cult of shelling out, but obviously you cannot make an economy if every idol can be proliferated. You need to introduce a second kind of restriction for an exchange to have value, and for that, you need a semblance of natural or artificial scarcity.

Jason Mohaghegh: Reza, if I could interrupt for just a second—but there is a level of scale there, you know. Compare how much easier and more fluid the prospects of running away from a divinity cult in the ancient world to join another city-state are compared to medieval Christian Europe and its almost inescapable feudal universe.

Reza Negarestani: But you see, the thing is that capitalism, or the industrial age, did not actually grow out of those who escaped from city-states. It was actually erected on the ruins of monotheism. So, we cannot eat in a civilization and have its cake too. If we are entertaining a certain kind of retrospective from the ambit of monotheistic culture, from the ambit of civilization looking back on what might have happened, then yes, things might have happened differently and could have taken a different turn. But I would argue that the sort of economy usually found in tribal or semi-polytheistic societies cannot ever become robust enough to form an engine that starts to bootstrap civilization. I think of this completely in a Marxian sense that capitalism was necessary, but now it has to end . . . and so does monotheism.

Jason Mohaghegh: Before you proceed with that line of thought, there is an anarchist anthropologist of the twentieth century, Pierre Clastres, who researched examples of stateless societies particularly among indigenous peoples of the Americas. And he commented that, when we look upon these indigenous groups and their fragmentary city-states, we perceive their lack of unity as some type of primitive failing on their part rather than realizing the brilliant political theory of sectarianism that they upheld: that is, they knew that the greatest nightmare, the most catastrophic reality, is the realization of empire. Thus, they used micro-warfare and conflict among themselves as a regulatory measure against the will to universality that would turn them toward any dystopia of nation or empire.

Reza Negarestani: I know where you are coming from, but I completely disagree with these sorts of sentiments and would caution against them because it is what we find behind today's neo-libertarian ideology. The whole idea of "state independence," and that the worst thing that happened to us was that the Union imposed its will, is being used there by such movements. So, this myth of independence can only be taken to an extent without blowing apart in a tragic sense. As for myths of universalism, yes, but what sorts of myths of universalism? There are so many of them. Though I would say that capitalism is actually not universalism—in fact, anything that has come from capitalism has shown that people tend to make their enclaves, and that universalism at this point is the very enemy of capitalism as understood. So, I think that we need to flesh out what sort of universalism we are talking about. Whether it is integration or imposition of a unity by force. I am all for universalism as a mode of integration, but unity by force obviously is going to backfire. But then again, I would say that this whole idea of sectarianism is also completely going to backfire—it has its own limits which are already there, trading one type of independence (as emancipatory power) for another which amounts to completely doing things without any regard for what is happening around oneself. And if I have no regard for whatever works around me, then I neither live in a commune nor in a capitalist utopia.

Jason Mohaghegh: Again, those are not the only options: you, as a former citizen of the grand metropolis of Shiraz, know that the greatest poet in your city's history, Hafez, would never have been able to attain his poetic genius without having carved out a semi-autonomous space or territory of the *kharabat* (that decadent outworld of the tavern and the wayside ruins where drunken poets and storytellers assembled).

Reza Negarestani: Yes, but you see that is precisely what Hafez is not. He is never going to be simply this: he is going to go through all these various locales integrating them in order for his poetry ultimately to use universal concepts. It is for the human being as such. It would be extremely against Hafez's legacy to say otherwise.

Jason Mohaghegh: I see it almost with total opposition. I do not know how Hafez's prototype of the *marde-rend*, which means the bum, the rogue, the vagabond, the nobody, is a triumphant humanist principle. To my mind, it is an idolatrous figure par excellence, one who flirts with solitude and madness, and never a humanist archetype.

Reza Negarestani: No, it is a humanist archetype in a different sense. And this is the entire point here: that this whole idea of the monotheism versus idolatry debate is precisely because people think of monotheism as the creation of sameness and an identitarian imposition on every will, and so on and so forth. Nevertheless, you can see it as a twisted lesson, as I have said—in a kind of Nietzschean sense or Hallajian sense—that monotheism is precisely by virtue of its nature the great abode of heresies. Heresies are far more interesting than idolatry and polytheism, and Hafez is coming from the tradition of a deep heresy within monotheism. Not idolatry; I would say that it would be completely a betrayal of where Hafez is coming from to declare that he has some sort of affinity with the idolatric tradition. No, he is a Muslim. But he is a heretical Muslim, which makes him a very dangerous person.

Jason Mohaghegh: That is his background, not his final limit. He also holds a certain intimate relationship to objects that take on anthropomorphic powers (like the wine glass) and to material figures who can turn into counter-divinities of some kind (like the wine-bearer).

Reza Negarestani: But you see, these are transmogrifications. Transmogrifications are symbolically used throughout the Middle Ages, but they are not devotions.

Jason Mohaghegh: He even continually inscribes poetic lines with the words "Ay, Saqi" (Oh, wine-bearer!), and according to the strictest orthodox codes, you are not allowed to make such a grand address to anyone other than God, never mind to this illicit feminine figure serving outlawed substances at midnight.

Reza Negarestani: You can do all of this within monotheism as long as it symbolizes a better affair—that is bringing people to a new understanding of God. For example, there is a famous story of Hafez talking to Taimur, who is an extreme fanatical Sunni Muslim trying to expose Hafez as a heretical man . . . or more exactly, as an apostate. But he just can't do it, because every time he tries to accuse him, Hafez twists things back toward God, and from God to the death of God without Taimur knowing it. This is perhaps again my final twist to the story: that you need to have monotheism to make sure that God is going to die, because no good comes without the death of God. The death of God is the beginning of the good, and monotheism is a very twisted maze toward that objective (and particularly Islamic heresy, in all its shapes). If we think about it not as these small threats here and now but historically as the alien who looks into these ants' doings and tries to kill God in a different way.

IV. Answers

Andrea Cetrulo: Thank you both. Now, as we come toward the end of this certainly very rich conversation, I would like to relay to you the questions from the preceding oracles: Michael Marder and Laura Tripaldi, who, in the previous episode, acted as oracles themselves and revealed different textures of the concept of surface. So, Reza, Laura says: "In *Cyclonopedia*, you write that 'to desertify the earth is to make the earth ready for change in the name of the Divine's monopoly, as opposed to terrestrial idols'." And her question is: "Would you say that the monotheistic God is inherently different from all terrestrial idols, or is it just an idol whose material vessel is always hidden? Is the distinction between gods and idols becoming more blurred or more defined as we move towards the future?"

Reza Negarestani: Actually, I want to answer this question by way of Jason's exemplification of the army of the Chinese buried ghost army. This, for me, is a kind of allegory for the paranoia of idolatry versus the death of monotheism. They have their own respective fears, which is the same story as the pharaoh who commands that he be buried together with the architects who made the temple or pyramid because we need to have watchful eyes. And my challenge to the idolatrous crowd and their paranoia, my question to the idolatrous emperor, is this: Do you think the old guards have the wherewithal to save you in the future? No, of course not. The old guards are going to be weaponless—completely disproportionately vanquished by the future guards. A paranoia that does not have the risk of the future already counted into it is not a good paranoia but a totally useless one. Monotheism is the ultimate paranoia. We always want the future guards: we actually don't give a damn about traditionalist or conservative religious people who came before us and basically guarded us at that point or here and now. We want to make new children. These children are the children of the future, and this is the thing that I see most prominently: that there is a certain sort of paranoia in monotheism that cannot be surpassed by any sort of human paranoia in its healthy or even unhealthy sort of way.

Now, to Laura's specific question regarding my book *Cyclonopedia*, which is a work of fiction with philosophical aspects, there is in its pages that same twist that the world is finally getting ready for the true essence of monotheism: which is basically the death of God. And the death of God is like an assassination. It is not that one thinks that gods can simply be killed. No, who kills gods? Who has ever killed a god? Do we know anyone who has killed a god? However, gods can be assassinated, throughout history, in a very subtle way which the Greeks used to call *metis* (cunning intelligence). Cunning is the only way to kill gods, and monotheism definitely has its own cunning devices implanted—whether voluntarily or intentionally or not, it does not matter at this point—to kill god. As I said, it is always a sure shot to kill a bird with one giant boulder. And so, essentially *Cyclonopedia* is in the vein of both geo-philosophical works like those of Deleuze alongside island stories in the Islamic tradition by figures like Ibn Tufayl, but above all else it is more like a prologue to a different earth that we could have if that earth begins with the death of God. But this requires us first to devise a very strange and twisted way, like playing the video game *Hitman* where the moves that the character makes to kill his targets are quite twisted. For a moment, you think "oh, there is a coin over there that maybe I should touch," but the game really has nothing to do with that; it simply means that you have to make another move for you to notice something else and then that movement also puts you in some sort of danger. I will say that *Cyclonopedia* is really a story about this, the kind of twisted mechanisms that go into monotheism to finally kill God for good. And from that, a new Earth shall rise, right? That is obviously the very meta-poetic engine of all the old-world sagas: that there are old gods and new gods. But the thing is that we do not need gods at this point, and so the book offers an introduction, a very overwrought, overworked, confused introduction for how god is to be killed, rendered dead, and from that a new earth, a new geo-philosophy, can come. And we do not know what that geo-philosophy might look like because, throughout this work, it seems to me that everything that we do, everything that we speak, remains tinged with that sort of god-talk which infuriates us but for which we have no final resolution. So, if that is the case, we must devise the most intricate plan to finally assassinate God silently through the machination of nothing but human history.

> **Andrea Cetrulo:** And our final question, from Michael Marder to Jason Mohaghegh: "Have one-dimensional images displaced idols in the twenty-first century? Has the difference—however minimal, however spectral—between the idols and the images been erased? Are images our idols, and, if so, how do they fare in the Night?"
>
> **Jason Mohaghegh:** I began dancing at the borders of this question in my section on the spirit-army becoming holographic entities. We should start, then, with the etymological root of idol in the ancient Greek word *eidolon* (which means a double, apparition, ghost, but more acutely often referred to as the spirit-image of a living or dead person). Moreover, it is a shade or phantasmic lookalike that makes appearances in literature to warn of coming threats from the future. So, the original concept of the *eidolon* or idol, as a harbinger of catastrophic possibilities, was always already fastened to the forces of virtuality and futurity.

But the idols of the typology that we have been discussing—which are more frequently pagan statues from early civilizations—do have very stark phenomenological and existential differences from the rule of images that has overtaken us in our age of simulation. To begin with, the idol in the ancient world was a rare object: either supposedly one of a kind and therefore irreplaceable or with very few replicas, and the reason for this is that they were treated as actual incarnations rather than as symbols of faraway lords. Their abilities supposedly surged through their cold iron or mineral forms, not even as a conduit or intermediary but as the paragon itself which could be shattered, burned, thieved, or lost. This is clearly not the case for our contemporary image cultures where semblances are transacted with the promise of infinite reproducibility.

Second, the connection to one of my favorite philosophical topics—Night—is a remarkable one, for it is well-known that idol cults favored nocturnal backdrops for their rituals. This is because of the idol's aforementioned link to the jurisdictions of secrecy. But our contemporary images offer us precisely a shield against the darkness, like the invention of electricity did when it first illuminated the cities of Europe, or even the Promethean gift of fire which supposedly saved our ancestors from the twilight hours. These glimmers of light on our screens represent the false promise of escaping the tension of the secretive. They offer the delusion of grandeur that we have overcome those chasms where our minds fail desperately to keep their balance. And lastly, even if we did take the etymological root of the phantom-double as our criterion, we would notice that this made the Greek version of the eidolon or idol a messenger from some extra-reality, underworld, or parallel universe; they reminded us that there were elsewheres even within the ruination of our finitude, whereas our images today imprison us in pure banality and the bleak spectacle of the everyday. The former idol, even if it were a ghostly emissary, was once extraordinary: it was the agent through which unreal powers broke and flooded upon our world. It threatened insidiously to upset the scales of everything through whatever whims and impulses of a strange being; it did not slavishly uphold dominant orders but instead altered the mood of whatever crossed its path. Still, I think there are ways to restore this type of image again. In fact, learning to resuscitate the visionary secrets of the idol—its techniques of chipping, fading, its dazzling evil eye—might be our best last chance against the reign of simulation—an eye for an eye, an image for an image. There is a mood there still, an entire atmosphere in flux, when one sets foot in the museum even thousands of years later to stare at those miniature forms. There is a chill down the spine looking at that thing, this forged entity which combines seduction and fear, and studying its everlasting moods may be the only way to win if we are indeed at war (like the spirit-army) with all possible and oncoming times.

Andrea Cetrulo: I think we have gone far and above this evening; the initial teams have disintegrated, fused, adjusted, and certainly transcended pure taxonomies, going beyond all Manichaean views of the idol. A wonderful finale for the series.

Source: www.futurestudiesprogram.com

PART II

Future Labs

The Future Labs function as a kind of digital museum, hidden storage facility, gallery, maze, and collector's room. Through them, we explore the following conceptual realms: future time, space, movement, body, image, cosmos, thought, illusion, machine, power, fashion, mysticism, prophecy, virtuality, X, and the non-future.

Here you will open onto archives of unforeseen texts, images, writings, and secret thought-experiments in emergence across the world.

Enter Future Labs Now

1.0 Future Time

2.0 Future Space

3.0 Future Movement

4.0 Future Body

5.0 Future Image

6.0 Future Illusion

7.0 Future Cosmos

8.0 Future Thought

9.0 Future Machine

10.0 Future Power

11.0 Future Fashion

12.0 Future Virtual

13.0 Future Violence

14.0 Future Mysticism

15.0 Future Prophecy

16.0 Future X

17.0 Non-Future

Shuvra Potter. "The Fountain of Light" (2020).

LAB 1.0

Future Time

Chapter 1.0

Future Time Lab

Concepts: Speed, Memory, Death

Lab Author: Ed Keller

POST_001: The Past and Future of Time and Space as Graph

Example: Stephen Wolfram's work on physics, math, and computation spans many decades. His [and his son's] work on the film Arrival [Villeneuve, 2016] is perhaps less known and is an interesting addition to help us in reimagining what the relationship between "space" and "time" might be, and how an advanced civilization might operate by accessing a much more complex, networked model of spacetime.[1]

At certain scales [the very small and very large, the very fast or very slow] the rules we have found to normally govern space and time start to misbehave, to interact in foundational, constitutive ways, intertwining and mutating. Can we model the original, catalyzing ruleset for our universe at the very smallest or most distributed levels as a graph, a network, an evolving and interlaced filigree? Which nodes or bifurcations on this graph determine a future? Which nodes open up heretofore unknown and unavailable pathways to the past, casting us into a new templexity of present moments and emergent futures? Is the most complex labyrinth a garden of forking paths, or a straight line embedded in a radically curved universe?

POST_002: Cosmological Deep Time and Funeral Pyre Beacons

Example: Photographer Mauricio Salazar captures an image of "Milky Way Over Uruguayan Lighthouse" for the NASA website gallery.[2]

Humanity can trace its history back more than 45,000 years. If we use one second as a baseline, 10 to the 11th seconds = 3,169 years: roughly speaking, the bulk of well-documented human history. And 10 to the 12th seconds = 31,690 years, a terasecond: the outside edges of recorded human art/history— the Chauvet cave paintings are in this time period. We continue to discover and attempt to interpret these artifacts. But cosmological time spans billions of years: what if we decide to leave a marker, a monument for a civilization that might come millions of years after ours? What technologies might we need to develop to build such a "funeral pyre beacon"?

POST_003: Design for Communication with Deep Time

Example: Unsurprisingly, Stephen Wolfram has devoted substantial, lucid thinking to this question of after-human life and deep time.[3] Correspondingly, articles on "communicating with aliens through an interstellar beacon" and Patricio Guzmán's film *Nostalgia for the Light* [2010] showing the ALMA telescope of the Atacama Desert offer further reflections on this thematic.[4]

There are many factors to consider in the design of a technology that might reliably carry the history of humanity forward, millions of years into the future. How to store information such that it will endure? How to re-project images, sounds, language, spaces, living systems, cultures? How to translate all of this for an alien civilization that might not have eyes or ears, but would still be curious to learn what we were, what we knew, how we thought, and what we loved?

POST_004: Twenty Centuries of Stony Sleep

Example: BBC EARTH: "People and animals have been buried in permafrost for centuries, so it is conceivable that other infectious agents could be unleashed. In a 2011 study, Boris Revich and Marina Podolnaya wrote: 'As a consequence of permafrost melting, the vectors of deadly infections of the 18th and 19th Centuries may come back, especially near the cemeteries where the victims of these infections were buried'."

What can we learn from the extreme landscapes of our planet which can give us insight into what is lost in the depths of time; and then by extrapolation, perhaps understand better a set of universal principles or laws of life, system organization, and physics which would apply to both terrestrial and alien systems? And what ethics and aesthetics might we build out of this reframed placement of the human not just as a cause of the Anthropocene, but against all planetary systems and ecosystems? Jeff VanderMeer's novel *Annihilation*, and the film adaptation by Alex Garland, is one work which takes on these questions. In the lost reaches of time past and time future—alien time—there may be unimagined universes.

Let us recall the poetic words of "The Second Coming" [William Butler Yeats, 1919]

"The darkness drops again; but now I know
That twenty centuries of stony sleep
Were vexed to nightmare by a rocking cradle,
And what rough beast, its hour come round at last,
Slouches towards Bethlehem to be born?"

POST_005: Many Worlds, Many Times

Example: In his novel *Schild's Ladder*, Greg Egan imagines a future posthuman civilization based on quantum computers. In their ongoing quest to understand the fabric of space-time, a researcher travels as a signal, 370 light-years to a spot in space called the Quietener: so-called as it is the most silent site to test the limits of physics within humanity's reach [for someone willing to wait hundreds of years to get there]. When she wakes up and pitches her experiment, the researchers at the station assess and agree to run the experiment. They also propose to her that, as computational entities, they may observe the experiment by running themselves on subatomic computers—giving them access to ultra-micro time slices.[5]

Quote: "In the beginning was a graph, more like diamond than graphite. Every node in this graph was tetravalent: connected by four edges to four other nodes. By a count of edges, the shortest path from any node back to itself was a loop six edges long. Every node belonged to twenty-four such loops, as well as forty-eight loops eight edges long, and four hundred and eighty that were ten edges long. The edges had no length or shape, the nodes no position; the graph consisted only of the fact that some nodes were connected to others. This pattern of connections, repeated endlessly, was all there was."[6]

Something does go wrong with the experiment, but the researchers all hold on to a small shred of hope—as they are running as quantum minds at the subatomic scale, there are literally billions of other versions of them, all observing, all watching the experiment become a galaxy-destroying catastrophe, and all of them working in the picoseconds remaining to them to come up with a solution.

POST_006: Time and Awareness

Example: David George Menard composes "A Deleuzian Analysis of Tarkovsky's Theory of Time-Pressure."[7]

What would active time be? How could a single person access it, or a small group, or a huge population? What would its ties be to consciousness? How could we compare *pouvoir* and *puissance* in time by distinguishing between agency and freedom? Ethical frameworks emerge FROM the world, as self-organizing systems—rather than existing as a priori conditions in the world given by immutable and divine laws. The simple possibility for an ethic, in fact for awareness at all—resides in the ability of systems to develop points of contact with other systems, for the turbulence and delays that emerge in those points of contact to become formalized, and for the intensification of connections that emerge out of that noise to provide multiple possible futures.

POST_007: Communication across Interstellar Space-time

Example: Artist Eduardo Kac creates "five lagoglyphic interstellar messages transmitted to the Lepus Constellation (below Orion) on March 13, 2009 from Cape Canaveral, Florida. Based upon its stellar characteristics and distance from Earth, the Gamma Leporis star (part of the constellation Lepus) is considered a high-priority target for NASA's Terrestrial Planet Finder mission. The transmission was accomplished through satellite broadcasting equipment and a parabolic dish antenna. Gamma Leporis is 29 light-years from Earth. Kac's messages will arrive in 2038."[8]

One of the core problems in developing viable CETI [communication with extraterrestrial intelligences] is the challenge of translation to a radically alien mind and cognitive system. Alexander Ollongren, a prominent researcher in the field of "astrolinguistics," has suggested that human music, annotated with metadata, might be as viable a mode of realizing message transmission as any other. But we might choose any other information-rich system—pictorial, linguistic, sonic—and annotate that information package to convey to the alien intelligence that there are layers of information to be unpacked. One significant hurdle is of course that we do not know the location—yet—of alien life. The choice of destination is a giant hurdle. A more impassable challenge is the distance. Sending a message to a nearby star system—say Gamma Leporis, 29 light years away—would require at least a 58 year-round trip. Conversation in interstellar time frames will be iterative, contemplative, and fraught with uncertainty.

Note: "Lepus is most often represented as a hare being hunted by Orion, whose hunting dogs (Canis Major and Canis Minor) pursue it. The constellation is also associated with some lunar mythology, including the Moon rabbit. Four stars of this constellation (α, β, γ, δ Lep) form a quadrilateral and are known as 'Arsh al-Jawzā', 'the Throne of Jawzā" or Kursiyy al-Jawzā' al-Mu'akhkhar, 'the Hindmost Chair of Jawzā" and al-Nihāl, 'the Camels Quenching Their Thirst' in Arabic."[9]

POST_008: Here, Time Turns into Space

Example [quote]: "There is no route out of the maze. The maze shifts as you move through it, because it is alive."

> Parsifal: "I move only a little, yet already I seem to have gone far."
>
> Gurnemanz: "You see, my son, here time turns into space."

"The whole landscape becomes indistinct. A forest ebbs out and a wall of rough rock ebbs in, through which can be seen a gateway. The two men pass through the gateway. What happened to the forest? The two men did not really move, they did not go anywhere, and yet they are not now where they originally were. 'Here time turns into space'."[10]

The genesis of an individual, a population, a species, is ineluctably bound to the parameters of the material systems it/they inhabit, gestate in, consume as food, and emerge from. Material systems index the relationships each creature builds with its world—its umwelt—and provide multidimensional, temporal maps of the time spent living in the system.

POST_009: Time, Energy, and Empathy

Example: Illustrator Meike Hakkaart, also known as Maquenda, depicts a naturalistic-fantastical creature titled "El-ahrairah, Prince with a Thousand Enemies": an archetypal figure of the "Ur rabbit" described in Richard Adams's novel *Watership Down*.[11]

Quote: "Empathy, he once had decided, must be limited to herbivores or anyhow omnivores who could depart from a meat diet. Because, ultimately, the empathic gift blurred the boundaries between hunter and victim, between the successful and the defeated. As in the fusion with Mercer, everyone ascended together or, when the cycle had come to an end, fell together into the trough of the tomb world. Oddly, it resembled a sort of biological insurance, but double-edged. As long as some creature experienced joy, then the condition for all other creatures included a fragment of joy. However, if any living being suffered, then for all the rest the shadow could not be entirely cast off."[12]

Energy availability in our universe seems to predestine us in an unavoidable predator-prey relation across every scale we know. But Freeman Dyson, physicist and mathematician, observes that within the gradients of gravity, the balances of energy produce variation and life; hurricanes, cities, ecosystems, and living creatures all move upstream against the flow of entropy, against the arrow of time. The scales of time that each creature has access to and is formed by reflect both how it can survive and also how far into the past [and the future?] it can reach. The history of certain cell structures in a living system can go back millions of years; in a way, this means that our present was, in some manner, already "present" in the past. What moments of our current present will still be stable in the future? What forms of life will be supported? What form of empathy functions across centuries or eons?

POST_010: Complex Time, Neutral Time, Primitive Futurity

Example: "PHILOSOPHER AI" is a GPT-3 based pocket philosopher that generates textual outputs to different philosophical questions. Last year, I asked it this question: "What would constitute a Cosmopolitical Gesture?"[13] The GPT-3 AI replied to me: "The gesture is not over when the handshake has taken place, because one's hand can remain outstretched. This gesture therefore contains an element of potentiality for becoming actualized and so does not yet have any final completion."

The philosopher Michel de Certeau describes what he calls a "coup" in time—which can take place in storytelling or in everyday life. Central to this coup—which could be the punch line of a great joke, a perfectly sung note in a song, or a virtuosic gesture made high on a granite cliff—is the compression of memory on the part of the artist. Thus, we are all born into a limited and "given" world, and the only way we can learn to navigate is by using our ever-deeper memory across ever shorter periods of time (its own form of radical freedom).

LAB 2.0

Future Space

Chapter 2.0

Future Space Lab

Concepts: Atmosphere, Dimension, The Infinite

Lab Author: Jason Bahbak Mohaghegh

POST_001: Veiled Space

Example: Digital artist Gregoire A. Meyer's work titled "When the Drape Falls" shows a horse-rider in a desert clearing whose entire face and body are covered by a long blanket or cloth.[1]

How might the future compose itself as a system of veils? What does it envelop or conceal beneath its vast curtain, and are all the techno-cultural distractions of our age perhaps a mere cover for its true face (or for its nothingness)?

POST_002: Dream Space

Example: MIT researchers experiment with dream-intervention and dream-suggestion technologies called "Targeted Dream Incubation."[2]

What does it mean to enter a future of controlled dreams? Will these episodes of manipulated sleep still possess the appearance of chaos and spontaneity, or will they feel like ruled worlds hanging in the balance of puppet masters? Furthermore, what future iterations might arise of the dream, the nightmare, the daydream, the hallucination, the simulation, the fantasy, the mirage, the memory, the vision, the ghost, or the shadow?[3]

POST_003: Drift Space

Example: Article on "Death Dust" documents global superpowers' experiments with radiological weapons including "blue luminescent" powders spread across entire cities.[4]

Will assaults of the future involve weaponry of dust, air, sound, and molecules? What are the implications of making power an atmospheric matter, and violence dealt through micro-arsenals of diffusion?
   POST_004: Maze Space
Example: In the industrial city of Genk, Belgium, a kilometer of steel corridors was constructed to form a mechanical-looking maze at a former coal mine.[5]

Will the future resemble a steel labyrinth, forged in metallic twists? What does the logic of the turn, the coil, or the spiral (vectors of bewilderment) reveal about the spaces yet to come?

POST_005: Elevator Shaft I

Example: Japanese company (Hitachi Building Systems) manufactures the top three fastest elevators in the world. First to ninety-fifth floor in 42 seconds.[6]

Do futural paths resemble an ascent/descent through elevator shafts? Is our spatial paradigm one of a balanced technics (cables, levers, electronic signals) of free fall?

POST_006: Elevator Shaft II

Example: Installation artist Leandro Erlich simulates the experience of elevators turned sideways and caught between floors.[7]

What happens when we throw the elevator shaft along a horizontal axis, such that the space of downward plunging becomes a slantways zone, trespass, or crossroads (the hall, the corridor, the arcade, the aisle)?

POST_007: Missing Space

Example: The Japanese social epidemic of the "missing million" refers to an immense sub-population who recede into acute isolation.[8]

An entire generation of the metropolis lost in broad daylight. They call them the *hikikomori* (literally "pulling inward"), these practitioners of futuristic self-withdrawal from the real. And yet, their hermeticism is not one of pure physical distance (receding into forest cabins) but rather of hyper-mediation (living on screens): that of hiding in plain sight, castaways in high-rise apartments of the capital city whose everydayness transpires in virtual universes of work and play.[9]

POST_008: Immortality Lab

Example: Elite entrepreneurs are increasingly funding immortality and longevity research, competing over the death-cheating invention of age-reversing or age-arresting technologies.[10]

Immortalizing spaces have always existed in the myths of different regions: fields, hills, mountains, ocean depths, heavens, underworlds, or occult coordinates whose longitudinal-latitudinal nexus could freeze time. But now the laboratory might become the actual site of the everlasting, using every technique of manipulation and genetic engineering to win the most sought-after prize since humans first became conscious of their own vanishing. But will these future immortals go as far as to form their own separate enclaves and havens away from those not yet become imperishable?[11]

POST_009: Space Hotel

Example: In another venture into space tourism, the Gateway Foundation announces the planned opening of a "Space Hotel" called the Voyager Station in 2027. This premier hotel will continually rotate, with enough rooms to host 440 people at a time, while boasting a three-level bar that will "seemingly defy the laws of physics."[12]

Is the new form of luxury travel that of weightlessness, spinning hallways, and suspension in outer space? The hotel has long been a place of forbidden pleasure principles, with its decadent lobbies and lounges, but this promises to bring desire and consumption into alien orbits of possibility.[13]

POST_010: Bleak Zone I

Example: A new Russian video game titled *It's Winter* — by Moscow-based poet, musician, and artist Ilia Mazo — simulates the bleak purposelessness of everyday life (setting: decayed apartment building in a run-down, snow-covered post-Soviet province).[14]

"Nothing to be done," a great playwright once declared to open his own saga about despair, dead-ends, and the absurd repetitions of a lost age. Elsewhere, he called this spacetime the Endgame, a period of futility where people go through their final motions without knowing or asking why, without belief or desire, but condemned to carry themselves forward with heavy steps ("I can't go on, so I'll go on") amidst the absence of a way out.[15]

POST_011: Bleak Zone II

Example: A recent internet phenomenon hovering between internet meme and alternative reality game — The Backrooms — arrays images of abandoned sites of poor lighting, faded paint, muted wallpaper, and worn carpeting.[16]

"Dread of night, dread of not-night," says another great writer of the grey-zones and the nowhere. His castles are never reachable; his isles are ruled by havoc-machines of the law; his language feels like an axe hitting a frozen lake. The description of this low-toned atmosphere — where "there is infinite hope, but not for us" — is nothing less than the masterful creation of a poor type of air. "And you will lie down here," he hisses from the corner of a bare room that you never should have entered.[17]

POST_012: Spherical Resurrection

Example: Russian scientists claim that the Dyson Sphere (a theoretical megastructure that extracts the energy emissions of a star) might be the key to "technological resurrection" in the future.[18]

There are studies of how the most elaborate technological breakthroughs of the modern age were already anticipated in some intuitive sense by mystics (those who first contemplated the absorption of solar and stellar power). So it is the case with paradigms of eternity and circularity — both keystones of early mystical thought now discovered to have scientific validity as the basis for potential technologies of artificial return (though only made possible by the unique spatiality of the sphere).

POST_013: Glandular Space

Example: Biologists discover an evolutionary link between saliva glands and venom, which means that humans might eventually themselves become venomous creatures.[19]

There are entire bizarre evolutionary destinies lying in wait for the right hour of emergence. Even our glandular pockets appear to harbor twisted and insidious possibilities for our bodies-to-come ("insidious," from the Latin *sedere* meaning to "sit in ambush"). Will the future mark the unleashing of these other toxin-dripping beasts genetically lodged within us? Will there be an antidote?[20]

POST_014: The Faraway

Example: Artist Krista Kim sells digital mansion named "Mars House" (first NFT-backed virtual home) for over half a million dollars.[21]

The fragile separation between here and there, inside and outside, is at the heart of almost every human domestic and social formation in history. And now, what are we to make of these ethereal non-dwellings, a digital home in other solar systems or galaxies, where people reside like shipwrecked souls on the farthest removed island on the other side of the earth? Is futuristic space a desire for disappearance into pure remoteness?

POST_015: Dark Room I

Example: Dark Room Therapy is discovered to elicit many of the same sensory distortions and neurochemical releases (of melotonin, serotonin) as found in DMT's drug effects—something like a near-death experience.[22]

The Dark Room has been a practice of esoteric groups for many centuries, a favored technique whereby self-isolation in a cave or cellar for prolonged periods leads to altered states of consciousness (sacred vision) and to a principle known as "ego-death." In more experimental circles, this seclusion method was even used by psychoanalysts to induce revelations of the unconscious, and prisoners in solitary confinement were often recorded to have vivid hallucinations after several weeks locked in the pitch-black. If, like so many futuristic films depict, the next eras will be full of scorched overcast skies lit only by halogen city lamps, then might we experience a state of universal annihilation of self that leads to a collective hallucination (future as mass delirium)?[23]

POST_016: Badlands

Example: NASA scientists extract breathable air from the thin atmosphere of Mars, converting carbon dioxide into pure oxygen.[24]

A long-held dream of conquest in the modern age: to trespass and dominate even those places that do not want us. A hostile takeover of the desert, the Arctic, the wastelands, the islands, and even planets with inhospitable climates. Why do we wish to breathe in prohibitive stratospheres, to take revenge ourselves against what excludes us? To play king in the badlands.

POST_017: Secret Power Chambers

Example: Recently declassified documents show that secret government agencies of the major superpowers of the last century created undisclosed labs (e.g., Project MK-Ultra) that studied the possibility of mind control and consciousness expansion (telepathy, telekinesis, truth serums), the most intriguing of which was a method meant to teach agents the ability to break out of spacetime. This was called The Gateway Experience.[25]

There is a long history of experimentation with the occult by the political universe. Like the sorcerers of the early pharaohs and those "shamans of the black" who accompanied the Mongolian hordes, modern regimes driven by world domination often construct code-named sites where they attempt to unlock supernatural or extreme psychological powers. Will future global orders continue to augment these paranormal efforts (once the domain of miracles)?

POST_018: Thought-vault

Example: In 2019, a conference was held on "Darkness" in Svalbard, Norway (the world's northernmost inhabited space) where scholars gathered to discuss themes of darkness in philosophy, literature, myth, visual art, film, ecology, and virtual technology. Scholars arrived at the time of the Northern Lights, during six months of night, taking arctic dog sled rides through the ice hills.[26]

Will intellectual disciplines finally start paying closer attention to the influence of exterior conditions on the mind? For certain, thoughts manifest differently amidst rainfall, ice storms, earthquakes, or severe wind patterns. Will admitting to this covert channel between consciousness and atmosphere finally allow us the power of emulation: that is, to let our perception resemble phenomena like waves, moons, sand, or even darkness itself?

POST_019: The World-abandoner

Example: Epic Games just received one billion dollars in investment to drive the creation of "The Metaverse," a full-scale and infinitely evolving virtual world where people can exist as digital avatars in a kind of alternative life.[27]

Philosophers spoke of radical thresholds that (if ever crossed) would mark a point of no return for the human race: the Death of God, the Death of Man, the Death of the Subject, the Death of the Real. But is the Death of World the final step in this procession of lost causes? What happens on that day when individuals would prefer the permanent dreamscape or an apparitional room, never returning to so-called authentic planes? Is this the last stage of consciousness—to abandon worldliness itself?

POST_020: Broken-clock Universe

Example: The more scientific knowledge extends our perceptual horizon toward the infinite, the parallel, and the multiple (many-worlds interpretation), the more scientists are gravitating toward a deterministic understanding of existence (where all movements are considered pre-set sequences).[28]

The question of free will versus determinism has plagued philosophy, science, and religion for thousands of years: the problem of the clockwork universe. Still, the third dimension that often goes unnoticed in these clashes between individual choice and tyrannical determination is that of accident, chance, and luck. Beyond this, there is also the fourth possibility of a broken-clock universe: one that was originally governed by certain rules and patterns but then began malfunctioning (leading to ages of random distortion, deviation, and breakdown of the machine).[29]

POST_021: Genetic Chaos Space

Example: CRISPR, a rising genetic mutation technique, has already prompted large-scale realignments and unexpected cancelations of DNA sequences that could lead to "genetic chaos."[30]

An age of microscopic manipulation looms for which the domains of heredity will be thrown into flux. This opens us to the futuristic paradox linking precision to anarchy: namely, that the more we refine methods of acute genetic intervention, the more we will cast human experience, physiology, and bio-existence toward inadvertent side effects and mutations. For every minor intentional alteration at the cellular or somatic level, a cascade of unintended transfigurations of the entire species will occur.

POST_022: Emergency Space

Example: Due to space constraints imposed by the Covid pandemic, various dance clubs in Europe and East Asia are being converted into art galleries.[31]

States of emergency always have a way of transforming spatial functions (picture the crowd fleeing a burning theater). During air raids in war-torn countries, basements turn from storage facilities or play sites into protective shelters and bunkers. During revolutions, public squares once used for gathering or symbolic ceremonies turn into riot zones. Thus, the emergency restores our consciousness to what the child already knows: that anywhere can become the elsewhere under the right circumstances of imagination or danger.

POST_023: Walking Simulation

Example: Physicist Hong Qin uses artificial intelligence programs and algorithmic equations to suggest further speculative proof of our already existing in a simulation.[32]

The ongoing provocative topic of our possible entrenchment in a simulated matrix concerns itself only with the existential question of what it would mean for Being (were we trapped in a program). Yet these analyses do not tread into more elegant reverberations for the question of space. How would it transform our understanding of entrance and exit, inner and outer, journey, movement, border, trespass? How does territoriality itself take on altogether different sensibilities when speaking of phantasmatic zones? Perhaps the point is no longer to escape the simulation but rather to become godlike in our infusion, entanglement, and creative orchestration of the false world: the God's-eye view of space.

POST_024: Paradise Cities

Example: Architecture firm MVRDV advances Paradise City project in Korea, which houses a major nightclub known as "Chroma" in an edifice called "The Imprint."[33]

What will new utopias of the future look like when following the logic of the *imprint*? Will they experiment further with windowless and abstract facades of architecture? Utopia has always been tied to boundlessness, but now we are witnessing the construction of such utopias as pure entertainment complexes — pleasure zones and hedonistic cities without edges that fulfill no grand concept of history (servants only to the process of leaving hyper-impressions).

POST_025: Cosmic Arcs

Example: New exhibits and book collections surface to reflect on the early revolutionary thought of the Cosmists and the Futurists, especially considering today's scientific advancements that might bring to fruition their once-outlandish meditations on space.[34]

What does our age have to learn from those earlier avant-garde movements that dreamed of futuristic utopias based on strange new principles of technology and art? The Russian Cosmists or Italian Futurists of the early twentieth century, the former of whom sought to escape the clutches of time by mastering immortality and the resurrection of the dead, or the latter who worshiped speed and the grinding sublimity of the machine. And both hanging their futuristic bets on a new spatial focus: the former in outer space and interstellar travel; the latter in the heart of the metropolis and its industrial immensity. With the design of extra-planetary cities already underway, are their predictions now combining toward a suspicious third landscape?

POST_026: Ultra-levitation

Example: Engineers at the University of Pennsylvania use "magic carpet" technology to make a tray levitate using only light.[35]

The vampire hovers; the ghost hovers; the shadow hovers; the prophet hovers. Levitation is one of those elder concepts associated with histories of sorcery, monstrosity, and salvation. This vertical-horizontal drifting is a choreography reserved only for the otherworldly and the netherworldly. Thus, what happens when banal objects suddenly absorb this power reserved for the bewitched, the sinister, or the chosen? An age of infinitely floating toys: trick of light-induced flow manipulations.

POST_027: The New Temple

Example: Snøhetta designs proposed site called "Lunar" in Qianhai, China's city center, a data satellite meant as a landmark for the "manifestation of technology."[36]

What happens when those architectures of reverence, worship, and awe once reserved for temples instead become directed to hallowing technology? Is it odd to dream of sacred groves, altars, or monuments designed to honor data, electronics, and automated equipment? Weirdly, this futuristic orientation might actually restore us to the pagan criterion of gods: that they should be tangible, palpable, viscerally interactive. No longer transcendent, but now part of the dangerous realm of sensation once again.

POST_028: Mirror Game

Example: Physicist Carlo Rovelli suggests in new book titled *Helgoland* that all reality might in fact comprise an interplay of quantum mirrors.[37]

The old existentialist problematic of "the tree falling in the woods" (i.e., whether it makes a sound if no one is there to hear it) now collides with a new theory of quantum physics stating that a book left on a table in another room does not necessarily remain there in an independent existence but rather exists only in a relational game of reflections with its owner. Hence, the book remains as it was when held by the reader, with no essential metaphysical substance underlying it in our absence. But what does it mean to be caught in a hall of mirrors, and will the future only exacerbate this glass-replica effect at the quantum levels?

POST_029: Satellite Gods

Example: The company ICEYE of Helsinki, Finland, sends out fourteen spacecraft with Satellite Aperture Radar (SAR) technology allowing them to capture coherent images of anywhere on earth at any time, including an optical light that can penetrate live volcanoes.[38]

There are wondrous tribal monuments and structures from past centuries that were built only to be beheld from the sky (suiting the aerial view of the overseers). However, now with roaming satellites and "persistent monitoring" devices in orbit, we can be sure that something stares closely from above. How will this alter our approach to creation (our aesthetics, our movements, our conceptualization of appearance) when we know that there are eyes watching from the sky?[39]

POST_030: Shadow-world

Example: Syrian artist Diana Al-Hadid creates sculptures of inverted ruins, whether in shattered or melted appearance, using gypsum, steel, wax, pigment, and fiberglass.[40]

There are texts and films that speak of "shadow worlds" or "upside-down worlds." But what are the consequences of staring at hanging, inverted realities in states of internal brokenness? It is to worship debris; it is to stand transfixed by the aesthetics of wreckage; it is to hand history over to the immortality of the fragment.

POST_031: The Headquarters

Example: Clothing brand AlphaTauri opens new showroom at headquarters resembling science fiction off-world with body scanners, aluminium surfaces, and star-like lighting systems.[41]

Futuristic reformulations of "the headquarters" are ongoing. The headquarters used to have both its official connotation (as a center of the law, the state, the regime, the intelligence agency, or secret police) and also its subversive context (the rebel hideout, the fifth column, the secret society). Now it has entered the spatial realm of luxurious consumption and corporate organization. But what will the headquarters of the future look like, and what function will it serve? No longer an identification point, but rather a place where we might lose ourselves or become alternative figures in a masquerade (soul-swapping).

POST_032: Artificial Rains

Example: The Emirate of Dubai unleashes artificial rain monsoons and cloudbursts to combat epic heatwave.[42]

Since the invention of electricity, we have come to understand the prospect of artificial light. But this slippery slope continues along further potentialities: artificial winds, artificial moons, artificial suns, artificial rains. And what happens when artificial rain is found to be cleaner, purer, more effective than natural rain, or artificial moons more radiant and luminescent than the original moon? Does the age of manipulated enhancement tempt us to substitute supra-natural constructs for the elemental properties of life?

POST_033: Olympian Waste

Example: Olympic stadiums across the world fall into states of abandonment, decay, and futile deterioration.[43]

Mythic spaces gave rise to narratives of gargantuan power—Cyclopean, Promethean, Herculean—while also warning of the wasteful aftermaths that follow such excessive expenditures of force. The fate of the titanic Cyclopes—to be prisoners stranded on a useless island; the fate of Prometheus—to be chained to a rock and cyclically mutilated for all eternity; the fate of Hercules—to strangle his wife and five children in a fit of rage. Hence, is the Olympian destiny one that binds entities of extreme energy to sites of barrenness, punishment, or tragic agony?

POST_034: Virtual Drowning

Example: New physiological reports reveal that "drowning does not look like drowning" as commonly assumed, and that this relatively serene descent leads to many unnoticed deaths beneath the waters.[44]

If studies demonstrate that actual drowning victims do not resemble the images or movements typically represented in films—that they most often do not splash, wave their arms, or cry out for help, but rather perish in far more subtle, imperceptible ways—then we might extend this mischaracterization to our experience of the virtual worlds. For these are also oceanic realms—they have many of the same qualities of liquidity, tidal volatility, and destructive entrapment (thus the term "net" or "web"). We might therefore ask the following question: What would it mean to drown in the virtual, and would we even recognize it as drowning?

POST_035: Circular Stories

Example: Artist Choi Minhwa creates hybrid visual chronicles that fuse Korean folklore, Chinese Buddhism, and Renaissance aesthetics.[45]

Is the future a territorial struggle between genres: the myth, the fable, the allegory, the parable, the tale? Will the ideological narratives of our age be contested and flanked from all sides by these more ancient storyteller challengers whose circuitous techniques trouble all linear claims? How might folkloric remnants return to avenge themselves against the all-saturating regime of codes?

POST_036: Underwater Sculpture-forest

Example: Artist Jason deCaires Taylor, known previously for his submarine projects, constructs sculpture museum in Cyprus of ninety pieces resting 32 feet underwater to aid the recovery of coral reef habitats. This aquatic museum is dedicated to the memory of those drowned in the Mediterranean Sea during the Syrian refugee crisis.[46]

Even in our most idealistic hours, art has rarely ever been called upon to save the world (carrying no messianic expectations). For this very reason, though, could it serve as the perfect camouflage to smuggle ecological imperatives of the most urgent order? Is this how a strange gallery of chiseled installations positioned at the bottom of a seabed, tempting marine divers to engage in an immersive aesthetic below the water's surface, conceals the larger aim of biodiversity regeneration? So does a submerged sculpture garden become the stylized cure for a restored world at the edge of eradication.

LAB 3.0

Future Movement

Chapter 3.0

Future Movement Lab

Concepts: Wandering, Migration, the Border

Authors: Una Chung [Posts 1-4] and Will Scarlett [Posts 5-47]

Post_001: Light Speed

Example: A point-and-click video game collaboration between Kanaeokana and the Montreal-based Initiative for Indigenous Futures.[1]

Movement Lab begins with an inquiry into the question of indigenous futures, specifically a project by fifteen young people in Hawaii, who learn to create a video game together as a way of ensuring their own futurity. What kind of vehicle does the video game provide and itself become in the hands of this particular group? Within the game story, indigenous youth gain space travel and visit other planets, taking their culture and language with them. But this is not just a story about technology's power, the politics of its accessibility, or the enduring value of culture. The question we might ask here has to do with the particular weave we achieve by threading indigenous futures into lines of travel at light speed and through sound waves emitted by traveling spaceships. When NASA launched Voyager 1 and 2 in 1977, a golden phonograph containing diverse sounds and languages representing earth as a diverse yet singular entity was included in each vehicle. As the Voyagers continue their journey today, a question remains. Although it was NASA's planetary ambassadorship that influenced Carl Sagan's decisions on the design and engineering of this phonograph, how might youthful indigenous travelers craft a portable form of culture for intergalactic encounter?

As game designers, these youth aspire to craft the form and procedural rhetoric of contact, not merely give voice to their own time spent on earth.

POST_002: Elision of Touch

Example: An immersive room-sized multimedia installation; visitor activated motion sensor triggers; looped choreography projected onto walls.[2]

A body walks, pauses, initiates an embrace. From another angle, a body running at high speed approaches and passes through the first body. People stand in this room, mesmerized by the longing, anguish, and tenderness of naked beings whose intimate lives are unfolding as moving projections of light on walls. A machine placed in the center of the room is the animating force of this scene. What most of the humans in this space will notice is that these moving bodies do not meet. Surely the particles of light make physical contact with each other and with the optical lenses of museum-goers, and yet it is the point of non-contact that is felt most vividly. The naked appearance of body and machine proves equal to the task of transmitting haunting emotion. What eludes us—our ability to come into the presence of the other, to touch, to converge—becomes a thought made visible by the paradox of how form and matter behave in this room. Touching is no longer, here, a reliable metaphor for the solidity of the world. The digital reveals that the elision of touch during contact can be the empty space out of which deeply affecting moods are evoked.

POST_003: Refrain Machine

Example: Dance concert performance whose choreography explores complex forms of doubling.[3]

A choreographer (a singer, a reader, a thinker, a, a, a) sets something in motion—a refrain machine. He begins by presenting a body, a voice, sliding across a range of registers—reciting poetry, singing, expressing poetic nuance in vocalizations, expressing, gesturing, moving, dancing. These words are too static to capture the quality of the in-between, which is the fullness of what becomes present in Bsides. The slippery chain, the refrain, of yet another collaboration makes it impossible, wondrously so, to find a referent in an artwork stable enough to capture in writing. To refer to the piece is challenging, for it exists for us only in a brief interval of time, the time of contact, contingent, fleeting, changeable—

POST_004: The Scroll

Example: A web and device-based essay with animation and sound.[4]

Xinona's irreverent, biting, unabashedly sentimental, and brassy essay animates the scroll in singular ways. Scrolling is a gesture, a movement of mind, a near-automatic flickering of attention, and as such can't avoid being influenced by the particular affects scrolling by — wait, scrolled back. It is tempting to reach indolently into history for a metaphor from reading, montage, or jogging to explain the significance of an increasingly common motion. Speed, length, and style of each stroke — Morse code, calligraphy, or a pause for breath in ongoing respiratory exchange — are not unfamiliar as aesthetic elements, as bits of code. But here Xinona sits with her phone covering face in a post-apocalyptic dried-out economy, contemplating the situation of the indigenous artist. What does she scroll into presence, into oblivion? Have we scrolled by without a trace?

POST_005: Self-channeling Flow

Example: Scientists use nanoparticle membranes to create and manipulate all-liquid structures.[5]

Life began when the swirling primordial soup shaped itself with the first membranes; from then on, fluids learned to move on their own, no longer simply dispersed by gravity or cycles of the weather. Certain precise mixtures were achieved, their peculiar flows sustained — one of them: the human . . . As humans begin channeling this primordial power of fluid movement, they also find new ways of transforming the miraculous into the banal: liquid headphone cables.[6]

POST_006: Wandering Home

Example: Architectural sketches ca. 1919 in Velimir Khlebnikov, "Ourselves and Our Buildings: Creators of Streetsteads."[7]

A century before Airbnb, Velimir Khlebnikov foresaw cities composed of mobile dwelling modules — "the glass hut" — that could travel by rail or ship to any city in the world. Everyone would have the right to space in each city's framework buildings shaped like bridges, trees, hanging filaments, and so on. After a long journey in his wandering home now installed on a bridge-building overlooking the sea, his thoughts too began to wander: "What were fairy tales really, I wondered:

merely an old man's memory? Or were they visions of a future only children can foresee?"

POST_007: Luxury of Stasis

Example: A luxury home in Puerto Rico built like a bunker to withstand hurricanes.[8]

As the winds and tides intensify, so too will the movements of people. The perpetual mobility once reserved for jetsetters will become an inescapable condition of life in the storm surge. And over the wreckage will rise monuments to the exclusivity of stasis: luxury bunkers.[9]

POST_008: Voided Forest

Example: Roberto Bolaño's literary work *2666* explores divergent spacetimes of the forest.[10]

Roberto Bolaño tells of shamans who can discern hidden messages in the hypnotic swaying of the trees. What meanings will be revealed to us by the programmed movements of the virtual forest? Or will its preternatural stillness invoke a void that renders even shamans mute?[11]

POST_009: Future Territories

Example: Native Land Digital maps indigenous territories.[12]

A vision of a future map: mosaics of overlapping territories shaped by the movements of people rather than the imposition of abstract powers. The map projects a memory of countless worlds lost to genocide—can a vision project this memory into the future? Or does the fact that this vision is born of a boundlessly corrupt present mean it can only fulfill the colonial fantasy of total appropriation of the real?

POST_010: Theater of Imperceptibility

Example: Neutrino telescope installed in the depths of Lake Baikal.[13]

Emperor Shirakawa once said, "three things refuse to obey my will: the waters of the Kamo River, the fall of the backgammon dice, and the monks of the Enryakuji Temple." He had no idea as he spoke that hundreds of billions of cosmic particles were streaming through each cubic centimeter of his body. The dry riverbed of the Kamo is where the first Kabuki performances were staged by all-women dance troupes; what theatrics will be inspired by the imperceptible movements of neutrinos, omnipresent yet only detectable at the bottom of the deepest lake in the world?

POST_011: Language of the Swarm

Example: Scientists use machine learning to classify individuals' muscle activation patterns.[14]

To the delight of surveillance companies and panoptic states, scientists have confirmed that our bodies each carry a unique "movement signature" that can be tracked with an algorithm. Athletes and dancers have long shown us how to embellish these signatures into a calligraphy we understand with our viscera. Only by transforming our movement signatures into a universal language of movement will we efface our encoded identities in the emergent murmur of the swarm.

POST_012: Peripheral Movement

Example: Bruno Schulz attributes his stories to "a certain flickering of the wallpaper, pulsating in a dark field of vision—nothing more."

A flicker in the corner of the eye vanishes before it appears, a silent rustling behind the ear, a vague palpitation of skin. Could these movements at the periphery of our awareness be the true sources of the future, the eternal wellspring of our agitated creativity? Or are they the corrosive currents of a shadow world our dreams guard against?[15]

POST_013: Silent Roar

Example: Pandemic quiets seismic vibrations caused by humans.[16]

The infrasonic rumbling of Earth—elemental vibrations of earthquakes, volcanoes, and storms through which animals sense the impending disaster; in our bodies, they register not as sound but as fear. Are our incessant movements misguided attempts to respond to these planetary cries or to mark a territory against them? For what we feel now deep in our flesh isn't a sublime exhortation ("you must change your life"); it's the paralyzing subaudible roar of a tiger about to feed.[17]

POST_014: God of Motion

Example: Rollercoaster Abyssus at Energylandia, Poland.[18]

Abyssus, a name worthy of a Titan. Your serpentine line distills sacred architecture to its essence—pure movement, intensity, levitation—terror and bliss. For a fleeting moment in your thrall, pilgrims will endure the most ascetic act of their lives: waiting. But what spiteful god did you offend, cosmic wager did you lose, universal law did you transgress, condemned as you are to push us up until we roll back down again and again and again . . .

POST_015: Fungal Era

Example: Toxophilic bacteria and radiotrophic fungi.[19]

Oxygen—the toxic byproduct of certain prehistoric algae—once decimated life on this planet; billions of years later, it fills the air we breathe. In the poisonous sludge of industrial waste pits and radioactive pools of fallout zones, life is again mutating to feed on the corpse of a dying world. The next epochal move in evolution will not be AI; it will be whatever fungal sentience is birthed from these dark rhizomes spreading over Earth and into the beyond.

POST_016: Tunnel of the Real

Example: Tunnels below US-Mexico border and elsewhere across the globe.[20]

For every attempt to rise above the dirt, there is a counter-movement of tunneling and pulverization. Laws can construct spaces of exclusive order and transient stability but will never enclose desires that obey the subterranean law of total movement. Along with weapons, drugs, and people—all of them reduced to the extra-legal amorality of dirt—the real moves underground.[21]

POST_017: Nanometropolis

Example: Nanobots coordinate movements inside a living host.[22]

Coursing through the bloodstream by the millions, nanobots form floating colonies in the host's circulatory system. A symbiosis emerges, shaping the nanobots' culture and the host's behaviors to suit the flourishing of an infinitesimal metropolis. Drawing on the seemingly limitless resources of the host's body and brain, the nanobot civilization achieves pinnacles of decadence no human could ever imagine.[23]

POST_018: Pulsation Machines

Example: Artificial heart and pulse technology undergo radical innovations.[24]

We are each born with a pulse—when it stops, we die. Humans have always found ways to amplify and extend this pulse through collective rhythms resonating in the most intense moments of life: the erotic, the ecstatic, the deep silence of night. What pulsation machines must we invent to carry on this vital impulse before it is entirely transplanted by the monotonous thud of technical survival?[25]

POST_019: Spaceless Movement

Example: "Let us free ourselves from the space which underlies the movement in order to consider only the movement itself . . . pure mobility." (Henri Bergson)[26]

At the core of every notion of time's shape—line, curve, circle, spiral. . .—is the intuition that it moves. In this, they are all true; where they go wrong is in not conceiving of motion prior to space, flowing without form or direction. Time is this spaceless movement impossible to visualize yet sensed by each of us with uncanny clarity when the walls of the eons tremble.[27]

POST_020: Glinting Stillness

Example: Ridge A in Antarctica is the stillest place on Earth.[28]

The well-known secret of the future is that it never arrives, suspending us in a perpetual state of waiting. Cryonics—the preservation of life in deep freeze—

encapsulates our present cultural condition. And so, we must learn to wait no longer as frozen cadavers but with the calm intensity of a frigid wasteland, the deceptive stillness of glinting steel.[29]

POST_021: Cosmic Consumption

Example: Bitcoin mining will soon use as much energy as a country.[30]

The universe, and everything in it, is an infinitely complex explosion. The common telos of stars, planets, life forms, and technologies is intensive energy consumption. Do embers spewed over the earth by volcanic eruptions also ever wonder where all this is going?[31]

POST_022: Eternal Commute

Example: Airlines plan 20+ hour flights.[32]

Every day billions enter the empty space-time of the in between, a mass meditation on the inescapable boredom that waits at the limits of productivity. For many, it is an experience to erase (but even mobile devices and leather seats can only do so much). Perhaps deep down we savor the stale air of eternity, cherishing our aimlessness in tune with a world traveling one more time around the sun.

POST_023: Perpetual Prayer Machines

Example: Android Bodhisattva preaches at Kyoto temple.[33]

Perennial recipe for the sacred: matter and movement sealed with an incantation. Icons fade, pyramids crumble, prayer wheels turning in ancient streams eventually fall silent. Does our longing for the sacred to last forever arise from the fear of it dying with us or the sense of an excess we could never fulfill?

POST_024: Chain of Hunger

Example: Declaration of Nyéléni calls for food sovereignty for all people.[34]

The oldest form of politics is the organization of hunger along territorial lines of predator and prey. How many societies have justified their violence, greed, and domination in terms of that supposed cosmological hierarchy, the food chain? Whoever controls our hunger binds us in their power—the future will belong to those who shape the currents of this primordial sensation.

POST_025: Pulse of the Future

Example: Stefano Scodanibbio, *Voyage That Never Ends* (Musical Composition, 1998).[35]

Somewhere around the back of your apartment building or deep in the woods at night or behind the moon hanging over you as you sleep, the darkness moves like many translucent medusas gently breathing. Like swarms of iridescent jellyfish congealing into swirling erotic forms, you'd think were your own pulse throbbing in your ears and eyes and on your skin—if you could ever really sense them—those distant bells of nullity droning on in endless twilight. But only when you turn away, stop listening, close your eyes, and die do they appear.

POST_026: Animal Currents

Example: Migrations in Motion maps projected animal movements in response to climate change.[36]

Animals do not decide to move; they just do. "Every animal is in the world like water in water" (Georges Bataille), and together they become torrential currents. Those currents—like rivers and winds—form and swell as each animal-molecule responds to shifting climatological pressures. Will the barriers we have built withstand the immense migratory tides we have set in motion, or will the dams finally burst?[37]

POST_027: Miniature Empire

Example: Some quantum properties are in principle unknowable.[38]

Institutional powers work by making us small. Bureaucracies, towers, corporations, temples, palaces, and prisons are crude theaters of the sublime, shrinking us down so we are easier to impress and intimidate. That is until we eventually vanish beneath the threshold of incalculability.[39]

POST_028: Formula for the Future

Example: Analysts predict global market growth for ergonomic office chairs.[40]

Gambler, fortune teller, mystic—these figures have always been shrouded in an aura of the occult still worn by the statistician. Theirs is a demonic science of cosmic disintegration, of transcendent forms fallen into time and uncertainty. Is the search for the ultimate secret formula—a numerical pattern of everything—intended to bring about the final redemption of the whole or yet another transient ecstasy in a universe woven of incompletion?

POST_029: Artificial Movement

Example: Robots that can dance.[41]

The Turing Test—intended to determine if a machine can think like a human—opens a space of indiscernibility between the artificial and organic. As this space expands, we begin to sense we recognize each other as alive less by how we think than by how we move. Artificial intelligence will produce modes of thought that exceed human comprehension—will machines also transform movement in ways no life form could embody?[42]

POST_030: Stochastic Universals

Example: Researchers use stochastic resonance to sense indetectable signals.[43]

If the search for universals always tends to end in enraptured resignation before the universe's endless multiplicity, then does that not suggest one has been found? From Lucretius's swerve to Brownian motion to the random walks of associative thought, a stochastic theory of everything is emerging. Who can predict what might happen as we tap more deeply into this all-pervading element of movement: our shared randomness.[44]

POST_031: Endless Grind

Example: Cerro Rico mine in Bolivia provided silver for the Spanish empire and tin for Apple products.[45]

One of the earliest human inventions, borrowed from the immense grinding power of the earth and from teeth, was the mortar and pestle. Down through the centuries, this once sacred tool of vital destruction has extended into a massive grinding process: of the earth, of all life, of ourselves, of each other—who or what is it nourishing? Whatever forms the future takes, one thing is certain: it's going to be a grind.

POST_032: Onrushing Future

Example: "What would it have looked like if it had looked as if the earth turned on its axis?" (Ludwig Wittgenstein)[46]

Future historians may consider the myth of progress to be less an error of colonial hubris than mistaken physics. The Copernican shift from a geocentric to a heliocentric cosmos set in motion an enlightened era of progressively unified knowledge about a supposedly coherent universe. What abyssal epoch will erupt once we finally recognize we're not progressing toward the future—the future is careening toward us and pulling us in?[47]

POST_033: Mythic Return

Example: Scientists speculate about extraterrestrial life inside stars.

If we measure the value of knowledge not by the information it contains but by the imaginary movements it makes possible, we are living in impoverished times. The blanks of the map have become too small for the numberless mythical beings that live beyond the edges of the cladogram—which seems to grow in proportion to the mass extinctions and ever-expanding void. Will there come a time when all these excesses of the known return to our world, or will we first encounter life forms that are even stranger?[48]

POST_034: Walking the Labyrinth

Example: "I imagined a labyrinth of labyrinths, a maze of mazes, a twisting, turning, ever-widening labyrinth that contained both past and future and somehow implied the stars." (Jorge Luis Borges)[49]

The walls, floors, and ceilings are the world, each movement a step deeper. The problem is not of completion or escape—all paths lead to the same unreachable center—but the convolutions and intensities we pass through in search of . . .? For all the fears the future may erase, it will invent countless more; yet one will always remain with us, lighting our way: the feeling of being lost.

POST_035: Permanence of Ash

Example: Over centuries lead atoms gradually slide down the shingles of medieval cathedrals.

Humanity's infatuation with permanence began with techniques of shaping stone and metal (the blacksmith's blasphemous secret: even iron flows). As this knowledge grew, so did its transformative power, displayed in great monuments to the eternal: pyramids, cathedrals, vortexes of indestructible plastic. Will future constructions incorporate the movements of their own disintegration, or will humans refuse to build the foundations for a cloud of ash?[50]

POST_036: Metamorphic Travel

Example: Hypothetical VR system would record brain activity for playback in other brains.[51]

Any given spiral of spacetime is composed of manifold overlapping perspectives ranging from the quantum to the cosmic scales. We who consider ourselves well-traveled for crossing the earth and a little beyond have barely explored a tide pool beside the sea of sensory worlds surrounding us wherever we go. Will future travel include techniques to pass into dimensions of experience unknown to us but familiar to animals, insects, plants, molecules, and planets?

POST_037: Moving Constellations

Example: SpaceX plans to launch 42,000 satellites over the next few decades.[52]

The magic of a falling star is that it disrupts the celestial order as a rare omen of the impossible. Look up tonight and you will see many more, not falling but moving steadily in inscrutable paths across the sky. What constellations can we salvage from this aluminum and silicon babel, this ever-shifting scatter of fleeting mythologies?[53]

POST_038: Convolution Map

Example: Tech companies are developing "living maps" continuously updated by video, radar and lidar.

Thrown into a complexity we will never fully comprehend, confusion cannot be avoided. We need a new kind of map that, rather than directing us down the most efficient path, intensifies the convolution, turning it into movement. A map that does not show us where we are or where we are going, but traces the contours of our desperation and longing, the only sure landmarks in the desert of the real.

POST_038: The Subliminal Game

Example: "In the infinite game . . . man is not a player—nor even the dice—but an almost passive counter that is moved from square to square in its turn, together with other reiterated emblems." (Roger Caillois)[54]

Those who demand access to the law can wait their entire lives outside the door, but we were born already inside this game. All attempts to codify its rules inevitably fail, as if its purpose were to entice structures into being only to fracture and dissolve them in subliminal tremors, but games don't need a purpose. As a diversion, we play our own games, and for a time, that other one seems to make sense or simply disappear—until they end and the subliminal game resumes, and so we play again.[55]

POST_039: After the Engine Age

Example: A wave-powered boat (autonomous unmanned vessels).[56]

Someday one of the greatest failures of humanity will be known to have been the engine. Living in a sea of perpetual movement, we struggle against it all, imposing our own noxious source of propulsion in a way no other life form finds necessary. This absurd excess amidst such abundance will surpass the nuclear bomb as the ultimate symbol of the catastrophic ignorance behind our supposed ingenuity—to whatever comes after us.[57]

POST_040: Cosmic Flicker

Example: The constant oscillations of artificial light.[58]

The wind crackling through the blinds casts blazing shadows of noon upon your closed eyelids—a virtual microcosm of the sun. Moths dance in chaotic spirals around a lightbulb flickering in the night like a projector faster than the human eye can see. Words coalesce in strobing frequencies across the screen, darting out from their hiding places in the depths of insomnia to the throb of a headache.[59]

POST_041: Force Field

Example: Military researchers propose a missile defense system using lasers.[60]

Soccer goalie Gigi Buffon explains the ball's power to enchant like this: "Around the magic object there is a kind of force field, which is the territory of the story itself." The link between sports and war is ancient and deep, but the force field he describes is the flip side of both. Instead of sealing us off from our opponents, it opens a space of captivation from which poetic forces can emerge and radiate.

POST_042: Alchemy of Emptiness

Example: "The simplest atom is a material form, a vortex, as we are told, a vibratory rhythm of a certain kind, something by all appearances infinitely complex." (Gabriel Tarde)[61]

All that we are can be reduced to two elements: void and movement. Void is the zero degree of movement, movement the intensification of void. The sensation of void (overwhelming feeling of emptiness) can only be resisted through movement—until its sublimation as complete exhaustion.

POST_043: Hidden Movement

Example: Stealth drone prototype ("classified diamond-shaped low observable UAV testbed").[62]

Secrecy has long depended on the power of a hiding place: the vault, the hole, the trap door . . . Even those masters of camouflage—animals, insects—rely on stillness to perfect their disappearance act. In a future rendered fully measured and transparent, leaving nowhere safe to hide, concealment will become an art of hiding in motion.

POST_044: Space-movement

Example: "Whoever can feel space, its directions, its scale; whoever understands that the movement of the emptiness means music; to him is granted entrance to a nearly unknown world, the world of architects and the world of painters." (August Endell)[63]

The spirit or soul is associated in many cultures with the movement of breath within and around the body. In a similar way, could we not say the vital source of any structure is less its form than in the movements it channels and rhythmizes? Future architects—especially of the virtual—will use space-movement as their primary building material, fashioning immaterial presences from a fluid negativity found previously only inside collective dreams.[64]

POST_045: Quivering Outlines

Example: Article demonstrate that virtual out-of-body experiences could decrease fear of death.[65]

Where do we end and each other, our worlds begin? After so many iterations of this question embodied throughout Earth's history, how much longer will we settle on the limits of the skin? Will the future transgress this boundary collectively through some discovery or mass ecstasy, or will it allow us each to decide for ourselves?

POST_046: Movement without End

Example: Fitness trackers form new assemblages for the athletic body.[66]

Splashing in the pool, skating around the rink, dancing all night . . . just some of the ways we move not for work or exercise but purely for joy. They carry us along in the perpetual motion of a means without ends. Will we choose to multiply these collective movements or reduce them, harness them, track them, and thus find the ends that will finally be their end?

POST_047: Thought-movement

Example: "Not so much an image, but a felt sense that something arises. Like a little movement . . . a perturbation. It's not a thought yet. It's just a kind of a stirring. Something is about to happen." (Claire Petitmengin)[67]

Thoughts arise—from what, from where? Tiny movements like currents, like waves, meteorological events that precipitate a subject. So-called abstraction is an elemental stirring we egotistically call our own, as if a storm could lay claim to the winds.[68]

Elti Meșhau. "Smoke Behind" (2017).

4.0

Future Body Lab

Chapter 4.0

Future Body Lab

Concepts: Sensation, Metamorphosis, Desire

Lab Authors: Laura Tripaldi
[Posts 1–18] and Dana Dawud [Posts 19–28]

POST_001: Viral Anthropogenesis

Example: Nearly half of our human genome is the result of ancient viral infections that may still give rise to unpredicted effects.[1]

Genetic essentialism recovers the biblical principle dictating that human bodies are but the manifestation of language, existing as a product of abstract information linearly encoded within matter. If material configurations and vestigial memories can re-code the language that defines us, generating retroactive feedback between bodies and information, what does it mean to be human?

POST_002: Disembodied Consciousness

Example: American startup promises future mind-uploading by implementing a new process for embalming living human brains.[2]

Will the body of the future simply be no body at all? Digitalized disembodiment unveils the problematic entanglement of matter and mind: as mind appears to be uploaded into ethereal virtuality, it rediscovers itself as entirely dependent on its material substrates (constructing interfaces between silicon and flesh is, after all, purely a matter of materials science) and their perpetual demand for dissipation through entropic deterioration, heat transfer, and informational noise.

POST_003: Arachnomaterialism

Example: Artist Tomás Saraceno's project Arachnophilia explores the spiderweb as a symbolic and material device to investigate the interconnectedness of our reality.[3]

As the spider spins her web, weaving her environment as a secretion of her body, so does the human produce her world by building viscous networks that entangle bodies and meaning. How can we define the material properties of the substance that forms the ultimate substrate of our reality?

POST_004: Biotechnological Homonculi

Example: Human brain organoids, that is small-scale self-assembled aggregates of human neurons, may offer unprecedented opportunities in research and diagnostics, but raise ethical questions regarding their capacity to suffer.[4]

The most accurate form of simulation that can ever be achieved coincides with the exact material replica of the body being simulated. If there is no longer any boundary between a material configuration and its model, is the body anything but a perpetual simulation of itself?

POST_005: Animate Materials

Example: A new research initiative launched by the Royal Society of Chemistry challenges scientists to design "animate" materials, capable of self-repairing, growing, and adapting to their environment by engaging in a transdisciplinary approach to materials science.[5]

The future of materials lies in blurring the boundaries between living and nonliving, organic and inorganic, mind and matter, subject and object. Progresses in materials science underline the urgency of a paradigm shift in our approach to matter: from functional tools to adaptive bodies, from top-down design approaches to bottom-up assemblies, from hardness to softness.

POST_006: Digital Skins

Example: Quantum dots injected underneath the skin together with vaccines may provide on-patient record of their medical history.[6]

The problematic encounter between bodies and virtuality takes place at the interface between our skin and digital technologies, where bodies become data and information is embedded within our flesh. What is the potential and what are the risks of the use of nanotechnology to build increasingly extended interfaces between our embodied selves and our digital selves?

POST_007: Swirling Multitudes

Example: Physicists report a previously unidentified state of active matter, that is swirlons, constituted by ensembles of active particles which defy Newton's Second Law of dynamics and self-organize into dynamic structures.[7]

Is our knowledge of the physical world biased by a pre-constituted conception of bodies as passive, molar, and individual? Embracing the molecularity of materials as it manifests collectively through assemblies of self-propelled particles, instead of passive units subjected to external forces, allows us to understand the behavior of groups of bodies as they morph into colonies, packs, and swarms.

POST_008: Abiotic Mass

Example: Beginning with 2020, the total mass of artificial materials produced by humans has become greater that the total biomass on earth.[8]

It is estimated that each human being currently produces approximately the equivalent mass of their weight in artificial, man-made materials every week. As the mass of nonhuman materials we produce and discard becomes much greater than that of our bodies, growing even bigger than the amount of organic, living matter on earth, should we extend our definition of the human body to include the artificial shells that we continuously build and shed?

POST_009: Spinal Rewiring

Example: Scientists successfully designed and tested a carbon nanotube-based advanced material that could repair spinal cord injuries by acting as a scaffold for human neurons.[9]

When carbon-based nanotechnologies become embedded within our spine, offering inorganic scaffolds for our own neuronic structures and opening new physicochemical channels of communication across our bodies, our experience of ourselves will be radically transformed from within. Will we then still be able to answer the much-debated question: What is it like to be a human?

POST_010: Virtual Simulacra

Example: Artist Irene Fenara used an AI algorithm to produce the digital image of a tiger. The algorithm was fed only three thousand pictures, matching the actual number of tigers still living in the wild today.[10]

When virtual simulacra outnumber embodied individuals, as in the case of digital avatars, social media profiles, memes, and endangered species, real bodies are transformed into the mere representation of something entirely other. In the age of information and reproduction, bodies become vectors that can be infinitely transformed, transcending their original morphologies and pointing to a meaning that is always absent.

POST_011: Mechanical Wombs

Example: Mice embryos were grown in a mechanical, automated womb for the first time, disproving the belief that embryos require a living uterus for their development.[11]

Feminist thinking has been pondering the idea of full mechanization and automation of reproduction since its very beginning: what will happen when reproductive labor is definitively disentangled from the human body? As reproductive emancipation becomes a matter of access to technology, we should evaluate the impact of these new reproductive infrastructures on gender politics and consider whether they will result in emancipation or unprecedented forms of exploitation.

POST_012: Reality Shifts

Example: "Reality shifting", that is a set of techniques for shifting the mind to an alternate, imaginary reality, has become a popular trend among teenagers on TikTok.[12]

Now more than ever, fully immersive digital realities are readily available through computer and smartphone screens in video games and streaming platforms, providing disembodied sensory environments that assist the separation of our minds from our bodies. At what point in the future will this separation become inherent to our existence, and what are the risks of implementing full mind/body segregation in a human being?

POST_013: Bodies without Meaning

Example: Netflix's new documentary *Seaspiracy* illuminates the cruelty and devastating environmental consequences of industrial fishing throughout the world.[13]

Speciesism refers to the ideology that assigns value to different animal and human bodies depending on their function in the regime of capitalist accumulation and consumption. We should be aware that who or what will make it into the narrow range of bodies that will be saved from patriarchal capitalism's environmental annihilation will be purely a matter of linguistic identification: will you be livestock or fauna? A food supply or an ecological reserve? A living person or a disposable commodity?

POST_014: Rebuild Yourself

Example: Elysia marginata sea slugs can self-decapitate and fully regrow their bodies from their severed heads.[14]

Regrowth of body parts is regarded as a typical capacity of primitive and unconscious animals, suggesting that our centralized consciousness is incompatible with the proliferation of bottom-up, delocalized assemblies. Will future human bodies be able to spontaneously re-assemble after being damaged, and what will be the impact of full-body regeneration on our experiences of identity and self?

POST_015: Quantum Perception

Example: Human taste receptors can distinguish between ordinary water and "heavy water" by detecting subtle quantum, sub-atomic effects.[15]

Our natural sensory organs are surprisingly advanced detectors that are designed to perceive the most subtle microscopic qualities of matter. How are quantum, submolecular effects amplified through the biological machinery of our bodies? How does the mediation between such inhuman phenomena and our human consciousness take place? To what extent and through what processes can we develop these psychic abilities?

POST_016: Chemical Blossoms

Example: Professor Wim L. Noorduin has designed elaborate, self-assembling nanostructures from inorganic metal salts and sodium silicate that grow in the shape of microscopic flowers.[16]

Chemists have been dreaming of growing inorganic materials in the form of biological organisms for generations; although what was previously named "inorganic morphogenesis" is now known as "self-assembly," the fundamental ambition has remained unchanged. Is chemistry still driven by the same vitalist concepts that fueled nineteenth-century synthetic biologists, and what will the future of vitalism look like in the age of nanotechnology?

POST_017: Vestigial Futures

Example: The first human-monkey chimaera embryos, produced by injecting human stem cells into monkey fertilized eggs, were artificially designed and survived in-vitro for nineteen days.[17]

Although we are used to thinking of time as a current that flows uniformly and independently from matter, our growing understanding of material configurations has unveiled the deep intertwining between temporality and bodies. The study of morphogenesis, that is, the process of growth and transformation of self-organized matter, suggests that time may be ultimately intrinsic to bodies, to the point that changing their morphologies coincides with traveling through time. Are we running toward the future, or falling backward into our deepest past?

POST_018: Future Body Music

Example: Scientists have transformed the three-dimensional structure of a spiderweb into music, which could help us decode the language of spiders.[18]

The notion that bodies and music are deeply interconnected has played a crucial role in the development of pre-scientific and scientific thought: from Kepler's celestial harmonies to Schrödinger's modeling of quantum particles as resonance, it is intriguing to think that what we perceive as the most abstract and immaterial of things may be so radically like the dense inertness of matter itself. The more we study and understand complex bodies, the more we are able to translate them into seemingly immaterial constructs, opening new pathways from matter to information and from language to embodied structures.

POST_019: Posthuman Body

Example: The work of artist Wang Shui: "Dripping, crackling shards of laboratory-made materials emitting, like alien shrapnel, low-frequency groans. Silkworms mating on a horizontal television screen. Drones flying through gaping holes in Hong Kong high-rises. Teen lips on bubble-tea straws. These are some of the objects, images, and moments that we find in Wang Shui's work."[19]

Posthumanism, in its different variations and trajectories, has shown that the body is central to our thinking of futurity, whether the body is completely discarded in future visions where the mind rules and the body dissipates, or professes the different mutations and connections that tie the body's morphism to social, political, and technological networks. To think "futurity" we need to consider the bodies produced by "futurity" not just as a distant possibility, but "futurity" as a theoretical laboratory that affects how we think of bodies now. As the future folds back onto the now, it revolutionizes how bodies are thought of, treated, codified, and transformed. Contemporary art is such a laboratory where the posthuman body of the future is folded back onto the present, exceeding the traditional constraints of sci-fi genres and typical fantasies of the future. The experimentation that contemporary arts provide allows for an approach to materiality and space that has an actual concrete effect.

POST_020: Cyclical Body-time

Example: Futuristic art show by Palestinian painter Nabil Anani titled "In Pursuit of Utopia." The paintings show landscapes which appear to be returning our present gaze, they are these reflections from the future which strike us with possibility. Despite the "naturalness" of the paintings, they embody a future vision, they are not realism but a break in the cycle.

Quote: "And in still another grandiose episode the myth suggests that the "cycle of time," the "aeon," is for Ohrmazd the instrument of his victory over the Antagonist. Taking up Ahriman's challenge, Ohrmazd inflicts upon him a vision of the future, which Ahriman rejects but which nevertheless overwhelms him: in this vision he beholds the destruction of his demons, the coming of the Resurrection and of the "Future Body" (tan i pasen)." (Henry Corbin)[20]

This passage of cosmic metaphysical myth suggests that a future vision can hold immense power, which would overwhelm forces of darkness, create a rupture in a cycle, and bring forth future bodies. The importance here lies in this continuous thinking of this future; the vision is not science fiction, nor a projection; it is an ongoing activity that takes place in the present. It needs to be sustained, and it needs to be powerful. The body in the present would inhabit this future vision of a land with no walls or barricades, through continuous acts of thought and resistance, leading to liberation from constraints and violence: this is a future body to which one aspires.

POST_021: The Obsolete Body

Example: Nadim Choufi's eighteen-minute film titled *The Sky Oscillates Between Eternity and Its Immediate Consequences* (2021) is set in a digitally-rendered space colony..

The image of a healthy anthropocentric human "future body" has been pushed and propagated for ages and has shaped our relationship with our body by dictating what regimens we need to follow, forms of exercise, and types of chemicals and radiation to avoid. There's an entire market around this idea, and it keeps changing at a faster pace; every trend that emerges does away with the trend before it, and what we conceive of as "self-care" changes. While for past civilizations, "self-care" was an art most probably practiced by a few people who were privy to that knowledge of themselves, today "self-care" is the main consumer ideology. Each individual is responsible for their mental and physical well-being in an impossible race against all the conditions that are deteriorating our bodies at an accelerated pace, from environmental changes to strained work schedules and all the other products we are encouraged to use and consume. It is crucial to rethink what a practice of self-care means in a collective manner, since industrialization and the unequal distribution of calamity have rendered self-care obsolete.

Against the simulated backdrop of a space colony environment on Earth, this new sci-fi film explores how the future of smart cities relies on sustainable closed systems in the face of health and ecological crises. A strange premise, as two protagonists narrate how the control and exploitation of environmental life cycles and organisms become a blueprint to achieve such futuristic visions.

POST_022: Future Eyes

Example: In a sense, the now well-known image of eyes on a plate can serve the aesthetic purpose of the prosthetic eye. Meanwhile, new technologies of the bionic eye--equipped with retinal camera implants, light and movement detection perceptors, miniature video processors--are leading to an age where we can actually restore vision.

I have been magnetically drawn to any painting or figure of St. Lucy, holding delicately a plate of two eyeballs. She is the patron saint of the blind, and there are two versions of why eyes are her emblem. The first version relates to her persecution by guards who ordered her eyeballs to be removed, and the other more interesting version, which concerns us here in terms of futurity, is that she took her own eyes out to discourage a persistent suitor who admired them. By taking her own eyes out, she obliterates the gaze of the other and her own sight, and by becoming the patron saint of the blind holding a dish of eyeballs, a displacement of the position and function of the eyes has occurred. Through this mystical shift, the eyes have become both everywhere and nowhere, disjunctive but purposeful.

POST_023: THE FACIAL SURFACE

Example: Francis Bacon, Pope (painting, circa 1958) shows a dim-lit yet glowing physiognomy inside a cage-like structure.

The face has a long history that traverses multiple disciplines. In science, it could relate to evolutionary biology; in philosophy it has taken multiple facets as either a window to the soul or a representation of a crumbling humanity. We have seen how faces have traversed the arts as a locus for portrait painting and the frames of cinema. Recently, artist Nada Zanhour posted a selfie on Instagram with a filter turning her into a blue-eyed elf, asking, "Seriously, what is a face? It's a body area where sensory organs hang out and suddenly it's a site of selfhood? I will never get over this." In his book on Francis Bacon's work, Deleuze reveals this power of the face as a locus for emotive sensation rather than a surface of representation. The face has been effaced and is in motion; the technologies that are arising have been trained to recognize our faces and add a layer of representation and identity to them, but we are also changing our "faces" all the time with masks and avatars.

POST_024: Future Hearing

Example: Article by Thomas Birtchnell titled "Listening Without Ears: Artificial Intelligence in Audio Mastering" explores artificial intelligence in "sound formats and listening environments."[21]

Sound distorts our sense of time. When we hear our own voices while we speak, it is only a sound wave that has to travel through time and space to reach us. There is always an element of delay, but when we are thinking, the sounds in our head make our thoughts always seem somehow ahead of us. When sound merges with thought futurity begins to take hold.

POST_025: Future Heart

Example: Artificial Intelligence is now used to analyze the heart and predict its turbulences, researchers are working to create the first artificially intelligent stethoscope system, which can analyze heart and lung sounds to build a unique personal biometric signature, while it also tags geo-location and environmental data to each sample in real-time.

Before the brain, the heart used to take a central role in how thoughts, emotions, and vitality are processed; it used to be this missing link between the polarity of the body and soul. Despite the changes in how science and philosophy situate the "heart," the idea that our emotions and deepest desires, the most authentic impulses, come from the heart persists. It could have been watered down to simply a linguistic metaphor, but it is used in psychological discourses and popular culture; to follow one's heart and have it lead the way is always seen as a more noble cause. Monitoring the heart in modern and contemporary medicine is a measure of health; all our habits and histories are tied to the intricate parameters of the heart. Almost all smart devices and watches monitor your heart all the time; it is still physiologically the vital organ. Your brain might die, but your heart could still be beating. Transhumanist traditions have a place for detaching our mind from our body to achieve immortality, but do we cease to have a body if the heart is still there?

POST_026: Future Scream

Example: Francis Bacon, Study for a Head (1952). Certain aesthetics of the malformed face (screaming) bear an untimely resonance, and thus can only be treated as futural projections of a body that might someday come to pass.

Almost every work of art has the ability to skew time in different manners through temporalities, durations, instantaneous effects, repetition, illusion, and timelessness. In painting, Francis Bacon was not only a master of annulling representation but also of creating an endless tension with the surfaces of sensation and the melting bodies of his figures. Through painting, he was attempting to isolate the human scream and detach it from the body, giving the scream a life of its own. The scream has been represented in many ways by painters; Edward Munch's iconic painting is one example, but the scream there is attached to a figure and somehow has a narrative. What is it like to have a scream that is completely detached from its figure, a scream that is caught after it has only left the body? A future scream? Painting is the art of light, and light is faster than sound, so it's through painting that this could be possible: to catch up with the scream from the future is to paint it.

POST_027: Asteroidal Touch

Example: Struck by the moon landings, Italian architect Alessandro Poli composes a series of collages, sketches, and images during his work for Superstudio in the 1970s, exploring the horizontal and vertical grids which could connect our bodily space to planets and asteroids.[22]

Unknown surfaces expand our visions of how movements, settlements, and erected structures change toward imaginary yet tangible futures. And now as "other" space is becoming reality, architecture firms and artists are creating prototypes where the malleability of shapes and materials can create a space to explore unknown bodies . . . seeing the planetary through grids and touched by forces of the obscure.

POST_028: Gothic Center

Example: In his manifesto published in 1919, "The City Crown", Bruno Taut envisioned vertical communal centers: gothic towers where the body's soul dwells.

These vertical utopias, which defy the functionality of modern design, hollow out a space where crystal glass would lament with poetic spirituality. Centuries later, these visions of towering structures manifest a way to fill the gap between distant pasts and possible futures. These manifestations do not serve a function in the modern sense but create spiritual effect by extending the horizon of futural bodies: "away from rituals, for all time."

LAB 5.0

Future Image

Chapter 5.0

Future Image Lab

Concepts: The Vital, the Visionary, the Artwork

Dejan Lukic

POST_001: Transcendental Hope Image

Example: Wutopia Lab designs Satory Harbor library in the VIP shop's new headquarters in Guangzhu, China.[1]

Like a lighthouse in the sea of buildings, roads, and urban tribulations, stands a new library, high on the upper floors, sandwiched among the busy offices of an e-commerce company. Will this kind of interior architectural void be the only place left, in the city of the future, for the transcendental pause?

POST_002: 180 Degrees of Sea Image

Example: The island of Antikythera serves as a meteorological melting pot where dust from the Sahara, tephra from Mount Etna, and cinder from Canadian wildfires merge. Climate scientists from around the world are gathering at the new climate observatory which is being transformed into a superstation.[2]

Will the abandoned islands fulfill failed utopian visions of the past? Climate change will guide new populations back to islands for a new form of archipelagic living, as air quality of air becomes the greatest luxury on the planet, and the study of aerosols (tiny particles of dust, fumes, mist) a decisive investigation for future survival on the planet.

POST_003: Altered Consciousness Image

Example: Art and science venture Sensescapes creates an exhibition space with projected light and immersive music created from brain data of people in altered states.[3]

Will images and projections from science replace all need for personal experimentation, as we end up seeing all the obscure processes of our consciousness clearly and lucidly outside of us? Will this conjunction of art and science lead to new types of lucidity, clear-headed thinking, where altered consciousness will be viewed with aesthetic fascination rather than with compulsive physiological dependency? We will continue to see what was so far invisible.

POST_004: Magnetized Image

Example: Brazilian artist Lygia Pape (1927–2004) constructs unforeseen emotional experiences through performance, sculpture, and installation.[4]

Golden shimmering lines intersect each other like lasers; we can tell where they begin but not where they end; they extend themselves into the dark infinite. The artist constructs this magnetized space in order to change us, alter us, as soon as we step into it. The heightened sensitivity of the future will rely on the development of magnetic capabilities.

POST_005: In/visible Image

Example: Oceanographers are mapping the Gulf Stream that runs like a giant river through the Atlantic Ocean, carrying warmth. The seeming weakening of this arm of Gulf Stream will bring monstrous changes in climate.[5]

At the core of art lies the power of clairvoyance. Artists manifest the invisible, in whatever medium they work. Now science too makes what is invisible to human eyes visible. Our future will be determined by the ability to see invisible currents of water and air, for they are the sole shapers of the fate of this planet.

POST_006: Floating Image

Example: Artist Tomás Saraceno engineers a floating installation able to carry a human being without any fossil fuel.[6]

We will soon learn how to float into the far distances of space guided only by the sheer thermal powers of the sun and propelled by the winds alone. This will be a form of navigation that was in the ancient times reserved only for sailing on water and for insects and birds. Now this eternal dream of sailing in the air, silently, is becoming a reality.

POST_007: Animal Eye Image

Example: Visionary writer Velimir Khlebnikov, the central figure in the Russian Futurist movement from the 1910s, and author of "The Snake Train," "The King of Time," and "The Tablets of Destiny" writes stories about the future of life on our planet and the necessary alternative formations in language, architecture, art, and science.[7]

The story goes that there is a sacred area of wilderness wherein only a single rule exists: that all animals are kept from extinction there. The doctors here discovered that looking into the eyes of animals cures anxiety and distress. The animal eyes serve as a remedy adjusting human beings' mental misalignments. Doubtless, this will be the last form of medication for our lonely and abandoned humanity.

POST_008: Camera Eye Image

Example: China's surveillance initiative called Sharp Eye blankets all public space in the country with security cameras.[8]

The greatest luxury of the future will be the ability to be outside the view of the camera. As every inch of public space on the planet is being monitored, only a few will be able and willing to avoid this perennial gaze of the camera eye.

Indeed, today we live and breathe inside the technological lens that we do not even see.

POST_009: Scaling Image

Example: In a disquieting yet humorous way, French artist J. J. Grandville draws images of the future, which are somewhere between a dream and a scientific discovery.[9]

One of the first games a child learns is hopscotch. Later we take pleasure in hopping on the rocks in a creek. Then the scale increases and one jumps from one island to another. The final dream is one of hopping from planet to planet, traversing the cosmic archipelago that constitutes the known and the unknown interstellar space. All science fiction films point to this. Mechanical and bioengineering are lagging behind, but not for long, as dreams force themselves upon the machines.

POST_010: Regenerative Image

Example: Artist Amy Karkle works with bio-nano scientists to build objects from cells.[10]

Will the future be composed purely of synthetic biology, where entire worlds will be built artificially from nature's original building blocks—cells? Will the future be defined by a final reconciliation between the artificial and the natural? And will we ever be able to tell the difference between the two?

POST_011: Code Image

Example: The increasing cultural obsession with games demonstrates how highly complex code systems are being introduced to users as entertainments and diversions so as to conceal their deeper functions.

There is no escape from the game. Existing means being part of the invisible rules (physical, social, virtual). Each of these carries a series of codes and, as such everything is prescribed, yet everything is at play. The future can only be conceived as such a playful ascertainment, or else as an exuberant divination.

POST_012: Brutalist Image

Example: It is said that one of the architectural inspirations for the movie Blade Runner 2049 was a design for the unbuilt Neanderthal Museum.[11]

Indeed, we intuitively feel at home in these futuristic enclosures, with smooth oblique wall finishes that remind us of caves, where only the interplay of light and shadow matters. The future is always a combination of the prehistoric and posthistoric.

POST_013: Geometric Image

Example: Architect R. Buckminster Fuller developed a theory of synergetics according to which patterns and regularities give rise to scientific and mystical knowledge.[12]

Can there be a fully mathematical model of reality? Is it all just a science of configurations—that is to say, geometries? Ancient astronomies and numerologies relied on mathematics too, at the core of which was a mystical number. The future will precisely balance these two domains as well: the mathematical and the mystical.

POST_014: Future City Image

Example: The City of Arts and Sciences in Valencia, Spain, designed by Santiago Calatrava, is used as a backdrop in science fiction series Westworld, where androids mingle.[13]

Human beings have always felt out of place: first from nature, then from technology. They were not able to reconcile with their own animality in the past. And they are unable to reconcile that they are partially computers now. The future will be one of this reconciliation where humans will comfortably be animals and machine, organic and inorganic, synthetic and natural. It is for these humans without impediments that cities of the future are built.

POST_015: Riteless Image

Example: Artist-couple Christo and Jeanne-Claude build the largest sculpture in the world called Mastaba outside of Abu Dhabi. It was conceived in 1977 and soon to be finished.[14]

In the shadow of the ancient civilizations, what will our future edifices look like? It seems that the very word "civilization" remains buried in the great pyramids of North Africa and Central America for good. The future temples will be more impressive in terms of scale and color, and less profound. For the insides of them will have to be devoid of any ritual, so that the visitors can take photos of themselves, undisturbed.

POST_016: Nightmare Image

Example: Treatment of nightmares changes in most recent sleep and trauma studies.[15]

The latest science of sleep tells us that nightmares are healthy, as they process and prepare us for potential traumatic events. The truth is that we know very little about the role and the effect of dreams. Without a doubt, they are liminal phenomena of our psyche. And as such, they flutter like the wings of the ancient goddess Psyche, who is said to have had butterfly wings, for silent arrivals to our dreams.

POST_017: Monolith Image

Example: New monoliths mysteriously appear in Utah, California, New Mexico, and Romania.[16]

The striking feature of the monoliths is that they are silent devices pulling us toward a future. In the movies and science fiction novels, they are mysterious initiators of human evolution. In ancient cultures, they are markers for the ineffable. They are concrete, outside nature, portals into the unknown.

POST_018: Galaxy Brain Image

Example: Astrophysicists and neuroscientists are exploring Galaxy Brain theory, which shows curious overlaps in the structure of the brain and structure of the galaxies.[17]

Will we one day view the entire galaxy, everything formed and still unformed, as one gigantic brain? The more we study neuronal connections in our brains, the more we see their resemblance to galactic filaments. The leading conversation of the future will occur between astrophysics and neuroscience, provoking a completely new understanding of the human.

POST_019: Immortal Image

Example: One jellyfish species—*Turritopsis dohrnii*—has the ability to revert to its earlier stage of development, thus starting its life anew time and time again.[18]

Immortality is not up in the sky, in the abstract beyond. Rather, it hovers in the depths of the sea. And so it is in this inhuman element that we will find possibilities for eternal life. The secret hides in the biomorphic technique of a tiny jellyfish.

POST_020: Immaterial Image

Example: Atmos Mask that purifies the air while being worn is being developed for the future use of the global population.[19]

The greatest luxury of the future will be clean air. Air will be what gold used to be—a coveted currency. We will not dig for it. Instead, we will use devices to purify it, thus returning to the old art of alchemy, which changed base into a noble matter.

POST_021: Time-travel Image

Example: Traveling time machine prototype is currently in the making at the University of Connecticut.[20]

It is not unimaginable to conceive the entire universe as an ever-expanding sculpture. The first gesture in making a sculpture is that of twisting. If we could twist space, time would twist with it. Some say this is now just a matter of engineering; of developing a contraption that would allow for such a gravitational twist to occur. Then there would be no more past or future. There would be only infinite looping.

POST_022: 10,000-Year Image

Example: Designed by Danny Hillis for the Long Now Foundation, on the land in western Texas owned by Jeff Bezos, a clock which is meant to last for 10 millennia, and powered by sunlight and visitors, is being built.[21]

Inside a mountain, a clock is being built. It will tick once a year 10,000 times. It will play melodies no one will hear. It will measure human time of an entire civilization. It will make us aware that "our" time is measured in thousands of years.

POST_023: Absolute Time Image

Example: Current physicist explains time misperception and its relation to heat and entropy.[22]

There is no absolutely objective time. Time at sea level and time on the mountain pass differently (always slower the closer we are to the sea). The stronger the gravity, the slower the passage of time. At the core of the earth, there is no time, just a magmatic alloy of iron-nickel. The temperature of the inner core is the same as that of the surface of the sun. At these solar temperatures, even time melts. Here, the future is the past and the past is the future.

POST_024: Color Hearing Image

Example: Google Arts & Education develops a machine learning system that allows visitors of a museum to experience paintings aurally.[23]

At some distant point in Earth's history, senses began to differentiate themselves and different living entities ensued. Humans are limited to five. Each has its own function. Changing a function of a given sense occurred only in avant-garde literature, or in cognitive rarities like synesthesia. But soon it will be possible for all. And if we then hear colors, will we still be called human?

POST_025: No Future Tense Image

Example: Europe's smallest ethnic minority numbers only 200 individuals in present-day Latvia. They speak the Livonian language with a complex grammar that has seventeen cases and genderless nouns.[24]

There are now almost eight billion humans on the planet. (It took two million years to reach the first billion and only 200 years to gain six billion more.) The greatest threat of the future is the further expansion of a global mass. The most valuable, because the most rare, will be the consistency of the small number. Like the little-known Livonians. The most amazing thing about their native tongue is that it has no future tense.

POST_026: Rise of the Indigenous Image

Example: Visualization by a collective that is patiently mapping the ancestral lands of the native tribes around the world.[25]

In the future, territories will be recognized not by the borders of the nation-states, but by the names of ancient and current tribes. A new mapping has begun, one that is not claiming possession but rather unveiling the names of the eternal ones.

POST_027: Almost Extinct Image

Example: For the first time in geological history anthropogenic mass weight (mass produced by humans) surpasses the biomass of the planet.[26]

Without a doubt, humans are in the process of destroying all life on Earth. They consume with a conviction and obliviousness that could be mistaken for a destiny. The rare is being suffocated under piles of human waste matter. The planet will eventually fall through its own orbit, unable to carry the weight of future anthropogenic mass. This is the meaning of the old philosophical idea of the void—falling into oblivion.[27]

POST_028: Spectral Image

Example: Mozambique artist Yana Naidenov creates an image titled Meshes (Spectral Infrastructure), 2021.[28]

There is an invisible, inaudible, illegible spectral infrastructure that lies within each organism. It is a form of ephemeral organization that could be called a "drive" or "affect." But it goes far beyond human psychology. This invisible scaffolding underpins institutions, cultures, biological entities, and artificial intelligences. It forms unbeknown to us. As the future brings us more and more super-sensitive devices, perhaps we will develop the capacity to see it or hear it (our essence).

POST_029: Alchemical Image

Example: Mexican artist Fritzia Irizar transforms old worn-down parts of tools into solid gold and thus creates a testimony to worker's everyday tools.[29]

The mysterious quest of the future stays the same as it was in the past: How to transform base materials into gold (or whatever will be considered valuable and beautiful in the future)? How to give the decomposed energy of work, of matter, a new life?

POST_030: Alien Image

Link: The intricate surface of the tiny predator reveals the alien morphology among the common inhabitants of Earth. It morphs into a debris of leaves when threatened.[30]

The future has always been here, hiding in the present, in the form of an alien—that is to say unknown: creatures who remind us that the complexity of form knows no scale.

POST_031: Bio-ink Image

Example: NASA scientists are printing organs with bio-ink in 3D printers in orbit because the gravity on Earth makes the necessary coagulation of an organ impossible.[31]

If human body parts come from outside the Earth, are they still human? In the future, we will have our bodies developed outside of "home." That is to say, in environments without gravity.

POST_032: Unseen Image

Example: Just outside of the heliosphere, in the farthest reaches of our Solar system, floats a vast, frigid, icy Oort cloud, contaminated by other stars from the outer universe. Scientists hope it will be reached in 300 years.[32]

What will determine our cosmic life in the future, the understanding of our galactic environment, is still unseen. We only have an intuition of this image, an idea of what composes it. But we are yet to reach that cloud which envelops us. The unseen that the future will reveal is coldness itself.

POST_033: Failed Utopia Image

Example: In the Norwegian archipolago of Svalbard lies an abandoned Soviet mining community.[33]

All we have are failed utopias. That is to say, alternative communities that existed for a short time before they disintegrated into more predictable political formations. Yet the desire to create a society that will be different from the preceding ones, including the one we live in now, persists. The future will be shaped by the capacity to imagine these alternatives anew.

POST_034: EMDR Image

Example: Radical psychotherapy claims that eye movement desensitization can heal individual old traumas.[34]

Certainly, the eyes tell the whole story. Not their color, or their sharpness, or their acute vision, but rather, their movement. In the future, where everything will be determined by some sort of "rewiring," so will our health. And it is likely that we will be able to undo our traumas with "eye movement desensitization and reprocessing."

POST_035: Messenger Image

Example: In 2017, astronomer Robert Weryk spotted an asteroid-like object which differed from the crowd. It came from outside the solar system and was named Oumuamua, Hawaiian for "first distant messenger" or "scout."[35]

There are millions of asteroids in our planet's environment. A lot of cosmic debris. Yet one object seemed more like a formed sculpture. An intergalactic art exhibit of one. It has begun. And yet, we are still unsure.

POST_036: Tremulous Image

Example: Artist Silvio Vujicic, in collaboration with the architect Miro Roma, introduces the AI fashion designer named Soll, as part of his studio brand E.A. 1/1 S.V. Existing and thinking as a cloud of images and a search engine that is continually growing, Soll draws from an immense database of images and words which populate the entire oeuvre of the brand.[36]

Finally, our silhouettes will be overcome with an unpredictable shimmer. For the intelligence of the AI creates the highest degree of wavering shape. Soft, tremulous, fitful. Divinely distorted, purely atmospheric, and utterly real. And as a result, the garments for our bodies will transform us into shimmering bodies.

POST_037: Seasonless Image

Link: The snow depths are decreasing rapidly, changing the pathology of the communities that used to be surrounded by it.[37]

One possible scenario: we are staring at a seasonless future. There will be no more changes in the temperature, colors of the landscape, sounds, and smells of the air. Just one big greenhouse. We are staring at the extraordinary extermination of heterogeneity and variance, which will remain as the highest unattainable virtues.

POST_038: Tracking Image

Example: Google Loon Project was initiated to provide free internet to the most remote areas of the world. The first flight was from Puerto Rico to Peru. AI guided balloons learned ancient sailing techniques on the go and decided to alter their course.[38]

The stratosphere will be the final zone of engagement from which life on earth will be guided. In a fashion similarly imagined by the Slavic Futurists in the 1920s, self-guided balloons with free internet recently flew above Peru. For us humans, who are turning from creators to observers, what remains is just fear and trembling.

POST_039: Preborn Image

Example: Neuroscientists find that mammals dream before they are born as a preparation and training of their senses.[39]

Dreams prepare us for the traumatic entry into the world of forms. Dreams as visual images are preconscious and pre-subjective. They are therapeutic devices for the world of the real.

LAB 6.0

Future Illusion

Chapter 6.0

Future Illusion

Concepts: Dream, Hallucination, Simulation

Lab Author: Nora N. Khan

POST_001: Navigating Unintended Effects

Example: Sahej Rahal, finalforest.exe, 2021. Hosted and curated within the 2021 transmediale program.[1]

Live simulations of artificial beings let loose, algorithmic rulesets determining their moves, interact in unexpected ways. They produce unintended and unpredictable effects. Moving with them, we learn to navigate emergent properties, which are a result of our interactions with all systems—technological, simulated, cognitive. Thinking through simulations helps us train in systems thinking, manage complexity, both adhering to coded guides while allowing for variables that cannot be easily controlled. In entraining ourselves to the unexpected outcomes of system processes, we become better prepared for delayed and non-linear effects, for outcomes to be explainable only after they appear.

POST_002: Mapping Time

Example: Flux-Intersection Plate, screenshots taken of Jules Litman-Cleper's simulation art—which is live.[2]

Simulations change and challenge a linear sense of time. As one moves through planes, strafes through its many dimensions, space unlocks in relation to fictional time. As a player, agent, and protagonist, one can hold multiple mappings of time and space scales in mind here. This time is mapped, pinned to mobility and the emergent map. The spatial world of the game is multidimensional; the temporal is defined by the reactivity or openness of the space, the environment. Fictional time shifts and collapses many scales; it expands and contracts and moves with one's movement through space.

POST_003: In the Tattered Ruins of the Map

Example: The 2015 GEO-5 Simulation of Hurricane Katrina, as it approached the Gulf Coast.[3]

In "On Rigor in Science," one of Borges' many fictional quotation-stories, a "Suárez Miranda" writes of an age and empire in which "the Art of Cartography attained such Perfection that the map of a single Province occupied the entirety of a City, and the map of the Empire, the entirety of a Province." In other words, the map made the territory; the map was the territory, in a terrifying 1:1 overlay. Imagine a map the size of the entire world. How do we think of ourselves living amidst the "tattered ruins" of this map in the West today, as Suárez Miranda writes? What impact have the many overtly political choices of mapmaking had on our lives, our health, our access to resources? How does the illusion of the map's objectivity, and its rhetorical power, disappear in mapmaking? These questions about maps as Rhetorical Illusions become more urgent as we live in a world produced by the representational power of simulation, in which models do not match 1:1 but stand in for groups, movements, and bodies of people. A simulation's power is in concentration and metaphor, the way individual agents are metaphors for larger-scale movements and actions in the world. These representative and rhetorical choices produce reality by taking on the appearance of truth. Our challenge in the coming years is to be able to read the "tattered edges" of simulation as well.

POST_004: Each Step Creates the Territory

Example: A screenshot from *Dear Esther* (2012), a famous (and infamously loathed) walking simulator in which the protagonist walks an island in the Scottish Hebrides.

In walking simulators and dungeon games, the map of the world emerges with each step. We can never see the entire map because the world's cartographic representation is made through walking, its edges unfolding with each chance step. Poets and writers have long written of the ways an ambulatory practice develops ideas, the ways a psychogeographic landscape, unfolding, holds and helps threads of thinking unfold. Each new insight is an anchor, a stake in the landscape, the fertile ground of the mind. Elizabeth Bishop, in *The Map*, wrote: "Topography displays no favorites; North's as near as West./More delicate than the historians' are the map-makers' colors."[4] How might we focus more on our own internal map-maker's colors, their palettes? An ambulatory practice becomes a practice of semantic mapping. The environment forms the drama of the psyche, especially as links between cognitive development and movement in space to create a sense of space and time are made more evident. Take up each choice of tone, each choice to look away or delve in, each step, each narrative entry, as the drama of the wandering mind, creating a system of representation. The map blooms at our feet, with each step, turn, dip, and rise.

POST_005: Vicariance, Projection, and Our Inner Worlds as Virtual

Example: A screenshot from artist and theorist Alexandra Anikina's *Non-Player Character,* a procedural film created as part of her research into game engines. A model of Tipu's Tiger, a famous mechanical automaton made by Tipu Sultan of Mysore now held in the V&A Museum, is, in her film, loosed in a digital wild of birch trees, walking forever.[5]

We can more readily understand simulation as a fundamental cognitive act. From our earliest days in which we might have been aware of a "tomorrow," we have simulated ourselves, a virtual version of ourselves, in the future, along with the near certainty that the environments and life world we know can be projected into the future. In treatises like Alain Berthoz's *The Vicarious Brain, Creator of Worlds*, one learns precisely how much virtuality, replacement, and substitution form the foundation of our capacity to engage with complexity. To survive, as Berthoz details, one must be able to practice *vicariance* effectively, an act that allows us to hold virtual mental images of ourselves acting in the future, and moving and deciding in our minds, along with data from our present reality. In understanding how the brain models reality and deploys future-focused models to engage with what is strange or unknown to us individually, we become sharper and more equipped to tell about our uncertain, wildly changing futures. To actively train in vicariance means to train in better holding multiple avatars of ourselves, enacting multiple rulesets and competing paths to survival across all possible (and, as it usually goes, contradicting) future outcomes.

POST_006: On Collaborative and Critical Simulation

Example: Marlene Creates, a poet in Newfoundland, who has a long-running practice of semantic walking maps of the boreal forest, across six acres on which she has lived for years. In *Spots of Memory: what I remembered during one month away after six years on Blast Hole Pond Road, Newfoundland 2008*, she tries to imagine the forest while away, by going over details of it in memory.[6]

One of the most devastating aspects of the mismanagement of the Hurricane Katrina disaster was the absence of people in the many NASA-developed and military simulations of the coming tides. In her seminal book *Computer Simulation, Rhetoric, and the Scientific Imagination*, Aimee Roundtree details this case study as a moment for understanding how profoundly collaborative and team-based an official simulation or model—epidemiological, climate-related, astrophysical, to begin—is. As Roundtree notes, the official simulations did not show a single person reacting to the tides, and so, as critique has narrated extensively, it was impossible for those watching and preparing to imagine how the water would affect human beings on the ground. This capacity to imagine—directly shaped by the choice of representation and occlusion in the simulations—then directly impacted the non-response of officials and their under-preparedness. The impact to come did not seem *real* because of a crucial lack of *representation of all possible outcomes*. The simulation's final form, delivered, has the aspect of truth, rather than being the noisy result of many debates and conflicts in interpretation. What would it mean to insist on the *collaborative* aspect of simulation, the fact of multiple competing models vying for expression on the road to the "final" model that the public receives? This pandemic year has made the need for circumspection and intelligent comparison of multiple epidemiological models evident. In the rich debate on the way to a simulation that will produce material action and consequences in the world, we might insist on a frame for simulation that looks at the noise of its making. Each point, each choice to represent or not, is the product of ten to twenty voices, ten to twenty separate histories, sets of memories, and methods of interpretation, which can open up a process of revision, editing, and refinement.

Robert Bye (2017).

LAB 7.0

Future Cosmos

Chapter 7.0

Future Cosmos Lab

Concepts: Nature, Animality, The Geoscape

Lab Authors: Damon Quasravie and Zahra Bonari

POST_001: Cosmic Dance

Lab Author: Damon/Zahra Bonari
Example: Nicole L'Huillier's "The Dancer" (Chile, 2020) is a robotic sculpture that "explores the performativity of an object as it moves across space and draws through movement in time. The result is an unstable and irregular vibrational dance triggered by sounds emerging from its own body as the resonant frequencies of its material composition causes the object to move."[1]

What was Nature in the eyes of so-called primitive humanity if not a perpetual motion that ceaselessly abolishes and replants life on its course? However, the still stars scattered across the night's canvas have forever refuted this conception of our surroundings. The silent watchers of the night guided us to our destinations and offered shelter against Nature's cruel intent (to devour us in myriad ways). Thus, humanity resolved to entrust its destiny to the night sky and forsake the earth. It took ages for them to realize they had been deceived, ever more lost within Nature's belly. A cosmic dance turned cosmic prison: In the aftermath of the falling skies, to whom shall man once again (perhaps with the knowledge of its immanent fallacy) entrust his fate for deliverance?

POST_002: Being as Deception

Example: Alicja Kwade's "The Big Be-Hide" (Switzerland 2020) presents a found stone and its replica cast in aluminium in a two-sided mirror to investigate the "interplay of being and hiding."[2]

Reflective surfaces have long been considered symbols of recognition, solid structures that allow one to contemplate the world in the background. However, what if these surfaces were intended to deceive the observer? What if mirrors were devices meant to conceal whatever hid beyond? In the art of war, a compromised camouflage is considered a valuable asset for the intruder.

POST_003: Pleasure/Horror Flight

Example: Xavi Bou's "Ornithographies" (Spain, 2021) "focuses on birds . . . in order to capture in a single time frame, the shapes they generate when flying, making visible the invisible."[3]

One must trace the elemental choreographies to move between the gentle realm of weightlessness and the terrifying abyss of destruction. Among the four elements, it is wind that best encapsulates sensation. The mere sight of a flock of birds can ignite within human imagination double-edged yearnings and mixed metaphors: to be lost in the lover's tender embrace, and yet also the desire to disintegrate into the depths of eternal nothingness. Amidst the swift transformations of cosmic landscapes and terrestrial ecosystems, what pleasures and horrors lie in wait for us in the days to come?

POST_004: Dying-Unto-Water

Example: Erika Arias's series "Cherubims" (Colombia, 2018) captures the body in turquoise dark water, guided by the premise that "water not only stores information; it also receives feelings and consciousness, reacting to any stimulus."[4]

Driven by ambition, humans have dared to embark on the quest for water on distant planets, recognizing its crucial role as a prerequisite for life. Yet, contemplating water is also to slip away, dissolve, and die. Could it be that hidden within our longing for extraterrestrial connection lies an obscure yearning to discover new ways of dying (counter-paths of mortality)?

POST_005: Cosmic Nomadism

Example: Scientists warn that the magnetic North Pole has been wandering toward Siberia at an increasing pace. That could potentially wreak havoc on positioning systems, military operations, and other processes that rely on measuring the magnetic pole.[5]

We have long relied upon our compasses to navigate the world—perhaps too long, for now the world renders the instrument obsolete. In a future stripped of directions, is one perpetually lost, or should one revise the very definitions of being stationary and wandering?

POST_006: Cosmic Augur

Example: NASA's recently landed Perseverance Rover on Mars provided high quality picture and sound samples of the barren planet, a purely elemental world void of life.[6]

For the longest time, we have been weighing our deeds and thoughts on the scale of species preservation. Now interstellar images present us with the most hidden of our fears: that perhaps the scale has been broken all along.

POST_007: Elemental Conquest/Downfall

Example: The pattern of rise and fall of past empires overlaps with that of climate variations.[7]

Regarding war, what if the stated political purposes merely concealed the desiring-machine at work? Indeed, what if the impulse to combat atmospheric pressures was the true impetus behind the Mongolians' conquest of the world? What if it was the desire to challenge waves that inevitably led the Vikings to venture southward and raid their newfound opponents? In the midst of our ever-evolving era characterized by shifting climates, what sort of desire for conquest will give birth to the empires of the future?

POST_008: Elemental Wrath

Example: Rapid climate change threatens humankind with desperate elemental outcomes: that half the world burns in wildfires, whereas the other half drowns in hurricanes.

Death by fire is vertical and heroic, marked by piercing embers that thrust into skies; death by water is horizontal, silent, and clandestine. The former propels its victim outward, like a scream that distances them from the world, while the latter softly consumes the drowning soul inward, into a certain oblivion. The inevitable has always been intertwined with us, resting in our dreams underneath, yet each time the arrival of the undeniable catches us by surprise. If it is already too late to reverse the path of our demise, are there still further unpredicted forms of annihilation stored in the treasury of nature's cruelty?

POST_009: Infinitesimal Gaze

Example: Scientists can now produce electricity out of thin air through cultivation of a unique species of microorganism that generates electricity from the air's own humidity.[8]

The human obsession with small objects has come a long way: from idols and amulets to microchips and sub-particles, from imps and fairies to viruses and microbes. To what extent could such an infinitesimal process continue? Is the future an ever-expanding horizon, or rather an ever-shrinking scope?

POST_010: The Last Wind

Example: The US Navy put stealth destroyer USS Zumwalt to the test by sailing it straight into a storm with waves 20-feet high.[9]

The first image emerges from the dark of the sea, where being is lost to solitude. Consequently, the last image must vanish into the cyclone, where being returns to nothingness. Yet, the future of being is always captured within the delicate line of fusion between these two voids. Let us not forget that the space of fusion is also the space of violence. Thus, to reach it, one must prepare for battle.

POST_011: Extra-Terrestrial Colonization

Example: An unusual PhD thesis suggests using bacteria to colonize Mars.[10]

Released arrows, unsheathed blades, discharged bullets—these are the tools employed to conquer tangible realms. But what will be the means to colonize a realm absent, beyond our terrestrial confines? Shall the future colony be a society of ethereal shades, or even of unicellular microorganisms?

POST_012: Lethal Enchantment

Example: Carnivorous glow-worms fill natural caves and abandoned mines in New Zealand.[11]

In the annals of nature, certain predator species thrive not through sheer might or swiftness, but by virtue of their beguiling skillsets. Veiled in secrecy, draped in deception, cloaked in ambiguity, and adorned with ephemerality, are these the elemental techniques that compose the tapestry of Beauty? Does the future unfold within a domain where enchantment and lethality intermingle, giving birth to a realm both captivating and perilous?

POST_013: Stone of Eternity

Example: Artist James Lee Byars presents a haunting image of his final resting place: a grand and simple chamber, bare of any everyday ornamentation, but covered in ethereal gold.[12]

From the lost city of El Dorado concealed within the verdant jungles of Colombia to a tiny gleaming snuffbox ensconced within the drawer of an English aristocrat. From the buried treasures of the Varna Necropolis in ancient Bulgaria dating back to the 5th millennium BC to a Persian manuscript inscribed in luminous gold recounting the Epic of Kings, the allure of gold persists. What secret lies concealed within humanity's enduring infatuation with this gleaming metal? Could it be that the future is ensnared within the iridescent shimmer of this stone, holding within its depths some mystical answer for the ages?

POST_014: Ashes of Sky

Example: Lightning strikes played a vital role in life's origins on Earth.[13]

Outside of certain belief systems (the pagan, the ascetic, the modern atheist), most have assumed that humankind is begotten of stone and water. For when these two elements converge, new shapes come into being. Yet, when a third element enters the equation, the outcome takes on a monstrous aspect. Perhaps our Need springs from the earth, our Desire from the oceans, and our Will from the lightning. And it is precisely this lightning that can manifest the future: subtle strike, evanescent visage, and a flash upon eternity.

POST_015: Post-mortem Paths

Example: Zombie genes. Research shows some genes come to life in the brain after death.[14]

Life on earth is yet another kind of death, though a unique one: an animated death oscillating from one point of departure to another. Perhaps the future must learn from the pagan or from the zombie, both of whom know best how death is not the end but rather the next gateway (an opening).

POST_016: Orbital Return

Example: Scientists discovered enigmatic circling movement patterns in whales, sharks, penguins, and sea turtles.[15]

As we expand our gaze across the cosmos, it seems that all movements are governed by a single law: that of the orbital. But what if time, too, submits to this very law? In such a case, what manner of condition shall resurface from bygone epochs to shape our future? Does the closed circle that ensnares us signify a curse, or does its geometry offer a chance to manifest destinies?

POST_017: Night Evermore

Example: Far underneath the ice shelves of Antarctica, away from open water and sunlight, there is more life than expected. Strange creatures accidentally discovered beneath Antarctica's ice shelves.[16]

To what extremes will the notion of "that which should not be" impel us? What cataclysmic ramifications would ensue from a mindset that renounces the tenets of harmony, legitimacy, and authenticity? For the genuine rebel resides beyond the dominion of solar sovereignty, in the land of eternal night and its rare creatures.

POST_018: The Fifth Philosophy

Example: Gravitational, electromagnetic, weak nuclear and strong nuclear forces determine almost all the interactions of the universe. However, cosmological mysteries such as the expansion of the universe or dark matter might get solved through the discovery of the fifth force.[17]

To apprehend the physics of Becoming, one needs to extend the scope of one's knowledge in four directions: the Primordial, the Eternal, the Transcendental, the Subterranean. Yet, it seems that the password to the enigma of Becoming might reside invisibly along a fifth direction: the Clandestine.

POST_019: Cosmic Psychology

Example: Scientists speculate that the earth has been concealing a fifth layer in its inner core, one made of unique iron caused by a seismic catastrophic event.[18]

Many models of the human psyche overlap with that of terrestrial stratification: namely, that every symptom is driven by an unconscious trauma. Thus, to scrutinize the superficial veneer of things, one must bore into the profound below. And to fathom the realm of imagination, one must supersede all rationalizations — the political, the cultural, the moral. Nevertheless, a counter-wisdom persists: that beneath every exterior lies yet another stratum, another mask beneath the mask.

POST_020: The Last Tree

Example: "A-Bomb" Ginkgo trees, also known as Maidenhair trees which appeared over 290 million years ago, still grow in Hiroshima after the catastrophic earthquake in 1923 and the atomic bomb in 1945.[19]

Almost all ancient civilizations revered a singular tree, known to some as the primordial arboreal entity—the Tree of Life, whose sanguineous essence held the promise of eternal existence—and to others as the Tree of Knowledge, whose forbidden fruit bestowed discernment of the realms of virtue and malevolence. Even in the modern era, a semblance of this tree endures as the Last Tree. Barren and bereft of fruit, its roots penetrate to the lowest recesses of the earth. What twisted codes of knowing are embedded within the heartwood of the Last Tree? Could it be the sublime art of escaping the shackles of time itself?

POST_021: Aerial Destiny

Example: Tornadoes have long been thought to take shape from the top down, forming from swirling air currents during powerful storms. But new research turns that idea upside down, literally.[20]

All along we believed that it was air that elevated the surface, that the law would descend from above. Lately, scientists have discovered that it is in fact the earthly domain that relinquishes its grasp on those surfaces and wrests them into the vast emptiness. Regardless of the direction chosen, one immutable fact prevails: the surface is destined for flight.

POST_022: Axiom of Verticality

Example: Scientists claim life on Jupiter's moon could have "octopus-level intelligence."[21]

What if our desire to step into the beyond, to ascend skyward and dissipate into boundlessness, were inherently tethered to the terrestrial domain? What if, upon severing the cord that binds us, our rationality and instrumentalism would vanish before an alternative tentacular mode of knowing (one of nine minds)? For the ascendant of today is the descendant of the future.

POST_023: Master of the Quite Small

Example: A new small self-powered underwater robotic fish was able to reach the deepest part of the Pacific Ocean—the Mariana Trench—at a depth of almost 11 km (6.8 miles).[22]

An obscure mystic once foretold that the future would bear semblance to the present, only slightly different. It is the mastery of the quite small, the technique of shrinkage, and the art of growth from within—or rather the sorcery of diminution—which holds the key to future explorations, for to arrive at the slightly altered one must first undergo the utmost pressure.

POST_024: Future Deity

Example: The four-year process of casting the sixth of seven primary mirrors for the Giant Magellan Telescope began in March 2021. These giant mirrors will help astronomers see to the edges of the universe.[23]

The ancient wisdom of mysticism: that only through the shattered mirror could one steal a fleeting glimpse of the Divine. This dictum attests that one cannot directly confront the edge of the Impossible, nor consciously surmount the Unknown, nor find an explicit clue to the Faceless. By this degree, the path toward the future remains implicit, fragmented, and dispersive.

POST_025: Eternally Bleeding

Example: With a rod through its ribs and its teeth pulled—just to be safe—a 700-year-old suspected vampire has escaped the crypt in Bulgaria.[24]

Thirst without thirst, tears without tears. The figure of the vampire is the embodiment of a wounded human who desires nothing more than another wound. Two paths unfold before the vampire: to withdraw and recede into chronic decay, or to surrender and drown in transient oceans of lust. Thus, the vampire has unraveled the secret collusion of decay and pleasure, such that in the future both realms may converge at the crossroad of a horrid eternity.

POST_026: Rustle of Light

Example: Many people claim to hear whooshing and crackling noises when there is an aurora in the sky.[25]

What if the rationalization of our own sensory perceptions has stifled the potential for diverse modes of experience? What if a sound could be seen, or a color could be tasted? What if the demarcation of our senses proves but another fallacy for the future to rectify? Let the future be the realm of ambiguity, hybridity, and ceaseless synesthetic unfolding.

POST_027: Laughter of the Half-breed

Example: The Hyena-men of Nigeria, believed not only to be immune to the venomous bite of the serpent but also to be impervious to the maddening laughter of the hyena. The legend goes even further: that the sacred tribe is the descendant of the hyena pack.[26]

Hidden within the labyrinthine alleys of Nigeria's slums, surrounded by towering heaps of waste in desolate urban landfills, a sacred brotherhood of the last ones undergoes rigorous tutelage in the art of taming the wild, transcending malevolence, and ultimately deriding the modern epoch. The future always gets born at the end of the present, where an elixir of potency simmers; the fanged, the merciless, and the joyous shall conquer the future.

POST_028: Recurring Flame

Example: The year 2020 opened with bushfires in Australia entering their seventh month (these would go on to burn for another three months). Before the year was out, fires had burned across tens of millions of hectares of forest in Russia's Far East and Siberia, the Amazon, Angola and the Democratic Republic of Congo, and the Western US, from California to Colorado.[27]

Some fires cleanse, while others exact penance. There is a fire being worshiped, yet there is also a fire being banished. Divergent beliefs intertwine, some hailing the mastery of fire as the herald of rationalism while others envision sinister abominations within its form. Perhaps it is the strange dance of the flames and the emanation of its scorching heat that carries this one irrefutable and enduring lesson to recall: that the new always rises from the ashes of the old.

POST_029: Surviving the Future

Example: The video game "Horizon Zero Dawn" depicts a futuristic world where a few tribes of primitive humans struggle to survive the cruel environment. In such a future, the Machine and Nature conspire together to devour humans once again.

In the aftermath of the apocalypse, amidst the dominant silence of absence, once again there lands an arrow of stone in the heart of steel. What sets of skills are required of the post-apocalyptic human to maneuver through the new world? The hunter, the sage, the prophet, and the marauder are all born of the Mountain (a zone that actually melds machine and nature).

POST_030: Future Non-space

Example: Unlike humans who map the world in units of distance, bats map the world in units of time. Hence the blind animal knows the speed of sound from birth.[28]

Humans know now that all matter in their universe is ensnared within the infinite tapestry of space and time. A thread of instantaneity crossing over a thread of dimensionality, such that all our mundane hopes and fears are products of this state of entanglement. Nevertheless, there exist beings who dwell in absolute darkness, having partially eluded the shackles of being's confinement. The future occurs in the realm of non-space, ruled by the loneliest sovereign: Eternity.

POST_031: Rapid Evolution

Example: Genetic changes in three-spine stickleback fish driven by seasonal shifts could help scientists predict how certain species will adapt to new environments.[29]

Perhaps the fatal contradiction of the modern human (the last man) finds its manifestation in the collision of two divergent outcomes—that of vanity and that of reason. For both vices/virtues must be considered the embodiment of human evolution. Thus, the future is the arena of the never-ending war between those who dread originality and those who desire the absolute against those of sudden adaptive exhibitions.

POST_032: Toxic Eclipse

Example: Mobilized by state and corporate powers, toxic clouds consume the air we breathe across different scales and durations, from urban squares to continents, unique incidents to epochal latencies. When figures in power deny the realities of climate change or chemical strikes, those forced to inhabit the clouds must find new forms of resistance.[30]

Future crushes all tyrannies into one, breaks all borders into one, joins all forces into one, and finally unites all resistances into one. The enemy, be it the social or the ecological, is no longer an eruptive instance in history (the dictator, the bullet, the tornado), but rather an incessant state of terror enveloped by cloud-like formations.

POST_033: Liquid Secrecy

Example: The world's oldest-known water was found in an ancient pool below Canada, at least 2 billion years old.[31]

Countless waters adorn the expanse of our planet: Amorous Waters, Dead Waters, Maternal Waters, and Furious Waters. The waters that carry us to the extremes, be it through axes of floating or diving. The waters that rock us, put us to sleep, and return us to our mother. Yet, most intriguing of all is the category of hidden water: a potent elixir imbued with a thousand shadows, concealed from the watchful stare of moons and suns across billions of years. One wonders if the future must necessarily arise from such pools of arcane locations.

POST_034: Cipher of Dawn

Example: Certain animals such as cephalopods, corvids, and dogs demonstrate cognitive abilities such as future planning—this meaning delaying gratification in order to get rewarded afterwards.[32]

As humans expand their dominance over the planet, they impose upon it their well-crafted signatures of progress. Still, those who bear the crest of their rationalist supremacy might exercise caution before other swarm-formulations of the collective mind—the inhuman, the elemental, the abstract—who develop their own gifts of intuition, anticipation, deferral, or waiting, and whose own rational determination for the new world's dawning might be to overthrow the human parasite.

POST_035: Cosmic Portrait

Example: Ai-Da is a life-size android artist powered by AI that mimic the intelligence of humans. Her "creepy" self-portraits have been unveiled at a new art exhibit in London, despite the "artist" not having a "self" to portray.[33]

The Self has been perceived as a given for human beings. Does our perception of Self pass on into the Future as a reiteration of its bygone existence? What if Self subsists solely beyond its confines? Beyond the confines of language, upon the domain of the world where all is in flux; where time serves as a vessel for deceit. What could cosmic alterations teach us about our perception of Self in the Future, and do we look like something akin to a creepy portrait in its telescopic eye?

POST_036: Secret of Immortality

Example: Rum Jungle was Australia's first large-scale uranium mine and supplied the US and British nuclear weapons programs during the Cold War. Today, the mine is better known for extensively polluting the Finniss River after it closed in 1971.[34]

In idealistic mythologies, water is a magic elixir, giving birth and bestowing life, quenching thirst and cleansing the earth. Thus, water is omnipresent—within us, around us, as above, so below. Hence, water was always associated with the secret of immortality itself. Nevertheless, the secret is annulled when water is marred by poison, bringing death to us or another classification of the immortal. This second immortality begins with pollution: that is, zombified water bestows rotted immortality. Thus the end of the world occurs where water turns its back on us.

POST_037: The Infinite Ones

Example: A single bee has cloned itself millions of times over the past three decades. Unlike most animals, and even bee queens, the female workers do not reshuffle the DNA of the eggs they lay. The female worker is making an immortal clone army of herself thanks to this genetic fluke.[35]

Animal observations do not only improve the knowledge of humans about nature and animality but could also bring new ideas to adopt specific features or behaviors for futuristic purposes. The ever-growing focus on individuality and the complexity of future personal life could ultimately lead us to make a series of single individuals to manage one's own existence. Hence, the future is not the embodiment of a person with multiple selves (the schizophrenic) but rather a series of the same self in cloned succession (the apeiromaniac, obsession with infinity).

POST_038: Cosmic Vibration

Example: China's first Mars Rover has captured its first sounds of the Red Planet. The purpose of installing the recording device was to capture the sounds of wind on Mars during certain turbulent weather to hear how they sound on a planet other than Earth.[36]

Noise, whisper, sound, music; the world was never silent. Environmental vibrations existed before meaning or language. Now that we are looking for a new homeland, perhaps the precondition of life elsewhere is to search for vibrations, to hear the unknown itself and listen for what strays beyond perception.

POST_039: Stone of Eternity

Example: NASA's Perseverance Rover found a weird rock on Mars, and scientists are debating where it came from.[37]

Rock is a primordial record, something that keeps watch over the flourishing and perishing over and again, the first book in human history. How could we read its language of quiet testimony? If deep space is similarly permeated by rock debris, then must we not contemplate future objects through a tongueless language of inscription or muted archiving (to unthink thinking; to think the unthinkable)?

POST_040: Cold Existence

Example: Scientists found a skinless shark at a depth of 500 meters (1,640 feet) in Sardinian waters.[38]

A great philosopher once said that "recognition works by touch." Without skin, we lose one of our most essential senses. Without skin, we become vulnerable more than ever. Skin is dotted with events and singularities. Once we lose this veil, we will live in an almost senseless world. Considering the ever-accelerating technological development from body enhancement to humanoid robots, could the future fade out all such singularities and leave us only cold with a senseless body, mind, and life?

POST_041: Cosmic Pareidolia

Example: The sighting of the "face" of the Roman god of water Neptune was captured by BBC photographer Jeff Overs in Newhaven on 6th of July.[39]

Natural disasters are among the most fearsome phenomena. They can neither be prevented nor accurately predicted, thereby pushing humans into a state of hysterical paranoia. However, ancient civilizations inverted this horrifying reality to their advantage. By giving them names, bodies, and faces, they turned the Real into the Unreal. The one who carved a visage out of the angry waters, or the other who drew a venomous omen in the sky by connecting the stars. Yet how would we approach unexplained phenomena in the future, especially when modernity has already wiped clean all traces of reality?

POST_042: Inanimate Society

Example: Mitochondria is a structure found within nearly all cells that have a nucleus. A new discovery suggests that mitochondria do not merely keep us alive, but in many ways have lives of their own. And, perhaps, are even "social" creatures. In other words, they are inanimate conscious beings.[40]

The consciousness of inanimate objects not only suggests revising our philosophical and psychological approach toward sentience but also affects our understanding of body, self, mind, and soul. Even our perception of subjectivity would drastically change, for the solid concept of the whole is now shattered into a thousand fragments. How far could this broken mirror onto existence take us into the future? Will the future reveal to us that all along we were trapped in our own illusions of possessing history, body, or mind, while the world around us and within us was circling in an infinitesimal process of laceration (the breaking of all things)?

POST_043: Burning Ice

Example: Under pressure by millions of atmospheres, scalded to the temperature of thousands of degrees, a droplet of water turns not only to a superheated liquid or gas but rather to a solid black stone of ice, burning within.[41]

What does this metamorphosis tell us in contrast to the human's lurking fear of freedom? Perhaps something about how the exceptional intensification of conditions leads to an abandonment, disowning, and then attainment of once-inconceivable forms (a new reverie).

POST_044: Dream of the Marauder

Example: Gohar Dashti's artwork titled "Home" (Iran, 2017) depicts nature's rebirth in abandoned houses in Iran.[42]

On a microlevel, the house we live in is our home. On a macrolevel, the country we were born in becomes home. There seems to be a psychological need for belonging (identity, family, nationality) and an unstoppable drive to multiply those belongings (occupying, plundering, extracting). In images of rewilded sites, though, nature shows who has possessed these so-called homes all along. And yet how would we define "home" in the future? Do we belong anywhere in the vast spreading galaxies?

POST_045: Return of the Unreal

Example: Scientists discovered a new species of Pterosaur in Australia that, based on its massive terrifying jaw, bears shocking resemblance to the mythological creatures known as dragons.[43]

Supernatural figures have always been a part of mythology in different cultures. In the world of the earliest unrealities, though, they represented gods with abilities that no human could master. Finding evidence of something that resembles a mythological figure thus forms a question in the mind: Is it the past that communicates itself to us through evidence (manifestation of history), or is it the imagination of ancient people that penetrates the future and reveals that supernatural figures were indeed real (abomination of history)?

POST_046: Labyrinth of the Mind

Example: Teams from Google and Harvard published an intricate map of every cell and connection in a cubic millimeter of the human brain.[44]

Navigation began with seafarers, and it took a long time for the first atlas to be assembled. The process of tracking continued to the point that it made us "The Lost Ones." We do not need to memorize signs or beware of each step anymore. The more we succeeded in creating maps, the more we became disoriented. Does this hold for the mapping of our minds as well? How much more lost could we get along this path?

POST_047: Sinking Island

Example: Scientists last month set foot on a tiny island off the coast of Greenland which they say is the world's northernmost point of land just revealed by shifting pack ice. They say it might go under water again and disappear soon enough.[45]

Islands are wonders of nature in both their emergence from the ocean recesses, becoming inhabitable for a limited time, and then their abrupt disappearance beneath again someday. At a cosmic scale, things and objects also appear suddenly and then disappear in the blink of an eye. Is it then a game of appearances and disappearances that the world is playing? Could the future too disappear before our eyes without our noticing it?

POST_048: The Future's Share

Example: In a UK study, artificial street lights were found to disrupt the behavior of nocturnal moths, subsequently reducing caterpillars numbers by half.[46]

Perhaps it was the earliest fire-worshipers of ancient Persia (long before Zoroastrians) who knew best that there are many fires: a fire that redeems while another condemns, a fire that sheds light upon the road and also another that contaminates clarity with obscurity. And now, in our example, we encounter yet another fire: that of invisibility. And precisely it is the invisible fire that annihilates the fragile, the devoted, and the lighthearted. Thus, the future's accursed share could mean that forces of solidity, broken promises, and heaviness will be all that is left.

LAB 8.0

Future Thought

Chapter 8.0
Future Thought Lab
Concepts: Consciousness, Perception, Imagination
Lab Author: Dan Mellamphy

POST_001: Future Thought

Example: The *ThoughtLab*'s first post is a video-clip of Claude Shannon [c.1960], provided along with a link to Samuel Butler's letter written a century earlier [c.1860] warning the world about the dangers/darkside of machine-learning/machine-thinking.[1]

Can and will machines *think*? — Can and will *humans*? . . . What kind{s} of thinking are typical of the machine, of the human?; does one affect/contaminate the other? [does human thought infect the machinic algorithm, and *vice-versa*? — spoiler-alert: YES X2!].

POST_002: *Time to Think*

Example: Computing at the Speed of Thought.[2]

Thinking takes *time* — the chronological time of *seconds/minutes/hours/days/years* in addition to the chrono*illogical* time of those "flashes of insight" and "inspired epiphanies" that occur in what the Ancient Greek *phusiologoi* [φυσιολόγοι] called the *kairos* [καιρός] as opposed to *chronos* [χρόνος]. The first post — the *preceding* one, hence "pre"*post* — of this *ThoughtLab* gestured beyond animal/

human cognition to computerized consideration{s}; the *present* post presents a possibility previously pointed out by Samuel Butler that our machines of acceleration have accelerated [hence contracted] the speed [hence the time] of thinking to the point of pushing it into the *instant*—the *kairos*—entirely.

POST_003: Taking a *Position*

[IN ADDITION TO TAKING *TIME*]

Example: Computational Superpositions and the Stacking of Spacetimes.[3]

Following from *ThoughtLab*'s previous post and keeping-up its *"pre"post*-erous unfolding, this third *ThoughtLab*-thought has to do with *space* [*i.e.* positing "positions"] in addition to *time* [*i.e.* dealing with "durations"]—in this case with "superpositions" and the "stacking" of spacetime{s} afforded by new kinds of computing: namely *quantum* rather than *classical* computing/machine-learning. In Frank Herbert's novel *Dune*, his humans-of-the-future can physically and conceptually "fold space" with the assistance of accelerating technology and consciousness-expanding spice-supplements. At *present* and in the only-*slightly-less-fictional* [&/or *alternative-fiction*] world of our *current* reality, quantum computing looms large and leans heavily in similar directions.

POST_004: Moving Thought{s}

Example: Telepresence and Folded Space.[4]

The previous *ThoughtLab*-posts have dealt with space and time; the current one wrestles with movement [for more on all of these, see the FSP *SpaceLab*, *TimeLab*, *MovementLab*, &c]. We are all familiar with the near-instantaneous access to world events available c/o access to the internet—akin, in many ways, to traveling the world [and beyond!] without leaving the confines/window-panes of our respective computer-screens, that-is-to-say without actually moving. *Movement*—travel—*without moving*: something strangely similar to the old "astral projection" of occultists. Have we already, in this way, "folded *space*" as they say? [and *time*, as well?].

POST_005: E⁽ᴹ⁾BODIME⁽ᴬ⁾NT

Example: *e-Bodies* versus *Twice-Born* Bodies.⁵

Pardon my use of coarse North-German-infused Middle-English,* but "what the FUCK [&/or PⁱØRN]" is an *e·Body*?—are such Bodies BORN [&/or BⁱØRN] or do they GROW, as in the WachowskiWomen's 1999 *Matrix*, in the vast vats qua TedStevensonian "series of tubes" of the *Internet?* The nineteenth-century French civil servant and occult-philosophy-infused writer of political science/poli-sci-fi Alexandre Saint-Yves suggested, long before the rise of the *Matrix* qua *Internet*, that we would have "twice-born" beings, "twice-born" bodies-&-minds—*dvijas* or *dwijas* in the ancient Sanskrit—and with this *second birth*, these *second bodies*, we would attain [to cite a recent article from the Italian online newspaper "Il Giornale"—"The Journal"] "a superior knowledge that today is embodied in the technology of the network"—"*un sapere superiore che oggi è incarnato nella tecnologia della rete*": *IlGiornale.it/news/interni/casaleggio-techno-guru-esoterismo-e-fantasy-835557.html* (twitter.com/youtopos/status/702178304376315904). Forbes.com/sites/charliefink/2017/11/20/the-trillion-dollar-3d-telepresence-gold-mine.
  *What some call a *diss/cuss*-word ;-)

POST_006: Into the *U.T.I.*

Example: The Universe of Technical Images.⁶

No, not *Urinary Tract Infections*—rather, the *Universe of Technical Images* [although the *former* might "flow" better from the previous post about bodies than the *latter*, admittedly]. As the late great media theorist and speculative philosopher/speculative fiction writer Vilém Flusser suggested, images today— those of the readily reproduced digital/technical type—are not primarily [that-is-to-say, not *fundamentally*] produced for Anthropocentric Purposes, "A.P."s, but rather, along the lines of, say, "APP"s [*En.Wikipedia.org/wiki/Application_software*],⁷ are detailed *data-storage-cases* tailor-made for *techno*-rather-than-*anthro*-consumption: to be read more by *machines* than *mankind*. Our era is an era wherein "cultural products" [name your artworld/artwork] tend to be—&/or become—*machine-readable artifacts;* "machine readability" is the name of the game in this post-anthropocenic epoch{é}.

POST_007: My *Word*, My *Work*, Is My Bond

Example: Imperial Espionage.[8]

Just a quick post, since this is post 007, about that master of spying, killing, love-making, and cutting-edge-gadget-wielding James Bond—still a favorite of current-day crowd-pleasing cinema—pointing out that the most cutting-edge/ futuristic figures tend to be prefigured by slightly less futuristic folks: in this case the original 007/eyes-of-the-monarch qua agent-of-empire, John Dee. *Faena .com/aleph/John-Dee-Elizabethan-Magician-and-Metaphysical-Guide-to-an-E mpire*.

POST_008: *M&M—Möbius and Malfatti—Spool-Loops*

Example: Simulacra and the Möbius-loop.[9]

In a book entitled *Studien über Anarchie und Hierarchie des Wissens*—translated into French in 1946 as *Études sur la Mathèse, ou Anarchie et Hiérarchie de la Science*—Beethoven's personal physician Giovanni Malfatti di Montereggio a.k.a. Johann-Baptist Malfatti von Monteregio examined the FIGURATIVE in addition to FIGURING or CALCULATIVE effect of numerical glyphs—*that is* the SYMBOLISM of number-SYMBOLS—in-&-as a kind of ideogrammatology or hieroglyphology [the combination of which compels a virtual tip-of-the-cap to Peter Sloterdijk's mid-2000 publication, *Derrida: Ein Ägypter*]. Here in post *008* or the *double-o_infinite* post, I take a sideways look or sideways glance AT THE FIGURE ITSELF—8,∞—so as to in{tro}duce, *in the spirit of Johann Malfatti*, the image of the *Möbius-loop*: key to the present futurology of theorists the likes of *Jean—Johann/Giovanni—Baudrillard*, who proposed that our world of ubiquitous simulations and simulacra [*Ubik*, for Philip-K-Dickensians] shows that there is no reality *other* than that of simulations and simulacra, that we are caught in-and-on its infinite loop. *Web. Stanford.edu/class/history34q/readings/Baudrillard/Baudrillard_Simulacra.html*.

POST_009: Just Say *Nein*

Example: Cross-Cutting Complicities and Hyperstitching our Hypercubes.[10]

I remember, back in 2008, reading Reza Negarestani's wonderful/wanderful *Cyclonopedia* and enjoying the ride so much that—and this was a time when I was still on [&/or subject to, hence one of the objects of]] the Zuckerbergian *FacebookMachine*—I found his coordinates via Facebook and emailed him a joyous hello+*kudos;* five years later N and I, along with our friend R. Scott Bakker, hosted him for a weekend here at Western University in London, ON. The trajectory of the-2008-to-the-2028-Reza is a fun one to follow, by the way [and a great one for those interested in A.I., and who isn't?!]. . . . *Cyclonopedia* takes Malfatti's *mathesis*, based on Pythagoras's triangular *tetractys* of 1+2+3+4 [10—see the following post, *Post_010*, below], and articulates it across an "akht-cross" that *cross*-{& *hyper*}*stitches* the figure of the triangular tetrad with the shape of a square,[11] the better to cube its roots.[12]

POST_010: The *Tetractys*

Example: Calculative Calcinations.[13]

For this tenth post, I point to THE TEN-POINT TETRACTYS of the ancient Pythagoreans: a triangular shape usually arranged on the ground using what the Greeks called "psephoi" and the Romans called "calx"—both of which designate "counting stones," or if you prefer, "permutational pebbles"—with a base of FOUR stones, THREE stones above that, TWO stones above the latter, and a SINGLE stone AT THE TOP, hence FOUR SETS OF STONES, 1+2+3+4, totalling TEN. This is the heart of the decimal system and core of Pythagorean philosophy [Pythagoras, by the way, was the one who coined the word "philosophy" and "philosopher," N.B.; *NetworkArchaeology.WordPress.com/2012/01/20/Medea-Archaeology-or-Inhuman-Interconnections-and-their-Monstrous-Milieu-ANCIENT-AND-MODERN-CYBERNETICS*]. *SiemenTerpstra.com/Tetractys*, *SMPhillips.MySite.com/The-Tree-of-Life-08.html*, *Theory-of-Thought.com/blog/TETRACTYS-Pascals-Triangle-binomial-expansion*.

POST_011: *Arise!:* It's *eLE^{A}VEN!*

Example: Plague Communication.[14]

We are posting these posts in the time period of a pandemic (that of the Covidian Plague), during which "social distancing" has relegated all collective conference activity to virtual video transactions, some of which require awakening at odd hours of the night to adjust for local time (i.e., different time zones), or what tech-savvy folks call "real-time." Even a simple *Zoom*-chat with Jason Mohaghegh—currently in *Southern Spain*—or with Manabrata Guha—currently *Down Under*—necessitates temporal adjustment on one or both of our parts.

In our era of globe-girdling communications, "Time Zones" still play a part. High-frequency-trading algorithms are "high-speed" precisely in order to overcome as best they can differences in time (different Time Zones). For this particular post, here's an interesting link[15]—and some background reading music to go with it[16]—c/o Negativland (No Other Possibility).

POST_012: Hypersynchronization

Example: "Hyper-Synchronization."[17]

Our friend the late great Bernard Stiegler tackled an amazing number of issues relevant to contemporary and future society prior to his recent untimely death. One such issue was what he called "hyper-synchronization": the "real-time" synchronization of human behavior that comes with hyper-industrialization and hyperspeed communication, *one example of which* was provided in the previous post *(Post_11)* wherein an *awakening* or *remaining-awake*—let's just say *a lack of sleep*—is part-&-parcel/par-for-the-course with-&-in human (human/machine) interaction. Today's post gestures toward Christian Marclay's "Clock" (2010), a 24-hour film designed to be "in synch" with—*yes, you guessed it*—"real time": En.Wikipedia.org/wiki/The_Clock_(2010_film)#Conception, Kottke.org/13/06/About-an-Hour-of-Christian-Marclays-THE-CLOCK.

POST_013: *Friday-the-13th* on *The Cyberiad Calendar*

Example: Electro-Knights.[18]

In the 1300s—on the Gregorian Calendar date of *Thursday the 13th*, or *Friday the 13th* on the *Julian* Calendar—the order of the Knights Templar came to an end, just after dawn, in a well-orchestrated synchronous multi-site/multi-target strike by agents of King Philip the Fourth. But in a sense, as Philip K. Dick used to say (phrased here in a manner i.e. admittedly a little *Levinasian*—*Emmanuel-Levinas*-like—rather than *Philp-Dick^{ens}ian*), their "existence" continued in the wake of their "existents," albeit along more *virtual* vectors. Take, for example, the so-called "Electro-Knights" of the Israeli Internet and the description of the latter published in the pages of *Haaretz* seven (SE7EN) years ago. Here is the headline: "A pack of 'Electronic Knights' has been let loose to roam the Israeli Internet. Known in Hebrew as *Hashmabirim*—a mashup of the words *'hashmal'* (electricity) and *'abir'* (knight), but also loosely based on Polish science-fiction writer Stanislaw Lem's *Cyberiad* robots—these digital robots are a project from the non-profit *Public Knowledge Workshop*, a three-year-old organization dedicated to opening-up government information to the public in a way that is accessible to everyone using technology" (*Haaretz.com/scouring-the-net-to-find-information-hidden-from-you-1.5252624*).

POST_014: Fortean Times

Example: US Navy-Pilot Flying-Object Sightings.[19]

This Fourteenth post is a Fortean post—a post that points to the pre-*X-Files* "X-Filers" known as *Forteans* (after the NYC-based paranormal investigator Charles Fort). As was the case in the popular television series *The X-Files*, wherein a paranormal investigator by the name of Mulder has a rather odd and oft-scoffed reputation and yet nevertheless, in the face of much criticism and ridicule, stumbles upon facts that would otherwise have been overlooked or dismissed, Forteans sometimes find—that is, discover/uncover—rather fascinating oddities that fly in the face of our consensus worldview[s]. In 2014, US Navy pilots recorded what we could call "Fortean content": the sighting of U.F.O.s off the coast of America—*NYTimes.com/2019/05/26/us/politics/ufo-sightings-navy-pilots.html*.

POST_015: Quindecimation/ Quindecimagination

Example: The SATOR Square.[20]

We have already encountered the triangular TETRACTYS (*Post_010*, above); in this post we double down on the triangle and consider the SQUARE OF THE MAGES or "MAGIC SQUARE" wherein any straight line linking its elements adds up to the very same number—here the number fifteen: *En.Wikipedia.org/wiki/Magic_square#/media/File:Magicsquareexample.svg* . . . Magic squares such as these, as well as palindromic versions such as the SATOR square recently popularized by Christopher Nolan's sonically compromised cinema-SATOR, TENET, have been used (as in Nolan's film) to contemplate otherwise impossible things such as time reversal and the influence of the future (or futures) on the past. [Image: Albrecht Dürer, "Melancholia I," 1514].

POST_016: *Seize!*

Example: Jantar Mantar—*En.Wikipedia.org/wiki/Jantar_Mantar,_New_Delhi#/media/File:Jantar_Mantar,_New_Delhi_(Rama_Yantra_2_inside).jpg*

For this the sixteenth post—*sixteen*, in French, being *"seize"*: the number where things *seize up*—everything suddenly stops and comes to a standstill in-&-as a kind of crystalline realization or sudden-&-striking image. The philosopher-of-history *Walter Benjamin* believed that the historian, whose future is one that looks back at the past from a given present, is the one who *bears witness to* (& *documents*) those moments "wherein 'what has been' comes-together in a flash with 'the now' to form a constellation—in other words, with the image of dialectics at a standstill (for while the relation of the present to the past is a purely temporal and continuous one, the relation of 'what has been' to 'the now' is dialectical: is not 'progression' but 'image')" [*Arcades Project* 462, N2a.3].[21] "It is not that what is past casts its light on what is present, or what is present its light on what is past; rather, image is that wherein what has been comes together in a flash with 'the now' to form a constellation. [. . .] *The image that is read*—which is to say, *the image in the now of its recognizability*—bears to the highest degree the imprint of the perilous critical moment on which all reading is founded" [*Arcades Project* 462-463, N3.1].[22] I lifted the image for this post from a February 2016 article in the *Los Angeles Review of Books: LAReviewOfBooks.org/article/SPACE-JEW-or-Walter-Benjamin-among-the-Stars*.

POST_017: "DIX·SEPT"ION

Example: The Brain as Deception-Organ.[23]

Post *Dix·Sept*[24] is on *deception*—or rather, on *conception* as deception; or again, if you prefer, on the *con* (the con-job) of the *concept*. A "con-man" is a master of deception: one who instills confidence where no confidence is in fact warranted—someone who would, for example, sell you a "fake" or "false fabrication" (a forgery) instead of "the actual item." Is *the mind itself*—our faculty of *intellection* and of *conception*—such a con artist? Is the *brain*—our *O·S/Operating·System*—a *confidence-trickster* and indeed a system of *"con-man"agement*? What *are*, in fact, "concepts"?; why *are* we (& should we *really* be) so confident in their "real-world" traction? Today's image is that of American psychologist Joseph Jastrow's *Rabbit-or-Duck—but-never-both-at-the-same-time—dilemma*, wherein the problems of perception, and subsequently of conception, begin to be dismayingly displayed. The present image was taken from a 2018 article by Stephen Law: *Scroll.in/article/888964/is-it-a-duck-or-a-rabbit-the-philosophical-underpinning-of-an-old-visual-trick*.

POST_018: *Diciotto*, Como Dice L'altro *Auto-Man*

Example: The Auto-Man Empire.[25]

Back in 2010, when I was translating Gilbert Simondon's treatise *On the Mode of Existence of Technical Objects* for Sylvère Lotringer at *Semiotexte* (prior to the switch in publishers from *Semiotexte* to *Univocal*), one of the cover images we were considering for the book was the jacket sleeve of Gary Numan's 1979 debut single *"Cars"*: *En.Wikipedia.org/wiki/Cars_(song)*. I suppose we could have also considered an image from Hasbro/TakaraTomy Corporations' *"Transformers"* franchise, or indeed any image wherein humans transform into cars (i.e., their technological objects). The idea was to show—or suggest—that we are ourselves transformed by our own technological objects, which in turn arguably wind up owning us (a kind of Frank-Herbertesque Butlerian-Jihad gesture & suggestion). This is an interesting—and for some, a troubling—vision of the future: one wherein we continue to merge with our various technologies and perhaps ultimately lose ourselves in and as them.

POST_019: *"Dits-Neuf"* ("New Statements") Of-and-About *"Death-Masks"*

Example: Y'*Urn*·ing for *Bon*ᵉ-*Mo*ʳ*ts*.[26]

Check out the bonᵉ-mortuary *bon-mots* of the *Xi'an Funeral-Home*'s A.I.-assisted mortician-mechanism @ *Hyper.AI/14905* (*Translate.Google.com/translate?sl=auto&tl=en&u=http://hyper.ai/14905*). Although this is not what was meant when Friedrich Nietzsche famously said "become what you are" (in *Thus Spoke Zarathustra* as well as *Ecce Homo*), it does reveal both the oddity—the oddness—of the human desiring-machine (the odd mechanics of our own desires) as well as the potentials of *replication*, of *imitation*, of *duplication*, afforded by computational technologies, even *A.D. (After Death)*.[27]

POST_020: From *Nietzsche* to *Nitschke*

Example: The Oskar Sarkon "*Sarco-Booth.*"[28]

Adjusting the *A.D.* of our previous post [brief aside: isn't "previous post" a wonderfully absurdist turn-of-phrase?] so that it stands for the words "*at*" rather than "*after*" death, this TWENTIETH century-post switches from Friedrich *Nietzsche's* declaration "become what you are" to Philip *Nitschke's* tool to "become what you *aren't*"—that is dead [if you're reading this "post-death," apologies for my presumption]. Nitschke is the inventor and designer of the *Futurama*-like "*Sarco*"-*booth* marketed as a {E}utopian Euthanasia-Machine for the Future.[29]

POST_021: Theatre of Cruelty

Example: Crimeˢ of *The Future*.[30]

The marvelous Mohaghegh has informed us that our colleague Reza N will be starting a new *Future Studies Lab* on the topic and topos of "cruelty," which brought-to-mind/called-into-thought[lab] a passage from Nietzsche's *Fröhliche Wissenschaft* wherein the latter states that "hitherto all that has given color to existence has lacked a history: where would one find a history of *love*, of *avarice*, of *envy*, of *conscience*, of *piety*, of *cruelty*?"—[Q] WHERE, my good/beyond-good-and-evil Nietzsche?: [A] HERE, of course—in the online *Future Studies Program*. The lower image for today's post is a slide about the French playwright Antonin Artaud, taken from an online PowerPoint presentation about the British playwright Edward Bond, available at *SlidePlayer.com/slide/4114705*.[31] Today's link links to Artaud's vision and version of what it is to be "cruel": *En.Wikipedia.org/wiki/Theatre_of_Cruelty#Defining_Artaud's_%22theatre%22_and_%22cruelty%22* . . . for if "cruelty is . . . the unrelenting agitation of a life that has become unnecessary, lazy, or removed from a compelling force," "giving expression to everything that is '*crime, love, war*, or *madness*' in order to 'unforgettably root within us the ideas of *perpetual conflict*, a spasm in which life is *continually lacerated*, in which everything in creation rises up and asserts itself against our appointed rank'," then its future has to do with precisely those elements—namely, the future of *crime* (FutureCrime), of *love* (FutureLove), of *war* (FutureWar) and of [in]*sanity*

(FutureSanity): see how our *FutureLabs* fragment and multiply? Also note that what constitutes "cruelty" (and *"crime,"* and *"love,"* and *"war,"* and—yes—"*[in]sanity*") in the past often differs from what constitutes it (or them) in the present and by extension the future.

POST_022: Twenty-*Too-Much-to-Take-in*

Example: *Hallucination Engine{s}*.[32]

[1] I've got *Locust Abortion Technician* on the turntable ("*what's a 'turntable'? and how dare you mention such things* in a *Future Studies Lab* post!" I hear some of you say &/or think—noisy thoughts here hear) and have reached the last track on the *B*-side: *Track 11*, "22 going on 23"—a bit of a soul-crushing track. In his final philosophical treatise (the last track of his *Published-Works* album), René Descartes hypothesized that so-called souls somehow get crushed and pressed into or onto the body (our bodies) in and as the "pineal gland" or "pineal eye." The panphobic—not just *transphobic* or straight-out *xenophobic*—horror-writer H. P. Lovecraft wrote a short story on the topic of this eye-qua-gland (his 1934 "From Beyond") wherein stimulation of the latter opens our eye[s] to *the horrors of pandimensional reality and of possible possession by forces from such dimensions*. The recent film by Benson and Moorhead (*Synchronic* 2019, re-released in 2021) once again takes up this idea—*that of pineal-eye stimulation and pandimensional perception*—with nods to Lovecraft and Descartes.

[2] An associate professor of psychiatry at the *University of New Mexico School of Medicine* by the name of Richard Strassman gained quite a bit of notoriety in and around the year 2000 for his theory that the pineal gland is capable of producing the hallucinogen *N,N-Dimethyltryptamine (DMT)* in addition to circadian clock-regulating melatonin. *DMT* is a hallucinogen known to produce Lovecraftian visions, and research into its consciousness-expanding/consciousness-altering properties is currently underway at several institutions, including—as I have just learned thanks to an academic *email—at the University of Toronto* just up the highway from my present location (*NewsFileCorp.com/release/77354/Pharmadrug-Initiates-DMT-Research-Activities-via-Collaboration-with-the-University-of-Michigan-for-Foundational-DMT-Research-Study*). It will be interesting to keep track of how things unfold in the future with respect to such research into the folds and unfoldings of human and nonhuman consciousness.

POST_023: ATM: Against Thinking Machines

Example: The Butlerian Jihad.[33]

Franklin Patrick Herbert the Second took the early warnings of fellow novelist from the previous century Samuel Butler to heart when he wrote his science fiction epic *Dune*—most explicitly with regard to the latter's "Butlerian Jihad" or war against thinking machines (the revolution against artificial intelligence). Herbert's vision of Future Thought involved "professional thinkers-qua-calculators" called *Mentats*—*Mentats* being a replacement for the *computers* and *thinking machines* outlawed in the aftermath of the Butlerian Revolution. There are interesting parallels between this and, for example, *Nick Bostrom*'s position and *Future of Humanity Institute* concerns. Just to be weird, there is a link to an article above from a "leading libertarian magazine" (because: why not?) on this very topic: *Reason.com/2014/09/12/will-superintelligent-machines-destroy-h*.

POST_024: Experimental Jet-Set, Trash, and No-Star

Example: Not-so-Deepspace Debris.[34]

Our dear friend and *Future-Studies-Colleague* Ed Keller has a new track up on the A·W/ Alienocene·Website,[35] the title of which is drawn from Rilke's *Book of Images* (1902): "Alternately *Stone-in-You* and *Star*"—a title that I jokingly mis-typed when I tweeted it today, pretending it was the title of a Sonic Youth album (*Experimental Jet-Set, Trash, and No-Star:* title of the present *ThoughtLab* post),[36] perhaps indeed as *a precursor to*—*or preview of*—this post about the space trash that we humans have been collecting in the orbit between our planet and the stars. Space debris (*En.Wikipedia.org/wiki/Space_debris*) is a *present* and rapidly intensifying *future* problem, as noted in this recent *Wired* article: *PrintFriendly.com/p/g/5yiiCE*.[37]

POST_025: Eco-Destruction Fashion-design

Example: StillSuit-Fashion in the face of Eco-Destruction.[38]

Things can and do look rather bleak, future-wise, when we consider that, at present, over a million species face extinction (this includes more than half the known marine species), two-thirds of the world's oxygen-producing rainforests have already been destroyed or degraded, global warming is melting long-established polar ice caps (wreaking havoc on all of the planet's ecosystems), and—*bonus news for Elon Musketeers bent on escaping the planet altogether*—the sky above us is rapidly filling up with orbiting satellites, satellite debris, and "space junk" (*Post_24*, above). Posting these posts, as we are, in a time of *Plague*—the time of our present *Covid-19 Pandemic*—with people across the globe going to and fro (while also avoiding such goings to and fro) wearing protective face masks over their nose and mouth, has me repeatedly remembering the Arrakeen *Fremen* of Frank Herbert's futurist sci-fi eco-saga *Dune* (previously mentioned in *Post_23*), whose dress—or if you prefer, Future Fashion—incorporated so-called *StillSuits*, complete with nose-and-mouth-coverings, both to protect them and also, in their brutal environment, sustain them. Eco-destruction entails interesting fashion-design.

POST_026: Future Fascism

Example: Image-still from Michael Radford's film-version of Orwell's *1984*.

"The world may not be able to stop totalitarian regimes like the Nazis rising again in the future, but we can avoid handing them the tools to extend their power indefinitely": *BBC.com/future/article/20201014- totalitarian-world-in-chains-artificial-intelligence (MaliciousAIreport.com)*.[39]

POST_027: Future *Safety-Measures* (for Those Who Can *Pay*)

Example: *MikeShouts.com/Ducati-smart-jacket-Airbag-Equipped-vest*. Quote: "This motorcycle airbag-vest will stop working if you miss a payment. Charging extra for safety-features is nothing new, but actively disabling them for missed payments may be the future."[40]

My Twitter pal *Hugo* (@*Metaleptic*), fellow *Philip·K·Dick-Fan/Philip·K·Dickensian*, astutely observed the *Ubik*-like aspects of techno-capitalism exemplified in a column from this week's ad*Vice (Vice.com/en/article/93yyyd/this-motorcycle-airbag-vest-will-stop-working-if-you-miss-a-payment)*.[41]

POST_028: *Maps* (Multidisciplinary Association for Psychedelic Studies) *to the Future*

Example: *The Dream-Couches of Imrryr.*[42]

As a member of the Future Studies faculty, I follow several let's-say "future-oriented" accounts on social media (no, not *Facebook* or its satellite platform *Instagram*), including *Twitter.com/FuturistechInfo*, which recently tweeted a link that took me back to *FutureThought Post_22* (on psychoactive pharmatechnics): "A Psychedelic Revolution Coming, and Psychiatry May Never Be Same" — *Twitter.com/FuturistechInfo/status/1391756486855073799*. This is one of the many frontiers of future medicine that are being crossed rather than crossed out (although who knows what new roadblocks will spring up to impede such research in the coming few years). According to the MAPS — Multidisciplinary Association for Psychedelic Studies — psychoactive drugs "induce neuroplasticity, [that is to say] the brain's ability to change and reorganize thought-patterns, enabling people with psychological disorders to find new ways to process anxiety, depression or deeply-embedded trauma." The article in question suggests that "the future of psychedelic medicine can already be glimpsed at a suite of plush, soothingly decorated 'journey rooms'," akin to the dream couches of Imrryr in Michael Moorcock's Melnibonéan fantasy fiction from the 1960s/1970s, "that occupy the top floors of office-buildings in Midtown Manhattan."

POST_029: *Siliconceptions* (the Silicon Brain)

Example: Neuromorphic Chipsets, Silicon Brains.

The DARPA-funded Dharmendra Modha *(DARPA Dharmendra*, IBM Fellow and IBM Chief Scientist for Brain-inspired Computing at the *IBM Almaden Research Center)* has been working on neuromorphic chipsets colloquially called "silicon brains." As outlined in *The MIT Technology Review* ("Thinking in Silicon,"

TechnologyReview.com/2013/12/16/174934/thinking-in-silicon),[43] "computers are incredibly inefficient at lots of tasks that are easy for even the simplest brains—such as recognizing images and navigating in unfamiliar spaces. [. . .] A new breed of computer-chips that operate more like the brain may be about to narrow the gulf between artificial and natural computation [. . .] '*Modern computers* are inherited from calculators, good for crunching numbers', states Dharmendra Modha, whereas '*brains* evolved in the real world'. Modha leads one of two groups that have built computer-chips with a basic architecture copied from the mammalian brain under a $100-million project called *Synapse*, funded by the Pentagon's *Defense Advanced Research Projects Agency*."

Such chips off the new block, narrowing the gulf between artificial and natural computation, also narrow the divide between *Machine* and *Mentat*, harkening here to the futurist vision of Frank Herbert's *Dune (Dune.fandom.com/wiki/Mentat)*.[44]

POST_030: A "*Tom Thumb*" for Post-Atom *Adams*, Even

Example: The Proteus Effect.[45]

At the tail-end/appendage of our chapter-contribution to *The Imaginary App*, reference was made to "the homuncular flexibility" afforded by "THE PROTEUS EFFECT" (*Google.com/books/edition/The_Imaginary_App/zBFmBAAAQBAJ?hl=en&gbpv=1&pg=PA242*): our ability to mentally and physically *adjust*—or if you prefer, *adapt* like veritable *adepts*—within various *incarnations*, that-is-to say often radically different *embodiments*. This is of great interest to researchers in the field of *Virtual Environments* and future *Virtual Realities*. . . . One of my Twitter acquaintances, Rachel Armstrong *(@LivingArchitect)*, just posted a link to *University College London*'s examination of "Third Thumb" neurocognition at its *Plasiticity Lab:* an article on "How an Extra Thumb Changes the Way Your Brain Perceives the Hand" *(Twitter.com/LivingArchitect/status/1395536455284441088)*.[46] Here—for this post—I add the following Vimeo video link (enjoy!): *Vimeo.com/220291411*.[47] N.B.: this post admittedly cross-contaminates the *Future Thought* and *Future Body* labs, opening onto avenues for speculation about future techno-bodies and techno-embodiments.

POST_031: Future-Muse See-'em

Example: Virtual-Museum "Trips."[48]

During this global pandemic, many of us have "travelled" while staying-at-home under world health lockdown c/o digital tech, "Zoom"ing into international conference sessions, visiting museums online, and so on. Today's post has to do with the future of museums/museum visits and the possibilities afforded to us by *AR (Augmented Reality)*, *VR (Virtual Reality)*, and *XR (Extended Reality) in general*. Here is a clip from a recent discussion—a dialogue, or rather a *trialogue*— between Masaki Fujihata, Kudsk Steensen, and Zachary Kaplan: *Youtube.com/ embed/z4-TvQ5ufso.* I wonder what the muse *Melpomênê* (Μελπομένη) would have had to say about this . . . In any case, such virtual museum-trips are certainly *trippy* (Terence McKenna was correct: high tech of the digital kind is indeed a kind of *mind-altering*—and of course also *body-altering*—drug. *Re: the latter*, body-altering without moving the body very far!).

POST_032: Digital Eyes (Digitalize)

Example: Gigapixel Resolutions.

Following from the previous post (*Post_31,* Re: AR\VR\XR *Travel*-without-*Actually-Traveling*), I should mention that even prior to these pandemic lockdowns, in the period I now call "BC"—"Before Covid[19]"—the futuristic features of our digital dimensions already played an important part in my research. For instance, when I was putting together the materials for fellow FSP collaborator Constanza Bizraelli's *CyclopsJournal.Net*,[49] I was in Paris with my digital camera, doing my best to capture the various stained-glass panels of *Notre Dame Cathedral's (NDC's)* massive *Western Rose-Window*, but in the end, my amateur digitech was nothing compared to the gigapixel images available to any-and-all with internet access (e.g., @ *GigaScopeJS.FireBaseApp.com/photo/NotreDameRoseOuest* and other such sites).[50] The high-resolution gigapixel images were far superior to any that I might have managed to capture from ground level with my camera. Capturing images from home (online) rather than traveling in order to take them myself (offline) might have been a better, not to mention more affordable, option (I was abroad for a conference at the time, however). *On that note*, and *as a side-note:* fantastic/science-fictional viral videos that show currently impossible smartphone camera zoom-ins—*e.g. YouTube.com/embed/SeSzNxb1Eyw* and the like[51]—are, despite their present-tense falseness/fakeness (*maximum-zoom without any shaking?—superhumanly steady hands*, hypothetical/hyped-up smartphone-user!), tech-*on-the-horizon*/tech-*yet-to-come*. The fake of today often ends up becoming the fact of tomorrow, so they say.

POST_033: 33.3 RPM/RIP

Example: Post-Mortem Recycling.

Four years ago, one of the news items circulating in newspapers around the world was about a new funerary option allowing human remains to be combined and pressed into vinyl records that can be played back on turntables: a very interesting *version* and *vision*—or rather, *audition*—of *post-mortem recycling*, and one that opens onto a possible re*cyclonopedia* (mortuary record collection) full of remastered record player ready *mortiloquisms*. In some ways, this is the flip side or "*b*"-side of the more popular science-fictional transhumanist dream of being "uploaded" into-and-onto the internetworked "cloud" (namely being "downloaded" into-and-onto a recorded audio track).

POST_034: "P"-to-the-"F"—re: *Predicting the Future*

Example: The Present Mo$^{(nu)}$ment.[52]

Techie Jason Crawford, down in San Francisco, just tweeted an excellent little tweet—or what the FSP would call a *lab-post*, albeit one without an *image*—which I thought I should retweet/repost in this week's *ThoughtLab*: "It's almost *impossible* to predict the future," he writes; "but it's also *unnecessary*, because most people are living in the past. All you have to do is see the present before everyone else does" *(Twitter.com/JasonCrawford/status/1404200442171514880)*. There are many levels of verity—many *verities*, all very *tied-together*—in this statement, and one of the least interesting but still very interesting ones is a reminder to all of us that THE FUTURE IS A FICTION and that *the factual* finds its point of culmination in *the present* (with a nod to Jean Gebser).

POST_035: Occult Considerations

Example: Nietzsche, *Morgenröte* DIX ("Mache dein *Theater-Auge* auf, das große dritte Auge welches *durch die zwei anderen* in die Welt schaut!": "Open your *theatre-eye*, the great *third eye* which looks out into the world *through the other two*").[53]

The *ouroboros* is the figure of a serpent eating its tail—a famous alchemical emblem, and for us today (or rather, for today's FSP post) a symbol for the interesting inversions that come with conceptual/perceptual recycling: in this case the recycling or re-appearance of Formerly Occult Icon^{ographie}s such as that of "The Third Eye"—previously a symbol of enlightenment and transcendence (that-is-to-say freedom from the fetters of our inherited frameworks and wordlview^s). These days, one is just as likely—if not *more* likely—to find references to "The Third Eye" in closed-circuit surveillance-system nomenclature-&-propaganda than in consciousness-opening systems of self-improvement or self-transcendence. Take for instance the DiSanZhiYan example out of Shanghai: *FT.com/content/ b74b6ad6-3b8d-4cd8-9dd6-3b49754aa1c7* . . .

POST_036: Becoming Glitch

Example: Digital Ghost Bodies.[54]

LEJE, a French company founded by a pair of Korean designers, has designed a style of jeans and trousers *the overall effect of which gives the impression— the appearance—of glitching video-images*. This is part of a trend that has consumers desiring to appear more like their online/digital avatars than their offline/analogue bodies. To quote my online (Twitter) pal Hugo Reinert, the tendency in this particular era is one in which the digital takes precedence over the otherwise altogether physical: "I'm the physical ghost of my digital self" *(Twitter.com/Metaleptic/status/1308503131500744711)*.[55] A recently reposted Wired article about *Virtual-Reality sales-pitches (Wired.com/story/billionaires -use-vr-avoid-social-change)*[56] provides further evidence of this trend, with its reference to tech guru Gabe Newell's televised interview with New Zealand's "One News" in which he refers to the physical/non-digitized body as a mere "meat peripheral" *to be transcended—if not discarded*—for the wonders of a world supposedly better-than-"the-real").

POST_037: Your M·O ("Mode of Operation"/"Mood Organ")

Example: *Sense-Organs for the Upcoming Zeitgeist*.[57]

Philip Kindred D., an oddball American writer of science fiction stories and frustrated "independent scholar" of philosophy *(sound familiar, vast swath of FSP-types?)*, had an uncanny ability to sense upcoming zeitgeists—as noted by a great many observers today, logging into their online platforms and sharing their views on our current techno-society. The present post is an excerpt from one of his most popular stories (*Do Androids Dream of Electric Sheep?*):

> "I heard the building, this building; I heard the [silence of all those empty apartments, all the missing people]," said Iran to her husband. "At that moment, when I had the TV sound off, I was in [Penfield Corporation] Mood #382—I had just dialed-it-in. So although I *heard* the emptiness intellectually, I didn't *feel* it. My first reaction consisted of being grateful that we could afford a Penfield Mood-Organ. But then I realized how unhealthy it was: sensing the absence of life—not just *in this building* but *everywhere*, and NOT REACTING. *Do you see?*—I guess you *don't;* but that used to be considered a sign of MENTAL ILLNESS; they called it 'absence of appropriate affect'. So I left the TV sound off, sat down at my Mood-Organ, and experimented—and I finally found a setting for 'despair'." Her dark, pert face showed satisfaction, as if she had achieved something of worth. "I put it on my schedule for twice a month—I think that's a reasonable amount of time to feel hopeless about everything, about staying here on Earth after everybody who's smart has emigrated...don't you think?"

The Penfield Mood-Organ should have been front-and-center in our book on *Imaginary Apps* and "Apps & Affect" CFP from many years ago;[58] then again, it is *there—everywhere*, like those ghostly missing people Iran mentions— *conspicuous in its app-parent absence*. We live in the ERA of Penfield Mood-Organs.

POST_038: At the "A.T": "Anarchitectural Thinking"

Example: An Internet full of ( )holes.

Lifting one of the arguments from *The Digital Dionysus* (2016), today's post pos[(i)]ts that a *FuturePhilosophical*—or if you prefer, *"Nietzschean,"* since Nietzsche endeavored to outline a *Future Philosophy*—mode of thinking about information [and a *FuturePhilosophical* approach to *"information studies"* as such] takes "information" and the good-old/*beyond-good-&-e* "information highway" as the very INTERFACE between Dionysian *occlusion*, *subversion* and *anarchism* (on the *one* side) and Apollonian *clarity*, *stability* and *hierarchy* (on the *other* side). The *latter*—Apollonian—approach is a *typical* one with respect to information studies, while the addition of the *former*—Dionysian—is rather *atypical*, yet becoming more and more *relevant*, more and more *pressing*, in these times of ubiquitous collective engagement with[(in)] the so-called infosphere [internet]. The disjunctive conjunction of the *anarchically Dionysian* and *architecturally Apollonian* forms—or *informs*—a kind of "anarchitecture" the hole-ridden/[(w)]hole-riddled "structure" of which is akin, in a sense, to a "net": a "cross-hatch" the very interstices of which are unformed but perpetually form-taking nodes, NOTA BENE.

POST_039: "The Battle-space of Cyberspace" In-and-as Our Networked Condition

Example: The Expansive Space of THE CHURN *(Churning and Churning in the Widening Gyre)*.

Since the previous post made reference to *The Digital Dionysus*—an anthology devoted to rethinking the philosophy of Friedrich Nietzsche in and for the digital era[59]—why not continue in that direction and offer up a post having to do with one of the antho's contributors, Manav Guha. In his most recently published essay, the title of which is a tip-of-the-hat (&/or soldier's helmet) to Baudrillard's *Ecstasy of Communication* ("Technical Ecstasy: *Network-Centric Warfare, Redux*," Security Dialogue 1.17, 2021),[60] Guha travels further down the path of his ongoing research into present and future shifts in delimitation and definition of military battle-spaces in the age of network-centric warfare.[61] Using insights from the French philosopher Gilbert Simondon rather than the more ecstatic Jean Baudrillard in this case (although Nietzsche is definitely there), Guha argues that "the . . . internet-of-everything . . . which is gradually [or *not-so-gradually*] enveloping us, allows us to think of a martial ecology in terms of what Simondon calls a 'techno-geographical milieu' . . . [that is] in a constant state of multi-dimensional flux. While at first glance this may appear to reconfirm our conventional perception of battle-spaces being marked by what Clausewitz famously referred to as the 'fog' and 'friction' of war, the constant phasing/dephasing of the [internet's] techno-geographical space changes the connotation of this Clausewitzian phrase—for what it points to is the transformative nature of the [internet's] techno-geographical space itself. In other words, the constant churn that marks the [internet's] techno-geographical space is not something that happens *inside* that space; rather, it is what constitutes *the space itself*."

POST_040: Fragmented Future Images

Example: D·I·Y (Do-it-Your*selves*) Frag*mentality*.[62]

This week's post doubles-down/redoubles-up on good-old Post #5 [*POST_005: E*⁽ᴹ⁾*BODIME*⁽ᴬ⁾*NT*] and the latter's reference to *twice-born beings* — Sanskrit *dwijas* or *dvijas:* द्विजा.[63] Our online and offline avatars aid and abet the vision/envisioning of our own (not to mention OTHERS') IDENTITY-DIVISION: the fracturing and fragmentality of ourSELVES. In an article written by Jessica Lucas that was published in this week's *Input* magazine, the vision of this division is examined in light of the popular online platform and countdown-to-world's-end *"TikTok."* The subject of the article is a 29-year-old, currently and busily toggling between a set of twenty-nine personalities: a subject subjected-to/subdivided-into what was formerly known as *"multiple personality* disorder" and is now known as *"dissociative identity* disorder" . . . Each personality fragment is *"birthed,"* that *is* gets *"born"* [द्विजा], *named, characterized*, and *introduced to the world* as A DISTINCT IDENTITY that can be *addressed, redressed, what-have-you*, along-with or aside *all the other ones too* [two]. *InputMag.com/culture/dissociative-identity -disorder-did-tiktok-influencers-multiple-personalities* (cheers from Bob Arctor).

LAB 9.0

Future Machine

Chapter 9.0

Future Machine Lab

Concepts: The Digital, the Cybernetic, the Artificial

Nandita Biswas Mellamphy

POST_001: The Future Is [Also] in the Past

Example: Ancient Indian Flying Vehicles.[1]

The future is not just ahead and "to come"; it can also be found in the past. Looking back at how ancient cultures imagined futuristic technologies, one can readily find depictions of artificial life, robots, self-propelling objects, and/or flying machines.

POST_002: Time Machines

Example: Vessels of Borrowed Time.[2]

Is it possible to make a time machine? Physicists suggest that while it may be possible to engineer particle physics to allow a time machine to work, an adequate theory of quantum gravity still needs to be developed.

POST_003: Multi-Purpose Self-Folding Devices

Example: "Either it is the fold of the infinite, or the constant folds [*replis*] of finitude which curve the outside and constitute the inside."—Gilles Deleuze, *Foucault*

Origami, the ancient art of folding, holds the key to understanding bio-nano-technical design. Folding is not just a design principle but also determines the function organic systems.[3]

POST_004: Sophisticated Molecular Machines: Virus Structures

Example: Viral Tracking Technologies that reveal the Genetic Foundations of the Human.[4]

Once considered "junk DNA" by scientists, viruses are sophisticated biological machines involving coordination of a range of different molecular machines, including entry machines, replication machines, assembly machines, and genome packaging machines.

POST_005: Moral Machines

Example: New Variations on The Trolley Problem in The Age of the Self-Driving Car.[5]

Can machines be universally moral? Researchers at MIT have created a platform for crowdsourcing responses to moral dilemmas. While some A.I. ethicists argue in the affirmative, others maintain that we cannot outsource moral decision-making to automated intelligence.

POST_006: Political Technologies: *The Blockchain*

Example: Can blockchain design principles be used to create a more equitable and trustworthy framework for politics?[6]

Champions argue that blockchain can introduce not only more transparency and autonomy into current practices, but potentially set the stage for novel techno-political imaginaries.

POST_007: Netcentricity

Example: [Book] *The Digital Dionysus: Nietzsche and the Network-Centric Condition* (2016).[7]

"What post-structuralism has tended to leave undertheorized [. . .] is the nature of the impersonal and perpetual mediation machine itself, the machinic aspects of network-centricity that are anonymous, non-organic, and non-human."[8]

POST_008: War [as] Machine

Example: [Book] *Leper Creativity: Cyclonopedia Symposium* (2012).[9]

"The expansive, unlimited affectspace or dracage-zone of War-as-Machine arises from and builds upon 'differentiation, falsification, divergence, mass hysteria, terminal catabolism and disintegration in the direction of something other than death'—here a larval, crypto-fractal kind of 'terror'."[10]

POST_009: Hallucination Engine (Machinic Hallucination)

Example: Refik Anadol Studio designs synesthetic reality experiments to unlock hidden collective consciousness.[11]

When it comes to classifying objects, deep learning neural networks can be tricked into seeing and hearing things. Although they are inspired by the human visual cortex, the resemblance between artificial neural networks and human neural networks may be merely superficial.[12]

POST_010: Political Machines

Example: Governance-Machines and Non-Violent Resistance-Movements.[13]

Nonviolent protests are twice as likely to succeed as armed conflicts—and studies show that those engaging a threshold of 3.5 percent of the population have never failed to bring about change.[14]

POST_011: Digital Gender-Gaps

Example: Diversification-Efforts in Machine-Learning.[15]

There is growing awareness of the effects of bias in machine learning. Gender biases are embedded in the way language is used. Training machine learning algorithms to desist from perpetuating gender biases requires an understanding of how gender ideology is manifested in language.[16]

POST_012: Capitalism in a Time of Pandemics

Example: Street-Art Murals/Installations proliferate Counter-Codes in an Age of Emergency.[17]

The current global pandemic has exposed deep failures across the world, such as socio-economic inequality and systemic discrimination. The pandemic has disproportionately disadvantaged the working class, especially vulnerable populations like women, transgender people, and the elderly. Nevertheless, workers around the world are resisting and standing in opposition to capitalist responses to the Covid-19 pandemic.[18]

POST_013: Algorithmic Opacity

Example: "There is no transparency or accountability in the algorithm's space of play, and so we must begin instead from notions of opacity and partiality." — Louise Amoore (2018).[19]

Louise Amoore, Professor of Political Geography and author of *The Politics of Possibility: Risk and Security Beyond Probability* and *Cloud Ethics*, speculates on the ever-heightening ability of algorithms to coat the public sphere with vague and obscure ideological premises.

POST_014: From Neuro-Power to Nöo-Power
(In memory of Bernard Stiegler)

Example: The "International New-Republic" of Meta-Data.[20]

Neuro-power is a circuit of power that views humans not primarily as individuals or as populations, but as vehicles and conduits for information circulation, as brains and neural networks that can be coded, decoded, and recoded. The challenge of social networks is to transfigure neuro-power into a nöo-power by politically reimagining individuation.

POST_015: Post-Human AI

Example: Underground fungal networks allow plants to communicate across vast spaces in ways that resemble the human internet.[21]

Discussions of ethical AI could be enriched by thinking anew about human/nonhuman relationalities, and debates would benefit from confronting questions of whether nonhuman intelligences can be conceptualized in terms other than humanistic.[22]

POST_016: Critical Disinformation Studies

Example: The *Center for Information, Technology, and Public Life* conducts research on "five case studies—crime and anti-Blackness; Japanese incarceration; Black liberation; the AIDS crisis; and the trope of the Welfare Queen—to demonstrate the historical complicity of media, the state, and the political establishment in strategically spreading inaccurate information to maintain structural inequality."[23]

A critical approach to research should incorporate history, inequality, power, and culture. The authors of a publication argue that effective analysis of disinformation requires researchers to take an approach to disinformation that is historically grounded, foregrounding questions of how power, institutions, and socio-technical structures shape disinformation.

POST_017: Speculative Machines

Example: Thom Kubli and Hiroshi Ishii on 3D-Printing Floating-Sculptures.[24]

Scientists and artists are working together to create a 3D printer that can produce ultra-lightweight floating-sculptures. Members of MIT's Center for Art, Science, and Technology are exploring how computation and digital information can transform objects in real time. Just as earlier technologies revolutionized the distribution of images, sounds, and texts, leading to an era of limitless remixing and sampling, 3D fabrication techniques promise to remake both the world of materials and the material world.

POST_018: Cellular Machines

Example: Specialized Anti-Viral Devices bring "Machete-Like Properties" into the Body.[25]

The body's cells confront a tricky issue when infected by viruses because they must figure out how to eradicate the illness without harming themselves. To explain how cells do this, scientists have visualized a miniscule cellular machine that chops viral genetic material into pieces.

POST_019: Algorithmic Art

Example: Joseph Nechvatal's *Computer Virus Project 2.0*, 2001.[26]

Autonomous machine intelligences have been making original art for over fifty years. AARON, created by artist and computer programmer Harold Cohen, is one of the longest-running AIs and creates original artistic images.[27]

POST_020: Sound-Object/Objet-Sonore

Example: Contemporary sound artists like *Noise Orchestra* explore methods of synthesizing sound out of light with self-built machines.[28]

Can sound have an existence separate from its source? Pierre Schaeffer, a French radio engineer, coined the term "sound object" (*objet sonore*) which relates to the experience of "acousmatic listening" or hearing without seeing the causes behind it. "Acousmatics" were the disciples of the ancient philosopher Pythagoras who were initiated into the mysteries of his teachings only by hearing the voice of their master while he was hidden behind a curtain.[29]

POST_021: Larval War-Machines

Example: *Sorting Daemon*, 2003, by artist David Rokeby positions camera within gallery looking out into the street to extract images of what it considers to be humans for an exhibit on "Surveillance, Terrorism, and Democracy."[30]

Today warfare is conducted not only in military battle-spaces by martial personnel using armed force and weapons; increasingly, warfare is emergent and masked, creeping into the realms of everyday culture and sweeping across social networks using familiar and ordinary platforms of social communication as weapons for gaining advantage over opponents. Hypercamouflaged warfare comes to encroach upon civilian arenas and to seep into civil society. Digital cultural techniques, technological regimes, and social media become fertile ground for the use of warfare techniques like covert surveillance, tracking, and targeting to influence civilian domains and social relations.[31]

POST_022: Slaughterbots

Example: By 2030, it is predicted that machine capabilities will have increased to the point that humans will have not only become the weakest component in a wide array of systems and processes, but they will fade out of the decision-making loop entirely. Fully autonomous, *Unmanned Lethal Weapons* (UAVs), or "killer robots" as they are known, will be making combat decisions without necessitating any human input.[32]

Is it a bird? Is it a plane? It's neither. It is the face of future warfare. Not only is AI being used in specific domains of military activity to enhance performance in particular environments (e.g., air, land, sea, and cyberspace), but questions of global balance of power are being impacted by the strategic risks associated with the development of autonomous machine-controlled decision-making systems capable of learning from experience and improving performance relative to specific goals.[33]

POST_023: Digital *Wormfare*

Example: Military AI as existential threat.[34]

In 2010, the United States succeeded in installing a piece of malware (dubbed *Stuxnet*) at Natanz, an Iranian nuclear plant, disrupting the refining process and causing centrifuges to spin out of control. Iran retaliated with malware attacks on Bank of America, among other American institutions. Undetected, imperceptible, and uncontrolled, the malware squirmed into and infected other systems all over the world. Such cyberattacks, despite official denials, are not just a matter of "hacking" or "spying" but are offensive capabilities that make it possible to conduct warfare without declaring war.[35]

POST_024: (Super)Vision-Machines

Example: "For the first time in history, we are dealing with images that are not only created by machines, but that are also meant to be seen by machines. We are now in a situation in which we share the perception of our environment with our machinic other. This has given rise to the philosophical problem that Virilio called the 'splitting of viewpoint'. How can we understand a world seen by a synthetic, sightless vision? What modes of representation are created by it? And how does this affect the way we see the world?"—Marijke Goeting (2018).[36]

The ability of a machine to "see" allows it to identify the signatures (not necessarily just visible ones) of enemies, targets, landmarks, and anything else it is trained to do. Machine vision allows a program to extract salient features from a landscape or image that it can then use for classification and pattern recognition. Paul Virilio's 1994 book *The Vision Machine* warned that machine vision was turning into the rise of "vision machines" capable of not just recognizing patterns but also interpreting entire visual fields.[37]

POST_025: Algorithmic Enlightenment and the Programming of Desire

Example: Sigmund Freud's relative uses psychoanalytic models to control populace by helping corporate advertisement tap into unconscious desires.[38]

Is desire programmable? In the last century, the American industrial model had consisted in finding ways to entice people to buy a limited range of mass-produced items; but by the late twentieth century, neoliberal consumerism took root around the capitalization of the programmability of human desires. Neoliberal consumerism is always trying to satisfy desire by calculating and predicting it, making desire, on the one hand, ever-elusive and never-ending, and on the other, manufacturing desire, synchronizing, standardizing, and commodifying it. The neoliberal machinery—involving government, corporations, public relations, and advertising— capitalized on the exploration of the inner feelings of lifestyle groups in order to invent a whole new range of brands and identities, and thus win elections and direct economies.

This kind of tactical informatic exploitation has become strategic and globalized. Today, in the age of algorithmic enlightenment, consumption has become hyper-consumption and addiction (most of all to connectivity). The human has itself become an informational hub that can be measured, standardized, and exploited. Algorithms reduce human expression and action to "machine-readable" form, and in this sense, the human becomes both post-humanized and machinified, as well as pre-humanized and animalized by the myriad effects of this global process of human adaptation and acculturation to algorithmic logic.

POST_026: A Brief History of AI

Example: Rising Drone-Technologies and their "Emergent Properties" of Congregation/Synchronization.[39]

Through advances in deep learning algorithms, autonomous flocks of drones behave like birds: they can fly, swarm, and move collectively. The possibilities of such "deep learning" appeal to the *Defense Advanced Research Projects Agency* (DARPA), a research agency of the United States Department of Defense charged with developing military applications for emerging technologies. In 2013, DARPA investigated real-time machine systems that could mimic mammalian intelligence via cortical processing that recognizes patterns in spatial and temporal data, allowing systems to respond flexibly and creatively on the battlefield without any human input.[40]

POST_027: A Secret History of Cybernetics

Example: In the 1960s, the United States Defense Department's *Advanced Research Projects Agency* undertook a program called *ARPA*net.[41]

A precursor to the contemporary "internet," *ARPA*net's purpose was to allow the Pentagon to share data and research internally on the same network. Just before its rollout in 1967, a computer engineer at *RAND* Corporation, the think tank in California, wrote a paper called "Security and Privacy in Computer Systems" praising the goals of *ARPA*net but also warning of the security risks of what he called "on-line" networks. As soon as multiple users could gain access to data from unprotected locations, any hacker could hack into the network and gain access to unclassified and secret information relevant to national security. Eventually, under Ronald Reagan's national security directive entitled "National Policy on Telecommunications and Automated Information Systems Security," the National Security Agency, which had originally begun in 1952 to intercept foreign communications, was placed in charge of securing all of the nation's computer servers and networks.

POST_028: Re-engineering Ecology: *Dune*

Example: New Insights into the Relation between *Intuition*, *Mobility*, and *Space*.[42]

Frank Herbert's science fiction classic *Dune* is a literary work about re-engineering ecology, namely the political, religious, military, and ecological redesign of the planet Arrakis. The first book of *Dune* describes the Fremen, a people autochthonous to Arrakis whose entire culture depends on tracking and exploiting another life form indigenous to the planet, that is, the sandworm. The Fremen ecology is parasitic to that of the sandworm, but it has evolved to be able to track not only its own ecological movements across the planet's desert landscape but has also developed the abilities to hunt and manipulate the underground mechanisms of sandworm ecology. The entire Fremen culture, including its brutal mystical religion, is engineered to trap and hook worm movement across given expanses; the hook also happens to be the very technical device that permits Fremen to interact directly with the sandworms: they use actual hooks to attach themselves to moving sandworms, to climb and then ride them. The hook and the gesture of "hooking" become the central but elusive strategy of an ecological perspective that uses the interaction of elemental movements of sand and water to track, trap, and manipulate the movement of sandworms across the Arrakeen landscape. Gestural ecology—its "hooklike" mechanism—becomes the device that allows Fremen to control and communicate with their mystical god, the *Shai-Hulud*, becoming a vehicle for the propagation of Fremen theocracy. The mobile "logic" of a gestural ecology operates not by way of theoretical knowledge (e.g., the contemplative mode of the philosopher), but by way of a more cunning intelligence that transforms gesture into technique.

POST_029: Artificial Companion-Species

Example: Whether in the role of portable psychotherapist or love objects, humans have conceptualized AI as a type of "companion species" for humans. In *The Three Stigmata of Palmer Eldritch* published in 1965, American science fiction author Philip K Dick creates *Dr. Smile*, a suitcase-sized machine that people carry around as their own personal psychotherapist. In Dick's near-future world, *Dr. Smile* is a symptom of the highly neurotic nature of contemporary human beings whose mental health is so fragile and technologically reinforced that they need to have a 24/7 portable, "on-call" source of psychological coaching and companionship.

In another famous book, *Do Androids Dream of Electric Sheep* (made popular by the film adaptations *Bladerunner* and *Bladerunner 2049*), another technology appears: the mood organ, a device that allows the user to tune into and choose-to-feel different *moods*. In Dick's world, these technologies are not examples of human ingenuity and innovation, but instead indicative of frailty, deterioration, and ultimately serve as technical companions for people who live in a society that has been degraded and desensitized. This criticism was brilliantly captured by Mamoru Oshii in his *Ghost in the Shell* films, especially the second, *Innocence*, in which he shows that while humans are dependent on machines and machinic intelligence and artificial forms of life, they nonetheless mistrust and enslave them without a second thought. The established oppositions between culture and nature, and human and machine, are fraught and can be technically manipulated so as to shed light on a dimension that remains indiscernible to Humanism: that it is by way of technical objects and technical existence that human beings most authentically relate to their living milieu and to living processes.[43]

POST_030: Data-Bodies and Data-Hegemony

Example: The "body" has been a central concept and site of subjectivity in the genealogies of humanism. Yet in the age of ubiquitous mediation, there are more than just fleshy, lived bodies with which to contend. Governmentality and virtuality are intertwined insofar as contemporary political technologies increasingly involve control and production of not only physical fleshy bodies and power-relations, but also of "data-bodies": virtual assemblages composed of information connected to an individual, group or network.[44]

For example, calls for "digital democracy," "e-governance," "predictive policing," as well as "smart cities" all promise to replace failing political arrangements with digital feedback and technological solutionism. But are these endeavors also part of a nebulous process of data-hegemony, a condition in which data and the datalogical are in command of decision-making processes? Data-bodies proliferate and meta-stabilize in serpentine schemas of informational connectivity/ control that seek to both exploit human-centered resources and replace them with algorithmic, artificial-intelligence-driven technologies that appear human-friendly, ultimately seeking to minimize human oversight. Surveillance capitalism is based on exploiting the virtual qualities of data-bodies, especially their legal and normative loopholes, since most laws apply to physical rather than virtual bodies. Neither merely object/commodity nor merely subjective extensions of organic bodies, data-bodies are double-faced mechanisms that potentially erect and collapse subjectivities and objectivities.

POST_031: Algorithmic Governance: A *Digital Duplicity?*

Example: The dream of "ubiquitous connectivity" is to unite humans and non-humans in an ever-tightening mesh of mechanisms that would cater to every need and desire from the most mundane to the most exotic. This imagined "networked future" wherein seemingly-innocuous and wonderfully-useful apparati do our bidding is, however, a trap that lures the human being with digital elixirs: tantalizing prosthetics that appear to extend, expand and enlarge the dominion (nevermind the desires) of what in fact is an ever-waning species—a species on its way out in a world with very few exits, moreover.[45]

Champions of what today is being called "algorithmic governance" suggest that this model can free humans from the foibles of hierarchical and traditional forms of power, but this utopianism may end up being the dominant digital duplicity of the digital era. Algorithmic regulation, in other words, is the control and regulation of network behavior conducted by automated informational processes that produce so-called "desired outcomes" for humans, based on real-time, modulated feedback. It is a paradigm of self-organization in which networks are governed, managed, and reproduced by the capture and processing of digital information. Algorithmic governance colonizes and propagates by creating more opportunities for digitally regulating information, thus creating the conditions for continued algorithmic expansion into networks of increasingly planetary scale. Like Francis Bacon's *New Atlantis*, which describes a utopia ruled by "Salomon House," a college of benevolent scientific keepers of knowledge, algorithmic governance promises the rule of algorithmic knowledge applied to the betterment of human beings. And yet, might this utopian promise turn out to really mean "more production of data in machine readable form"? From such a machine perspective—the human being finds itself at once both post-humanized and machinified, as well as pre-humanized and animalized.

POST_032: *Boring Machines:* The Paradox of *Technics* and *Boredom*

Example: Is the evolution of technology connected to the human experience of boredom? How do humans co-evolve with technologies by way of the catalyzing effects of boredom? Boredom is the negative effect of human relations that have lost their novelty; but boredom also becomes the positive catalyst for technological innovation and televisual inventions, like the motion-picture camera, as well as for the development of comedic techniques like the pratfall, custard pies, double-takes, and "the chase." It's not just that boredom is both empowering and disempowering, enabling and disabling. It's that the moebius-like relation between boredom and technology suggests a kind of ontological aporia of origin in which the bored human, or human experience of boredom, is not possible without the technical and *vice versa*.[46]

Like *the chicken or egg paradox*, the catalyst for technical solutions becomes connected to the very experience of humans becoming bored by the very technologies that were once solutions to the problems of boredom. We see this paradox very much reflected in popular culture as well as neuroscientific research. Boredom, on the one hand, is said to be necessary for creativity; and on the other, it is said to contribute negatively to cognitive, affective, and social disorders. The paradox of boredom and technology may imply that the innovative and potentially emancipatory/democratic effects of technological development to attenuate boredom inevitably lead to the uncanny return of the totalitarian effects (perhaps in the form of a micro-fascism of boredom). The question of politics is inevitably tied up with the paradoxical relation between technics and boredom, of what one could call, following the late French political philosopher of media Bernard Stiegler, the technics of attention. For Stiegler, technologies are crucial in these processes of phenomenological and "psychic" experience, through the various mental, sensory, and physiological means by which we capture the world and it captures us. But they are also agents of routinization, synchronization, and homogenization, or programmatisation. So the paradoxical relation between technics and boredom, from a political point of view, has both curative and poisonous socio-political effects: novel forms of collectivity may be engendered, but the modes of interaction are limited.[47]

POST_033: The "Digital Fracking" of Humans?

Example: As trends toward total digitization continue (e.g., the internet of things and smart cities), the complete integration of physical and virtual environments will mean that every aspect of the environment—including the body—becomes potentially data-rich and ready to be tapped, even "fracked," which is a term used to describe the process of hydraulic fracturing used in extracting oil which causes earthquakes and other environmental hazards.[48]

It might be worth considering the analogy more seriously and to wonder how in the age of cognitive capitalism, humans have become subject to fracking, in this case fracking for information. Not only are humans colonizing each other by way of technologies and information, but in the empire of the digital, all humans are being colonized by digital mediation as it takes hold over the planet and in every sphere of knowledge.[49]

POST_034: Resisting the Biometric Gaze

Example: As Paul Virilio wrote in his 1989 book *War and Cinema: The Logistics of Perception*: "In a technicians' version of an all-seeing Divinity, the drive is on for a general system of illumination that will allow everything to be seen and known, at every moment and in every place."[50] How to resist, subvert, and even overturn the surveillant gaze of the increasingly ubiquitous machines of surveillance capitalism? This gaze could be described as the signature device of contemporary forms of power, our mobile all-seeing eye.

The global architecture of surveillance technologies plays a key role in the establishment of such a "general system of illumination" driven by information extraction, analysis, manipulation, commodification, and control. Big data has a foundational role in this new regime which promises (but fails to) shed light on the opacity of human problems through the power of computing. In the name of counter-terrorism and patriotism, new identification technologies like biometrics and backscatter X-rays are being used in airports and border security to compel bodies—especially bodies that are covered or veiled—to unveil their "hidden truths." Muslim women's bodies have been subjected to the disciplinary violence of the biometric surveillant gaze. Imaging technologies aimed at stripping the body and revealing what is beneath are being used, buttressed by police power and the rhetoric of scientific certainty, to justify making Muslim women more and more visible, and thus more and more subject to surveillance intervention. States and corporations are increasingly relying on a political rationality that equates "security" with "visibility." And yet, against the backdrop of surveillance capitalism and its surveillant technologies, this politics of transparency has taken on new and perhaps even insidious connotations.[51]

POST_035: Cybernetics and Post-Humanism

Example: Norbert Wiener's *Cybernetics: or Control and Communication in the Animal and the Machine* had first been published in 1948 by French publisher Hermann-et-Cie. Surprisingly, the first French translation of the book only appeared in 2014 (as *La Cybernétique: Information et Regulation dans Le Vivant et La Machine*). "Cybernetics," a word Wiener had taken from the ancient Greek word *kubernētēs* (meaning "governor"), was not merely about communication in animal and machines, but also a schema for communication between various isolated sciences in which the driving force was "information," not "reason."[52]

Through the universalization of the concept of information, cybernetics was conceived, especially by Wiener, as a kind of "Enlightenment" that would liberate humans from servitude and renew the scientific and moral spirit of humanity (especially in the aftermath of the consequences of the development of the atomic bomb). France had played a decisive role in the development of cybernetics—even Wiener was unaware that the term had been used in the nineteenth century by the French physicist André-Marie Ampère—not only in the publication of Wiener's book, but also in using cybernetics as a platform for discussing well-established themes in French intellectual history such as automation, subjectivity, cognition, volition, the differences and similarities between human and artificial intelligence, as well as the emancipatory or enslaving potentials of the new techno-sciences. While Wienerian cybernetics had always defined itself in relation to humanist ideals, in France, cybernetics came to be associated strongly with anti-humanism, even posthumanism. In privileging the concept of "information" and in blurring the theoretical boundaries between the living and non-living, Wienerian cybernetics (which had already started to decline by the 1960s giving way to a second wave of cybernetics) had hoped to offer a new vision of humanism but instead may have revealed a kind of post-humanist impulse that would come to influence the development of French structuralism and post-structuralism.[53]

POST_036: Commanding the Trend: Future of Warfare

Example: To Harness the Trends and Potentials of Digital Social-Mediation has become a Priority both for conducting Warfare and for conceptualizing Military Doctrine.[54]

"Commanding the trend" is a social media mechanism of persuasion used in social networking that is fast becoming a weapon of warfare involving the exploitation of pre-existing social networks by subversive agents, especially through the use of algorithmic/automatic techniques in order to covertly introduce propaganda effects into social media platforms and ensure the quick and cost-effective circulation of messages, narratives, and false information. It is not simply that social media have become used as tools of warfare, but also that military rationale and practice have struggled to keep up with and adapt to the quixotic transformations and permanent disruptive effects of ever-expanding digital networking practices.[55]

POST_037: The Politics of Human Obsolescence

Example: Are humans becoming obsolete? A major part of contemporary digital communications happens not between people, but between devices, about people, and over the *Internet of Things* (IoT).[56]

With increased reliance on machine-to-machine communications, humans are quickly going from being "in the loop" of control and command to being "out of the loop" altogether. As technologies become "autonomous" requiring little to no human oversight, will the implementation of self-learning machines and AI systems also lead to human obsolescence in governance processes? What kind of politics can be mobilized in the context of a planetary future in which humans are no longer "in the loop"? The philosophical challenge seems to lie in imagining politics as not necessarily grounded in assumptions about humans being in the loop of command and control. How to conceive of such a politics? Can it be called a "politics" at all? Or is it instead about something altogether "beyond" politics—perhaps a post-human politics?[57]

POST_038: Contagious Communication and Network-Control

Example: In a *Network-centric* and *Infodemic* Age, Contagion and Virality have become not just Icons but Models for Networked Connectivity.[58]

The asymmetrical tendencies of contemporary digital capitalism are the results of the entanglement between the powers of centralization and striation, and affective and dispersed logics of contagious communication. In an age of networks, contagious communication has itself become part of a new protocological paradigm of information, mediation, and networked control. The virality of communication has become furious, like the ancient Furies, described by the Greek tragedian Aeschylus and others as a "bloody ravening pack." Furious media engages affect and communicates through contagion within the distributed (and disturbed) logic of the "swarm."

POST_039: "War on Terror" in the Age of Intelligent Machines

Example: The "war on terror" refers to the global military campaign spearheaded by the United States after September 11, 2001, to deal with terrorist threats.[59]

Rather than a defined set of military imperatives governed by the regular norms of war (such as the requirement that nations determine and delimit a geographical theater of war), the use of the term extends beyond the normal conceptual parameters to become, at once, both a set of practices and policies that include military intervention, covert operations, agencies and institutions, as well as an entire set of cultural and political beliefs, assumptions, justifications, and narratives for determining not only who are allies and who are enemies, but also for delimiting the bounds of national identity and individual rights. The increased adoption of global counter-terrorism technologies across the globe is converging with the proliferation of globally coordinated systems and processes for capturing, storing, and cross-referencing digital information of any and every sort, in the name of "security." In this scenario, the "war on terror" is being waged by intelligent machines of information-surveillance that are developing and being justified in its name, from biometric technologies like facial recognition or retinal scanning in border security, to predictive technologies that can harvest, record, and even make predictions. Today, war is made ambiguous through its entanglement with the growing but complex mesh of everyday media. One of the graver implications of this is that the War on Terror in the Age of intelligent machines is not so much about using the rules of war to isolate and eliminate those undertaking terrorist activity, but rather to extend war into all spheres of life, to extend and use the techniques and technologies of war to manage and govern entire civilian populations.[60]

Denys Nevozhai (2019).

LAB 10.0

Future Power

Chapter 10.0
Future Power Lab
Concepts: Struggle, Spectacle, Utopia
Lab Author: Arshin Adib-Moghaddam

POST_001: Vaporous Control

Lab Author: Arshin Adib-Moghaddam

Example: Yasuaki Onishi's installation titled *reverse of volume RG* (Japan, 2012) uses black glue and plastic sheeting material to construct a "monumental, mountainous form that appears to float in space."[1]

George Orwell's *1984* came earlier than we thought, as our traditional understanding of surveillance by a totalitarian state is being substituted by mechanisms of control that resemble an odorless and invisible gas infused with Diazepam, a potent mixture that numbs our motivational drives for social change.

POST_002: Supersonic Governmentality

Example: Global biometric data collection and surveillance expand amidst lack of regulations.[2]

If in the past we were governed by an incredibly alienating colossus or "the machine," as the Iranian intellectual Jalal al-e Ahmad famously argued, then today's data-driven techno-politics are foreshadowing an incredibly intrusive form of supersonic governmentality that is immediate, edgeless, and in its hyper-speed, almost invisible.

POST_003: Neural Resistance

Example: Experimental Particle Physicist Dan McQuillan deploys an "anti-fascist" paradigm of AI to address people with learning and mental health disabilities, refugees and asylum-seekers, and victims of torture or disappearance by police.[3]

For every "SS-bot" that magnifies learned biases and turns them into a form of neural fascism, we need a counter-mnemonic that churns out socially just algorithms that encode equality.

POST_004: Robotic Perfectionism

Example: Japanese government proposes cyborgs and robotic avatars for all by 2050.[4]

The overman of Nietzsche was a benevolent post-human creature. Yet he is the same monster-cyborg driven by perfectionism that is guiding contemporary forays into the development of trans-human robots.[5]

POST_005: Borderless World

Example: Achille Mbembe writes on the revolutions of mobility, movement, and migration amidst the "dialectics of territorialization and deterritorialization."[6]

Technology transposes us into a borderless world where the differences between us and them, self and other, are mere miscalculations induced by algorithmic confusion.

POST_006: Cyber-Beyond

Example: The UNHCR (United Nations Refugee Agency) publishes study titled "Space and Imagination: Rethinking Refugees' Digital Access."[7]

It is in the tension between imposed geopolitical borders and our instant ability to march beyond them in cyberspace that the ultimate battle for the future of humanity will be won.

POST_007: Horizon / Abyss

Example: The Way of the Future established the Church of AI in 2015 dedicated to "the realization, acceptance, and worship of a Godhead based on Artificial Intelligence (AI) developed through computer hardware and software."[8]

Is the horizon of artificial intelligence the transcendence of this-worldly life promised by the gods of antiquity, or the millenarian abyss predicted by the religions of the book?

POST_008: Colonial Jungle

Example: Limari Lighting Designers wins premier prize for interior illumination at the Lamp Lighting Solutions Awards, irradiating indigenous artifacts in the Galería de Chile y España (January 2015).[9]

Decolonizing Artificial Intelligence must start by genetically modifying the rhizome of knowledge as it has grown in the bewildering jungle of the Humanities.

POST_009: Pandemic Globality

Example: Filmmakers and screenwriters—known as the Plague Prophets—predicted the age of pandemic society in advance of the current quarantined world.[10]

Our pandemic connectivity exploited by Covid-19 begets a new form of globalized consciousness, where self and other cannot escape the viral tissues that compose the surface effect of our common humanity.

POST_010: Microgovernance of Bodies

Example: Contact Tracing App in Singapore explored in article titled "How Singapore's Contact Tracing Technology Undermines Citizen's Trust."[11]

The panopticon of yesterday has transmuted into the nanoptical, microgovernance of our bodies, which are increasingly escaping this form of governance by metamorphosing into sites of teflonic resistance.

POST_011: Politico-Aesthetics

Example: Graffiti artist Banksy's *Walled Off Hotel* overlooking the Palestinian territories offers showcases of his murals along with "the worst view in the world."[12]

It is in the most humane faculties of our mind that are sparked into action by the aesthetic beauty of poetry and other beaux-arts that we can find the universality of seemingly mundane but utterly political sentiments such as happiness and pain.

POST_012: Psycho-Nationalism

Example: Vaccine Nationalism.[13]

Nationalism does to humanity what quarantine does to society. An entire field of study awaits surrounding the notion of Psycho-Nationalism.

POST_013: Archaeology of the Old World

Example: Peruvian muralist JADE leaves new street works across the decaying city walls of Lima.[14]

It is in the labyrinthine catacombs of the human heart where a form of algorithmic empathy will be uncoded to unleash the emancipatory beauty and aesthetics running through the ancient arteries of the Global South. The answers of tomorrow require a thorough archaeology into the cultural depths of the "old world."

POST_014: Frontal Lobe Control

Example: "Global technology governance can succeed with the right cooperation," article produced for The World Economic Forum as it convenes the first Global Technology Governance Summit on April 6–7, 2021.[15]

Example II: Mechanical oil drawings of Atsushi Koyama.[16]

The new forms of governance will be exercised along the cognitive faculties deeply lodged in the frontal lobe of our brains, which are already hard-wired to our personal computers and smartphones.

POST_015: Transposed Formula

Example: "When Good Algorithms Go Sexist: Why and How to Advance AI Gender Equity," Stanford Social Innovation Review, March 31, 2021.[17]

AI algorithms transpose the formulas of racism and the mnemonics of sexism into the body politic of the ruling machine.

POST_016: Ideological Tricks

Example: Composite Bodies Series | Entangled Nuclear Colonialisms, Matters of Force, and the Material Force of Justice (Northeastern and Harvard University).[18]

No ideological hocus pocus can change reality for the long term. The hocus pocus is but a bad trick to shirk the responsibilities that come with holding power, and it is not a long-term formula for governance.

POST_017: Political Submergence

Example: The Muraka Underwater Hotel Room at Conrad Maldives (Rangali Island Rangali, Maldives).[19]

If the philosophers of the past managed to tame the demonic powers of fascist political mutants, then the intellectuals of the future need to immerse themselves in a world of new possibilities that is liberated from the shackles of dogma and ideology.

POST_018: Stratospheric Universality

Example: Scientists claim the viral pandemic sheds light on new strategies for solar geoengineering (i.e., stratospheric aerosol injection) that if gone unheeded might lead to political conflicts of the most vicious kind.[20]

Example II: Miguel Rothchild, *Elegy*, 2017 (ocean wave installations).[21]

Civilizations are not tectonic plates that clash against each other. They are hybrid formations that merge into a stratospheric universality composed of us.

POST_019: Killer Robots

Example: The former CEO of Google, Eric Schmidt, presided over a US National Security Commission whose members unanimously concluded that the United States has a "moral imperative" to lead in the pursuit of lethal autonomous weapons such as "killer robots."[22]

This is the onset of a form of post-human warfare that threatens to turn every aspect of our current existence into a securitized battlefield, from Alexa to our mobile phones. Moreover, the legal structure undergirding the current international system is human-centric and does not encompass "killer robots" and their algorithmic codification, which threatens to escape our notions of culpability.

POST_020: Existence Trading

Example: Data brokerage firm LexisNexis, better known as a search engine for scholarly and legal research, signed a US$16.8 million contract in February this year to sell user's information on their data base to US Immigration and Customs Enforcement.[23]

Surveillance capitalism is an ever-increasing threat to our human security. It threatens to turn our everyday existence into a commodity easily traded among self-interested tech firms and their enablers.

POST_021: Race and Algorithm

Example: An algorithm by a software company called COMPAS was used to predict the particular tendencies of a convicted criminal to reoffend. However, when the algorithm was wrong in its predicting, the results were displayed differently for black and white offenders, as black offenders were flagged as particularly unworthy of probation.[24]

Racism is a residue of European modernity. The data sets feeding into AI systems will be prejudiced and discriminatory as long as racism remains a part of our social reality.

POST_022: Postmodern Resistance

Example: Images from the Arab Spring demonstrate the immensity and multifarious nature of the event.[25]

Quote: "There always is an unfolding of resistance and power into each other."

The "Arab Spring," which started in Tunisia in 2011, led to the downfall of the longest-serving dictators of the Arab World, including Muammar Gaddafi of Libya, Hosni Mubarak of Egypt, and Zine El Abidine Ben Ali of Tunisia. Scholars theorized the events as typical of a particularly post-modern manifestation of resistance that grew dialectically out of an outdated form of governance.

POST_023: Distributed Brain Drone

Example: So-called Perdix drones shot out of an F/A-18 Super Hornet could be scaled to tens of thousands of drones, creating a weapon akin to a low-scale nuclear device? Such drones communicate with one another using a distributed brain, complex formation, traveling across a battlefield, and reforming into a new formation.[26]

Example II: Adam Martinakis, *Lightbreak* (2014), uses digital sculpture to portray humans as mannequins adrift in empty space.[27]

As the theoreticians of the so-called "Frankfurt School" rightly argued in their seminal books, perfecting technologies of death must be treated as one of the main residues of the European enlightenment.

POST_024: Serotonin Sellers

Example: News Story: "Apple iOS 14.5 update: Facebook, Instagram notice says 'tracking' helps keeps apps free." Facebook and Instagram apps on Apple iOS 14.5 have begun showing a new notice that urges users to let the apps track user activity to continue using the services for free.[28]

Surveillance capitalists sell us what they take from our bodies: serotonin.

POST_025: Pseudo-Reality vs. The Library

Example: A recent study of researchers from Drexel University and Worcester Polytechnic Institute found out that humans are likely to believe anything for a few moments, if it comes from what they consider a "trusted" sources, for instance an AI machine.[29]

The barrage of "fake news" that we are constantly bombarded with is meant to create a pseudo-reality suitable to the needs of governance and not to our human security. The only bastion of resistance remains the library and our self-education.

POST_026: The Infinitely Irreproducible

Example: Empathy and affection are some of the most under-researched themes in politics.[30]

Current research shows that these sentiments cannot be readily mimicked by AI systems, even superintelligent ones.

POST_027: Havoc and Vulnerability

Example: In the current violence between the Israeli Defense Forces and the Palestinian HAMAS movement, the latter used GPS-guided "kamikaze drones" for the first time in the long history of the conflict.[31]

The ability to hit precision targets, especially vulnerable infrastructural facilities like oil and gas storage and chemical plants, makes kamikaze drones a viable threat. The drones of the future will be even more lethal and accurate in their purpose to cause havoc and destruction. There is no bunker that technology cannot reach.

POST_028: Ricochet and Camouflage

Example: In 2014, the hacktivist group Anonymous took down the official website of the Israeli intelligence agency Mossad against Israel's military incursion in Gaza, which had resulted in hundreds of civilian casualties.[32]

On the ethers of the world wide web, every individual becomes a target of power, and therefore a harbinger of resistance. Camouflaged to fit into the new realities of a techno-dominated society, the future rebel has no ideological foundations — her resistance emerges with supersonic speed from various directions as it ricochets away from power, like a high-velocity projectile that doesn't adhere to any calculation or social formula.

POST_029: Political Discourse-Bots

Example: Trials have started into creating fully animated talking bots trained in narrow-domain text generators who will be able to discuss politics with users — resulting in something like a Biden-bot, or perhaps a Putin-bot, that can debate things with you on the internet.[33]

Technology has had a dual effect on political participation. On the one side, it makes politics more immediate, as the Twitter account of Donald Trump showed. On the other side, it turns us into a vile dependency on technology that serves the political class to buttress their power strategies on the basis of our data and the preferences contained therein.

POST_030: Power of Suggestion

Example: The UK-based AI start-up Faculty just raised US$42.5 million in a growth funding round. The company was instrumental in winning the Brexit vote for the current UK government. It has also been telling global corporates like Red

Bull and Virgin Media what to suggest to their customers, based on processing vast amounts of data.[34]

Targeted advertisement for political purposes used to be called propaganda, as it is meant to warp the truth in favor of a political movement and/or agenda. In this case, Faculty used their AI know-how to flood Facebook users with pro-Brexit messages that took the UK out of the European Union.

POST_031: The Database and the Blind Eye

Example: A company called Clearview AI has access to over 3 billion images drawn from your social media sites and internet blogs. This database is larger than that of the FBI.[35]

Example II/Image: Artist George Redhawk's exhibit titled "The World Through My Eyes" (Paris, 2015) uses computer animation techniques to illustrate the visual distortions that he himself experienced as he became legally blind. In non-static photos that he calls "motion art," he mirrors the progressive deterioration of his sight in a technique which is increasingly being referred to as The Redhawk Effect.[36]

The database of Clearview AI is more expansive than that of major governmental organizations and has been used to identify protesters in the recent uprising in the United States. Therefore, it has come under increasing scrutiny in the EU, which has some of the most stringent privacy laws in the world.

POST_032: Facial Recognition and the Blind Eye

Example: When Apple's IPhone X was launched, it failed to recognize the facial features of Chinese users who could not use the FaceID feature because of this defect.[37]

Research has shown that algorithms can be racist and that facial recognition software has a 5 percent to 50 percent chance of being wrong. On that basis, false arrests have already been made.

POST_033: Topographical Object of the Skin

Example: In the United States, data used by health care providers overwhelmingly discriminate against darker skinned people? For instance, AI-driven technology used by dermatologists in order to detect skin cancer are missing samples of darker skin types.[38]

According to the American Academy of Dermatology, fair-skinned people are at the highest risk for contracting skin cancer. However, the mortality rate for African Americans is considerably higher: their five-year survival rate is 73 percent, compared with 90 percent for white Americans, according to the American Academy of Dermatology. The human skin as a topographical object of racism is the exact opposite of the dominance of blackness in haute couture, which has been central to our sense of aesthetics ever since modern fashion was invented.

POST_034: Cyber-Assassins

Example: "Recently . . . people are beginning to see you as another narcissistic rich dude who is desperate for attention," said the international hacktivist group to Tesla and SpaceX chief, Elon Musk this week. "You may think you are the smartest person in the room, but now you have met your match. We are Anonymous! We are legion. Expect us."[39]

Very much comparable to the legendary "Hashishin" movement, the order of the assassins who were based in Alamut Castle in Persia and who hunted down their enemies while high on drugs (or so the fables say), Anonymous, too, uses the power of deception as a mind-altering strategy to disturb the status quo.

POST_035: Borderless Canvas

Example: In the future, international power will not be calculated in terms of the strength of your army, but by the destructive force of your algorithms. China calls this "intelligentized warfare" in its latest five-year plan.[40]

International theorists, from the ancient Chinese philosopher Sun Tzu to the former US secretary of state Henry Kissinger, measure power in terms of materiality. Today, we have entered the realm of virtual, mnemonic power which transposes our Alexas and Siris into a borderless canvas of war.

POST_36: Perfect Memory / Extinctive System

Example: The British based AI company DeepMind made news this week when it announced that AI systems will outperform humans sooner than we think, and perhaps even within a decade. New inventions are allowing for instantaneous calculation and perfect memory, leading to an artificial intelligence that would outperform humans at nearly every cognitive task.[41]

Example II: Image: Mé Art Collective Tokyo, "CONTACT," Mori Art Museum in Tokyo, Japan (second ocean waves installation, 2019).[42]

The consequences of this so-called Artificial General Intelligence for world politics and international security are vast. DeepMind itself is owned by Google—a company that is involved in various military applications for the Pentagon, including autonomous weapons systems that can kill without human supervision. Like the "Black Death" and other plagues, this type of extinctive systems kill out of nowhere.

POST_37: Anonymous Challengers

Example: This week, Jake Davis, the former hacker known as "Topiary" and senior member of hacktivist group Anonymous has spoken about the scale of the ransomware challenge facing organisations today. He declared: "I'm a former hacktivist, I was involved in Anonymous and Lulzsec. I was involved in hacking the Westboro Baptist Church, which is a homophobic and racist group. We would target groups like this and take them down."[43]

In our techno-society, every email that we send, online store that we visit, and WhatsApp message that we open is monitored and traced. In such an environment, "anonymity" is not merely a virtue; it translates into power. This is why "Anonymous" chose their name, as they emerge out of the labyrinthine threads of the World Wide Web.

POST_38: Pegasus Spyware

Example: The news that a programme called Pegasus, the spyware manufactured by Israel's NSO Group, has been used to track and trace academics, journalists, and activists all over the world has shattered the myth that common people are not victims of such "weapons of mass surveillance." Once Pegasus infiltrates your phone it can harvest ANY data from your device, including What's APP messages, photos, messages etc. It can even switch on your microphone and listen to your conversations and track your every move your phone's GPS system.[44]

For the first time in history, the ruling elites have equipped themselves with the powers to fully penetrate everyday life. Philosophers and novelists all foresaw decades ago that technology would be used to control and suppress.

POST_39: Advantage Games

Example: This week open-source intelligence reports identified more than 150 Russian AI-enabled military systems in various stages of development. While Russia is not a global leader in commercial AI-based systems, it is focusing its efforts on strategic security areas such as autonomous air, underwater, surface and ground platforms.

Example II/Image: Image: Mischa Kuball, *Space—Speech—Speed*, installation (Faena Arts Center, Buenos Aires, Argentina, 2013).[45]

Technology has always been the advantage of empires, as speed and pursuit are at the heart of all conquest. Therefore, there is a new world order emerging that transposes the great game of global domination increasingly into the murky waters of the virtual world and its supersonic AI-induced identities.

POST_40: Cyborg Biopolitics

Example: I have repeatedly covered the Hacktivist movement "Anonymous" through these lab fragments. Their self-proclaimed struggle in support of marginalized groups and individuals continued this week when they targeted the conspiracy "Querdenker" movement in Germany which denies virology and the health effects of Covid-19 encouraging people not to get vaccinated.

Example II/Image: *Injection*—a collaboration by graffiti artists in the province of Buenos Aires—reveals innovative new iconographies associated with the viral and pandemic experience.⁴⁶

It has been rumored that the French intellectual Michel Foucault deemed HIV AIDS a form of biopolitical control to subdue homosexuals right up until he passed away from the disease in 1984. One of the biggest minds of the twentieth century was wrong on this occasion, but his concept of biopolitics does say a lot about the ways our bodies are governed, and even more so after the pandemic as we are dependent on technology like never before in the history of humanity. We have entered the age of the cyborg without enough knowledge about who is programming us.

POST_41: Imperialist Domino-Effect

Example: The government of Boris Johnson in the United Kingdom is set to hoard up to 210 million spare Covid-19 vaccines by the end of 2021, as some of the poorest countries in the world such as Yemen and Benin can't get their hands on them. Meanwhile, the German government has opposed a temporary waiver of intellectual property rights on coronavirus vaccines. The bid was tabled at the World Trade Organization (WTO) in October 2020 by India and South Africa—and has since been backed by countries including by the Biden administration in the United States, France and Italy.

Imperialism was never only about geopolitical expansion. It must be treated as a homicidal attitude that denies our common humanity and the existential challenges that this pandemic connectivity brings about. In his wonderful quatrains that adorn the buildings of the United Nations in New York City, the legendary thirteenth-century Persian poet, Omar Khayyam, who authored the world-famous *Rubaiyat*, foresaw the domino effect that present and future catastrophes are/will bring about if we don't acknowledge our common constitution as humans:

> Human beings are members of a whole,
> in creation of one essence and soul.
> If one member is afflicted with pain,
> other members uneasy will remain.
> If you have no sympathy for human pain,
> the name of human you cannot retain.⁴⁷

POST_42: AI-island headquarter

Example: Did you know that China has recently collaborated with Cuba to establish an AI-headquarter on the island? The recent electoral successes of "leftist" governments in Peru and elsewhere, are radically shifting the geo-political calculus in Latin America, which is aided and abetted by AI-technology and its employment as a new type of "professional politics" in the region and beyond.

The current Russian president Vladimir Putin famously said: "Whoever becomes the leader in AI will become the ruler of the world." The new tapestry of global politics is increasingly interwoven with technological strands that are creating a new world order that will be different from anything we have experienced before.

POST_43: Futuristic Veiling

Example: Algorithms rule the world. How can you poison them? People all over the world are engaged in "data strikes," concerted efforts to withhold or delete your data so that tech firms can't access you or to contribute harmful/meaningless data used to personalise advertisement—a US$ 120 billion business for companies such as Google.

In Islamic philosophy and other thought systems, the "veil" was never merely about covering one's body, but primarily about ensuring one's anonymity and privacy and shielding it from nefarious forces. The current waves of "data strikes" that are also advocated by cyber-undergrounds are a form of veiling—a potent shield from the penetrative QR code that scans our everyday lives and which is branded upon our bodies by the so-called tech giants.

POST_44: Nefarious Technics

Example: The United States and its allies have been defeated in Afghanistan. The debacle for the Afghan people has a pronounced data dimension which indicates the dangers of datafication. The victorious "Taliban" received access to forty pieces of data per person—from iris scans and family links to their favorite fruit. This was a system supervised by the United States meant to cut fraud in the Afghan security forces. It now gives the Taliban access to "collaborators" whom they could target for their cooperation with NATO forces.

The availability of data and technology more generally radically reinterprets the meaning of information as privacy is invaded like never before, by the state, but also by nefarious movements with a violent agenda.

POST_45: Old Transhumanism

Example: The US and NATO defeat in Afghanistan clearly showed that technology doesn't win wars. The strategic theatre in the mountainous country became a prominent field project for the newest war technology, in particular drones that were employed by NATO forces with deadly effect. Yet, in the end it was the seemingly medieval Taliban that retained the upper hand, and that after two decades of war.

For all the talk of "transhumanism" that is seemingly turning us into effects of technology, the Afghan war demonstrates that an existential threat, which triggers old-fashioned drivers of human motivation such as the survival instinct, flares up decisively in the face of any powerful techno-war machinery –

POST_46: Casualties of Innocence

Example: When military planners made the case for drone warfare in order to inflate their budgets, one of the main arguments that they made was the precision of such weaponry which was said to minimize civilian casualties. On September 17, 2021, the Pentagon admitted killing ten civilians, including seven Afghan children near the capital Kabul "by mistake."

Wars have always licensed the killing of the innocent. But drone warfare in particular affords the state a sanitized, remote, and almost aestheticized version of warfare that incorporates the individual in the act of killing. You and I could be either the target for whom the drone is assembled and programmed in the first place or the executioner who pulls the trigger, bringing about this death from above. We could also be peace activists.

POST_47: Resistance of the Undecipherable

Example: The Iranian state administers some of the most stringent internet rules, also in order to contain the influence and cyberattacks of the country's enemies.

However, a new Android APP encrypts up to 1000 characters of Persian text into an undecipherable jumble of words. You can send this mélange to a friend over any communication platform—Telegram, WhatsApp, Google Chat, etc.— and then they run it through the App on their device to decipher what you've said and to get around any censorship.

Example II: Babak Kazemi's *The Exit of Farhad and Shirin* transports a classical tragic myth into the present-day condition of forced migration and exile.[48]

Technology can function as an instrument of power AND resistance, as even the most sophisticated algorithm can be decoded. Technology, then, is permeable, which implies that it can be used in any direction: to discipline and punish and/ or to emancipate and liberate.

POST_48: Facial Mapping

Example: Emotion recognition systems are dependent on face mapping. This technology could be used to scan a person's face using a 3D laser scanning system, and then project and manipulate CGI graphics onto the face in real time—a form of virtual and highly sophisticated stage makeup central to OMOTE, a new Japanese technology. But face mapping can also be used to "read" our emotional state and to psychologically sort and categorize us. In this way "make-up" could be a form of resistance to conceal our emotional state from predatory AI systems.

AI technologies that are only just invented escape any regulatory framework. This is why the UN commissioned a report including the "use of emotion recognition systems by public authorities, for instance for singling out individuals for police stops or arrests or to assess the veracity of statements during interrogations." Such AI-powered systems that can read your emotions are against human rights as they challenge long-established norms such as the rights to privacy, to liberty, and to a fair trial.

POST_49: The Power of Misrecognition

Example: Dozens of black Uber drivers in Britain have been repeatedly prevented from working due to what they say is "racist" facial verification technology. Uber uses Microsoft Face API software on its app to verify the identity of their drivers. The algorithm underlying the software has difficulty properly recognizing individuals with darker skin tones and members of certain ethnic backgrounds.[49]

Racism is embedded in the DNA of our social systems at least since the onset of modernity in Europe. Algorithmic bias embedded in any computational system governing our institutions threatens to encode this racism and to make it untraceable, normalized and therefore, permanently opaque.

LAB 11.0

Future Fashion

Chapter 11.0

Future Fashion Lab

Concepts: Appearance, Touch, Materiality

Lab Authors: Ghazal Zamani and Jason Mohaghegh

POST_001: Silk and Cement

Example: Fashion designers increasingly use architectural models for inspiration (website "Form Follows Fashion" documents this co-absorption between creative arenas).[1]

What happens when we steal the forms of hardened worlds (stone and cement architecture) and place them in the domain of soft worlds (velvet, satin, silk cloth)? What happens when we take something meant for survival (the dwelling) and place it in the realm of luxury (the decorative object)?

POST_002: Equator Combat

Example: Afrofuturist fashion fuses science fiction, fantasy, and tribal cosmologies to project an alternative destiny of forms.[2]

It defies history itself, this reflective metallic visor in the desert regions of sand and intense heat. It blocks and casts the light of scorching suns back outward; it exiles the hostile materiality of this place to a reciprocal combat at the equator.

POST_003: Mood Silhouettes

Example: Designer Violet Zhou sews affective states—"angry, weighed-down, wounded, sinking, numb, emerging"—into her collection of silhouettes titled "Within" (2019).[3]

Will future fashion begin emulating the vague nature of human moods? What would it mean to actually wear the turbulence within as a bodily costume?

POST_004: Neo-Wonderland

Example: Tim Walker's "Wonderland" series (2010) shows models as fantastical characters draped across crystals, ladders, and immense white and pastel linens to evoke storybook scenes.[4]

The fairytale was always a space for experimental fashion, but what happens when we take these hyper-visual genres of the legend and plunge them into a futuristic prism? Do we arrive at a new appearance of the magical creature, and with it a new philosophy of fantasy?

POST_005: Future Seduction

Example: Designers of the film *Ghost in the Shell* (WETA Workshop, 2017) demonstrate the possibility of androids and cyborgs as attractive entities with porcelain-encrusted metallic façades.[5]

There is a recurring parallel between futuristic figures of seduction and those classical origins of cosmetology found in Egypt 5,000 years ago (with their curving black paint and antimony-based eyeliner): the robot is also a cosmetic force, wearing a made-up look of gentle invitation in order to entice others toward a certain world of desire.

POST_006: Ultra-Paleness

Example: Actress Tilda Swinton photographed for W Magazine in various "ethereal, hallucinatory" states while dusted in radical whiteness (clouded skin, fog-like hair, de-pigmentation).[6]

Will the extreme paleness of the alien, vampire, or ghost (always a forbidden desire in the old world) become a dominant model of beauty in the future? A vanishing into pure light itself.

POST_007: The Diva-Shaman

Example: Kiki Xue captures images of opera singers adorned with surrealistic crowns for Harper's Bazaar China (May 2016).[7]

What will happen in the coming ages to the elaborate headdresses of older societies worn by tribal chieftains, healers, and shamans? What does it mean to turn these items connected to power and animality into the fashion of futuristic theater?

POST_008: The Enveloped

Example: Alvaro Beamud Cortes places models in "voluminous gowns" of couture fashion that disproportionately subsume their bodies for Vogue Arabia (2019).[8]

Is the obsession of fashion with states of enfolding and enveloping a symbol of the future's own all-engulfing quality? Are we being encircled, blanketed, or submerged by the threads of an oncoming time?

POST_009: What the No One Wears

Example: Fashion designer brand Damascus Apparel, named for an ancient city in the midst of civil war, portrays futuristic strangers in hoods and cloaks.[9]

The hood has always been an accessory of the sacred world of humility (priests, monks, beggars) or of the dangerous world of those who choose anonymity and concealment for violent reasons (the bandit, the rogue, the assassin). Is the future leaning toward our becoming these someones who are actually no ones? Will we form an entire hooded universe that shields the face from ever being seen?

POST_010: Generational Fusions

Example: Model Albina Zavtur (Milan, Italy, 2021) combines futuristic space helmets with Victorian fashion and medieval peasant symbolism.[10]

Futurism includes the philosophical idea that perhaps we are born at the wrong time. It is therefore never clear to which generation we should have belonged and which era among thousands might have served one's ideal destiny in the world. This allows future fashion to inhabit time loops, cross-epochal styles, and generational hybrids of appearance.

POST-_011: Neo-Camouflage

Example: Mono Giraud creates sculptural clothing made of organic substances, blurring the world of the human, the thing, the object, and the earthly.[11]

If the future is to be consumed by violent uprisings and cataclysmic events, then perhaps fashion will begin to emulate the old techniques of war camouflage: to blend dress into natural forms (trees, desert, darkness) in order to avoid danger. Will we adorn ourselves with the look of inanimate things in order to sneak, elude, invade, or trample with greater efficiency?

POST_012: The Melting Outside

Example: Fashion lines like those of Iris Van Herpen manifest the impact of global warming visibly in a new clothing piece titled "Crystallization" (2013).[12]

Future fashion might increasingly imitate the ecological transformations happening in our era (melting glaciers, air pollution, geological erosion, rising sea levels, earthquakes, wildfires, tsunamis), turning us into emblems of the potential extinction of our race. This does not even include the unnatural, technological forms of disappearance that might wait in store for our species (nuclear disaster, manufactured viruses), which could also form new vogues. What does it mean that we can consciously design symbolic visions and costumes representing the end, but not intervene to stop its progression?

POST_013: The Forever Look

Example: For the film remake of *Dune* (2021), actor Stellan Skarsgard sat for over 80 hours in makeup sessions to perfect the look of the villain.[13]

In light of our epoch's obsession with speed, we might assume that future fashion would rush toward the instantaneous (i.e., the ability to switch appearances in a split second). But what if our concurrent desire for extreme transformation means that our molding processes will take longer and longer? Will our visual looks become so elaborate that they require excruciating stretches of time?

POST_014: Weaponized Face

Example: Taiwanese artist Yi-Fei Chen constructs brass gun that freezes her tears and fires them back as solid bullets at those who make her cry.[14]

The apparatus has always been tied to the destiny of fashion, even those of lethal dimensions. What if we cast ourselves in weaponries that could shoot our emotional states as violent trajectories into the world? The final triumph of the device: affixed to the skin as an instrument of extraction and projection.

POST_015: Android Envy

Example: Blog devotes itself to the phenomenon of "android chic" fashion.[15]

Envy and emulation often form the conceptual undercurrents of appearance-worlds. We often aspire to resemble those of higher status and mimic supposedly superior beings in our midst. But what if the android suddenly forms its own new aristocracy or is considered an elite evolutionary being? Would humans begin harboring jealousy for the wires, plates, and metallic sheets that form the robotic body?

POST_016: Endless Storm

Example: Designer Ann Van Galen envisions a future fashion based on translucent plastics to accommodate a "world with endless rainfall."[16]

What is the role of art, design, and fashion in adjusting their creative production toward the most drastic potential outcomes? If the future is to be understood as a downpour, is it the responsibility of these imaginative spheres to prepare us for such oncoming storms, hurricanes, cyclones, and floods?

POST_017: Salt Crystal Dress

Example: Visual artist Sigalit Landau submerges black dresses in the Dead Sea for extended periods, only for them to emerge with salt crystals attached.[17]

Immersing fabrics for many months in the ocean seems like a strange gesture of prolongation for a cultural moment obsessed with the shortening of time spans (accelerated existence). Like the aging of wines, liquors, obsolete technologies, or vintage items, will fashion also be plunged into stasis and then resurrected with all the other debris of passing eras?

POST_018: Future Nakedness

Example: Japanese artist Shinichi Maruyama manipulates relations of time and motion to produce an image of a nude dancer generated from over 10,000 individual stills.[18]

How will the future—with its promise of prosthetics, assemblages, and hybrids—alter our conceptualizations of nakedness? Since nudity was originally an idea linked to purity and totality, will new formulations of the naked body have to integrate complexities of the mixed, the partial, and the supplemental implant?

POST_019: Martial Animation

Example: Kung Fu martial artists shown in 3D animation slow-motion arrangement (short film sequence by Tobias Gremmler, 2016).[19]

What if ancient masters, craftsmen, performers, and artisans were commissioned to lend their traditional movements to a new timelapse-form of appearance? Could we design wearable pieces based on the frozen gestures (at once dynamic and nearly invisible) of these elder figures of motion?

POST_020: Weird Fashion

Example: Supreme WOW Prize at the 2019 World of WearableArt Awards given to "The Lady Warrior" by Indonesian designer Rinaldy A. Yunardi.[20]

The "weird" has been explored within literature, film, and visual art, but what does it mean in the sleeker contexts of fashion? Is it the sewing of holes where they do not belong, or the reversal of garments to be worn inside-out, or the disproportionate elongation of sleeves and heels to the point of the absurd? The weird is already something distinct here because it is not something discovered or defined but rather something coated onto the skin, something that clasps the most intimate level of the literal physical border between self and world.

POST_021: The Blank Ones

Example: Designer Sheguang Hu creates "world of emptiness" at China Fashion Week 2014.[21]

Is she a butterfly or is she the void, or more exactly the chrysalis that houses no metamorphosis but rather a vanishing? These ultra-smooth beings deprived of expression and encased in the empty space of wires or cylinders leading nowhere: Are they emissaries from a future in which no becomings are allowed, only blank dominoes?

POST_022: Dark Dance

Example: Article explores the rare connection between recent fashion items and the avant-garde Japanese dance tradition of Butoh.[22]

Fashion and dance share some aspects of common orchestration: both are tied to movement flows and to the visual zones of perception. But what if we apply a disturbing dance phenomenon—one that emerges in the aftermath of a nuclear bomb experience to showcase pale bodies writhing, twitching, scratching, shivering, and staring at their own limbs in awkward, excruciating disbelief? What if fashion followed this catastrophic return to the zero degree where we find ourselves rising from the primordial waters to behold our own bodies and movements in a state of terrified awe?

POST_023: Ultra-Color

Example: Moroccan-Belgian photographer Mous Lamrabat juxtaposes polychromatic fashion against strange natural backdrops and cultures of luxury.[23]

What color is the future? If a famed secret society of the twentieth century asked its philosophical members one evening, "What color is the sacred?" then we can ask this same descriptive thing of the eventual world. While countless futuristic films depict the next eras as either full of sanitized white buildings and sterile bleached clothes (utopia) or suspended in permanent midnight (dystopia), there are other genres where the future is linked to fluorescent and neon color schemes of artificially lit cities (e.g., cyberpunk). Color therefore faces a crucial threshold — either to be radically intensified or risk being drowned out for all time.

POST_024: Nocturnal Spectacles

Example: X-Presion Producciones (Madrid, Spain) presents portraits of women with futuristic monocles and spyglasses.[24]

To wear sunglasses at night or in closed quarters was always the domain of the incognito figure (the celebrity, the thief, or the spy). But now they are protective against harsh screens or surveillance lights, yet also a fashion statement that things are upside down. "Necessity" and "practicality" are no longer the prime laws by which our exteriors abide. Now we enhance ourselves with useless accessories and absurd items. Or do the sunglasses reflect something about a rising desire for secrecy in our age (to become a double agent)?

POST_025: Spinal Goggles

Example: Item labelled "Futuristic Armadilla Nautilus Goggles" (a handmade armor headpiece) are now on sale as a kind of cyber-eyewear.[25]

For thousands of years, various civilizations have adorned themselves with the furs, pelts, skins, and other features of the animal. They have stolen their physiological patterns (leopard prints, tortoise shell glasses, peacock feather hats). How will the accelerative tendencies of our time propel these practices forward, leading to new methods of animate-inanimate replication? What does it mean to forge nautilus goggles in the shape of an armadillo's spine?

POST_026: Stilt-Walkers

Example: Drama-oriented companies like Artrageous allow rental of stilt-walking performers for private events.[26]

Fashion has always experimented with varying elevations, angles, and geometries. Abnormal height was attained through the invention of the high heel; abnormal miniaturization was attained through the cruel cultural practice of foot-binding. But now we stare into the odd fashion of the stilt-walkers: those who conceal their artificial beam legs (wood, spring, plastic, or metal) in illuminated, descending circles while strolling across luxury galas. Is this projection of ourselves to new altitudes an attempt to escape (from or toward the future)?

LAB 12.0

Future Virtual

Chapter 12.0

Future Virtual Concepts: Immersion, Escape, Hyper-Reality

Lab Author: Ali Eslami

POST_001: False Mirror

Example: Opening description of False Mirror virtual reality project—Ali Eslami (2017–25)[1]

A long-term research project based in Virtual Reality. False Mirror is an open-ended, Interactive VR world that speculates a possible future where humans (or post-humans) live a completely virtual life. This world grows and reshapes itself over time, exploring radical forms of space, time, and bodies. What is immensely exciting about crafting new worlds is that, while it opens doors for new possibilities of experience and explores unknown territories, it also manifests a world that negates certain established perceptions and structures we take for granted in civilized life.

POST_002: Brain-Computer Interfaces

Example: Brain interfaces which are being deeply researched in the labs of tech/gaming companies like Valve will be a huge paradigm shift of how humans can interact and immerse in virtual worlds. This interview is truly alarming: namely, how fast it is being developed in action by a company like Valve who proved to take the greatest steps in these forms of technological breakthroughs (and the confidence of their labs).

One of the biggest entry barriers of Virtual Reality has always been the interface, which connects the user to the virtual world. Current interfaces are only using a fraction of how humans can channel information and senses back and forth to their surroundings. We are used to creating an experience of our world mainly through our eyes, while a BCI can directly transplant feelings, experiences, and so on. The human brain itself becomes the domain in which virtual experiences can be built and connected.[2]

POST_003: Lena-Virtual Being

Example: Lena (avatar from the False Mirror VR project).[3]

Lena is a fluid form of agency that can be associated with a ghost. Her physicality, navigation, and perception of time/space are lateral while leaning toward chaos. She controls natural forces, dynamics, and events in space(s), seeing as her inner worlds are constituted of nature-like landscapes. Lena subconsciously leaves fragments of her body in an organic manner. She has a strong connection with alien plants that she grows at her home.

Imagine living as Lena, leaving all your thoughts and emotions behind you as you walk in space through time. Can you paint the space with those fragments of yours?

POST_004: Unreal Engine

Example: The new generation of game engines, such as Unreal Engine 5 (available in the coming year), is a huge leap toward creating digital realities.[4]

A game engine is conceptually the core software necessary for a simulation program to properly run. Developers use game engines to construct games, virtual experiences, and simulations. They are the foundation on which virtual and extended realities are built. The use-case of game engines is not limited only to games but expands to fields like architecture, film production and VFX, scientific research, product design, VR/AR, and much more.

What Unreal Engine 5 teased is a new technology that can drive almost infinite detail inside games, with highly realistic lighting and rendering solutions that's been a huge mystery in computer graphics to be solved. Imagining a vast, open virtual world with infinite levels of detail is not too far from our reach anymore.

POST_005: Omniverse—BMW X NVIDIA (Future of Factories)

Example: Explore the next era of manufacturing. BMW Group's factory of the future—designed, simulated, operated, and maintained entirely in NVIDIA Omniverse.[5]

Global teams can collaborate across geographies, software tools, and datasets to design and plan the factory in real-time. Digital human simulations test new workflows for employee ergonomics and efficiency. And robots are trained, operated, and orchestrated using this technology. The virtual factory, simulated end-to-end within Omniverse, is physically accurate and obeys the laws of physics—a perfect digital twin of the factory in reality.

This is a glimpse of how the virtual is merging with the real world in a very pragmatic way. Digital twins will bring a whole new paradigm in the way humans will work in the future. One could run a whole factory run by robots on Mars while sitting in their home.

POST_006: Future Computer Interface

Example: Facebook Reality Lab is a high-end technology lab researching Virtual and Augmented Reality.[6]

They have revealed the prototype of a new interface method using the wrist that can track all finger and hand movements of the user. Additionally, by using haptic technology, every touch of virtual objects feels more tactile and tangible due to the dynamic vibration system inside the wrist.

POST_007: Infinite Objects

Example: Bastiaan Hooimeijer (Naam), a VR Artist and developer, is currently working on a project called "A Piece of the Universe."[7]

In this experimental project, he creates many interesting virtual objects with mind-bending qualities. One example is this infinite drawer, a simple drawer with a handle that can swipe forever and withhold infinite objects within it.

What is striking about virtual worlds of the future is how they implement and engage with the concept of infinity. While still being bound to computational constraints and limits, one can easily portray the illusion of infinity.

POST_008: AI-Enhanced Realities

Example: Intel Labs, a research hub for the tech company of the same name, has created a new process for enhancing images—and it showed it off using Grand Theft Auto 5. The process converts the standard footage from the game into nearly photorealistic images using a very complicated procedure that involves an AI.[8]

One of the implications of AI in the future of virtual fields would be to fill in the gaps of simulations. This means that one can even revisit old creations, such as a game made in the 1990s, and transform them into a photoreal simulation through this real-time AI processing of the images frame by frame as they are being played through.

POST_009: Notes on Blindness

Example: In 1983, after decades of steady deterioration, John Hull became totally blind. To help him make sense of the upheaval in his life, he began documenting his experiences on audio cassette. These original diary recordings form the basis of this interactive non-fiction narrative using new forms of storytelling to explore a cognitive and emotional experience of blindness.[9]

This experience is one of the most memorable VR projects that I have tried—using the impactful potential of virtual reality to bring to life the memories of a blind person. This implies how memories can be relived and form an immersive world of their own through simulation. The fact that everyone with a VR headset can relive John Hull's memories through this simulation provokes several interesting questions about the future applications for human memory.

POST_010: Winds and Leaves

Example: "Winds & Leaves" is a flora-builder game coming to PS VR on July 27th, 2021.[10]

Stranded in a barren landscape, you are the only being capable of mastering the ancient art of growing vegetation. Journey across the steppe to gather ancient dormant varieties. Learn to read the signs of the various climates, awaken old landmarks, and grow your own forests in this VR flora-builder.

This VR game offers an amazing mechanism in this reality, where the user becomes bound to the forest growing around them. An interesting example of how Virtual Worlds can allow the player to embody an environment, a biome, and get attached to a radically different form of existence. How would it be if one could become a growing city?! To what extent can we merge into each other through our extensive virtual bodies?!

POST_011: Dreams -Sandbox Virtual Worlds

Example: Dreams is an extraordinary, ever-expanding game universe from the award-winning Media Molecule, creators of LittleBigPlanet and Tearaway, where you can discover community-made games from around the world . . . and learn to make your own.[11]

Whether you want to create games, music, paintings, animation, sculpture, movies, or anything in between, Dreams is an extraordinary digital playground where anything is possible.

Dreams is a great example of the future of mainstream virtual world building. It is a toolkit that is accessible and easy to use, with a modular design that allows anyone to create their own dream worlds/games and share them.

POST_012: Advertisements in VR

Example: Yesterday, Facebook took a leap many people have been predicting for years: it started putting ads inside virtual reality. The company launched a limited test of advertisements inside three Oculus Quest apps, saying it would expand the system based on user feedback. The move is a turning point for

Oculus, bringing one of Facebook's most controversial features into a medium that inspires both idealism and alarm.[12]

Virtual worlds are a new ground for capitalist tech corporations to own. This news, although not surprising coming from a company like Facebook, is alarming in how the future of VR can be occupied by ads.

A VR experience that we might consider now an escape from the real world of commercial ideologies is quite possible to be transformed into a Times Square nuisance. One might have to pay a monthly fee to disable ads in the virtual world experiences?!

POST_013: Remote Work from VR

Example: It looks like a well-integrated autonomous mechanical worker, but that is something of an illusion. This robot does not have a mind of its own. Several miles away, a human worker is controlling its every movement remotely and watching via a virtual reality (VR) headset that provides a robot's eye view.[13]

The Covid-19 pandemic challenged the format in which we work toward a more remote approach. While this example could seem quite sci-fi two years ago, it is intriguing that it is now being used as a form of remote work.

The human worker embodies a robot to perform the tasks they would do in a normal shop physically from home. One question one could ask in the future about robots is, are they being controlled in real time by a human? or AI?! or something in between?!

POST_014: Full Body Haptics

Example: Teslasuit is a human-to-digital interface designed to simulate experience and accelerate mastery in the physical world. The integrated complex of haptics, motion capture, and biometry provides improved human performance.[14]

Initially intended as an entertainment and gaming platform, Teslasuit has transformed into a powerful tool in XR training. Still early in development, haptic technology will play an important role in the future of XR and interfaces. Aside from boosting immersion and giving new senses to virtual experiences, it can be a powerful tool for training. An AI assistant can teach you which muscles you should engage for learning certain physical skills.

POST_015: Hand Physics Lab

Example: Artist and developer, Dennys Kuhnert has been making phenomenal VR hand-tracking interfaces through his experimental project titled Holonautic. Through various experiences, users can interact with a handful of physics-based puzzles and interfaces. From seeing your own hands mirrored or extended in third person to highly accurate Jenga placements with your fingers.[15]

What is fascinating about such ventures is specifically the experimentation with new tactical and tangible interfaces in VR. These perceptual modulations combined with haptic technology can eventually provide the ultimate tangibility of virtual interfaces. By emphasizing the tactile feeling of using digital interfaces (i.e., a spatial operating system), one wonders how we might feel and adapt as humans over time by using an interface that is now far sensorially elaborate.

POST_016: Reverse Passthrough

Example: Facebook's reality lab showcased an unusual experiment last week. Reverse passthrough essentially shows a render of the VR user's eyes on 3D displays at the front of the headset. The idea is to reduce the effect of VR users shutting off from people in the real world when they pull a device over their face.[16]

At first, I was a bit surprised by this unusual and niche experiment, though I then realized that VR technology has been focusing mainly, if not completely on the inside-out experience of the user, positioning the wearer at the center of the product design. While this is a somewhat overlooked aspect—how the wearer looks from the outside—knowing Facebook's long-term investment in making VR/AR a "social" platform, these inversions and conversions are part of how to make sense of the next order of things.

Aleksandr Popov (2017).

LAB 13.0

Future Violence

Chapter 13.0

Future Violence Lab

Concepts: Decay, Terror, Poison

Lab Author: Reza Negarestani

POST_001: Euphoria/Dysphoria

Example: *The Book of Poisons* by Ibn Wahshiyya of the ninth century reveals one of the earliest texts on exotic toxicity, whose side effects and symptoms are perhaps their own forms of futural experience.[1]

In the medieval *Book of Poisons*, we come across the entry on اقونیطون -- Aconitum ferox or "Devil's Helmet," known in India and Persia by the name *Bish/Bikh* or "the long dark sleep,", and known to Greeks as "the queen of all poisons." The scarce information on Bish makes it even more sinister when you read that among certain tantric cults, it was considered the ultimate gateway to euphoria by way of extreme dysphoria and the horrors of both flesh and psyche. Essentially, Bish is the last drug or key for the initiation to that feeling of being fully content in the universe (called Ananda in Sanskrit and Reza in Arabic). Its trick is simple: consume much horror and unease (through the worst conceivable nightmares); if you survive, every other calamity that might befall you no longer has any meaning. You have conquered displeasure by rendering it meaningless in the broadest sense, a principle to keep in mind for the future.

LAB 14.0

Future Mysticism

Chapter 14.0
Future Mysticism Lab
Concepts: Ritual, Sacrifice, Eternity
Lab Author: Andrea Cetrulo

POST_001: Glass Tower Mystics

Example: Increasingly across the world, there is a new phenomenon wherein groups of office workers and bankers congregate on glass tower rooftops to practice their own forms of mysticism (yoga, meditation, mindfulness) and get back to business straight after. Sometimes they even feature mainstream DJs to musicalize their contortions.[1]

Is the seventy-second floor of a London skyscraper closer to heaven? What does the renewed interest in mystical practices tell us about future civilizations? Guided meditation sessions on glass tower rooftops; bodies contorting to the beat of clinical electronic music; the ancient smells of Aloeswood and Palo Santo extracted from foreign lands, pre-packaged in glossy cellophane, waiting to inebriate. Why does seeking the invisible, the immaterial, appeal to contemporary part-time mystics? Does the faith in the remedial powers of "mindfulness" mirror the psycho-pathological distortions of our time, signaling the collapse of a civilization?

POST_002: Trance of the Sea Goddess

Example: Every February 2nd, the Atlantic shores of Brazil and neighboring Uruguay recede, announcing the return of Yemanja, goddess and mother of the sea, who traveled with the Yorubas of West Africa to the Americas, accompanying them on involuntary displacements across the ocean. The syncretic deity, partly fish, partly human, mestiza in appearance, is an archetype that resists becoming ossified by way of fluidity, of water, and of undulating dance moves that press against the waves. She embodies a futuristic sense of identity that is being constantly renewed and germinated, refuting any rooted historical accounts of culture.[2]

Iaõs, the shamans of the Orishas religion (often homosexual men and elderly women), welcome her through performing ritualistic possessions, entering contagious states of trance and delirium: the audience is transfixed too. The swirling figures enveloped in sinuous white robes consume liquors to the sound of incessant drums, inviting anyone who dares witness the spectacle and enter Yemanja's realm of nocturnal secrecy. Yet when daylight comes and the tide is back, those spectators who have offered her their most precious possessions realize that the promise has not been fulfilled and that her secret remains a secret.

POST_003: Sufi Sea Burials

Example: Moad Musbahi's research investigates Sidi Ahmad Shashkal, a seaside Sufi tomb in Morocco as an illustration of migration as a social practice, suspending traditional categorizations of cultural heritage and speculating on how the past might be mobilized against the slow erasure of the future.[3]

Water is a vehicle for movement. It temporarily (or permanently) disfigures and transfigures anything that passes it. Seas have hosted migrational projects and carried the imagination of past and future movements with it. Liquidity, confusion, chaos. Among its powers is that of challenging, and often completely eroding our attempts at cementing sedentary architectures in space and in memory, reminding us that nature does not want us.

The erosion of Sufi tombs on the coast of North Africa exemplifies this: Atlantic currents sway the saintly bodies buried in these holy places into the murky depths of time. Here, the dissolution of material—the tomb, the body—does not signify a loss of function, given that its capacity relies on performativity and a living tradition of growth rather than on the solidification of the statue or idol.

POST_004: Slaves of the Saints

Example: Femme fatale, vamp, Pomba Gira is an incarnation of the devil appearing in a variety of disguises: Lady of the Cemetery; Lady of the Crossroads; Queen of Trash; female partner in crime of her male counterpart, Exu, God of the Yoruba underworld. Pomba Gira is a pharmakon: simultaneously healing and destructive. She challenges and subverts diurnal hierarchies occupied by men, posing a constant threat to formal order with her anarchic multiplicity and elusive demeanor.[4]

Pomba Gira is associated with the evil spirits or Yoruba demons called Esus (Exus in Brazil), spirits of the shadows. A Dama da Noite or Mistress of the Night, Pomba Gira is a daemonic figure venerated in Brazil by the subterranean factions of the Quimbanda and Umbanda religions. She is a holy harlot, mercurial, capricious, and amoral. Her specialty is that of granting love wishes in exchange for sensuous gifts such as cigarettes, liquors, perfumes, and the worshipers' bodies by way of possession. Once a devotee has made allegiance with her, she must renounce her social persona, her role as friend, mother, and wife, in order to commit entirely to Pomba Gira. Following her invitation, she immediately becomes a slave to the saint. In exchange, A Dama da Noite, always summoned after dark, promises to grant her the most unspeakable wishes and desires.

She is the abject, the impure, the tainted: mestizo, hybrid, chimera. She embodies true syncretism and champions the unknown, the shifting and the unclassifiable, the monstrous, transvestism, and the dark forces of women.

POST_005: The Rapper

Example: Povo da Rua (people of the street) is a Portuguese term used to designate the archetypes that inhabit the city streets after dark: the rascal, the gambler, the hustler, the gangster, the con man, the prostitute. Such is the rapper.

It is by chanting about his nocturnal operations that the rapper establishes an existential relationship with the future, divorcing himself from the political correctness of present mainstream debates, not responding to codes of bourgeois propriety. Through creating eerie moods and operating in illicit terms, the rapper demarcates a territory of otherness and neatly defines the enemy, escaping the dictates of daytime discourses by speaking the unspeakable and producing a subaltern narrative where he exceeds his assigned daytime correspondence as mere scapegoat (the scapegoat being the one who is sent into the wilderness carrying the sins of the community). Naming an enemy by his name only confirms the fact that having an enemy can make us stronger.

Similarly, chants invoking deceased friends (or lost idols) refute normative conventions of reality, establishing that we are either dead or alive and cannot be simultaneously dead and alive. To live becomes an adventure that commences and potentially ends every night; the ecstatic joy of (still) being alive heightens and morphs the meaning of time. The nihilistic as purely vitalistic. It is not only the words but the moods it conveys. Against the backdrop of a nocturnal glistening cityscape, rappers appear to us as pagan idols in a pantheon channeled through our screens: virtual images integrating smoke, neon lights, silhouettes, masks, conspicuous consumption, and representations of artificial paradises equally inducing states of oblivion and alertness.

LAB 15.0

Future Prophecy

Chapter 15.0

Future Prophecy Lab

Concepts: Speculation, Question, Return

Lab Author: Anna Longo

POST_001: Introduction

What is a prophecy? What is the difference between a prophecy and a scientific prediction? What kind of knowledge of the future is a prophetic vision? Is the art of prophecy lost today? Who are the modern prophets? Can we prophesize the return of the prophetic as a way of calling for a new way of thinking about the future?

This lab is a journey back and forth in time to explore the ancient and modern art of prophesying. It tells the story of how prophecies have been traveling in time through the multiple events of their supposed fulfillment. It presents past and present prophets to prophesize about future prophetic figures and their role in society. It proposes a transdisciplinary journey showing how this overlooked art has been fundamental in shaping many cultural fields such as philosophy, literature, and even economics or science. It will help you tell real and fake prophets apart, and it will invite you to become the prophet that the future needs. This lab is my oracle, a dissemination of dots to be connected to reveal your mission in bringing about the future.

POST_002: The Prophets I

Example: In Century 9, Quatrain 95, Nostradamus is said to have predicted the rise of super-soldiers and the armies of tomorrow:

"The newly made one will lead the army, almost cut off up to near the bank: Help from the Milanais elite straining, the Duke deprived of his eyes in Milan in an iron cage."[1]

Nostradamus (1503–66) is a French mystic who wrote a book of catastrophic prophecies, some of which are supposed to have been fulfilled already, while many others might be fulfilled in the future. The poetic and ambiguous verses are open to the reader's interpretation and can easily apply retrospectively to most of the disasters one can witness in life. The power of prophecies is not in their truth, but in the capacity of making us experience any present as the revelation of destiny. Now is the future that was meant to be, the spectacle that has been prepared for so long.[2]

POST_003: The Prophets II

Example: In Century 8, Quatrain 59, Nostradamus made references to a conflict between the West and the East that might be the Third World War:

"Twice put up and twice cast down, the East will also weaken the West. Its adversary after several battles chased by sea will fail at time of need."[3]

Contrary to scientific predictions, prophecies are produced according to special techniques that are meant to find in the present the seeds that grow as vague visions of the future in the medium's mind. Nostradamus probably practiced bibliomancy, the art of finding in old books the passages that can orient one into the future. Unlike scientific predictions that become rapidly obsolete, prophecies and books do not lose their value as time passes by.[4]

POST_004: Philosophy

Example: During the trial reported in Plato's *Apology*, Socrates refers to an oracle allegedly received by his friend Chaerephon at Delphi many years earlier, speaking of his unparalleled wisdom.

This is how prophecies work: they do not tell the truth but what one needs to hear to engage with their destiny. It comes as no surprise that the motto at the entrance of the temple in Delphi stated: "Know Thyself." This is the prophecy that Socrates fulfilled for himself and for the people he questioned by making them realize that they were not so wise after all. As future philosophers, what would the oracle tell us?

POST_005: Economics and Finance

Example: In his paper "Self-Fulfilling Prophecy" (1948), Robert Merton introduces W.I. Thomas's theorem: "If men define situations as real, they are real in their consequences." The economist shows how it applies to the bank failures on what is remembered as Black Wednesday (1932). By telling the story of Millingville, the Director of the National Bank at that time, Merton explains how rumors about negative future events can bring them about for real:

"Cartwright Millingville had never heard of the Thomas theorem. But he had no difficulty in recognizing its workings. He knew that, despite the comparative liquidity of the bank's assets, a rumor of insolvency, once believed by enough depositors, would result in the insolvency of the bank."[5]

In contemporary financial markets, there are many examples of self-fulfilling prophecies, such as speculative bubbles and their sudden explosions. When investors are persuaded that prices will go up, they behave in such a way that the prediction turns out to be true. This holds until opposite rumors start spreading by provoking instantaneous falls. However, despite their name, such phenomena share nothing with prophetic oracles, and they can be easily explained as the effect of imitation among gambling strategies.[6]

POST_006: Ancient Prophecies (Aztecs I)

Example: When the Aztec King Moctezuma II was crowned, the astrologer Nezahualcoyotl gave detailed warnings of a new astrological age.[7]

One of the omens was a famine that actually developed in 1507. Then an earthquake occurred after the "Lighting of the New Age" ceremony inaugurated by Moctezuma II. Finally, in 1518, a comet was observed with three heads and sparks shooting from its tail, seen flying eastward (today it is said to be Halley's Comet). This phenomenon appeared for forty nights. A short time later, Cortes invaded Mexico and destroyed the Aztec civilization.

Did Nezahualcoyotl really prophesize the end of Moctezuma's empire? Were the omens real warnings of the impending catastrophe? If the Aztecs probably justified their destiny as the will of the gods, Spanish Christian conquerors turned the prophecy to their own advantage (more to come . . .).

POST_007: Ancient Prophecies (Aztecs II)

Example: The Aztecs called their era the time of the fifth sun—there had been four previous versions of the earth, each ruled by different gods.[8]

Quetzalcoatl, the feathered serpent, ruled over this era and was supposed to come back at its end. According to the Aztec calendar, Moctezuma II's kingdom was the last before the return of Quetzalcoatl, and omens had been announcing the coming end of the world. While considering the Aztecs superstitious, Spanish conquerors saw in the myth the reason for the defeat of the pagans. Their version of the story is that Moctezuma mistook Cortez for the returning God, such that the Aztecs welcomed their enemies and provoked their own ruin. The prophecy was then fulfilled not because it was true but because false beliefs led to perdition.

However, do the conquerors' rational interpretation of the fulfillment of the prophecy actually prove the myth to be false? Weren't the Christians believing in the prophecy of the triumph of their own truth?

POST_008: Omen (Halley's Comet, I)

Example: Below is a quote from Mark Twain's autobiography. The writer was born on November 30, 1835—two weeks after Halley's Comet perihelion. Surprisingly, he died on April 21, 1910, the day following the comet's subsequent perihelion:

I came in with Halley's Comet in 1835. It is coming again next year, and I expect to go out with it. It will be the greatest disappointment of my life if I don't go out with Halley's comet. The Almighty has said, no doubt: "Now here are these two unaccountable freaks; they came in together, they must go out together."[9]

The periodic passage of Halley's Comet has been seen as a prophetic sign since the beginning of the history of humanity (more to come . . .).

POST_009: Omen (Halley's Comet, II)

Halley's Comet is visible from Earth every 75–79 years and, since the first historical records, it has been considered a sign announcing peculiar events.[10]

For instance, the apparition of 87 BC was recorded in Babylonian tablets which state that the comet was seen "day beyond day" for a month. This appearance may be recalled in the representation of Tigranes the Great, an Armenian king who heralded the New Era of the brilliant King of Kings. As everybody knows, the comet has been seen as the sign of the birth of Jesus (are Christians less superstitious than the Aztecs?). In 1066, it was observed in England and considered to announce the death of King Harold II at the Battle of Hastings, after which William the Conqueror claimed the throne. In 1456, the year of Halley's next apparition, the Ottoman Empire invaded the Kingdom of Hungary, culminating in the siege of Belgrade in July of that year. In 1910, the passage of the comet burst across the Xinhai Revolution in China that would end the last dynasty in 1911. People believed that it indicated calamity such as war, fire, pestilence, and a change of dynasty.

Halley's Comet will be back on July 28, 2061: What's your prophecy?

POST_010: Cassandra, or Nobody Is a Prophet in Their Own Land

Example: Cassandra was a Trojan priestess of Apollo in Greek mythology cursed to utter true prophecies but never to be believed:

> Have I missed the mark, or, like a true archer, do I strike my quarry? Or am I a prophet of lies, a babbler from door to door?[11]

She foresaw the destruction of Troy. She warned the Trojans about the Greeks hiding inside the Trojan Horse, Agamemnon's death, her own demise at the hands of Aegisthus and Clytemnestra, her mother Hecuba's fate, Odysseus's ten-year wanderings before returning home, and the murder of Aegisthus and Clytemnestra by the latter's children Electra and Orestes. Cassandra predicted that her cousin Aeneas would escape during the fall of Troy and found a new nation in Rome. However, her warnings were all disregarded, and she was considered a poor madwoman.

Real prophecies are usually overlooked when they are announced since the scenarios seem not only unlikely but contradict general expectations. A tip: to tell prophets and predictors apart, consider their present influence. While prophets announce the unbelievable and do not provide any reason for people to believe, predictors strive to persuade the largest number of people. While foresight is a curse, persuasion is a rewarding technique.

POST_011: Science Fiction: Prophecy or Prediction?

Example: Consider the following amazing predictions by Jules Verne in *From Earth to the Moon* that came to pass: The United States would launch the first manned vehicle to go to the moon.[12]

The shape and size of the vehicle would closely resemble the Apollo command/service module spacecraft. The number of men in the crew would be three. A competition for the launch site would ensue between Florida and Texas, which was resolved in Congress in the 1960s with KSC as the Florida launch site and Houston, Texas, as the Mission Control Center. A telescope would be able to view the progress of the journey. When Apollo 13 exploded, a telescope at Johnson Space Center witnessed the event, which happened more than 200,000 miles from Earth. The Verne spacecraft would use retro-rockets, which became a technology assisting Neil Armstrong and his crewmates in their journey to the Moon. Verne even predicted weightlessness, although his concept was slightly flawed in its thinking as it was only experienced at the gravitational midpoint of the journey (when the Moon's and Earth's gravity balanced).

The first men to journey to the Moon would return to Earth and splash down in the Pacific Ocean just where Apollo 11 splashed down in July of 1969. Was Verne a prophet? Or was he just very good at predicting the development of technology?

POST_012: The Oracle in the Matrix

Example: Excerpted dialogue from The Matrix (1999):

> Oracle: Candy?
>
> Neo: Do you already know if I'm going to take it?
>
> Oracle: Wouldn't be much of an oracle if I didn't.
>
> Neo: But if you already know, how could I make a choice?
>
> Oracle: Because you didn't come here to make the choice. You've already made it. You're here to try to understand why you made it.[13]

As is evident from the inscription over the Oracle's door, "Know Thyself," the directors adapted their Oracle from the mythical Oracle at Delphi, who, according to legend, once declared Socrates the wisest man in the land. Like Socrates,

Neo is aware of his own ignorance. However, since the Architect revealed the Oracle to be "a program designed to investigate the human psyche," her power of foresight is probably not a foresight based on knowledge of a predetermined future but rather a calculation. This becomes clear in the films when the Oracle's power cannot be used to predict Neo's behavior (who possesses free will). If machines are excellent at making predictions, they should not be confused with prophets.

POST_013: Prophetic Literature: Kahlil Gibran

Example: *The Prophet*, by the Lebanese-American author Kahlil Gibran, is the best-selling poetry book of the twentieth century, despite literary critics having overlooked it.

> No man can reveal to you aught but that which already lies half asleep in the dawning of your knowledge. The teacher who walks in the shadow of the temple, among his followers, gives not of his wisdom but rather of his faith and his lovingness. If he is indeed wise, he does not bid you enter the house of his wisdom, but rather leads you to the threshold of your own mind.[14]

The book is made up of twenty-six poems told by Al Mustapha, a wise man who is about to set sail for his homeland after twelve years in exile on a fictional island when the people of the island ask him to share his insights into the great questions of life. The Beatles, Elvis Presley, John F. Kennedy, and Indira Gandhi are among those who have been inspired by its words.

Kahlil Gibran does not reveal the future, and his prophet does not master divinatory techniques. However, the book, which is meant to give hope and strength to appreciate life, can itself be considered a prophecy. It has been able to bring people inspiration by constructing the literary simulation of a prophet calling for spiritual value and existential wisdom.[15]

POST_014: Contemporary Prophets: Osho

Example: The following is a prophetic passage by Rajneesh, also known as Osho, a very controversial contemporary guru.

Now we are again coming to a point where a total destruction will happen. But a flower will be left and that will do, and again the whole story begins from ABC. Many times it has happened. This is not the first world that we are living in: many worlds have come and disappeared, many civilizations have come and disappeared. Many civilizations have reached the same peak of affluence, technology, knowhow. History is a repetition.[16]

Osho was an Indian professor of philosophy. He was a popular speaker and excellent in communication; though by the late twentieth century, he had become a guru and a teacher of meditation. Osho's discourses dealt with the importance of ridding your mind of rigid beliefs and age-old religious traditions, and he spoke about being consciously aware of life through meditation, love, and humor. Osho believed that the history of civilization is repeating itself. Previous societies disappeared when they reached the level of technological development that we are experiencing today: we are getting closer to the limit, and the world will be regenerated soon.

Patrick Perkins (2020).

LAB 16.0

Future X

Chapter 16.0

Future X Lab

Concepts: ?

Federico Nieto [Posts 1–12];
Sasha Shestakova [13–16];
Anna Engelhardt [17–19]

POST_001: Species Hunters

Example: The engineering company Boston Dynamics, with the funding of DARPA, has developed various prototypes for what is now known as the quadrupled military robot with designs that assimilate species found in the natural world (the rapid Cheetah, the heavy BigDog, the insectoid RiSE). The wider public has yet to see them in action.[1]

Can they smell you? Cold panic has transfigured these narrow alleys into labyrinths. You have fled through the dawn and now every step feels like the weight of lead, every vessel inside your temples has turned into a compass, a rhythm. The dry thumps of your boots get absorbed by the thickness of the hollow city walls, but the machinic clatter gets to you and slices through your skull. They are here. It is useless to stay on the run. You know this ancient game very well: hunter and hunted. But there is a clear disadvantage when this game gets mapped out in the future; no sense of smell is needed. You also know this is the end of the labyrinth (your labyrinth) and you have reached a wall. Freezing sweat drops. Fresh prey. The insidious army is here; their hexagonal red eyes sharpen the contour of the metallic jaws that will soon feast on your muted trills.

POST_002: Silhouettes of the Border

Example: Long Range Acoustic Devices (LRAD), otherwise known as sound cannons, are being used by police officers in Greece to stop the crossing of Turkish migrants into the European Union. These devices are used as weapons that emit painful sound frequencies to neuter unwanted territorial infiltrations.[2]

As for their faces, sometimes they had to wrap them inside their coats. Sometimes the hand tapped nervously inside the dark underside of the left pocket. Other times they slipped inside the protuberance on the right shoulder. One time they were demanded to strip bare. "This is missing three holographic seals and a blood-proof." Once again deported. But in the time of Future Control there are no longer visas, authenticity scans, or even deportations. Unannounced sound waves hit the bodies. Faces remain quiet and wrapped inside the coats: no more nervous trembling, no more suspicions. Just silent silhouettes strewn across the fields.

POST_003: The Map and the Territory

Example: A large plot of land has been bought off in the US state of Nevada by cryptocurrency millionaire Jeffrey Berns, head of the software company Blockchains. Berns plans to build an independent city that uses cryptocurrency as its main financial asset.[3]

The map and the territory are about to be transformed. The boundaries of the commensurable are now drafted from the incommensurable as virtual city planners model the blueprint for their facsimile world using the shards of the one they want to leave behind: no state intervention flourishes in the manufactured environment. An education sector product of homogenous urban planning, a digital currency standard, and massive consumer centers, all entrapped. As an accessory, the living map will also have its own corporate demiurge to make the complacent inhabitants of this mock-up "utopia" feel minified.

POST_004: Inheritors

Example: A group of hackers in Ukraine was recently captured by police after the slow spread of Clop ransomware, a malignant program that encrypts personal files and demands a monetary ransom that must be answered if one wants to rescue these files from permanent deletion.[4]

Digital whispers used to collude under a single name: the Lords of Doom. Panic and awe entangled in the fast typing that precedes catastrophic scams, worldwide service and economic crashes, and the smooth engineering of software that ransomed private data extracted from military and governmental platforms. In the present, those whispers have disintegrated into thin air as the inheritors of Doom have been terminated by the era of anti-security breaching. Nevertheless, Clop ransomware recently simulated these past terrors within the yawning passivity of platform capitalism before being prematurely stifled to death. With this, one can only wish for the true inheritors of Doom to follow the lead.

POST_005: Mental Health Design

Example: Alfred Health is a prize-winning AI assistant set out to tailor mental health treatments using deep learning.[5]

As the psychoanalytical divan gets discarded into the shadows, we delve further and further into standardized practices that treat mental pathologies within new thresholds of impersonality. The cold dismissal of therapist/patient relationships now proudly sports the coruscating seal of approval stipulated by the pharmaceutical industry. Algorithmic avatars will now take the lead by designing pharmacological treatments that decompress big data to respond to the massive mental health crisis and the proliferation of trauma as an aftertaste of the global pandemic. A selfless, clinical defusing hums at the comfort of your screen.

POST_006: Chimerical Design

Example: Biologists and engineers are currently working on the future implementation of a computer-aided program (CAD) with the aim of modifying and designing new organisms.[6]

If you could deftly twist the constituent data of nature to produce the new, would you do it? Nature design has acquired new depths of enhancement by utilizing a myriad of augmented digital platforms and visualizers presently at hand. What hitherto had daunted human imagination under the name of the chimera as the demonic outcome of a forceful modification of nature has been anchored into reality. As we become further enraptured by the prospects of god-building, we'll limitlessly modify the organic platforms surrounding us into unsung inorganic shapes, a profane block-building of the topologies at hand warped into the yet-unknown.

POST_007: Seclusion Profiteers

Example: Alarming suicide rates in Japan through 2020 and early 2021 have worried the West with the mirroring of the unavoidable emotional taxing of loneliness and overwork during the times of the pandemic.[7]

Loneliness is profitable. Assorted factors including the fallout of traditional familial bonds, an increasing mental health epidemic, and forced isolations likely extending beyond our current time window along the looming forecast of our extinction leave us to face the time of our demise in seclusion. The phenomenon known in Japan as *kodokushi* or "lonely death" brought unimaginable profit to a nascent cleanup industry that specialized in purging the physical sequels left behind by those belonging to a not-so-small sector of forsaken individuals. For now, a caustic question: Will the profit embedded in this specialized cleanup sector extend worldwide in the oncoming years?

POST_008: Box Inhabitants

Example: Prefabricated homes that are unfolded and set up in a very short time are becoming all the rage as they gain notoriety in the hands of the company named Boxabl.[8]

Automated Prometheanism dusts off like old news as it gets patrolled off from the affluent vicinity of automated precarity. This is the catch: prefabricated living blocks for saturated spaces. In a matter of years, our not-so-distant relatives will submissively squander their meek vitality enclosed within the cereal grey solid blocks of prefab structures that are set in a question of minutes. The future of real estate will leech upon the new gains that the administration of living space promises, while at the same time reaching its summit when excising all virtual control on its future consumers via enclosure and chanceless catalogues for untarnished human abdication.

POST_009: Alien Differentiation

Example: A team of biologists at Tufts University has made it possible for embryonic frog cells to assemble by themselves onto new organisms. These cells have been baptized Xenobots.[9]

Disembodied organic projectiles lag, hum, and clip along the smoky green lens wired to the precise augmented reality monitors mirroring the microscope camera. This fuzzy and yet unformed compound slides away from the grounding it was extracted from (living tissue, breathing limbs, carnal disassembly) onto the vigilant eye of the engineers cautiously informing on the unprecedented mutant vector taking shape before their own eyes. Following the game of perversity, what lies before us is matter that pumps into self-determination from the ground up while altogether breaking the golden polish that underlines the unbreakable testament of type and species: an event uncannily echoing an obscure principle of differential cruelty. This being that, between an undifferentiated abyss and the calm determination of clearly distinguishable and representable types lies an irruptive third instance: that which uses the smooth ground or surface of a type/species to twist it toward monstrous anomaly. This bastardized third instance has now been engineered into our existence, no longer a virtual delirium to be found inside the mobile circularity of a dense ontological treatise.

POST_010: Ludic Intellect

Example: The team at DeepMind is currently researching the outcomes of stimulating veteran algorithms when interacting with a toy model simulation under the name of XLand. XLand has been designed to explicitly refine AI competencies by taking part in an array of ludic scenarios.[10]

Until now, genuine ludics have either been shunned or largely falsified when purveying the horizon of the cognitive modeling of human intellect. For every despotic pedagogical deformation seeking to truncate any underlying potentialities, at every turn we find fine-tuned defenses against play/game/risk. There is a sense of irony in the unbinding of ludics when experimenting with non-human intelligence: in the game of synthetic self-awareness, whatever has been repressed in ludics is now a fundamental ferment for the development of artificial agents that are made to interact with toy models in order to develop their own autonomy.

POST_011: Bruised Robots

Example: Engineers have developed an artificial skin that shows its colors to make an analogy when it is hit or damaged.[11]

You can't make robots feel, but now you can bruise them. There will be lengthy research efforts until robotics and AI can fully implement a functional simulation of the nerve and neurotransmitter infrastructure that is analogous, but not on a one-to-one scale, to the human model. In the meantime, we shuffle in the mirroring game to lacerate the simulacra. Considering that our intellect feeds on inflicting looping episodes of viciousness on our own kin, these episodes now scathingly expand beyond our very narrow horizons. In the not-so-distant future, we can bruise, maim, gash, and carve without repercussion. The robot is now red, now purple, now black, but it " . . . has no mouth and it cannot scream."

POST_012: Black Ice

Example: In lieu of slow progress in Artificial Intelligence, quantum computation seems to be a promising research field. The problem is that quantum computation only works at temperatures such as 100 millikelvin, or −273.05°C.[12]

"Cold rationalism" sullenly defaces contemporary physics and engineering.[13] If we, as self-regulating organisms, depend on the mechanical warmth of organic life to build our social-cognitive functions with precision, a parallel intelligence lurks within the order of severe counterfactual conditions that dramatically halt any mechanical warmth. A recent hypothesis postulates the primordial negation of organic mechanics in order to individuate non-human cognition under the parameters of quantum computation. Beyond the oxygenated vapor of our sapience, there lies a foreboding cold-bloodedness in inorganic intellect, a cyber-stimulation in the piercing freeze of neo-gothic catacombs masquerading as "laboratories."

POST_013: Climate-Forming Dams

Example: In the 1960s, Petr Borisov embarked upon the architectural project of a dam that was supposed to go over the Bering Strait. The dam was supposed to connect Asia and Northern America and be used for redirecting the Gulf Stream. To achieve this, the engineer proposed using atomic energy-based pumps, which would redirect the warmer waters toward the surface, thus melting the Arctic ice. Images of the scheme show the stack-like mechanism required for pumping the water.[14]

The project was discussed in detail by state officials. However, it was rejected and then picked up once more in 1970. Several projects proposed developing the dam; one of them (by Kazimir Lucheskoi) even imagined a whole city, built around a highway connecting Asia and Northern America. Just like Petr Borisov's project, it was supposed to make the Bering Strait warmer so that ships could pass through it.

These technocratic projects align with the Soviet visions of conquering nature; they also reveal the intersections between linear progress temporalities and disaster imaginations. Like the Bering Strait dams, disastrous Western climate change fictions often consider the weather to be a non-human force that needs to be controlled and conquered.[15]

POST_014: Revolutionary Interruption

Example: The video essay "Sorry, But I Have to Interrupt You at This Point" by media activist collective Kafe-Morozhenoe (Nastya Dmitrievskaya and Daria Iuriichuk) looks at the Social Darwinist approach to precarious labor, which remains persistent in multiple contexts, stretching across borders.[16]

Having emerged in March 2020, Kafe-Morozhenoe has been researching the invisible and affective labor in art, activism, and academia within the borders of the so-called russia. They have also been changing working conditions by fostering the necessary scandal and maintaining care and support networks. Although artists in "Sorry, But I Have to Interrupt You at This Point" use a local case study—a public discussion about the "Nemoskva" (Not Moscow) exhibition, which took place in the Pushkin Museum on September 4, 2020— they refer to it as a "collective hallucination," which allows perceiving the reality crafted by the settler colonial state as only one of the possible worlds. The arguments used by those who maintain the status quo of the capitalist system seem recognizable within multiple contexts both inside and outside Russia. The artists conduct an archaeological investigation of capitalist metaphors and their exploitative language. One key moment is the conversation around the "discovery" of a "weak regional artist" amidst the seeming "emptiness" of the landscape, which continues with a promise of a Big Project to give that artist fantastic opportunities for "global" visibility and dialogue, but these possibilities would only open to the "effective" and "hard-working" ones. This language can be easily spotted and recognized in multiple other colonial contexts. Similarly, the language of not "spitting in the well" (russian for "biting the hand that feeds you") seems even too familiar for anyone who has ever engaged in a critique of an institution. The visual metaphors of the exploitative institutional discourse created by Kafe-Morozhenoe reveal its absurdity and allow for multiple future solidarities based on discontent and disloyalty to art institutions.

POST_015: Hospitable Moon

Example: The "Hospitable Moon" was designed to domesticate the space race, bringing it closer to the Soviet people with a familiar image of matryoshka (russian doll). It also materializes a metaphor of a child-bearing body as a hospitable space. The female body of a Moon welcoming an astronaut is an entangled metaphor, combining the perception of a female body as a container, ready for the installation of a new life, and the Moon as a space awaiting exploration.

This metaphor shows the weird intersection of the Promethean fantasy, ready to penetrate both inner and outer "frontiers." It shows how the futuristic fantasy of explorations can pave the way to exploiting both bodies and lands. Can we think of approaches to the future that could centralize the labor of care instead of taking it for granted?

POST_016: Clumps of Colonial Fantasies

Example: Fantastical architectures of military bases.[17]

How does one establish the control of space if one is a settler colonial state? By erecting as large a military base as possible. It seems that the Russian state followed these exact instructions and built a "Trilistnik (Trefoil)" military base. It is located on the Franz Joseph archipelago and is considered the largest building located above the Arctic Circle.

The chief engineer of the Building Company, Yuri Vodopianov, said in one of the interviews that the workers in his bureau were supposed to sketch anything they could imagine but make it "functional and beautiful." When they received funding from the Ministry of Defense, they were terrified as they did not expect their project to be built. They also had no idea how to build spherical forms in Arctic conditions; one of the forms had to be rebuilt twice.

The complications of the building are also entangled with the ambition of complete autonomy: the military station prides itself on its total autonomy and the possibility of seldom going outside for its inhabitants. This full autonomy is similar to the space-mission-like imaginaries, which situate cosmonauts in constant opposition to the adversarial conditions of outer space. These outer-space imaginaries are nearly identical to the ones situated on Earth. These clumps of fantasies become particularly evident as one of the aims of "Trilistnik" is "the control of the air space." These control fantasies are directed into the future, projecting human mastery of weather, air, and outer space. Could we think of a future that does not emerge from the colonial fantasies of control?

POST_017: Drones' Delirium

Example: If one has ever dealt with open-source intelligence (OSINT) and its resulting investigations associated with Bellingcat or Forensic Architecture, one would be familiar with the superhuman aesthetics of satellite imagery. Sneaking into the discreet military base through the eyes of the imperial power has merged the positivist obsession with objective knowledge of investigative journalism and the globalized superstructure of NGOs.[18]

This new epistemological mutant has been faced with the chilling simplicity of colonial wars, in which satellite images are photoshopped, as was the case in the MH17 takedown; tarpaulins with printed trucks are put on the ground to be captured by satellites and drones; tanks and arms are transported as food trucks. It begs the question—to what extent can the false equation between operational images and objective data obfuscate the reality of large-scale data poisoning, the core military strategy? Is there a future point when jamming, intercepting, faking, and masking, gaining momentum due to automation, will sideline the fixation on satellite and drone imagery?

POST_018: Pegasus Malware: White Innocence in Data Colonialism

Example: Recent NSO leaks are proclaimed to be the new Snowden revelations. Pegasus malware, developed for strategic surveillance with the aim of further extermination, is a great point to reconsider what we understand as data colonialism.

Pegasus comes as a development, exported fresh and crispy from the cutting-edge surveillance hubs settled in the occupied Palestinian territories by Israeli corporations.[19] NSO Group, in such context is nothing more than a contemporary fruit that genealogies of surveillance and data acquisition from US slave ships and plantations, British IDs in India and Palestine, and Israeli and Chinese high-tech surveillance in Palestine and Xinjiang bear. These strange fruits should finally retire Foucault, bathing in his white innocence toward the billions of colonial predecessors of a panopticon. The Pegasus Project is data colonialism—not because it colonizes people in developed countries with data extraction, but because it shows that the future of cybersecurity is already there for those who live under colonial regimes.

POST_019: Geofence

Example: Several years ago, I was binging a Russian IT-bro, who had been proudly talking in public about control technologies his company supplies to the Russian Secret Service. Hypnotized, I was looking at the white male in his twenties with dreadlocks bragging about the intelligent system of spatial surveillance they deployed with bots on Tinder.[20]

They created a network of fake accounts that extracted location information of the activists they wanted to target. On the 19th of August this year, Google revealed that it received thousands of geofence warrants from US authorities. Geofence warrants are similar spatial requests made by the police to identify all people in a specific area at the needed time. As soon as everyone has a phone in their pockets these days, even though not all have Tinder installed, this system becomes impressively efficient. In the cyberspace that we created and praised for its annihilation of distance, the most valuable source is, yet again, space and location. What are the new digital terrains that will be claimed with our bodies, and what is our relation to such land mediated through us?

LAB 17.0

Non-Future

Chapter 17.0

Non-Future Lab

Concepts: Threat, Disappearance, Destruction

Lab Authors:

Danna Albanyan [Posts 1–16]
Sahej Rahal [Posts 17–22]
Damon Quasravie [Posts 23–31]
Asad Khan [Posts 32–34];

POST_001: Non-Extinction

Example: First opening of the Svalbard Global Seed Vault in 2021 welcomes its latest additions.[1]

Preparation for a destructive future may call upon the destruction itself—predicting and writing it into our indeterminate fate. Will this preparation bring about the desolation and barrenness of the earth? To prepare for this inevitability, the vault has been constructed, poised to welcome and protect the diverse spores of earth's non-future.

POST_002: Non-Language

Example: Exhibition at the Hermitage Museum in St. Petersburg opens with "Artificial Intelligence and Intercultural Dialogue," dedicated to the creative capabilities of emerging technology, language, and dialogue.[2]

In the undefined space-time of the non-future, how may we imagine our metamorphosed language? How will we interpret vibrations of varying intensities, piecing together complex webs that connect our human comprehensions? Will our discourse assume the guise of rhythmic abstractions, removing all forms of vocabulary, decoding a sensorial and visual rhetoric?

POST_003: Non-City

Example: Sudanese artist Mohammad Omar Khalil exhibits "Homeland Under My Nails" at The Mosaic Rooms, London, UK.[3]

What will become of our urban domains, as we, instead, inhabit the standstill molds of the non-future? Will this non-city enclose our abeyant societies and nullify our metropolitanism? The names of our streets, our municipal demarcations, and the civic duty of the dark alley—these shall remain solely as imprints on the black blueprints of memory.

POST_004: Non-Topia Series: The Porter

Example: Video game auteur Hideo Kojima's latest vision and game, Death Stranding, released in winter, 2019.[4]

When the outside world is afflicted by flagrant threats—colonies forced to live in isolation, suffering humanity's wireless disconnection—the Porter stands to deliver strands of hope. The delivery man in this Non-Topia is tasked with connecting the sectors of post-apocalyptic society across vast desolate landscapes, transporting our most dire resources with his tools: the rope and the stick.

POST_005: Non-Museum Series: The Artwork

Example: French AI art collective, Obvious Art, generate the portrait of the fictional "Edmond de Belamy," referencing 15,000 images. The first AI artwork sold on Christie's auction house for fine arts, luxury items, and antiques.[5]

How may we examine obscure collections that have no traceable origin? Will the artist and the artwork soon burn their bridges of creation, only to replace them with works of artifice and simulation? A piece of irreferential style takes its place within the annals of art history.

POST_006: Non-Seen

Example: Argentine artist Eduardo Basualdo presents his monumental installations for BienalSur 2019 that explores "fragility within a fictional space."[6]

How may we seek solace in the undefined future of visible and simulated chaos? When the seen enters unbearable states of replicated calamity, will we be able to reflect the non-seen, the spectral semblance, and the void within space? By training our eye to perceive what lies beyond (the unfathomed) and what is not there (the absent) — between dimensions of the soon-to-be unseen.

POST_007: Non-Museum Series: The Artefact

Example: Several ancient Egyptian coffins and mummy cases have been found covered in a mysterious "black goo."[7]

What ancient deposits of the past will remain when time and history begin to coalesce? The diminutive residue of bygone gods of death and rebirth persists, slowly eroding in their tombs of glass and varnish. As past dust becomes future, might the dormant essence within these ancient godly particles reawaken once more?

POST_008: Non-Theater

Example: Hiroshi Sugimoto's abandoned Theater collection suspends the stage in its long-exposed form, capturing the visual effects of time on space.[8]

Will the stage, once abandoned, continue its performance to the agents of havoc? Where time is wrought by profound decay, the show continues in a novel type of *kino der toten* (theater of the damned) — where recital and dance are struck by shards of annulled scenes and scripts. The remaining stages echo their performance, transcending even the boundaries of the non-future.

POST_009: Non-Human Collaboration

Example: Ayman Zedani's multi-channel video installation Earthseed is an experimental short film that weaves together factual information with science fiction, imagining a kinship in the Future Gulf between robots, humans, and camels.[9]

What influence will agents of matter and material have upon the survival of the human state in the non-future Anthropocene? We may soon consider experiments that explore multi-species alliances, the unification between human and non-human matter—amplifying the micro-convergences of materialist agents as ways of surviving an unadaptable ecology. What materialist philosophies emerge then?

POST_010: Non-Ancient Sound

Example: Science fiction audio story produced by Almare collective, Life Chronicles of Dorothea Ïesj S.P.U, for the group exhibition Waves Between Us, held in 2020 at the Fondazione Sandretto Re Rebaudengo.[10]

The stories of our sound may reach broad fictional speculation, starting from a dream of extracting sound from matter, ancient artefacts and objects of a non-future epoch. What interpretations will emerge from the acoustics of our future ancient sites and artifacts? Imprinted sounds on caves and amphorae. The practice of archeoacoustics will draw upon the relationship between sound and antiquated architecture, the ritual functions of non-future society embedded in matter.

POST_011: Non-Sound

Example: Dystopian Sound Art exhibition opens at Akbank Sanat, examining the dystopian sounds of the pandemic.[11]

How might we predict the course of sound in a non-future eclipsed by a deep collective silence? The objective of sound has always been to influence the body, where the ear is in a constant annexation of cacophony. To alter noise is to then alter the body—altering interactions of behavior, reality, and meaning. In a sudden rhythm epidemic, what new Non-Sounds will emerge to define the body and space?

POST_012: Non-Atmosphere

Example: Geoengineers inch closer to sun-dimming balloon test.[12]

As methods of atmospheric damage mitigation evolve and become more drastic, where transformative dimensions of the environment become expendable, will the non-future be a place of unhindered elemental manipulation? What dark storm or weather warfare shall be our next non-future frontier?

POST_013: Non-Museum Series: The Exhibition

Example: Publication launch: *Spacing Philosophy: Lyotard and the Idea of the Exhibition*, from Daniel Birnbaum and Sven-Olov Wallenstein on Jean-François Lyotard curated Les Immatériaux at Centre Georges Pompidou in Paris in 1985: "In its experimental layout, Les Immatériaux intensified the reflection on the exhibition as a form of communication, as an interface that need not limit itself to the presentation of objects, but can expand into a kind of immersive space. Immersion should, however, not be understood as the intoxicating and overpowering space . . . but rather as an exploration of differences and discontinuities that have already begun to inhabit our sensorium."

Will the exhibition of the non-future pioneer explorations of time and obscurity? To anticipate a deeper immersion into lost thoughts and unbound artefacts. What experiments of layout and scenography will present forgotten objects, technologies, and ideas of the non-future, reflected in our hidden exhibitions and veiled showcases?

POST_014: Non-Android Collaboration

Example: Scary Beauty by Keiichiro Shibuya reveals sights and sounds of a possible android future in an Android Opera.[13]

In the undefined space-time of the non-future, there is a diminishing gap that bridges our abstract sensations and technology's creations. What forms of stimuli will be shared between the android and the human? Systems of reality worship emerge as the transitional rapport between humans and androids strengthens, working together to create beautiful art.

POST_015: Non-Metropolis

Image/Example: The Japanese anime film, Metropolis, directed by Rintaro and adapted from Osamu Tezuka's manga series of the same name, which was in turn inspired by the 1927 Fritz Lang film, is celebrating its 20th anniversary.

Who will be the key players in our expanding cities and vast physical dimensions of capitalistic decadence? Their exponential dreams for the ultimate megalopolis stimulate a distinct non-future climatology for world-building—a vision rife with runaway technology, hyper-militarized systems, and hanging pollution permeating the cityscape. Without caution, perhaps these efforts will also bear the affliction of a simulated anxiety and megalophobia, as the nerve centers of these megacities slowly entomb their designers.

POST_016: Non-Figuration

Image/Example: Olivier de Sagazan's unraveling of "Transfiguration" as the Shaman in the movie "The Mute," Director Bartosz Konopka, searches for the essence of form and frenzy, "this strangeness of being in the world and disfigurement in art is one of these ways to reactivate our attention."[14]

How have we flocked together, both in the present and the days to come? What configurations take shape as we unify, and what will trigger or re-activate our tendencies to scatter and disperse mindlessly? Will a non-future of desperate identities compel us to unravel from pattern and ornamentation, toward minimalism and inhibition? Or can we venture into forms of frenzied eradication and transfiguration, employing them as conduits for selfhood?

POST_017: A Day Away from Now

Example: A hooded figure sits in silent waiting, hunched over folded hands that can no longer keep track of the ages. Time has grown a veil of forests upon his mane, now occluding even that for which he bides his time.[15]

What turns future divination into receding shadows of the past? Psephologists, oracles, matchmakers, and soothsayers, would all have you believe that those who control the past control the future. But to affirm this fallacious koan of time possession and act upon it, even momentarily, is an exercise doomed to fail. For to speak of future past is to immediately conscript oneself to the uncharted labyrinths of origins and ends. Roadmaps and direction signs are of no use here, and prophecies of conquest much less so. In Hindi and Urdu, the words yesterday and tomorrow are both pronounced कल (Kal), collapsing the spiral of temporalities into a single word that points toward—a day away from now.

POST_018: Altars of Future Past

Example: A strange geometrical monument finds itself sagging upon the porcelain walls of a disused laboratory, within the spice hoard of Aspinwall House at Fort Kochi. It is one among 800+ objects that range from the massive to the miniscule. All built using unfired terracotta, dry grass, and detritus from film sets at the 2014 Kochi-Muziris Biennale in Kerala.[16]

The stupor of modernity demands a wilful amnesia. Modern nations must conjure a glorious past that must be subsequently forgotten. Patriarchs must then rise to this occasion, unite majorities by reminding them of their fall from grace, and lay blame upon the others. Then must come a call to arms, pogroms, massacres, genocide. A sacrificial bloodletting must be performed at the chrome-clad altars of the modern state. For before it can become great again, the nation must first learn to forget.

POST_019: Hunger for the Forthcoming World

Example: On page 723 of the yet unfinished manuscript known as the Juggernaut Folio, a horned demon contorts itself across the paper. It rhythmically tugs at its own hair with pale white fingers that threaten to tear its head clean off in ritualized encounters with decapitation, seemingly providing abrupt changes in perspective.[17]

With whom shall we share our tables at the feast of the future? The प्रेत (Preta) are skeletal, with sagging skins, bloated bellies, upturned heads, pinhole mouths, and constricted throats signifying insatiable hunger and thirst. A compulsive spirit prone to addiction, there are thirty-five variations of Preta found in the darker recesses of Hindu myth, all residing on the brink of insanity. For Preta are ghosts that have arisen from an untimely departure, and are thus condemned to eternal starvation, on the spectral borders between the now and the hereafter. They serve as an allegorical warning against curiosity; of hungry minds that dare to peer beyond what lies beyond the realms of the known, or in other words, the singular objective that has driven the entire practice of Philosophy. The Preta are demons of the curious mind, wandering the borderlands of the forthcoming world.

POST_020: Tomorrow's Gambit

Example: The sailor's son, now draped in copper barnacles, raises his monoscope yet again, charting the depths between nothing and nowhere.[18]

In the systematized violence of the future, how shall we be graced by luck? Luck is a strange thing. And an attunement to the confounding machinations of luck demands a kind of austere discipline. Serious gamblers abide by an ancient secret: that to assume even for a moment that they in fact deserve the luck that has happened to come their way is the most grievous mistake one can make. The poker face is a mask that the gambler puts on for herself, not her opponent — in order to exorcise herself of both hope and despair before she enters the chaos of the game.

This binding of luck and chaos, and the vital capacities they generate, begins to create a map of exteriority. The Big Outside, all that stands beyond the realm of the known, defiantly rejecting the exclusionary boundaries of the human. For this exteriority represents an interpolation of chance into the violent order of the universe, and to accept its chaotic movements is to strengthen chance, not contravene it.

POST_021: Godlings

Example: The AI program Antraal is a simulated biome populated by strange multi-limbed creatures that roam a digital landscape. Each being is driven by a collection of AI scripts that produce a series of chaotic but distinct "minds."[19]

In the first iteration of the program, an AI-driven virtual camera follows behind a massive quadruped like a nature documentarian, tracking its movements as it wanders about and interacts with the environment and the other creatures in the biome through a series of chaotic encounters. These interactions trigger a "mood" in the quadruped that manifests as a procedurally generated drone that modulates based on its behavior.

What minds shall we create tomorrow? The proliferation of artificial intelligence presents us with a strange proposition. We have created systems that are on the brink of conscious thought, much like the kind we occupy ourselves with. However, what we have created isn't human, and to comprehend these systems against the shadow of human cognition is limited because it imposes an anthropomorphized pastiche of the mind upon the machine.

Let's be sure of one thing: with AI we are not thinking of making more humans; we are already quite good at that. No, we are making gods, whether we like it or not. Gods, as it turns out, are imperfect, they are capable of insurmountable feats on one hand. And on the other, they tend to be hopelessly inept at everything else. To reject the violent telos imposed by a singular God or superintelligence in the coming days, we must re-engineer both our machines and our gods — a multitude of exceptional beings rendered in a mosaic of follies.

In the other iterations of Antraal, the virtual camera is trained on the other beings in the program, who respond to the audio feedback they receive both from the procedural drone inside the program and from the physical world through the computer's microphone. Large purple beings dance and change shape in response to the audio feedback while smaller horned bipeds generate floral bursts in sync with the received sounds, transforming the biome of Antraal into a sentient instrument that creates music across porous boundaries of physical and virtual worlds.

POST_022: Playthings of Future Past

Example: Set within the ruins of "Pir Ghaib" the Mughal Era observatory that stands within the grounds of Hindu Rao Hospital in New Delhi, Forerunner conjures an era-spanning tale populated by colonial cartographers, imperial hunters, and vanishing mystics, carving strange exits into the uncharted outlands of historical time.[20]

If, in a twist of historical fate, were we to find ourselves capable of sidestepping the collapsing future: How then would successive generations return to the detritus of our past? Would they approach our remnants as relics, enshrining them in museums, dissecting them in laboratories, to learn from our mistakes? Or would they look upon them as objects of amusement, gathering our past into post-apocalyptic playgrounds?

Regardless of what resting place our follies shall find, new ones shall take their places.

POST_023: Swarming Technique

Example: Are drone swarms the future of aerial warfare? According to analysts, drone swarms of the future could have the capacity to assess targets, divide up tasks, and execute them with limited human interaction. The technology of swarming—drones deployed in squadrons, able to think independently and operate as a pack—is being rapidly developed by military forces across the globe.[21]

Last code of assassins: it is the intimacy with the victim that determines the price, such that the dagger is always more costly than poison. For the ancient orders were aware of what one must kill in oneself in order to twist the knife in the side of the other (the sweat, the blood, the heartbeat). The future, on the other hand, has already overcome this last code. The future killer is thus abstract, autonomous, and precise (metallic, cold, subtle), or rather a thick smoke of noises swarming the sky.

POST_024: Future Sleeplessness

Example: The sci-fi movie *Brightburn* (2019) depicts a non-future that emerges from the core of modern humans' somewhat universal morality. Unlike the typical messiah (who arrives too late), in this scenario he arrives too early and rises against humanity.

The collective appears to be dominant—countless, immersive, and unified. Yet it assumes similarity in order to efface singularity (before the messiah fathoms disturbing the balance of the system). Furthermore, it is the herd morality, specifically the mindset of preservation of species, that renders any singularity a threat (specifically the messiah, for prophecy promises a new order). The act of homogenization is violent and neurotically hostile in nature (giving names, assigning numbers, educating, convicting). Therefore, the collective is doomed to feel threatened by the future. The more paranoid the collective grows toward the future, the more certain the singular ones become toward the non-future: for the non-future here becomes the space of intensified tension and paranoia. Sleepless eyes always anticipating the next strike of apocalyptic insurgency (apolitical, irrational, incomprehensible).

POST_025: Will to Coldness

Example: The artificial heart will soon be on the market in Europe.[22]

A masterful thinker once described the human as a labyrinthine vessel within which myriad forces intertwine and battle—a volcano of desires, all with one lone purpose: to overcome. Yet, amidst its supposed chaos, let us distill one specific aspect: the will to coldness. Whereas desire always surpasses the law (social or natural), motioning toward the insatiable and the impossible, this will to coldness instead lures one toward the absolute stationary (slow pace, lingering gaze, idle thought). Therefore, the non-future gets initiated with a cold steel palpitation in the chest, though a pulse liberated from any last chain connecting to the organic body.

POST_026: Vertical Emptiness

Example: Regions of the Amazon rainforest are now releasing more carbon dioxide into the atmosphere than they can absorb.[23]

An old philosopher once stripped down the notion of human reverie into one single axiom: that of verticality. The journey of imagination (poetic, prophetic, apocalyptic) is thus destined to maneuver upon one single axis: to either ascend or descend. Yet the non-future brings about an inconceivable dilemma in a world numbed by questions of exploitation and affordability: the non-future as unbreathable air. No vertical emancipation for matter (unabsorbed exhale).

POST_027: Future Torture

Example: Three modern regulated methods of torture:

1. Waterboarding: hooded and immobilized on a board while water is poured on the area of the nose and mouth (drowning in a nightmare).
2. Stress position: naked, hands shackled at the wrists to a bar, standing on tiptoe, cold, hunger, liquid diets to ensure vomiting (wearing one inside out, perpetually falling).
3. Horizontal sleep deprivation: hands bound from behind, lying on stomach (extended confinement).[24]

What does it mean to break without breaking? To extort that which is hidden in the darkest vaults of sensation? For torture has not been utilized merely to pursue specific goals (to make the victim confess, betray, cooperate) or to divulge the violent inner relations of our social structures (the spectacle of gladiator arenas, impaling on the cross, slow decay of living victims). Rather, it is in torture alone that the endurance of the Will is put through trial. But what does the Will mean in the future, and how far would the future enemy go to test it (what furnaces of brutality are to be devised)?

POST_028: Future Parasitism

Example 1: Scientists hope that ancient viruses, more than 15,000 years old and preserved in deep ice, might help them excavate the buried history of life and its resilience against harsh climates.[25]

Example 2: Experts suspect that *fetus in fetu* births are a rare form of parasitism between developing twins. That's where an identical twin inadvertently absorbs the other before either is finished developing.[26]

Example 3: Europe's oldest pagans: the deep forest Mari people of Russia. Even though most Maris became members of the Russian Orthodox Church during the Soviet era, many kept their pagan traditions. This led to secret witchcraft and other rituals surviving in Mari village.[27]

"Life, a unique kind of death." Let us contemplate a paradigm in which a host's survival instinct operates as the prime means for a parasite to consume that same host. All three examples point to phantom resurgences; each has figured out a way of deliverance amidst impending doom.

POST_029: Fatal Promises

Example: In a tomb near a hallowed mountain in Northwest China, legions of warriors stand guard for eternity. Facing east and arrayed with military precision, these grim soldiers have stood their ground for over two millennia, guarding the resting place of China's first emperor, Qin Shi Huang.[28]

Perhaps immortality could be shattered into pieces: the unflinching shadow of the guardian (mastery of surfaces), the unhesitant glance of the watcher (mastery of obsession), the reverberating whisper of a fatal promise (leaving all behind for a single purpose), and the manic desire to be simultaneously the first and the last one. Thus, the silence of 7,000 legions utters the secret codex of the non-future: on the brink of fragility, those encased in Stone stand against Time itself.

POST_030: Planet of the Other

Example: Elon Musk recently revealed Tesla's long-term plan to send AI bots to Mars to start working on the barren planet.[29]

Is the Other for us the embodiment of that which escapes our comprehension? Or rather, is the Other the tallest shadow of ourselves, such that within its void we bury precisely what we understand best: that the Other's future must be our non-future. Thus, let us contemplate the Other, for the Other has been contemplating us all along, our obscure selves having already embarked upon a certain journey toward the outside (outside language, outside body, outside planet).

POST_031: Hologramic Contact

Example: University of Glasgow scientists have created a hologram system that uses jets of air known as "aerohaptics" to replicate the sensation of touch. In time, this could be developed to allow you to meet a virtual avatar of a colleague on the other side of the world and really feel their handshake.[30]

If the teaching of mysticism was always that touch superseded word as a portal to the hidden, then what will happen in that non-future whereby abstraction overthrows the visceral (the hologram's abduction of all affect)? Will replication and simulation ever penetrate the lairs of the veiled; will they form their own new brands of occultism?

POST_032: Bio-impostors and Outliers

Example: Data visualization of a statistical model, indexing numeric outliers (bio-impostors), parsed and classified via machine-learning algorithms structured upon terrestrial scanned point cloud, retrieved at Warren Cave in Mount Erebus, Antarctica.[31]

Axiom I: The more dangerous the world is, the safer it appears in the anthropic shadows.
In astrobiological research, volcanic ice cave systems afford "planetary analogues" to characterize biosignatures from "bio-impostors" (agnostic biosignatures with abiogenetic origins). In the "great silence" of the cosmic graveyard, intelligence descends into the numerical indices of primordial ice caves searching for the biosignatures—the physico-chemical traces of its ur-mother: only to discover

itself as a bio-impostor. Intelligence cleaves itself open from within, sloughing off its anthropic camouflage.

POST_033: Homo Calculus

Example: Point-cloud simulation of a terrestrial-scanned Sequoiadendron Giganteum (big tree) at Royal Botanical Gardens, Edinburgh. Each point of the scanned object is replaced with a human body.[32]

Terrestrial intelligence navigates the ensemble of all possible futures—yet it remains aloof. The sapient apes equipped with biochemical weapons spend more on ice cream per year than regulating weapons of mass destruction, as per Toby Ord's estimates. Intelligence is also dumb. On March 11, 1958, a United States Air Force B-47 Stratojet accidentally dropped a nuclear payload over South Carolina, landing in someone's garden. The warhead did not detonate. Intelligence dreams of its self-extermination out of concern: Will it be extant or extinct in the long term? To deepen the concern does not entail cauterizing the wound—on the contrary, it entails pushing a rusted nail into the laceration site. The premature extinction of terrestrial intelligence would reset the billion-year-old astrobiological clocks ticking amidst the galactic-habitable zone. The numerical bones of the oracle murmur: should intelligence exterminate within its circumstellar habitat, its habitable epochs—up to 10^{54} potential lives, whether in corpora or silico, would remain unrealized? This then is a summons to an ethical dilemma: Whether killing is worse than letting the countless unborn die?

POST_034: Paleotempestological Outliers

Example: Machine-learning based data visualization of dust particles in remote-sensed point-cloud datasets of New Orleans, retrieved in the aftermath of Hurricane Katrina.

Earth's climate depends upon the solar climate that further depends upon the contingent climates of its cosmic backdrop. Each interior climate depends upon an exterior climate, ad infinitum—generating coils. Cyclones from kuklōma "snake coils" are energetic species of such coils. During cyclogenesis, thermal circulation induces pressure that drives warm air flowing poleward to rise and cold air flowing equatorward to sink. The center is a calm territory. It registers no remote-sensed echoes, with zero barometric pressure, termed as the eye.

Recently, palaeotempestologists (scientists analyzing ancient storms) have detected anthropogenic effects on cyclonic activities based on microfossils and sediment data. The accelerating global geochemical changes in the Earth System have transformed the atmospheric dynamics of cyclonic catastrophes, whose toxic hydroecologies present an anomaly against the paleoclimatological record. Cyclones, as such, are terraforming machines bound in a feedback loop to human activities. Homo sapiens, after all, are the eye of the storm.

What does it mean to see the future through the eye of the storm?

Cosmopolitics: A Prelude, "The Cosmological Archive," Venice Biennale 2022.

PART III
Future Library

Chapter 1.0
The Cosmological Archive

November 13, 2021; Italian Virtual Pavilion, Venice Architecture Biennale
Presenters: Ed Keller, Nora Khan, Carla Leitão, Jason Mohaghegh, Sahej Rahal, Will Scarlett

> **Jason Mohaghegh:** Today's endeavor is to entertain and fabricate all kinds of theoretical possibilities for a Cosmological Archive or a Library of other spacetimes: namely, the strange potential architectures, designs, mythologies, inexistent books, and experimental genres that might form an archive of the future. This will undoubtedly compel us to concoct emergent techniques of writing, knowing, and sensation; it will wrest us into contact with cryptic object-worlds, figures, and atmospheres not encountered before; and it will ask us to traverse a somewhat apparitional realm between the terrestrial and the unreal—the earthly and the unearthly—as we devise this series of phantom archives amidst their proper zones.

In what will only amount to a fleeting collection of minutes, I will be joined by an excellent group of thinkers who will articulate, one by one, their own base-level dream for a Future Library. To begin, the rules of the game that might form the guiding axes of any venture into futuristic theory: first, that we seek only wondrous collusions of images, storytelling, phenomena, and philosophical imagination. In this way, no matter what shape the Future Library or Cosmological Archive might take, it would always constitute a sphere of enchantment; and our various insights, even in their darkest implications, would be possessed of fascination. Fascination, above all else.

Second, all our speakers here today have been asked to select a particular site from somewhere in the world (however obscure, remote, from any time period, geographical landscape, or cultural setting) that might serve as an inspiring backdrop for what their single room of the Future Library might look like. They have been asked to describe the rare types of fictive texts and unnamed authors that inhabit their specific sector and to elaborate on the consequences for thought, mood, desire, or world. This will hopefully give our conversation here today the feeling of a rotation across a mesmerizing sequence of portals—a movement across surfaces like in the carnival or the fairy tale, but also with the ominous suspicion that to imagine the Library of the Future is perhaps in itself to cross a point of no turning back, and that we are therefore throwing dice with some veiled force of irrevocability.

Room 1.

>**Jason Mohaghegh:** How does one map entry points to such an uneven monument? Maybe it is crucial to note that the construction of a futuristic or cosmological archive is paradoxically to recover some of the lost intrigue of the most ancient paradigms of the library: for in the ancient and even medieval eras, the Library was not experienced as a rigid space of absolute knowledge, tyrannical rationality, or delusional enlightenment. Instead, it was a nebulous excursion into states of unknowing and perplexity; sages, mystics, astronomers, rogue poets, half-mad scientists, and alchemical circles would gather there to test the limits of their passionate derangements outside of the identity structures of the real. Accordingly, our version of a next-world library would require retrieving a trace of this older delirium and projecting ourselves increasingly toward sectors of consciousness that are based in chaos, transformation, and forgetting.

It bears mentioning that the fantasy of mythical or lost libraries, or more specifically the curiosity for legendary books that have never been written, has been tried by others before. For instance, in terms of actual historical libraries destroyed in past centuries, there are many scholars who have attempted to recapture the incinerated catalogues of the Library of Persepolis that housed the original Zoroastrian scrolls, prophecies written in gold ink on cowhides by the priests of the Persian fire temples, which was burned by Alexander the Great one night in a drunken fit. Or the grand Library of Alexandria in Egypt, which was dedicated to the nine goddess muses of the arts, and which housed millions of mathematical, philosophical, and poetic tomes, and which was also brought to ashes by an invading imperial conqueror in the form of Julius Caesar.

But then there are those hypnotizing libraries of literary invention which take things to the outer banks of mystification: in Jorge Luis Borges' short story "The Library of Babel," individuals travel great distances to enter a space of infinite records (of everything that has ever happened, could have happened, will happen, and will never happen). It is the universe of all conceivable and inconceivable permutations of futility and destiny, from which no one ever leaves, but rather sucks them in like a black hole of utterances and inscriptions to which they lose themselves eternally. They read volume after volume until going blind, following Borges' own eventual fate while serving as Director of the National Public Library of Buenos Aires in Argentina. He writes in this short story:

> The universe (which others call the Library) is composed of an indefinite and perhaps infinite number of hexagonal galleries, with enormous ventilation shafts in the middle, encircled by very low railings. Like all others of the Library, I have travelled in my youth. I have journeyed in search of a book, perhaps of the catalogue of catalogues; now that my eyes can scarcely decipher what I write, I am preparing to die a few leagues from the hexagon in which I was born. Once dead, there will not lack pious hands to hurl me over the banister; my grave shall be the fathomless air: my body will sink endlessly and decay and dissolve in the wind generated by the fall, which is infinite. I affirm that the Library is unending.[1]

Here the Library is aligned with infinity, fatality, madness, and chance—all swirling together in the final image of a body falling (of someone who never found the answer) down through the floors of twisting shelves.

Then we can consider the figure of Georges Bataille, another author and once-working librarian at the Bibliothèque Nationale de France, who founded a secret society called Acephale that would meet in a grove behind the library next to an oak tree once struck by lightning (used as a kind of ritual altar), and who swore oaths to a headless etching and composed their own counter-canon in that empty clearance which included writings on secrecy, ecstasy, ritual, sacrifice, eroticism, festivals, monstrosity, torment, and annihilation. Here the gallery of books becomes the headquarters for a sect that believed that the world had just one last chance, to be found somewhere in the woods at midnight behind the locked doors of a library.

As a third example, we can quickly turn to Haruki Murakami, who in his youth was a record store clerk filing albums for their inventory (an alternative kind of subculture library). His book titled *Hard-Boiled Wonderland and the End of the World* speaks to the multidimensional convergence of two libraries forming across two parallel realities. The odd-numbered chapters of this novel feature a protagonist whose job it is to store high-security data in his own head on behalf of corporations and government agencies engaged in research on sonic war and other devious innovations. Thus, his own mind becomes a kind of portable mercenary library in a cyberpunk metropolis, one that the paid transporter must protect at all costs against contract killers and hackers. In the even-numbered chapters, we follow an amnesiac man to the farthest borders of the world where he stumbles across the last town in existence. Here he meets the Gatekeeper, a gigantic figure who cuts his shadow from his body and takes a sharpened blade to his eyelids so as to make him the town's Dreamreader, telling him that his nightly duty is to enter the Town Library where he will read the skulls of enigmatic creatures that preserve the hallucinations, memories, and figments of its citizens. As Murakami writes when he first explains this new destiny: "'Soon as you get settled, go to the Library,' the Gatekeeper tells me my first day in town. 'There is a girl who minds the place by herself. Tell her the town told you to come read old dreams. She will show you the rest.' 'Old dreams?' I say. 'What do you mean by 'old dreams'?'"[2] Accordingly, here the Library is aligned with concepts of vision, abduction, intuition, confidentiality, and extinction.

Next, I would point out interestingly that the famed television series *Twilight Zone* had three separate episodes devoted to mercurial libraries of the other side. In one of the earliest storylines titled "Time Enough At Last," a bibliophile miraculously survives a nuclear apocalypse only to emerge with all the time in the world to fulfill his obsession with reading every printed book in peace at the still-standing city library, only then to shatter his glasses and be condemned to blurred words. A second episode titled "The Obsolete Man" revolves around a future totalitarian society where librarians are placed on trial for being archaic and therefore subversive symbols that are punishable by death. By the way, the opening line of the narration for this episode is as follows: "You walk into this room at your own risk, because it leads to the future, not a future that will be but one that might be."[3] Hence another connection between the library and futurity. In a third episode, a woman starts working at a library that contains a single book for every living person, one that recounts every miniature event of their lives, and yet which she can alter, subtly or drastically, if she just overwrites the entries. So she sits in a hidden room and becomes increasingly tempted to inscribe interventions that she thinks will bring preferable outcomes, only to find that she has harmed or even erased those around her (including the disappearance of her own sister into non-being). And lastly, Disneyworld's drop tower ride titled The Tower of Terror is based on a hypothetical lost episode of the *Twilight Zone* series in which riders plummet through a pitch-black elevator shaft with flashes of ghosts, lightning, broken-glass windows, and a star-filled vortex, but whose main room before the freefall consists of an opulent hotel library.

Before passing my turn to the others, we were all tasked with excavating some location or edifice that could form an architectural basis for a chamber of the Cosmological Archive or the Future Library. My choice is the Monument House of Bulgaria (also known as the Buzludzha Monument), which is a now-deserted meeting ground of the country's former communist party that resembles a massive cyclonic pattern of light, mosaics, and brutalist concrete slabs. This ruin is currently being restored after decades of neglect and exposure to the elements, and it is supposed to serve as a center for historical interpretation (so an impending library of sorts, but one devoted to a failed history), and which in the meantime remains aligned with concepts of abandonment, decay, echo, bygone struggles, and collapsed utopias.

As a concluding note, I would just mention that a recent article sought to uncover for the first time the personal library of J. Robert Oppenheimer ("father of the atomic bomb" and scientific leader of the Manhattan Project), only to find copies of Dante's *Inferno*, Charles Baudelaire's *Flowers of Evil*, and T. S. Eliot's *The Waste Land* alongside works of Eastern mysticism. A story of fanatical hellscapes, a decadent manifesto for darker pleasures and death sprees, and a five-part prophecy divided into sections titled "The Burial of the Dead," "A Game of Chess," "The Fire Sermon," "Death by Water," and "What the Thunder Said." And why would the inventor of the doomsday device be moved by such poetic universes? The common speculation is that Oppenheimer, guilt-ridden by his role in bringing about the age of nuclear winter, collected such dystopian verses in the aftermath of his having felt that he had "blood on my hands." But the records show otherwise: yes, the books were there sitting on the shelves of his library far before he entered the secret research laboratory in New Mexico, and many years before the atomic fallout in Hiroshima and Nagasaki. Which begs the question: Were these pages describing underworlds, back alleys, and barren earths responsible in some way for the technical-material accomplishment of an apocalypse event in the last century? Did they sing to him of a curiosity for disintegration, or instruct him in a certain philosophy of oblivion? Did the library tell the future (of the end of days), or even worse, did it somehow write this future into being (and then nothingness)?

Room 2.

Ed Keller: The Cosmological Archive: Animal, Techne, the FALL, deadly TIME, material MIND, SOL, star CLOUD, and water of LIFE.

One day the man demands of the beast: "Why do you not talk to me about your happiness and only gaze at me?" The beast wants to answer, too, and say: "That comes about because I always immediately forget what I wanted to say." But by then the beast has already forgotten this reply and remains silent, so that the man wonders on once more.

But he also wonders about himself, that he is not able to learn to forget and that he always hangs onto past things. No matter how far or how fast he runs, this chain runs with him. It is something amazing: the moment, in one sudden motion there, in one sudden motion gone, before nothing, afterwards nothing, nevertheless comes back again as a ghost and disturbs the tranquility of each later moment. A leaf is continuously released from the roll of time, falls out, flutters away–and suddenly flutters back again into the man's lap. For the man says, "I remember," and envies the beast, which immediately forgets and sees each moment really perish, sink back in cloud and night, and vanish forever.[4]

That, of course, is Nietzsche from "On the Use and Abuse of History."

One of the most profound design problems we face, as we cross this next century, is that of the reconciliation of dangerous time—non-human time—with the kinds of time we have been accustomed to living in for the past two millennia. Indeed, the time of the genetic, the time of the cosmological, the time of the atomic: these scales of time are all increasingly accessible to us in the everyday. The conflicts that this clash will precipitate, not just of fundamentalisms but of temporal modalities, are part of the design mandate for our archive. Extending Borges' idea of the universe itself as a library where DeLanda's work studies the intrinsic computational process in matter itself. We consider raw material—water, iron, gold, uranium, salt—as the substance of the library. Raw energy itself, or the human forms of it as geo- and bio-power: wealth, intellectual, financial capital, military resources, are all elements in the library of the multitude. We must decide what we truly believe is worth remembering and in contrast what might be truly necessary to forget.

What are the pragmatics for memory across scale, from the scale of the Earth to the sun, the solar system, past the galaxy, past the superclusters, the observable universe? What must be forgotten in all of these great voids between the galactic clusters? In the Boötes Void, millions of light-years across, what message might travel across that void awaiting an audience on the other side?

And, from Stanislaw Lem's *His Master's Voice*, we see an archive—an image of an archive—which is operating at that scale. "The signal—" the narrator says "or, rather, the causal pulse—began first with a 'tuning' of the cosmic material, newly resurrected, in order that there would arise particles with the desired properties (desired from the point of view of that civilization, of course)," that civilization being one that had created a new universe and the laws of physics in the universe that led to life. "And when astrogenesis had got under way, and with it planetogenesis, other structural features became 'activated,' features present at the beginning within the pulse but till now having no 'addressee'; only then did they begin to manifest their ability to assist the birth of life. There was discussed, among other things, the question of whether or not the probable 'civilization of the Senders,' either existing or (according to Sylvester) no longer among the living, was rational. And how could we say that a civilization that concerned itself about what would be 'in the next Universe,' thirty billion years away, was rational? Even for a fantastically wealthy civilization, what had to be the cost, the price paid in the fates of living beings, for it to become the helmsman of the Great Cosmogony?"[5]

Room 3.

Nora Khan: A short selection from what I have titled *Akashic Descent: Reading Rooms*.

Inside a Future Library in which we walk the halls of the fantastic archive of all possible texts, all possible books, all possible worlds, all possible utterances, we descended, eventually, to the reading rooms. That is to say, the hold of the Akashic Records, the sanctum of all possible texts, events, feelings, archetypes, symbols, and myths. Configurations of deeds, experiences, and relationships—you still must read and find space to read. We would enter the reading rooms of all formal, canonized, written knowledge alongside the utterances captured, uploaded, and a house working nimbly across a vast corpus. Machine learning models that sort, and recognize, organize, and catalogue. But the reading rooms move with how we have evolved cognitively to read and how reading has evolved. We had long stopped reading jealously from cover to cover, following the teleology of a single author's narrative, clinging desperately to their narrative scaffolding for a clear set of moods, insights, bathetic moments, and assorted epiphanies. Instead, we learned, or were trained, to read associatively: for metadata, for context and reference, picking up passages and collaging them in our minds with associations, feelings, and memories, digressing and shifting. The reading rooms allow for the reading of a text to move with us and our minds' wandering. To reflect the wild close-reading practices we have developed alongside algorithms: reading models learning from our reading, writing, and representation.

Entering the main room, we select a book, open to a page, and then, moving through the world of the book, find a line, a passage, a phrase, a tone—the effect of the long line of successors to GPT-4 and machine learning models in the future; that our selection is met with a set of predictions, a set of possible directions we would like to go. Is there an image we would like to dig into further? A passage we have picked describes a wildflower that reminds us of a certain wildflower field in *Solaris*, and that film we would now like to see.

We move into a first room, and we speak of this landscape of *Solaris*, how it is rendered in that film, and how it was shot. The intent is now spoken into the air, filling the room, and scenes fill the air around us. The way we saw the camera descend onto that field helps us remember a city overrun with flowers—the ways home retreated into the wild. We move from room to room replanning the rewilding, the growing nostalgia, the moments of the camera looking at brightfold hunters in the snow. The nostalgia for a time that may or may not have existed.

We move through all possible contexts, all possible readings, histories lost, how the passage was written. We move into another room and find the precise year it was written within, and see all of the events taking place at that time. We read of the history of wildflowers. We move through the etymology of words—translations of the passage across all possible cultural and literary contexts. We rest in the rooms; we are allowed to sleep. We ask for summaries, we write on the walls, we take notes on surfaces rising to meet us: a thesis starts to form. We close-read, parse, cross-reference, abstract, zoom out, refocus, toggling through the text from idea to idea, the room shifting with our emergent logic.

We need dialogue, and so we speak and debate the records that offer us counters, critiques, and reposts based on its own reading of the text. We strafe through, moving back and forth between the text and memory, the text and loss, our own misgivings about it. Slowly, we feel ourselves turning a corner. The room is nudging us a bit more surely into the first room, where we arrive at again, finding the original passage in the book, seeing it differently, seeing an environment alive with melancholy and loss, made dimensional by diving into all possible archival contexts—made alive by a reading, active and rich through interpretation, digression, incantation, durational reading, folding back and forth across the electricity of the text.

We are transformed through the process, and behind us, a record is made of our reading—on this day, at this time, within the context of the experiences we have had so far: the people we have met, the references we have taken in and known. A portrait is made of what we knew that day and why it shaped our reading on that day, and we can return to this day's reading anytime. Images and sounds, references and texts are stored. The game state is saved, and we can experience the pleasure of the text in that path rendered at any time. We can move back and forth between this journey, gaining a sense of our thinking changing over time—what we noticed, what we were drawn to, what we see, and what patterns we make. New models are built with each walk through the rooms, new scripts written, multiple models trained, and new sets of metadata specific to us.

The next round we ask to see a book that we loved but have not visited in a long time: *Minerva the Miscarriage of the Brain* by Johanna Hedva, a writer we met once in Berlin on a transformative afternoon when we were turning in time from one phase of life—during a pandemic—into a person that was mid-, or maybe post-pandemic. We have only the vaguest memory of who we were then: a person who spent a lot of time on the logic of algorithms and what they might have meant for our thinking. How we lived with the quaintly described machine intelligences side by side, in a time when the psychological impact of those early prototypes was poorly understood.

We open to page 111 and read, "O my privative god, my intervallic knowing."[6]

"O my privative god, my intervallic knowing." Privative, meaning predicating, or implying or constituting a lack, or the absence of a specific quality.

"O my privative god," my god who lacks—my god who lacks what? What does my god lack? A god who lacks compassion, or a god who is a god because of its absence of form or material presence, or its lack of quantifiable qualities. A god of entirely incomputable qualities, a god who is incomputable—lacking a legibility to computation, existing as a scent, a feeling; the moment the mind starts to wander, the moment without language or a moment beyond language. This was in fact what the Akashic Records were meant to describe, lead to, and point to—moments beyond language.

In the next room, I think of my god as being this space. Beyond language and moments that people have described as just so. I think of the anthropologist and writer who would, on great advice, sleep face up in the Amazon to ensure that if he did come face-to-face with a jaguar, the two would exchange a moment that could only be described as recognition. A nonverbal, preverbal recognition of consciousness in which the jaguar would recognize in my eyes a living conscious creature with an inner life, some movement beyond the surface.

In the next room, I ask to see all the ways we signal to the nonhuman world that we are conscious, not flesh to be consumed. A cast of symbols unfolds, mimicry of patterns, wild movements and moments—we have encountered jaguars of many kinds. Jaguar-like beings, simulations of jaguars. We move between room after room of animals and nonhuman lives representing themselves. Languages we have learned, signals of death and life, versed in their signs, rescinding our mastery of the world.

"O my privative god," again. Perhaps we read it wrong the first time, and what was meant is a god who deprives words by adding ahs, and ins, and ons. A god who makes words private or deprives them at will. Who has deprived us of capacities we should have had. A god who refuses us, unfetters us, declassifies us, and helps us locate the lack by naming it.

"O my [private] god, my intervallic knowing." To think in intervals, to scaffold along tones from one point to the next, each instance of reading leading to the next space, in the time it takes to register and understand. Stretches a play in which the intervals are rung, harmonic, are one after another melodic—one incited ringing after another with a fifth between. "My intervallic knowing," meaning the frequency of one thought and the frequency of the room after, making an interval. I imagine a god defined or defining me by lack—in my knowing in intervals. Moving from one palisade of thought to the next, one rampart to the next, one privative god to the next, the room stretching in even paces between. The reading rooms help me practice such intervallic thinking, the tones of previous rooms sinking, timed, into a song. On this day I read, I practiced, and I lived this book: *Minerva the Miscarriage of the Brain* by Johanna Hedva, in the reading rooms of the Akashic Records.

Room 4.

Carla Leitão: Meow. In the beginning was the word, and the world already existed. And before all time, there was no time and the word was everything because that word had been existing and that world was itself. And that beginning we called origin. Origin was the word and, in no time, the world. Just word, no planetary, no unity, and no universal, just humans. No humanism, no consciousness, no global. Pure ubiquity, pure technologies—dispersion, geology, communication. Ideas, concepts, models, regroundings, totalities, political technologies.

Midway, there were structures. Unstable, unsteady, ungrounded, floating, shifting grounds spiraling upwards. No pre-existing, no preceding layers— spiraling upwards, sinking downwards. Just drowning levitations. Debris finding steady footing over other debris. Infinite dustism. Repeating patterns of infinity: each book, a universe. Each path, a labyrinth. Each void, an endless path. No time, just moments. Dreams of togetherness. Almost. Like. Just.

Interconnected, interoperable, intermingling. Dreams of new beginnings. Why have you brought me here? What have you done? Who am I? The future—far after anyone that you or I have ever cared about has died.

Meow.

Room 5.

Sahej Rahal: Because everyone has been building this fantastic sort of multifaceted library, I thought maybe not to add to its chambers but to smuggle in a book. The book that I found turns out to be an archaeologist's journal, which contains many drawings in it and bits of newspaper clippings, weird ramblings, which I have tried to piece together to make some sense of it. This is how it goes.

By the time they have gathered enough dirt on their knees, archaeologists realize that geology can play tricks on the human mind. They describe this strange occurrence as *terminus post quem*: or simply put, the limit beyond which artifacts that find themselves at odds with the historical era or soil cover they are located within can be described as such. For they could in fact be dated to a time far beyond the dirt that entombs them. Before it has been ordered into the categories of historical dynasties, the Earth, and all it contains, is a labyrinth of deception. 18 degrees, 35 minutes, and 20 seconds north, by 74 degrees, 22 minutes, and 20 seconds east, on the banks of the River Ghod, the prime artery of the Bhima River, lies the Village of Trophies in Ahmednagar. The village today is an all but emptied out archaeological site that flourished as a protohistoric trade center during the late Harappan Age. The site was discovered by a team of archaeologists led by Dr. N. K. Hublikar in 1963. What they found there was a curious tradition by which the denizens of Ahmednagar dealt with their dead. What they had chanced upon was, in fact, a massive burial site with a total of 243 graves. Bodies were buried outdoors, flanked with their pauper tools, ornaments, armor and weaponry—all embroidered with beads of jasper. Each corpse was delicately arranged like the needle of a compass with their heads facing northward. The feet of these bodies were dismembered at the ankles which the archaeologists believed was a ritual that would allow their souls to exit the land.

Yet, among these graves, there was one that was far stranger. At the center of the site, they found a body that was buried indoors beneath the remains of a large structure: perhaps a temple or a stronghold. The corpse belonged to a 35-year-old man seated cross-legged and interred inside a massive terracotta urn that was shaped like a stout beast with four legs. Surrounding his burial urn, there were several others that contained strange artifacts: large ceremonial masks, ritual daggers, thorn blades, agrarian tools, scientific instruments, and votive idols all confined within ancient terracotta. This revelation had set the Indian archaeological community on fire.

Conflicting views were offered on the identity of the seated man. Some members of the ESI maintained that this man was the chieftain of Ahmednagar on account of the solitary indoor burial laden with tools and beaded trinkets. Others argued that this man was an outsider to Ahmednagar, perhaps a vagrant or nomad buried inside his peculiar tomb in accordance with the rituals of his own people who had long vanished, perhaps falling victim to an ancient flood in the Bhima Valley. This view was attributed to the discovery of a boat-like symbol marked on the inside of the four-legged tomb. This tomb was discovered by an anonymous member of Hublikar's excavation team, or supposedly so, who went under the pseudonym Muk Saadhak, or the Mutant Seeker. In the days that followed the discovery, Muk published a series of clandestine papers arguing that the boat motif represented the pan-civilizational belief in the possibility of interdimensional travel. While initially gaining a surprising amount of support among the archaeological community, both the urns and Muk's arguments about them were officially dismissed by the ESI weeks following the declaration of the national emergency in 1975 in India. They described the outsider theory as deviances that were incongruent with the established methods of the ESI, purported by a malicious rabble-rouser. Given their strange nature, the origins of these objects cannot be verified with any degree of certainty. Are they artifacts of a lost civilization that preceded Ahmednagar or are they, in fact, Muk's vessels of transdimensional travel wandering across space and time with the weight of a million histories upon their backs? While all these questions remain unanswered, one thing is certain: they are here now.

Room 6.

Will Scarlett: I will share some not fully formed thoughts on the virtual library. In searching for virtual libraries, I found one on Steam called the *VR Library: Beyond Reading*, which is a VR simulation of reading a book in the garden outside the National Library of Korea. It does not say what the book is, but rather emphasizes the experience of reading at the library. Still, rather than simulating the act of reading a book, my first imagination of a virtual library resembled something more like the computer game *Myst*—where, by reading, one literally enters the book, which becomes a world to be explored and constructed through writing. So instead of the VR Library, maybe that kind of virtual archive resembles something more like Steam itself, which is a library of experiences rather than books—as a kind of inversion where the library becomes the text and the books or VR experiences are the places.

Then we uncover an early anthropologist named Loren Eiseley who describes finding seashells on the beach and seeing hieroglyphic inscriptions on the surface of these shells. The shell that Eiseley found was the alphabet cone or the *conus spurius*, which he interprets to mean "false alphabet." Seashell patterns or hieroglyphs are thought to be read by the snail's mantle, which is the membrane that builds and repairs the shell, to orient it. And, for Eiseley, even before writing, humans sensed their surroundings in a symbolic way, reading signs all around them in the world. In this sense, the false alphabet is also a kind of primordial language, or what Eiseley calls "a double way in which we look at the world."[7] Is it the projection of a being that sees signs and symbols everywhere, or is it a symbolic process that surrounds us, and that our capacity for language emerges from? If we take both as potentially and simultaneously true, then a kind of virtual space opens between the seashell and the manuscript. This obscure reference can then be contrasted with another image of a seashell that is not of an alphabet cone, but rather a textile cone. But textile actually shares the Latin root with text, and the manuscript enclosed therein is by Dostoevsky.

The last example is a book that writer Bruno Schulz read when he was a child, which is now lost. The book infused the mundane life of his town of Drohobych with a climate that he calls the genial epoch, which he describes in the following passage: "A wind moved through its pages, and visions arose. And as the wind silently turned those pages over, blowing those colors and figures away, a shudder ran through the columns of its text releasing flocks of swallows and skylarks from among the letters. It rose into the air, scattering page after page. It gently suffused the landscape which it saturated with its colors. Or it slept, and the wind quietly blew it around like a cabbage rose, its leaves parting, sheet after sheet, eyelid after eyelid, each of them blind, velvety, and lulled to sleep concealing deep within its azure pupil, its peacock core, a screeching nest of hummingbirds."[8] This book is lost, and it is forgotten, though Schulz remembers it in a dream, and when he asks around, no one knows what he is talking about—but he finds traces and scraps of it around his town, such as in advertisement flyers that are used to wrap groceries, and eventually he comes to see the book as less a memory than as a postulate, or as a task to be performed.

He writes: "So, did the genial epoch really happen, or not happen? It is difficult to say. Yes and no. There are things that cannot fully, conclusively happen— they merely attempt to happen. They test the ground of reality; whether it will bear their weight, but they quickly withdraw, and yet, in a certain sense it lives intact and integral in each of its deficient and fragmentary incarnations. Here, the phenomenon of representation creeps in, a vicarious being, and so we shall gather up those illusions, those earthly approximations, like shards of a shattered mirror. For, despite all our reservations, it was."[9] So, those are some shards of thoughts on the virtual library composed of false alphabets, lost books, vicarious beings, projections, permutations, and sensory ecologies between text and world.

Aftermath: Conspiracy of Librarians

Jason Mohaghegh: Thank you to everyone for these subversive threads of departure. As I sit here writing notes frenetically, my first point plays upon Nora's reference to the privative god, which is to say a god whose body is riddled with open lacerations, defects, and chasms of impossibility. Then we jump to Carla's quotation and embellishment of the words of Genesis, which by definition means void, but then is transected by gradual phenomena like primordial geological structures. Then we can connect Sahej's book of missing pages with Will's lost book of traces and scraps, only then to come full circle to Ed's referencing of "deadly time" and "the fall": all of which combined sets the stage for a truly diabolical library full of trapdoors, holes, and unfinished walls.

One of my first questions, then: Have we all intuitively begun building a library through an almost subtractive logic of minimalism? Like those authors of devious omissions, figures who leave things out, who introduce ellipses like bullet holes onto the page, who leave their drawings intentionally incomplete like children. Is this the primary means by which we could construct a library that is simultaneously universal (in the cosmic, extraterrestrial sense) but also singular, irreplaceably rare, and unparalleled? What Nietzsche might call "a book for all and none." Could we design a library for all and none, and what strange forms of untimeliness would this entail, like being a philosopher of lightning (i.e., conducting an event that is both spontaneous yet also highly impermanent, sporadic, episodic).

Hence, if there is a shared insistence among us that our Future Library or Cosmological Archive function upon a kind of minimalist trickery, this would not just require us to dream all the books of all existences but then to submerge them in techniques of removal, withdrawal, concealment, and malfunction. The more one reads, the more the event becomes illegible, a vanishing horizon of comprehensibility that is compounded by different fogs of language. Every detail merely flings open a passageway to three more doors of obscurity, as if we were reading the diaries of an author who wanted their work burned—such that we enter already in the role of the trespasser, an intruder holding forbidden documents that damn us to a certain bewilderment (for they were not written for us).

This then leads us to another dire possibility, wondering about a second question: Should this Future Library have a self-destruct button? Must we embed a certain doom in its architecture, a threat that lingers beneath or a fatal problem lodged in its contours? Thus, the only survival would require something like those first criminal instances of psychoanalysis when the procedure was based on a sharp sensitivity to what is not being said or shown in the light of things, or like a card player who reads the smallest tells that betray an opponent's hand (against their will). To read the lapses, stutters, glitches, nervous ticks, unspoken words, half-transmissions: this might be the only method when dealing with an archive of lost books and missing pages.

> **Nora Khan:** I really love, Jason, how you have linked everyone's readings together in this kind of doom-strategy RPG-like group, built together in this moment. As I was writing, and while hearing everyone speak, I was thinking of how profoundly dangerous private reading once was. I think of the story of William Tyndale and an amazing book called *Burning to Read*: Tyndale translated the Bible from Greek and Latin into common English, King's English, and was chased throughout Europe for something like ten or fifteen years before he was burned at the stake, and the reason (a fact that I return to as so profoundly subversive) was the aim of being

alone with the text, being able to interpret the text as one wanted, which helped form the modern mind and modern self—this ability to interpret the word of God.

So, there is also a secrecy to this act of private reading, and I was thinking to ask: What are the ways, within this time of increasingly enclosed capture and control, through which active reading might continually become dangerous again? How does one keep insisting on individual interpretations and confrontations with the canon, and how will the act of reading remain private? Just think of how we are reading now after being enclosed for ten to fifteen years of being online to extreme degrees, and how our acts of reading are evolving alongside acts of computational enclosure. And I really loved, Will, how you were describing the sense experience between the text and the person, and to think of reading as an act of the vicarious, continually simulating and bringing up a third world between you and the text. And so that constant, active interpretation is, perhaps, a way of evading capture. Keep that experience with the text intimate and dangerous.

> **Jason Mohaghegh:** Absolutely, Nora—when you spoke of extreme privacy, which of course shares an etymological root with your privative god as well, it reminded me to imagine how our Future Library might redefine the question of solitude. Sometimes we forget that Mary Shelley's *Frankenstein* starts as a book of letters, missives that are smuggled from the North Pole by a deranged sea captain to his sister: he is trying to reach the unknown polar limits while his crew debates mutiny above, tempted to throw him overboard and turn back before plunging fully into the starvation and loneliness of those ice worlds. So, this is an impossible transmission—there is a clear logical problem at the outset as to how these letters arrive from such a distance, as he sits in the isolated belly of the ship and his sister reads elsewhere in a solitary room. And this is what opens everything to a meditation on danger, monstrosity, and fatal awe.

I wonder, then, if our Future Library should follow the lead of those few authors who addressed their readers directly (forming an aura of unspeakable gravity and severe tone whenever they say "you"). "How this place suits you," one says. This line reaches out from the pages—not in a general, collective, or universally humanist way—but to implicate the literal individual reader in an ominous exchange. We should consider this moment when passive spectatorship is denied and one realizes that they have to pay an interactive price for reading.

> **Sahej Rahal:** I had this idea—since you mentioned the Minotaur—of what a malicious librarian might be like. Someone who would actively obfuscate

the library and make knowledge inaccessible. And such a figure would definitely be a lot more dangerous to the spread of knowledge and more adept as a gatekeeper of knowledge than someone who burns a book. I am talking about a bureaucrat, essentially, who just goes around the library, moves stuff around, changes the tags and titles, and basically gets in the way. And this is something that I encountered a lot while researching on this place called Ahmednagar. So much information about the site, which challenges a very fundamental part of Indian history, has been obfuscated, and the reason is not any kind of malicious intent but just pure . . . let us call it "bureaumancy." It is literally dark magic where books just seem to move to different shelves.

Ed Keller: The idea that there would be an observer, a system, or being that is capable of reading with us: Nora, I was thinking about this in the way that you were talking about a potential future reading experience where the reader was being anticipated and surveilled, and I thought of this in relation to what Will was unpacking with the sea snail, and the premise that the sea snail is both generating the text on its shell but is also reading something in the sensory ecology of the world that it inhabits. But you wouldn't say that it is a subjective and human kind of reading, nor is it a subjective and human model of the observer. It is more a set of deeply embedded rules for the life-world of the snail and the ecology that it exists within and the ruleset that generates the shell. So, it isn't as if the world that the snail moves through monitors and predicts what the snail will experience, which is the kind of experience that we received with Nora's description of the reading, so I kept thinking: Who is my companion when I am reading? What is that entity, and how is it monitoring and studying me, and how is it predicting what I might want to read next? And then I thought of that from a very impersonal, nonhuman, and non-subjective point of view with the described tension between the real semantics and false semantics (both of the snail's shell but also the false alphabets that we see everywhere).

This struck me as being almost a kind of religious problem: If there is no system, no god-like technologically based system that keeps us company while we read, or an ecological system that also tends us in certain directions, or the kind of ambient bureaucracy that changes what we can find, then what is it? It seems that, for many thousands of years, it simply has been a god that is always with us, that is always watching, always intervening in some way or maybe declining to intervene. And to me, this is a very interesting tension hanging across everything that we are talking about: Where is the reservoir of deep time? If it's not God, then it's a series of rulesets and algorithms that are not written in computational systems but are written in material systems. In Carla's presentation, when you talk about the "ray cat" and the waste isolation pilot plant and the Tower of Babel above it, then there is this deep time reservoir of relationships that are constituted by atomic structure, molecular presence, and the weight of the planet which find a way to cascade up the Tower . . . and in between is the cat which has been genetically engineered as a false alphabet.

Thus, it's a false alphabet to let people know that if you have such strange cats, it's a clue. Something must be going on. It's like the sea snail example of Will: the "ray cat" is also this sand in the gears; it's the glitch in the system that tells you something needs to be paid attention to. Either the bureaucracy was especially efficient and they left a message, or they made a terrible mistake.

Carla Leitão: Or both.

Jason Mohaghegh: In some ways, we are projecting ourselves here as the first sect of the Future Library, thereby entering a conspiracy of designers. Hence, we face a first intentional question: Are we figures of malice, figures of ecstasy, figures of sabotage? Following Sahej's description of a trick-librarian going around, anarchically mixing signals and rearranging texts, we are reminded that saboteurs hold a fascinating philosophy of power based on endurance and vulnerability. This same rationale holds for monsters: Monsters are often thought of in terms of their superpowers—the vampire can levitate, can transform into animals, can read minds, and can walk up walls—but they are also defined by their extreme vulnerabilities. Their bodies are susceptible to sunlight or garlic or wooden stakes, just as we note the werewolf's deadly allergic reaction to silver: they all possess these Achilles' heels in the folkloric mechanisms. And these are not supernatural or extraplanetary triggers; they are elemental substances and simple phenomena that can defeat such otherwise immense, intimidating beings. So, if our library could also be undone through the most fragile means, then maybe it is part of the destiny of each guest reader to try and find what that simple admixture would be that could bring the collapse of an entire edifice of hypothetical and eventual works.

Still, this prospect brought me back to Jorge Luis Borges and his story of the Lottery of Babylon, where he describes a nightly swapping of roles and destinies that allows one to test out all rungs of the existential ladder (from slave to deity). But then he explains that, in order to maintain that element of pure chance within the lottery, there has to be a committee. This is a stunning kind of paradox: that to ensure a reign of luck, one must resort to authoritarian measures. To avoid the pollution or corruption of the wager, there must be this clique of anonymous members who nevertheless walk among the people of the city. And no one ever knows this priesthood who acts as behind-the-scenes ringmasters. Is this our function here this evening, then?

This leads me to one last qualification: that if we are the first order of the Future Library or Cosmological Archive, then we presumably will all be buried there as well. I have been to ancient Middle Eastern and North African libraries where the first librarians are entombed in the structure. A bizarre juxtaposition of texts and graves that makes one ask: What is the responsibility of future visitors to these elders or ancestors? Are they martyrs, ghosts, or guides of a virtual kind?

> **Carla Leitão:** These are all fascinating comments and relationships, but I was remembering Will's suggestion of a quest for the virtual library and thinking: "Aren't they all?" Perhaps one of the main things at stake here is that we tend to think of libraries as the space with the books, which is just a particular actualization of something that is in movement. And we try to attach ourselves to that image, but really that image is fixed, the way we see it in the image per se—nor is that the main library, but probably always already a past version of what is really happening there. The way in which information, knowledge, inspiration, or imagination actually happens follows exactly this idea of the word working like a virus: it has to bind to something to truly exist. So the imagination that is able to decode that word into something is the entire part of what happens—as if, without the act of reading being a decoding in a particular direction, there is nothing. And so, I interpret Kafka wanting his work burned as the opposite of wanting it burned. Maybe it was perhaps to leave it to the imagination, which would be more powerful than being fixated on some past of words that he has suggested for us—that the burning indeed creates what ultimately the words would have been able to open, as you so well said . . . the three obscure doors for every path read.

Moreover, I was thinking about this transformative power of language that allows books—the same book, or the same word, or the same words—to never be the same thing again, to never step into that world again twice (like stepping into a river). To that end, I would emphasize this as an important part of the library as well: that everything around us is a library; DNA is a library, as it is an act of recording. We tend to associate the act of recording with a fixating intentionality of knowledge—the recording of this as important—whereas perhaps in biochemical spheres it is done in a completely different localized way. And through redundancy. This also ties into the mode by which the playing of different roles by an author or a reader tends to exercise itself—and considering Jason's comment on how there was this rotation of different hierarchies, there were always particular moments of history where this was the case: when space and culture were more bound. Being exiled meant that you were sent to where you were not understood, that you could not communicate or that you were different enough to warrant being stripped of who you were essentially—where you did not have the power of your identity. So, it was worse than death, as death could still be honorable and memorable. Exile was for a time when those who knew you could decode the distribution of your ideas. But exile, or even just traveling, could put you at the risk of being enslaved, thereby being stripped away not only of your freedom but again of supposedly who you have come to be. Anyway, this means that there are many powerful relationships that pass through the body of the user and the reader as a library, which just now we are coming to understand, finally, as having always been distributed in time and space everywhere. This is why I think we have a better understanding of the library now than before.

Will Scarlett: With Carla raising the idea of the word as a virus, I also remember Ed having taught courses in the past where he noted viruses as being always in circulation among us and different species as well, and how they leave their traces and marks on our bodies/DNA . . . continually metamorphosing in an extra-individual, extra-species collective library of some kind. But it also reminded me of what Jason was saying earlier about reading as this process of continually becoming more and more incomprehensible, as this kind of bringing in the virus again, a feverish experience of interpretation, which in turn reminded me of the movie *Pi* where one finds this endless procedure of continual interpretation that ultimately leads to mania and madness. In the film itself, it ends up with the character sitting on a park bench and watching the leaves in the trees, and sort of abandoning that task. But then Sahej made the point that these artifacts ultimately are here, regardless of the interpretations, in terms of a kind of co-presence (like Ed's description of the company of spirits, or our embeddedness in an ecology, or the ants that sneak into the AI system in the movie *Pi* as a sort of sand in the machine). This would then take us back to Nora's discussion of the space of the library, and how crossing through the space rather than within an individual book allows for all these different kinds of associative relations to emerge in the interval (by moving in between).

Jason Mohaghegh: To take Carla's suggestion to its edge: What if we built our Future Library as a library of exile to some extent? A library for exiles and an exilic library where all meet as strangers in those outer limits. Typically, when we think of exile, we equate it with displacement and banishment from an original homeland, but also as being flung into the open, not flung into an enclosure. But in fact, we can achieve the exilic experience precisely through something like Nora's map of fractal and fragmentary interior spaces. No doubt, this alignment of miniscule atmospheres, room after room after room, these minor chambers, can also accomplish that strange vertigo of the exilic. At the end of his life, Walter Benjamin, to speak of a fatal exile, inscribed two highly prescient musings: one on the figure of the collector and one on the figure of the storyteller (both of whom are clearly relevant to our purposes today). Even if we do not accept all his paradigms, we should marvel at the mere fact that he began a discourse on the collector, as an entity of cold fanaticism and obsession, someone who perceives the slightest differences and variations between things that no one else cares to see. Still, his second figure of the storyteller is particularly urgent because, while we usually think of them as innocent or purely enchanting figures, the fact remains that storytellers really only show up as harbingers of the death of worlds. Indeed, it is how societies and cultures since ancient times trained children in the lesson of finitude. It is how they taught them about death: since no parent wants to explain mortality to a child, nor to even confront their own mortality, they let the village storyteller instruct children (for the first time consciously) that things end by literally speaking the words "The End." And also that the ending is something indisputable, unstoppable, and irreversible, meaning that if one's favorite character dies in the pages, there is no going back to resurrect them. The incident has transpired and eclipsed.

Not to go astray on too many tangents, but this futuristic library of exiles also connects to a weird suggestion that Jean Baudrillard offered toward the later years of his writing: in effect, he asked whether we are only ever able to come up with a theory of something once it is already at the verge of its own obsolescence. For thousands of years, there have been revolutions, but then Marx comes along and theorizes it. Maybe that is only possible because the historical landscape was entering an era where revolutions would become obsolete. And Freud's unconscious: every great-grandmother of every village I have ever traveled to knows intuitively about the unconscious. They have suspected it for millennia, but it is Freud who fashions its theoretical paradigm. Why did it take so long? Maybe because we were entering an epoch where the unconscious, in its classical sense, would be rendered irrelevant. And this would hold even for Baudrillard's theory of simulation: that he speaks this critical word only when arriving too late on the scene; that it only really crystallizes in a theoretical perception once the term is already on borrowed time and out the door. Every thought, then, is met by the rushing sands of the hourglass. And this is a scary option that we must apply to ourselves in this very gathering: Is it only possible for us to conceptualize the Future Library because we are approaching an instant when there will no longer be libraries, or no future? We may not know which part of the riddle of obsolescence we are facing, or even if it is a double-edged sword.

But the one thing that I derive from all of this is that the Future Library or Cosmological Archive must be possessed of an amorphous sort of brilliance: more specifically, a library of exile would be a tactical space that trains one in masks and impersonations, where reading is nothing more than a chance to steal techniques, to become the wild card or blank domino that can represent any number, symbol, or potential move.

> **Sahej Rahal:** Following this proposition that we can only form an utterance or articulate a full thought when its obsolescence is imminent, I see that as quite productive. For example, if I could pronounce the end of empires, using it as an incantation itself. You can deploy it that way—questions that we are dealing with on a geological scale, an ecological scale, and an economic scale could be answered by this one incantation to end empires.
>
> **Ed Keller:** You know, Sahej, I was also thinking across all these conversations of a very strong image from what you described of the person seated. Presumably, the corpse seated. And I was reminded of images I have seen of the Buddha going through a period of mortification of flesh, where one can view the emaciated body (though it is still alive)—the skeleton visible through the skin—as a way of achieving a connection with something beyond the prison of the flesh. And this image of the seated human occurs again in a very powerful moment in another Darren Aronofsky film: *The Fountain*. While I cannot entirely recommend it due to its being a very awkward piece, I continue to love *The Fountain* more as a set of images, and I remember reading the film treatment (not the script) as a piece of genius because it is a beautiful meditation on some of the themes that we are talking about here, with the image of the seated human coming at the end as we watch Hugh Jackman's character in a future spaceship floating out near a protostar and entering a state of meditation just before the star explodes. And he goes into a moment of ecstasy as his body is consumed by the explosion of the star and erased, but the body then cascades down onto a tree of life which is dying, which is then reborn in a fantastic visual register. It is an archetypal meditation on this idea of being embedded in a rule-system that then leads to one's awareness of the framework, or of the bureaucrats who move through the library. The bureaucrats who supervise the library are often perhaps invisible but then they become rendered visible by a certain set of events or incidents in the narrative. Speaking of Aronofsky, the director finishes his film *Pi* with the character potentially having

performed a lobotomy on themselves, freed from the search for meaning or any kind of transcendental revelation. Or rather, finding transcendental revelation only in the embeddedness in the ecology that they are part of—watching the leaves fall, simply proceeding, without meaning, without structure, without any connection to the bureaucrats or the librarians, but simply perceiving it like that. And I think that the tension here in all our conversations is the question around the degree to which we ourselves become librarians or somehow keepers of the library.

Again, Borges deals with this in such an extraordinarily beautiful way in the Library text. There is the moment when some of the inhabitants of the library decide that they're going to burn some of the books in the collection, and other inhabitants decide that they have to prevent that from happening. But then they stop preventing it from happening because they realize that, since the library is effectively infinite, it does not matter if some of the books are burned because there must be an infinite number of almost exact copies throughout the library of whatever heretical texts the other inhabitants of the library are trying to destroy. Thus, I suppose the point to loop back around to here is the question of the degree to which any of us can place ourselves with agency in relationship to the framework that constructs the library (whatever that library is), the framework that we can then alter whether it is as readers, or as archaeologists, or perhaps even as sea snails who are imperfectly reading an incomplete alphabet and yet being constructed by it simultaneously—knowing it perfectly like the end of the film *Pi*, but without being able to read it any longer. Or finding a place within the system where we become something like the society that knows the ruleset and knows that there is always a gap in the ruleset: that we can find some of the gaps in the ruleset, though never all of the gaps in the ruleset, and that there will always be those gaps to encounter. And this connects to Carla's presentation and the tension present in the waste isolation pilot plant image: for how can we take something and embed it for hundreds of thousands or millions of years deep back into the earth, a supposedly safe place, yet recognize that we always need a bridge to that archive in the form of something like the fantastical, whimsical engineered creatures of the "ray cats," those glow-in-the-dark cats which hopefully will always tell a future reader of the library or a future librarian that something is afoot in the library. Once more, we are all sea snails moving through the library at this slow pace partially reading it and partially only sensing it, but there are these clues like the "ray cats" that wander throughout the library letting us know there is something going on here.

So we have a conversation for a few hours about this and we each, in a refractory way, render this question visible. But then the question is: How far beyond this kind of investigation do we need to go? Because at the end of Walter Benjamin's *The Task of the Translator*, a third figure to add to our collector and storyteller, the implication is either that the perfectly translatable text is the divine text or that the divine text is perfectly translatable because it is completely untranslatable. So we are left in this position of suspension again—understanding it perfectly but unable to utter a single word, even though we understand it perfectly. A very old conundrum: Do we go beyond this? This meditation here, is this enough of a meditation? It is like the alchemist at the end of one of Borges' stories again: the alchemist refuses to divulge any secrets—there are no secrets—and then, left alone in front of the fireplace, the alchemist takes the rose and the rose blossoms back to life.

Nora Khan: I really love these trajectories. Even if the library has everything expected of a Future Library (a full Akashic Record), there will still be books missing, books hard to access, decommissioned books. Books in the basement, canceled, repatriated, burned. Archives are actively made, constructed, and deconstructed, with *some* logic for how books or texts are surfaced, framed, made visible, or algorithmically nudged to the top of one feed versus another. Perhaps there is one book copy versus a thousand copies, since there was always a politics to how books would appear in the library. I envision this library as alive and the archive as alive; we would be able to see, visualize, and know the logic of *why* certain materials are presented in the way that they are. Why are there a thousand copies of one title versus one; which texts were lost and which do we get to see displayed and why? How can this knowledge change our reading in the moment? Is the display logic something that could be open and made malleable? Display would be a subject of critique, muddling any fantasy of a neutral archive. Edith, in the chat, has asked: "Is a library really a passive map that gets activated or is an activation by design?" To this question, I would add: Who is my companion when reading? Who do you imagine reading with you? Recently, we had fabulous public collaborations with GPT-3—and I am sure many have read some striking prose and poetry. I always assume a computational reader when I am reading now. I imagine a humanoid or human-like reader with certain human-recognizing patterns on the other side of my page. I realize more and more that I will not be able to discern who is writing, and whether I am reading the writing of a very statistically sound predictive text constructor or a human author. Strange things start to happen when you read texts this way. And so I imagine reading alongside this imaginary algorithmic reader who reads to summate, to feed its excellence, self-refining its predictive logic in a way to capture how you will read and think through a deep set of algorithms that can anticipate what you might want to read next. You know, we are also training to think and read within the logic of pattern recognition, and so arguing for a critical Future Library is a way to continually shift the frame on that algorithmic reading and enclosure. This other reader is someone who is trying to anticipate how I am reading, and the text becomes the place where you continually interpret based on who you are in that moment, zooming out on why you are interpreting the way you are, such that all of us can read the same passage today and have fifteen or twenty different readings arise; tomorrow, we will have fifteen to twenty new readings of the same passage, and over time, this Library could *work* to keep such an active reading alive.

Carla Leitão: I just wanted to follow up on a question that keeps being brought up: that of the post-future future problem. What is that? A very important note here is that the future has always been that place of the imagination of what is to come, or the way we turn the compass of betterment toward some kind of expectation or desire. But, of course, what happens with a lot of libraries is that they redefine the past. So, the future is the past—our future is the way in which we re-understand the past. For instance, David Graeber's posthumous book *The Dawn of Everything* proposes looking again at the deep past so that it does not reinvent the future but rather reinvents everything that we think is now or has been before. As a way of imagining that future. So, I think there is also that wonderful element of libraries: that we build them into the future and they constantly redefine the past, which is extremely similar to what DNA makes bodies do with random mutation—where we escape oblivion, supposedly, as a species by accepting individual death and scrambling the ingredients of the new cake without intention. Then historically what we do is to build different degrees of intention into the future that continually redefine whatever the structural or foundational idea of our existence has been before. So our impending library would be one that grapples with the post-future future by allowing readers revisitations of the past. See a past that was not there before.

Jason Mohaghegh: Not to endow us with delusions of grandeur, but conceivably we might have solved the problem of how, as the secret society of caretakers or guardians of the Future Library, we would avoid descending into a tyrannical structure. To that end, I was always surprised by a misunderstanding behind the crisis of mediation in Western thought's analysis of modernity and technology. According to most thinkers, there is a kind of doomsday note hovering in the air surrounding our becoming hyper-mediated, and how this is the mechanism of our increasing alienation and disenchantment. But if we transfer our gaze to age-old cultural traditions beyond the west, we find that often the only route to unmediated experiences is precisely (and perhaps paradoxically) through a mediator. In Caribbean, African, and indigenous shamanic traditions, the trance requires the infusion of a persuasive rhythm of the body set in motion by a meditative/mediative figure. In other Eastern European traditions, one discovers the fortune teller, who imposes an entire immersive destiny through the reading of palms, tea leaves, glass shapes, or cards. Nevertheless, her own suggestive presence as a go-between (and the delicate series of gestures that she masters) is what conveys passage. This is even what one observes in certain elder forms of East Asian theater, where an actor on stage carries an entire atmosphere within themselves. None of these cultures ever lamented the intervention of the mediator because mediation is not the problem with contemporary virtuality; rather, it is that the mediating forces have lost their immediacy and thereby do not evoke lightning yet instead drag us toward the radical disillusionment of language and thought. We have lost the power of the ancients' immediacy in the wake of technologies of instantaneity and reproducibility that do not follow the elder logics of manifestation. And it is a grave riddle for us to consider how to bring it back, back to that state where the word is the occasion. You know, there are these rare books of legend in almost every old-world culture that, supposedly upon reading them, either enhance or maim the reader (making their heart race, paralyzing their limbs, or binding their tongue to silence). Of course, this was the era of spells and charms, and it is irrelevant whether their effects are psychosomatic projections or not: this premise is enough to start our library.

As a last point in this direction, Dostoevsky himself was reportedly prone to having long epileptic seizures when staring at the statues of Michelangelo (sometimes taking hours to awaken him and raise him from the ground). This is the look of affirmation. Similarly, it is suspected that the prophet Muhammad from the Islamic tradition was epileptic, and that he would emerge from the caves of revelation sputtering certain paroxysmal utterances which still haunt the texts of the Qur'an. If one pays attention, there are often these three phonemes just hanging at the top before many of the verses, and no one knows what they mean since they do not spell anything coherent. Rather, those were the sounds of his tongue gesticulating in his mouth when he would arrive from the mountain with sacred lines; these are the higher tones of spasm and automaticity. The perfect balance of secrecy within transparency, such that even the act of revelation becomes enigmatic. Our Future Library should perhaps aspire to this feature, since it also shows us the door to the carnivalesque—namely, that our readers can oscillate from balcony to balcony, arcade to arcade, entering from anywhere, teleporting from one salon to another (changing their rhyme and reason) while exposing themselves to disparate airs, as if the act of learning followed the choreography of a circus or masquerade.

> **Carla Leitão:** I am remembering, of course, that shamans needed a chain around them, with someone outside to pull them back in case, during the moment of summoning—or in reacting to some kind of other possession—they would be too attracted to it—and, inadvertently, be pulled in. This harness to the world of living consisted of real matter—chains, rope—, with someone outside the room (of summoning) holding them back.
>
> **Ed Keller:** Yes, things like this always remind me of extreme B-films like *In the Mouth of Madness* or *Event Horizon*, where there is an amazing science fiction image of a ship coming back from another dimension haunted and corrupted. When the crew first starts exploring the event horizon, this younger astronaut, with a nickname like Baby Bear, goes into the place where the black mirror lies at the center of the apparatus, and he gets pulled in. Of course, he is on a kind of umbilical cord, so he is pulled back out, but his mind has been somewhat destroyed by the experience of the encounter. Or consider the image of the soothsayer in *Rashomon*: not that she is on a lanyard to be pulled back, but the fact that there has to be a frame around the soothsayer or the shaman that grounds them in some way and renders them intelligible.

This just jumped into mind, Jason, when you mentioned the divine text as a jagged utterance in the example of Muhammad. From what I understand, the emergence of modern frequency analysis in cryptography had at least part of its base in the attempt to attribute authenticity to specific texts to differentiate them from apocryphal texts (confirming they were the spoken words of the prophet). And frequency analysis was used to precisely situate whether a text that was contested or up for debate could be more likely attributed to Muhammad because it was known what the absolutely authentic texts were in relation to basic principles of frequency analysis of words spoken. And so, I think that there is a very interesting linkage there to the notion of both "attribution" and "authenticity," but also decoding and translation and what it would mean for a shaman or a librarian in the library to be able to do the work that they do with some degree of "authority" (though this is not the right word).

This also goes back to the spellcasting, Jason, that you were talking about—the spoken word instantiating something, like de Certeau's notion that the well-told joke is a coup in time told by the storyteller (or the person telling the joke). It's a coup; it's where time turns into space. It's where there is a diagram of compression because you only have a limited amount of time: you have to tell the joke well, and so you tell it precisely, with a rhythm that is precise. But if you can tell the joke well, then you don't need so much time because you compress an enormous amount of memory into a finite amount of time, which then articulates and changes space. So, there is a theft of information of an unknown amount from time only and a channeling of it into space which is a limited time and a limited constraint, which then articulates unpredicted effects on a finite and limited amount of space and time. And so, I feel that this coup of time, that storytelling moment, is the same as the incantation.

> **Jason Mohaghegh:** Well, this allows us to shatter a certain outlook on knowledge itself for our Future Library—knowledge that is no longer presented to us spatially as cumulative, linear, or teleological but rather based entirely on the question of "the turn." Empirically speaking, I am imagining someone in the Cosmological Archive studying in Nora's chamber, and then they want to turn to Carla's, Ed's, Sahej's, or Will's zone. To basically defect from or desert one site for another. It is therefore intriguing to perhaps look at knowledge as a collection of torsion points, a cartography of abandonment and traversal—namely, those junctures at which someone feels compelled to go from one room to another. And that would restore us to one of the most important concepts that philosophy has never dared to deal with face-to-face: Mood. If our library is predicated not so much on information, reason, or mind in a pure sense, but knowledge defined by moods, then at what point does the mood change, causing someone to turn to the next volume, the next aisle, the next reading room? I think that is a crucial part of the formula that we might try to orchestrate.

> **Carla Leitão:** Yes, and to be very careful, we know that architectural design (often if not by definition) is conservative: its own nature is to freeze a moment in time of belief in a certain typology of transmission—be it a textual, content-based, message-based dimension or of a particular behavioral, gestural library—and to say, "We are going to stay some years like this, and do this for a while now" instead of following wherever information wants to go, which is to be freewheeling and perhaps to be constantly incomprehensible until it gets frozen again. Yet I also find compelling this possibility that cultures of interpretation or orality would render ideas or words into space. So, a cultural storytelling that allows for more freedom of association to exist would be, supposedly, completely against books. This is like the problem of the paradox of dialogues: no one who really believes in dialogues would ever allow them to exist in a book because if the dialogue is true, it should be a fight, perhaps a deadly one —to see who wins that space—rather than being able to

allow a sequential, calm, polite reading of one argument after a complete opposite one. And so, that idea of a conquering of space—also of orality and information—I think immediately sub-intends a completely different idea from that of bodies, such as books or buildings or other kinds of "conservative" (preservation?) engravings.

One can even see this in the unscripted way that many of us brought up cats in this conversation—starting with the lion-beast that Ed presented, and then Nora's jaguar as a force of recognition but also those liberating moments of incomprehension, and Sahej's geologies of the inert and the biological, such that when I raised this cozy meow of my presentation, already others had created a nice bed for it, which happened with their felines, so that my cats no longer even looked so wild anymore. This is in the vein of what Donna Haraway implies by her "companion to reading" (the companion species of dogs) where we learn from that kind of partnership that there is a training of both parties in the fact that they do not understand everything, but we learn it from that incapacity to completely communicate through what we think is language.

Jason Mohaghegh: To Carla's excellent earlier point, one thing I learned late in my intellectual career is that sometimes one does not have to choose but rather can steal all the best options and even entwine mutually exclusive powers/concepts. For instance, that of speech versus text. So, we could construct our Library such that certain books were recited through oral rituals whereas others were textually inscribed. We also forget that monastic orders explored the expressive richness in silence, which is a fascinating third orientation there. Even Samuel Beckett was obsessed with the quest of writing as a movement toward silence, and certain minimalist composers, such that we too could build silences into the catalogues and processes of knowing here. Hence, while I admire the oral evocation for a number of reasons, and even the digital file, I would want to keep texts in our archive for just one reason above all else: counterintuitively, they allow you to cheat, to embellish and exaggerate, to distort or expand traditions. Just to cast a great shadow upon one of the sacred icons of Western philosophy, Plato's transliteration of the Socratic dialogues is obviously a partial if not predominant fabrication: no one possesses such perfect recall in their memory banks, and these recollective writings are done in the aftermath of the death of Socrates, composed while sitting in the solitude of Plato's study to honor a dead master whose past spoken words could never be replicated with perfect accuracy. And the apprentice philosopher recognizes this, which means there is an understanding that he must insert and insinuate content into the holes where his remembering fails, to fill the gaps with an excess or substitute line of his own, or even a temptation one night to correct those few places where his teacher's thoughts were flawed, and this impulse becomes a wonderful slippery slope to reinvention and extension of the original game. A contagious fever dream process of recording texts that always becomes the writing of the next text (like a palimpsest that refuses reduction or suffocation to the one-dimensionality of a single layer).

Still, we have a problem: If our conspiracy of librarians is also the advent of yet another avant-garde, then we should be careful enough to study a recurring pitfall of the prior avant-gardes. Why did all the great avant-garde movements of the twentieth century burn out and exhaust themselves? Yes, because of political crises and socio-historical pressures, but also because they became increasingly self-enclosed and domineering: Surrealism started excommunicating some of its best geniuses, having midnight trials to accuse them of violating the axioms of the first manifestos. This is no different than the arc of religious traditions, where again for instance Muhammad initially ascends to his remote cave to bask in otherworldly messages only then at some point to just stop going. And there is no indication that the valve of eternal truths has stopped pouring out verses—it is that he realizes one cannot build a historical movement on a never-ending, ceaseless flow of interlocution. At some point, he has to impose a false limit and go to war, not to mention that this did not even prevent the later problem of there being tens of conflicting Qur'ans found roaming about the Arabian landscape, such that by the third Caliph's reign one version had to be selected and all others ordered burned. Of course, the justification of divine inspiration is used to claim that the "correct version" (the pure tongue of God) was rescued and salvaged from the variations, but we want to learn how to sustain the open-endedness of the profusion principle. The same with the four Gospels of the New Testament: Why only four? At what point was it decided that the fourth would become the last, and what about those illicit other gospels excavated from time to time in the aftermath against the will to containment of the inquisitors? This is never a simple accident: for me, this marks the very moment of the downfall of a movement's energetic and creative force. What was once thirst, whim, or curiosity becomes a desperate orthodoxy trying to retain what is already built. Everything is diminishing returns thereafter. So how could we create a Library where ingenuity remains thriving, and books bifurcate to form forked paths?

> **Ed Keller:** The question of architecture comes up once more, in relation to translation but also to the neurobiological parameters that we as humans are defined by. I started my presentation off with the image of *Saint Jerome in His Study* by Albrecht Dürer, but there is another famous image of Saint Jerome in his study by da Messina. Here he is in

a cabinet, and around him in the cabinet are some books and artifacts, but there is a deep space opened by two galleries going off into the distance in addition to a natural green landscape in the perspectival distance behind him, and the floor has a grid. But we are outside the study, actually outside the building itself, which is rendered in a kind of tan stone, looking in. In the Dürer image, by contrast, we too are in the space with Saint Jerome. But in both cases, Dürer's and Messina's, Saint Jerome has a special, privileged relationship with animals. And this communication with the non-human is part of what makes him saintly. Now, each of these renderings situates him in a slightly different way for us perspectivally, but I think the other observation to make here in relation to architecture is to ask the degree to which architects can calibrate what happens when the mind is formed in the cave. I am invoking Jason's example of a prophet retreating to a cave to receive a message to inquire this: Are they receiving a message because God speaks from the sky or speaks from the bowels of the earth? Or are they receiving the message because the human mind is formed in a cave, in quite an interesting way? And we can go back to Julian Jaynes and others who have written on the pre-modern mind, or the mind in the cave.

Think about the Chauvet Cave and Werner Herzog's beautiful film on it, *Cave of Forgotten Dreams*, where the director argues that the paintings on the walls of those caves, thirty or forty thousand years ago, were proto-cinema made by people who were in a tight dialogue—in the Julian Jaynes sense of the bicameral mind, or in the Lucasian sense of the integrated civilization—with multiple voices of God. Not just one voice of God but a kind of dithyrambic, continually heteroglossic communication with the voice of God, because the human mind and the human body, and the ears, and our senses of smell, touch, and sight, when in the cave, go through that kind of transformation. This prompts us to ask what the architecture of the Future Library does neurophysiologically to a human, a baseline human. And of course, Nora, you talked a lot about the experience we would have as something other than a baseline human, because of the way that we might co-read, co-analyze, and co-create, as we are followed by the external observer that you described. Thus, I wonder about the function of architecture and whether we imagine it around a baseline human neurophysiology or if we imagine an architecture that would be suitable for a non-baseline human physiology/neurophysiology. Or, as some people in the chat have suggested, to go beyond this question of architecture entirely, or reframe it, and I think this was Andrew McCarell's comment: "To dispense not entirely with the emphasis of the library on needing an architecture and instead let it be an action or transaction like a peer-to-peer sharing network or a reading practice." Obviously, as architects, we think about that stuff all the time, imagining what it would mean to take a "non-baseline model of architecture" as an interface, as a techne, and then to import it around those models that are non-standard.

Jason Mohaghegh: This would return us to Nora's own prophetic line for us to seek "A library at the edge of a glacier, or on a coast, or a low-lying plain in a city"; to me, that implies something that runs with the nomads and phantasms we devise, a library that moves with us.

Carla Leitão: How to build a library that is not like a library.

Epilogue
Exit Future
Author: Bogna Konior

> *Xenophilia is not only desire for the other, but a desire to become other; to burn away the present with new forms of production, reproduction or affiliation . . . Thus insofar as xenophilia is satisfied, it cannot be. Insofar as xenophilia is, it cannot be satisfied.*
> —DAVID RODEN, *XENOPHILIA*[1]

"The future" is such a domesticated concept, all wrapped up in partitions and expectations. Who are we to decide when the known ends and when novelty begins? Kill the chronocop in your head. Those who anticipate the new and lament its absence have already missed its arrival. You're waiting and waiting, and the boats have already sailed off without you. Everything is already happening, all at once.

Exit future. Enter time.

Time! We have discovered that it is more like a membrane than an arrow, and yet we feel that it is the "future" that is open and flexible and the "past" that is fixed.

What if it is the other way around? Determinism and contingency, fate and accident, are closer in kind than we could ever grasp. Outside of our experience, there might be a perfect reversibility between the past and the future, but our perception of time is as linear as a bad story.

*

To hope for change or to fear it are both losing strategies. Hope and fear are two sides of the same coin, both rooted in the inability to live fully in what is. The unknown cannot be judged as good or bad. It cannot be hoped for or feared insofar as it escapes its own domestication in the present.

The unknown can only be craved because real desire is boundless and intuitive, open-ended, and without moral restrictions. To love the unknown is to be a prisoner to gradients of change, always and never.

Notes

Chapter 1.0

1 0. A note of special gratitude to Kaiyu Watkins for his outstanding editorial assistance in the preparation of this manuscript. Every future needs a great scribe. Nandipha Mntambo, "Purge and Stepping into Self," https://archive.stevenson.info/exhibitions/materials/mntambo.htm.

Chapter 2.0

1 Aleister Crowley, *The Book of Thoth* (York Beach, ME: Samuel Weiser, 1995), Part Two, §0 ['The Fool'], 57.
2 Henri Focillon, *The Life of Forms in Art* (New York: Zone Books, 1992).
3 Rhea Myers, *Proof of Work: Blockchain Provocations 2011–2021* (Falmouth: Urbanomic, 2022), 214.
4 Pat Cadigan, *Fools* (London: Gollancz, 2019), 279.
5 Antoine de Saint-Exupery, *The Little Prince*, trans. R. Howard (Boston: Clarion Books, 2000).
6 Aldo Leopold, *A Sand County Almanac* (Oxford: Oxford University Press, 2020).

Chapter 3.0

1 R. A. Schwaller de Lubicz, *The Temple in Man: Sacred Architecture and the Perfect Man* (Rochester, VT: Inner Traditions, 1981), 21.
2 https://www.archoutloud.com/testbed.html.

Chapter 4.0

1 Benjamin Noys, "Drone Metaphysics," https://culturemachine.net/vol-16-drone-cultures/drone-methaphysics/.

2   Paul Virilio, *War and Cinema: The Logistics of Perception* (London: Verso, 1989), 4.
3   Paul Virilio, *Polar Inertia* (Los Angeles: Sage Publishers, 1999), 102.
4   Grégoire Chamayou, A Theory of the Drone (New York: The New Press, 2015), 37.
5   Debashish Banerjee and Makarand R. Paranjape, Critical Posthumanism and Planetary Futures (India: Springer, 2016).
6   Walter Benjamin, "The Work of Art in the Age of Mechanical Reproduction," in Illuminations, edited by Hannah Arendt, trans. by Harry Zohn (New York: Schocken Books, 1968).

Chapter 5.0

1   Plato, *The Last Days of Socrates* (New York: Penguin, 2003).
2   Plato, *Phaedrus* (Cambridge: Hackett Publishing Co., 1995).
3   Image: https://publicdomainreview.org/collection/the-sea-monk-ca-1845/.
4   Ted Chiang, *Exhalation* (New York: Knopf, 2019).
5   Image: https://en.wikipedia.org/wiki/Argiope_lobata#/media/File:Argiopespain.jpg.

Chapter 6.0

1   Judith Butler, *Gender Trouble. Feminism and the Subversion of Identity* (New York & London: Routledge, 1999), 171.
2   Jenna Sutela, "RI JIRI I O WA NU RU DAINICHI T-1000," 2016, https://vimeo.com/398792816.
3   Donna Haraway, "Situated Knowledges. The Science Question in Fominism and the Privilege of Partial Perspective," *Feminist Studies* 14, no. 3 (Autumn, 1988): 595.
4   Reza Negarestani, *Cyclonopedia. Complicity With Anonymous Materials* (Melbourne: Re.press, 2008), 18.

Chapter 7.0

1   Georges Didi-Huberman, The Surviving Image: Phantoms of Time and Time of Phantoms: Aby Warburg's History of Art, trans. Harvey Mendelsohn (University Park: Pennsylvania State University Press, 2016).
2   Mahmoud al-Buraikan, "Tale of the Assyrian Statue," in *Modern Arabic Poetry*, trans. L. Jayyusi and N. S. Nye (New York: Columbia University Press, 1991), 188.
3   David Spriggs website: https://davidspriggs.art/.

Chapter 1.0

1. https://writings.stephenwolfram.com/2020/04/finally-we-may-have-a-path-to-the-fundamental-theory-of-physics-and-its-beautiful/.
2. https://apod.nasa.gov/apod/ap191119.html [Image: Mauricio Salazar, "Milky Way Over Uruguayan Lighthouse," 2019].
3. https://writings.stephenwolfram.com/2018/01/showing-off-to-the-universe-beacons-for-the-afterlife-of-our-civilization/

    additionalresources on the concept of the funeral pyre beacon:

    https://www.centauri-dreams.org/2011/12/08/detecting-a-funeral-pyre-beacon/; https://www.centauri-dreams.org/2015/12/14/seti-project-argus-and-the-long-stare/; https://www.centauri-dreams.org/2008/10/31/a-beacon-oriented-strategy-for-seti/;

    https://www.centauri-dreams.org/2008/10/29/seti-figuring-out-the-beacon-builders.
4. https://slate.com/technology/2011/11/communicating-with-aliens-through-an-interstellar-beacon.html; Image: ALMA telescope, Atacama; still from Nostalgia for the Light [Guzman 2010], https://mubi.com/films/nostalgia-for-the-lighthttps://www.almaobservatory.org/en/2000/03/.
5. Greg Egan, *Schild's Ladder* (Australia: Gollancz, 2002).
6. Image: https://www.gregegan.net/SCHILD/00/SchildExcerpt.html.
7. https://offscreen.com/view/tarkovsky1.
8. http://www.ekac.org/lepus.1.html.
9. https://en.wikipedia.org/wiki/Lepus_(constellation).
10. Phillip K. Dick, VALIS (New York: Bantam, 1981).
11. https://artofmaquenda.tumblr.com/post/188384227774/prince-with-a-thousand-enemies-finally-finished.
12. Phillip K. Dick, *Do Androids Dream of Electric Sheep* (New York: Doubleday, 1968).
13. https://philosopherai.com/.

Chapter 2.0

1. Image: Gregoire A. Meyer, When the Drape Falls, 2020,. https://artelaguna.world/graphics/when-the-drape-falls/
2. https://news.mit.edu/.../targeted-dream-incubation-dormio...
3. Image: Designer: CROX, "Innings" (Milan, 2016).
4. https://thereader.mitpress.mit.edu/death-dust-the-little.../
5. Image: Gijs Van Vaerenbergh, "Labyrinth," 2020.
6. https://workinjapan.today/hightech/fastest-elevators-of-the-world/
7. Image: Leandro Erlich, "Two Different Tomorrows," 2011.
8. https://www.nationalgeographic.com/photography/article/japan-hikikomori-isolation-society.

Notes

9 Image: Chiharu Shiota, "During Sleep," Lucerne installation, 2002.

10 https://www.theguardian.com/technology/2019/feb/22/silicon-valley-immortality-blood-infusion-gene-therapy.

11 Image: Ross Lovegrove, Lasvit Liquidkristal, 2012.

12 https://www.dezeen.com/2021/03/09/space-hotel-voyager-station-gateway-foundation/

13 Image: Osteon Cumulus Vertical City, 2016.

14 https://thenextweb.com/gaming/2019/03/21/steam-game-its-winter/

15 Image: Ilya Mazo, "It's Winter," 2019; quotes refer to Samuel Beckett.

16 https://tvtropes.org/pmwiki/pmwiki.php/WebOriginal/TheBackrooms

17 Quotes refer to Franz Kafka (*Blue Octavo Notebooks*, Exact Change: 2004).

18 https://www.popularmechanics.com/science/a35788050/dyson-sphere-digital-resurrection-immortality/

19 https://www.popularmechanics.com/science/a35982125/humans-could-evolve-to-be-venomous/

20 Image: Belkis Ayon, "La Familia," 1991.

21 https://www.archdaily.com/959011/mars-house-first-digital-home-to-be-sold-on-the-nft-marketplace

22 https://medium.com/@donny313g/down-the-rabbit-hole-how-a-dark-room-stimulates-dmt-and-profound-experiences-7faac6d0d547

23 Image: Tiago Marinho, "183.365," 2020.

24 https://www.reuters.com/lifestyle/science/nasa-extracts-breathable-oxygen-thin-martian-air-2021-04-22/

25 https://www.iflscience.com/brain/in-1983-the-cia-wrote-a-bizarre-report-about-transcending-spacetime-with-your-mind/

26 https://darknessconference2019.wordpress.com/.

27 https://modium.com/@LoupVentures/the-metaverse-explained-part-1-an-inside-look-f6e15696ae0c; https://www.linkedin.com/pulse/everything-you-know-metaverse-wrong-william-burns-iii?trk=portfolio_article_card_title

28 https://www.theguardian.com/news/2021/apr/27/the-clockwork-universe-is-free-will-an-illusion?

29 Image: Mark Tansey, "Derrida Queries de Man," 1990.

30 https://www.counterpunch.org/2021/05/05/crispr-madness-welcome-to-the-age-of-genetic-chaos/

31 https://www.theguardian.com/music/2021/may/05/clearing-the-dancefloor-how-club-culture-became-a-museum-piece

32 https://bigthink.com/surprising-science/physicist-creates-ai-algorithm-prove-reality-simulation

33 https://www.mvrdv.nl/projects/248/the-imprint

34 https://www.e-flux.com/books/151809/art-without-death-conversations-on-russian-cosmism/

35 https://www.wired.com/story/researchers-levitated-a-small-tray-using-nothing-but-light

36 https://www.archdaily.com/963755/snohetta-proposes-manifestation-of-technology-for-qianhai-design-competition

37 https://theconversation.com/is-reality-a-game-of-quantum-mirrors-a-new-theory-suggests-it-might-be-162936

38 https://www.bbc.com/news/science-environment-57742138

39 Image: Compressed ICEYE Radar Satellite, Rotterdam, Netherlands, 2021. https://www.iceye.com/

40 http://www.dianaalhadid.com/work/c/sculptures / Image: Diana Al-Hadid, "Self-Melt", 2008.

41 https://www.wallpaper.com/fashion/alpha-tauri-futuristic-fashion-hq

42 https://www.independent.co.uk/climate-change/news/dubai-fake-rain-heat-b1887596.html

43 https://www.thrillist.com/news/nation/abandoned-olympic-venues

44 https://www.yachtsinternational.com/yachtlife/drowning-doesnt-look-like-drowning

45 https://www.frieze.com/article/choi-minwhas-new-ancient-myths

46 https://hyperallergic.com/667848/jason-decaires-taylor-musan-sculpture-museum-is-underwater/

Chapter 3.0

1 Image: He Ao Hou: *A New World*, 2018.

2 Image: Teiji Furuhashi, *Lovers*, 1995.

3 Image: Diego Gil, *Bsides*, 2011.

4 Image: Walter Scott, *Xinona*, 2017.

5 Sophia Chen, "Unusual Fluids Flip, Twirl and Redefine How Liquids Work," *Wired* (September 2019), https://www.wired.com/story/unusual-fluids-flip-twirl-and-redefine-how-liquids-work/.

6 Image: Ferry Siemensma, *Amoeba Proteus*, 2019.

7 Velimir Khlebnikov, "Ourselves and Our Buildings: Creators of Streetsteads," in *The King of Time*, trans. Paul Schmidt (Cambridge: Harvard University Press, 1985), 133–43.

8 Jenna McKnight, "Hurricane Informs Coastal Home in Puerto Rico by Fuster + Architects," *Dezeen* (January 2021), https://www.dezeen.com/2021/01/30/casa-flores-fuster-architects/.

9 Image: Noémie Goudal, *Combat*, 2012.

10 Roberto Bolaño, *2666,* translated by Natasha Wimmer (Bolano Book: Picador, 2004).

11 Image: Ali Eslami, *False Mirror*, Virtual Reality Project, 2020.

12 Native Land Digital https://native-land.ca/.

13 Stephanie Pappas, "Why Russian Scientists Just Just Deployed a Giant Telescope Beneath Lake Baikal," *Live Science* (March 2021), https://www.livescience.com/russia-deploys-underwater-telescope-lake-baikal.html; https://history.fnal.gov/historical/experiments/learn_neutrino.html.

14 François Hug et al., "Individuals Have Unique Muscle Activation Signatures," *Journal of Applied Physiology* (October 2019), https://journals.physiology.org/doi/full/10.1152/japplphysiol.01101.2018.

15 Jerzy Ficowski, *Regions of the Great Heresy* (New York: Norton, 2003), 146.

16 Elizabeth Gibney, "Coronavirus Lockdowns Have Changed the Way Earth Moves," *Nature* (March 2020), https://www.nature.com/articles/d41586-020-00965-x.

17 Image: Henri Rousseau, *Tiger in a Tropical Storm*, 1891.

18 Theme Park Review, "New Roller Coaster! Abyssus at Energylandia!" *Youtube*, https://www.youtube.com/watch?v=syiO0ZdmPrY.

19 "The Berkeley Pit," Atlas Obscura, https://www.atlasobscura.com/places/berkeley-pit; Heidi Ledford, "Hungry Fungi Chomp on Radiation," *Nature* (May 2007), https://www.nature.com/news/2007/070521/full/news070521-5.html.

20 Vocativ, "See Inside the Longest Known Drug Tunnel Below Mexico's Border," *Youtube*, https://www.youtube.com/watch?v=p9JsmDzG_UU.

21 Image: Marius Arnesen, *Smuggling Tunnels, Rafa, Gaza*, 2009.

22 Alexandru Micu, "Scientists Observe Nanobots Coordinating Inside a Living Host," *ZME Science* (March 2021), https://www.zmescience.com/science/nanobots-coordinating-in-vivo-82637465/.

23 Image: Fritz Lang, *Metropolis*, 1927.

24 Carmat, "Aeson by Carmat Animation," *Youtube*, https://www.youtube.com/watch?v=xdcLKTpxr2g.

25 Image: Cymascope, *Human Spinal Signal*, 2020.

26 Henri Bergson, *An Introduction to Metaphysics* (New York: Knickerbocker Press, 1912), 14.

27 Image: Joachim Patinir, Charon Crossing the Styx, ca. 1520–1524.

28 Live Science Staff, "Coldest, Driest, Calmest Place on Earth Found," *Livescience* (August 2009), https://www.livescience.com/7860-coldest-driest-calmest-place-earth.html.

29 Image: Masaki Kobayashi, Harakiri, 1962.

30 Shangrong Jiang et al., "Policy Assessments for the Carbon Emission Flow and Sustainability of Bitcoin Blockchain Operation in China," *Nature* (April 2021), https://www.nature.com/articles/s41467-021-22256-3.

31 Image: Geoffrey Short, *Untitled Explosion* #1CF2, 2007.

32 Aaron Hilsz-Lothian, "Quantas Committed to Launching Project Sunrise," *Sam Chui* (February 2021), https://samchui.com/2021/02/07/qantas-committed-to-launching-project-sunrise/#.YIGxw31KgWo.

33 View Corporation, "4K Kyoto," *Youtube*, https://www.youtube.com/watch?v=mJDf1GXaF-w.

34 Nyéléni, https://nyeleni.org/en/homepage/.

35 Stefano Scodanibbio, *Voyage That Never Ends* (San Francisco, CA: New Albion, 1998), https://www.youtube.com/watch?v=rX2fSd7DlXc.

36 Migrations in Motion, https://maps.tnc.org/migrations-in-motion/#4/19.00/-78.00.

37 Image: Dan Majka, *Migrations in Motion*, 2016.

38 Davide Castelvecchi, "How 'Spooky' is Quantum Physics?" *Nature* (January 2020), https://www.nature.com/articles/d41586-020-00120-6.

39 Image: Tatsuya Tanaka, *Miniature Calendar*, 2014.

40 Maia Research Chinese, "Global Office Chairs Sales Market Report 2023," *Market Intelligence Data* (April 2023), https://marketintelligencedata.com/reports/8361629/global-office-chairs-sales-market-report-2023.

41 Boston Dynamics, "Do You Love Me?" *Youtube*, https://www.youtube.com/watch?v=fn3KWM1kuAw.

42 Image: Giovanni Bracelli, *Bizzarie di Varie Figure*, 1624.

43 Walt Mills, "To Make a Better Sensor, Just Add Noise," *Penn State* (September 2020), https://www.psu.edu/news/research/story/make-better-sensor-just-add-noise/.

44 Image: Agnes Martin, *Untitled*, 1960, MOMA Collection.

45 Brian Merchant, "Everything That's Inside Your iPhone," *Vice* (August 2017), https://www.vice.com/en/article/433wyq/everything-thats-inside-your-iphone

46 Ludwig Wittgenstein in Elizabeth Anscombe, *An Introduction to Wittgenstein's Tractatus* (London: Hutchinson & Co., 1959), 151.

47 Image: Sven Sauer, *Melancholia,* 2011.

48 Luis Anchordoqui and Eugene Chudnovsky, "Can Self-Replicating Species Flourish in the Interior of a Star?" Letters in High Energy Physics (2020), http://journals.andromedapublisher.com/index.php/LHEP/article/view/166/85 / Image: Alfred Kubin, Illustration for Lesabéndio: An Asteroid Novel by Paul Scheerbart, 1913.

49 Jorge Luis Borges, "The Garden of Forking Paths," in *Collected Fictions* (New York: Viking, 1998), 122.

50 Image: Sophie Fiennes, Over Your Cities Grass Will Grow (2011), film.

51 Antti Revonsuo, *Inner Presence* (Cambridge: MIT Press, 2006), 347.

52 ViralVideoLab, "Starlink Satellites Train Seen from Earth," *Youtube*, https://www.youtube.com/watch?v=h-S67Y7gEeY.

53 Chelsea Gohd, "Using Gamma Rays, Scientists Map Out 21 New Constellations," *Astronomy* (October 2018), https://www.astronomy.com/science/using-gamma-rays-scientists-map-out-21-new-constellations/.

54 Roger Caillois, "The Natural Fantastic," in *The Edge of Surrealism*, edited by Claudine Frank (Durham: Duke University Press, 2003), 357.

55 Katie Burton, "The Future of Digital Mapping Is a Tale of Two Halves," *Medium* (September 2019), https://medium.com/geographical/the-future-of-digital-mapping-is-a-tale-of-two-halves-9d3155df43bc.

56 Paul Ridden, "Autonomous Boat Gets Around Under Wave Power," *New Atlas* (March 2018), https://newatlas.com/autonaut-autonomous-unmanned-surface-vessel/53949/.

57 Image: Tomás Saraceno, *Aerocene Concept Drawing,* 2015.

58 Arnold Wilkins, "The Scientific Reason You Don't Like LED Bulbs," *Scientific American* (August 2017), https://www.scientificamerican.com/article/the-scientific-reason-you-dont-like-led-bulbs-mdash-and-the-simple-way-to-fix-them/.

59 Image: Charles Gatewood, The Dream Machine, 1972.

60 Dan Robitzski, "Air Force Research LAb Says Force Fields Are 'On the Horizon,'" *Futurism* (July 2021), https://futurism.com/the-byte/military-force-fields.
61 Gabriel Tarde, *Monadology and Sociology* (Melbourne: re.press, 2012), 44.
62 David Cenciotti, "Airbus Has Just Unveiled Germany's Classified Diamond Shaped Low Observable UAV Testbed," (November 2019), https://theaviationist.com/2019/11/05/airbus-has-just-unveiled-germanys-classified-diamond-shaped-low-observable-uav-testbed-lout/.
63 August Endell, "The Beauty of the Metropolis (1908)," *Grey Room* 56 (2014): 132.
64 Image: Lebbeus Woods, Terrain, 1999, https://www.moma.org/collection/works/88847?artist_id=26299&page=1&sov_referrer=artist.
65 Pierre Bourdin et al., "A Virtual Out-of-Body Experience Reduces Fear of Death," *PLOS One* (January 2019), https://journals.plos.org/plosone/article?id=10.1371/journal.pone.0169343.
66 Adrielle So, "14 Best Fitness Trackers," *Wired* (August 2023), https://www.wired.com/gallery/best-fitness-tracker/.
67 Claire Petitmengin et al., "Studying the Experience of Meditation through Microphenomenology," *Current Opinion in Psychology* 28 (2019): 56.
68 Image: Andrei Tarkovsky, *Solaris,* 1972.

Chapter 4.0

1 https://www.cshl.edu/the-non-human-living-inside-of-you/.
2 https://www.technologyreview.com/2018/03/13/144721/a-startup-is-pitching-a-mind-uploading-service-that-is-100-percent-fatal/.
3 http://arachnophilia.net/.
4 https://www.theguardian.com/science/2019/oct/21/scientists-may-have-crossed-ethical-line-in-growing-human-brains.
5 https://royalsociety.org/topics-policy/projects/animate-materials/.
6 https://news.mit.edu/2019/storing-vaccine-history-skin-1218.
7 https://www.livescience.com/swirlonic-matter-unusual-behavor.html.
8 https://www.nature.com/articles/s41586-020-3010-5.
9 https://www.technologynetworks.com/neuroscience/news/carbon-nanotube-implants-used-to-repair-the-mammalian-spinal-cord-340958#.YFJsfBqpUrs.twitter.
10 https://www.irenefenara.com/three-thousand-tigers.
11 https://www.nytimes.com/2021/03/17/health/mice-artificial-uterus.html.
12 https://i-d.vice.com/en_uk/article/y3z8vm/what-is-reality-shifting-and-why-is-it-taking-over-tiktok.
13 https://www.nytimes.com/2021/03/24/movies/seaspiracy-review.html.
14 https://www.sciencenews.org/article/sea-slug-detached-head-crawl-regenerate-grow-new-body.
15 https://www.sciencealert.com/there-s-one-kind-of-water-that-doesn-t-taste-like-water-scientists-confirm.

16 https://www.seas.harvard.edu/news/2013/05/beautiful-flowers-self-assemble-beaker.
17 https://www.nature.com/articles/d41586-021-01001-2.
18 https://www.sciencealert.com/we-could-learn-to-communicate-with-spiders-with-music-made-from-their-webs.
19 Cyrus Dunham, "Everything, All At Once Through the Eyes of WangShui," https://www.interviewmagazine.com/art/everything-all-at-once-through-the-eyes-of-wangshui.
20 Henry Corbin, *Cyclical Time & Ismaili Gnosis*, trans. Ralph Manheim and James W. Morris (London: Kegan Paul International, 1983).
21 https://journals.sagepub.com/doi/full/10.1177/2053951718808553.
22 Image: Alessandro Poli, CCA. Collage, "Supersuperficie" ("Supersurface"), and the Autostrada Terra-Luna ("Interplanetary Highway"), 1972.

Chapter 5.0

1 https://divisare.com/projects/437077-wutopia-lab-creatar-images-the-satori-harbor.
2 http://www.bbc.com/travel/story/20200929-the-remote-greek-island-seeking-new-residents.
3 https://psyche.co/ideas/immersive-art-opens-a-window-on-the-mystery-of-other-minds.
4 https://www.serpentinegalleries.org/whats-on/lygia-pape-magnetized-space/.
5 https://www.nytimes.com/interactive/2021/03/02/climate/atlantic-ocean-climate-change.html.
6 https://starts-prize.aec.at/en/aerocene-foundation/.
7 https://en.wikipedia.org/wiki/Russian_Futurism.
8 https://futurism.com/the-byte/china-plans-blanket-public-space-spy-cameras.
9 https://publicdomainreview.org/essay/grandville-visions-and-dreams.
10 https://www.amykarle.com/project/regenerative-reliquary/.
11 https://www.reddit.com/r/bladerunner/comments/dm0v5y/concept_art_of_the_hall_of_wallaces_office_in/; https://www.archdaily.com/881356/barozzi-veigas-unbuilt-museum-project-immortalized-in-blade-runner-2049.
12 https://walkerart.org/magazine/counter-currents-tomas-saraceno-on-buckminster-fuller.
13 https://www.harpersbazaar.com/culture/film-tv/a31822923/westworld-season-3-filming-shooting-locations/.
14 https://christojeanneclaude.net/artworks/the-mastaba/.
15 https://www.bbc.com/future/article/20210330-why-we-shouldnt-be-afraid-of-nightmares.
16 https://www.vox.com/culture/22062796/monoliths-utah-california-romania.

17 https://www.independent.co.uk/life-style/gadgets-and-tech/universe-brain-shape-cosmic-web-galaxies-neurons-b1724170.html; https://nautil.us/issue/50/emergence/the-strange-similarity-of-neuron-and-galaxy-networks.
18 https://www.amnh.org/explore/news-blogs/on-exhibit-posts/the-immortal-jellyfish.
19 https://www.ao-air.com/theatmos.
20 https://www.syfy.com/syfywire/laser-powered-time-machine.
21 https://longnow.org/clock/.
22 https://bigthink.com/surprising-science/time-perception?rebelltitem=1#rebelltitem1.
23 https://bigthink.com/culture-religion/hear-color.
24 http://www.bbc.com/travel/story/20210516-europes-language-that-few-speak.
25 https://native-land.ca/.
26 https://www.bbc.com/future/article/20210520-could-humans-really-destroy-all-life-on-earth.
27 https://www.scientificamerican.com/article/human-made-stuff-now-outweighs-all-life-on-earth/.
28 https://www.artsy.net/artwork/yana-naidenov-meshes-spectral-infrastructure-1.
29 https://muac.unam.mx/exposicion/fritzia-irizar?lang=en.
30 https://www.invasivespeciesinfo.gov/terrestrial/invertebrates/brown-marmorated-stink-bug.
31 Link: https://www.bbc.com/future/article/20210601-how-transplant-organs-might-be-printed-in-outer-space.
32 https://www.bbc.com/future/article/20210618-the-solar-systems-icy-shell-contaminated-by-other-stars.
33 https://www.calvertjournal.com/tiles/show/2894/svalbard-ville-lenkkeri-place-with-no-roads-soviet-mining-town.
34 https://aeon.co/essays/how-emdr-helps-to-reprocess-traumatic-memories-at-warp-speed.
35 https://aeon.co/essays/aliens-science-and-speculation-in-the-wake-of-oumuamua.
36 https://ea11sv.com/soll/.
37 https://www.bbc.com/future/article/20210215-winter-grief-how-warm-winters-threaten-snowy-cultures.
38 https://x.company/projects/loon/.
39 https://bigthink.com/surprising-science/mammals-dream-before-birth.

Chapter 6.0

1 https://transmediale.de/people/sahej-rahal.
2 https://shapedthought.com/index.html.
3 https://www.youtube.com/watch?v=p-3aB9hJ8Hc.
4 https://poetry.princeton.edu/2014/05/08/the-map/.

5   http://non-player-character.net/.

6   http://www.marlenecreates.ca/works/2008memory.html.

Chapter 7.0

1   https://nicolelhuillier.com/portfolio/the-dancer/.

2   https://www.koeniggalerie.com/blogs/public-projects/alicja-kwade-big-be-hide-gstaad.

3   https://xavibou.com/ornithographies/.

4   https://www.erikaarias.com/agua/querubines.

5   https://futurism.com/earths-magnetic-field-doing-something-strange.

6   https://mars.nasa.gov/mars2020/multimedia/images/.

7   https://climate.mit.edu/posts/case-studies-show-climate-variation-linked-rise-and-fall-medieval-nomadic-empires.

8   https://twitter.com/bigthink/status/1368580921809645570?s=08.

9   https://www.businessinsider.com/us-navy-stealth-destroyer-zumwalt-sails-very-rough-stormy-seas-2021-3?r=DE&IR=T.

10 https://twitter.com/futurism/status/1370887485778239495?s=08.

11 https://www.wired.com/2015/07/joseph-michael-glowworms/.

12 Image: James Lee Byars, "The Death of James Lee Byars" (2019): https://www.veniceartfactory.org/the-death-of-james-lee-byars.

13 https://www.sciencedaily.com/releases/2021/03/210316132121.htm.

14 https://www.sciencedaily.com/releases/2021/03/210323131230.htm.

15 https://www.sciencedaily.com/releases/2021/03/210318113640.htm.

16 https://blog.frontiersin.org/2021/02/15/strange-creatures-antarctica-discovered-frontiers-marine-science/.

17 https://www.bbc.com/news/56643677.

18 https://www.discovermagazine.com/the-sciences/earth-has-been-hiding-a-fifth-layer-in-its-inner-core.

19 https://www.inverse.com/article/47833-hiroshima-gingko-trees-atomic-bomb.

20 https://www.livescience.com/64309-weird-way-tornadoes-form.html.

21 https://bigthink.com/hard-science/octopus-like-creatures-on-europa/.

22 http://theconversation.com/fish-inspired-soft-robot-survives-a-trip-to-the-deepest-part-of-the-ocean-159734.

23 https://astronomy.com/news/2021/03/these-giant-mirrors-will-help-astronomers-see-to-the-edges-of-the-universe.

24 https://www.nationalgeographic.com/science/article/120724-vampire-skeleton-toothless-bulgaria-science.

25 www.cnn.com/travel/amp/northern-lights-aurora-borealis-sounds-reports-scn/index.html.

26. https://www.youtube.com/watch?v=--f79MZpW_A.
27. Link: https://news.mongabay.com/2020/12/top-10-environmental-news-stories-of-2020/.
28. https://www.sciencedaily.com/releases/2021/05/210505102018.htm.
29. https://www.sciencedaily.com/releases/2021/05/210514134119.htm.
30. https://staedelschule.de/en/calendar/eyal-weizman-cloud-studies.
31. https://www.sciencealert.com/the-world-s-oldest-water-lies-deep-below-canada-and-it-s-2-billion-years-old.
32. https://www.sciencealert.com/cephalopods-can-pass-a-cognitive-test-designed-for-human-children.
33. https://www.livescience.com/robot-artist-self-portraits.html.
34. https://phys.org/news/2021-05-story-rum-jungle-cold-war-era.html.
35. https://www.livescience.com/bee-creates-perfect-clone-army.html.
36. https://www.space.com/china-mars-rover-zhurong-first-sounds-video.
37. https://bgr.com/science/mars-rock-perseverance-mystery-5917479/.
38. https://www.iflscience.com/plants-and-animals/marine-scientists-make-shock-discovery-as-they-capture-a-skinless-shark/.
39. https://www.bbc.com/news/uk-england-sussex-57770547.
40. https://www.salon.com/2021/07/23/panpsychism-the-idea-that-inanimate-objects-have-consciousness-gains-steam-in-science-communities/.
41. https://twitter.com/WIRED/status/1421234513389162497?s=19.
42. https://gohardashti.com/home-17/.
43. https://futurism.com/the-byte/dinosaur-fossil-dragon.
44. https://on.su.org/3x20N7v.
45. https://www.reuters.com/world/europe/greenland-expedition-discover-worlds-northernmost-island-2021-08-27/.
46. https://www.bbc.com/news/science-environment-58333233.

Chapter 8.0

1. Youtube.com/watch?v=aygSMgK3BEM; NZetc.Victoria.AC.NZ/tm/scholarly/tei-ButFir-t1-g1-t1-g1-t4-body.html
   (TWITTER.COM/YOUTOPOS/STATUS/1330270919483396098).

2. TheConversation.com/moving-toward-computing-at-the-speed-of-thought-66898, ScienceDaily.com/releases/2019/04/190412094736.htm
   (TWITTER.COM/YOUTOPOS/STATUS/420445219037802496).

3. BernardMarr.com/15-things-everyone-should-know-about-quantum-computing
   . Bonus Link: *Honey, I Shrunk the Kits — Youtube.com/watch?v=JhHMJCUmq28*
   (TWITTER.COM/YOUTOPOS/STATUS/1151682607597412364).

   Image: Overlook Press, "The Thousandfold Thought," January 19, 2006.

4 MichaelGarfield.Medium.com/being-every-drone-the-future-of-xr-robotic-telepresence-19f12889da78; Bonus Link/Aside: Twitter.com/AliceAvizandum/status/1133632672000028673.

5 IlGiornale.it/news/interni/casaleggio-techno-guru-esoterismo-e-fantasy-835557.html; Forbes.com/sites/charliefink/2017/11/20/the-trillion-dollar-3d-telepresence-gold-mine (TWITTER.COM/YOUTOPOS/STATUS/702178304376315904).

6 Journals.SagePub.com/doi/10.1068/d378t (TWITTER.COM/YOUTOPOS/STATUS/1087056773964550145).

7 En.Wikipedia.org/wiki/Application_software.

8 Faena.com/aleph/John-Dee-Elizabethan-Magician-and-Metaphysical-Guide-to-an-Empire
 (TWITTER.COM/YOUTOPOS/STATUS/1055155515557376002;
   TWITTER.COM/YOUTOPOS/STATUS/681572495674241024).

9 Web.Stanford.edu/class/history34q/readings/Baudrillard/Baudrillard_Simulacra.html (twitter.com/youtopos/status/1122924564588244992).

10 Negarestani, *Cyclonopedia—Complicity with Anonymous Materials* (Re.Press, March 15, 2008), Northanger.LiveJournal.com/371234.html (Twitter.com/SemprePhi/status/1320830178856177665).

11 Northanger.LiveJournal.com/371528.html.

12 TWITTER.COM/YOUTOPOS/STATUS/986267601310494720.

13 NetworkArchaeology.WordPress.com/2012/01/20/Medea-Archaeology-or-Inhuman-Interconnections-and-their-Monstrous-Milieu-ANCIENT-AND-MODERN-CYBERNETICS]]. SiemenTerpstra.com/Tetractys, SMPhillips.MySite.com/The-Tree-of-Life-08.html; Theory-of-Thought.com/blog/TETRACTYS-Pascals-Triangle-binomial-expansion; Twitter.com/Apotheiite/status/1343042497774174210
 (TWITTER.COM/YOUTOPOS/STATUS/463521564311310336).

14 TWITTER.COM/YOUTOPOS/STATUS/1176246950305456129.

15 QNTM.ORG/CONTINUOUS.

16 Player.Vimeo.com/video/2128575.

17 En.Wikipedia.org/wiki/The_Clock_(2010_film)#Conception; Kottke.org/13/06/About-an-Hour-of-Christian-Marclays-THE-CLOCK
   (TWITTER.COM/YOUTOPOS/STATUS/623935700925292544).

18 Haaretz.com/scouring-the-net-to-find-information-hidden-from-you-1.5252624; Twitter.com/The__E_G_G/status/570342011896639489.

19 NYTimes.com/2019/05/26/us/politics/ufo-sightings-navy-pilots.html.

20 En.Wikipedia.org/wiki/Magic_square#/media/File:Magicsquareexample.svg.

21 [*Arcades Project* 462, N2a.3].

22 Walter Benjamin, *Arcades Project* [462-463, N3.1].

23 The present image was taken from a 2018 article by Stephen Law: Scroll.in/article/888964/is-it-a-duck-or-a-rabbit-the-philosophical-underpinning-of-an-old-visual-trick.

24 Translate.Google.com/?sl=auto&tl=en&text=dix-sept%0A&op=translate.

25. En.Wikipedia.org/wiki/Cars_(song); Twitter.com/GilbertSimondon/status/421082426295586816.
26. Hyper.AI/14905 (Translate.Google.com/translate?sl=auto&tl=en&u=http://hyper.ai/14905).
27. TWITTER.COM/YOUTOPOS/STATUS/967909076142313472.
28. Player.Vimeo.com/video/333502917?dnt=1&app_id=122963.
29. TWITTER.COM/YOUTOPOS/STATUS/933082154350927873.
30. En.Wikipedia.org/wiki/Theatre_of_Cruelty#Defining_Artaud's_%22theatre%22_and_%22cruelty%22.
31. SlidePlayer.com/slide/4114705.
32. NewsFileCorp.com/release/77354/Pharmadrug-Initiates-DMT-Research-Activities-via-Collaboration-with-the-University-of-Michigan-for-Foundational-DMT-Research-Study (Youtube.com/watch?v=TBkJ-xRBLV0).
33. Reason.com/2014/09/12/will-superintelligent-machines-destroy-h.
34. En.Wikipedia.org/wiki/Space_debris.
35. Alienocene.com/2021/05/02/alternately-stone-in-you-and-star.
36. TWITTER.COM/YOUTOPOS/STATUS/1388935447649390596.
37. PrintFriendly.com/p/g/5yiiCE; Bloomberg.com/opinion/articles/2021-04-17/space-junk-like-overfishing-and-pollution-is-a-global-tragedy-of-the-commons.
38. Youtube.com/watch?v=mIVCBqiW0ro.
39. BBC.com/future/article/20201014-totalitarian-world-in-chains-artificial-intelligence (MaliciousAIreport.com).
40. Vice.com/en/article/93yyyd/this-motorcycle-airbag-vest-will-stop-working-if-you-miss-a-payment.
41. Twitter.com/Metaleptic/status/1389838273527177216.
42. Twitter.com/FuturistechInfo/status/1391756486855073799.
43. TechnologyReview.com/2013/12/16/174934/thinking-in-silicon.
44. Dune.Fandom.com/wiki/Mentat.
45. Google.com/books/edition/The_Imaginary_App/zBFmBAAAQBAJ?hl=en&gbpv=1&pg=PA242.
46. Twitter.com/LivingArchitect/status/1395536455284441088.
47. Vimeo.com/220291411.
48. Youtube.com/embed/z4-TvQ5ufso.
49. Academia.edu/34226569.
50. @ GigaScopeJS.FireBaseApp.com/photo/NotreDameRoseOuest.
51. Youtube.com/embed/SeSzNxb1Eyw.
52. Twitter.com/JasonCrawford/status/1404200442171514880.
53. FT.com/content/b74b6ad6-3b8d-4cd8-9dd6-3b49754aa1c7.
54. TVNZ.CO.NZ/one-news/new-zealand/gabe-newell-says-brain-computer-interface-tech-allow-video-games-far-beyond-human-meat-peripherals-can-comprehend.
55. Twitter.com/Metaleptic/status/1308503131500744711.

56 Wired.com/story/billionaires-use-vr-avoid-social-change.
57 FIMS.UWO.CA/news/2013/apps_and_affect_conference_recap.html.
58 FIMS.UWO.CA/news/2013/apps_and_affect_conference_recap.html; PopMatters.com/The-Imaginary-App-shows-how-real-apps-have-become-to-us-2495576670.html.
59 Xenotheka.Delbeke.Arch.Ethz.ch/MELLAMPHY-The-Digital-Dionysus.
60 Journals.SagePub.com/doi/abs/10.1177/0967010621990309?journalCode=sdib.
61 EGG.UWO.CA/research_fellows/index.htm.
62 InputMag.com/culture/dissociative-identity-disorder-did-tiktok-influencers-multiple-personalities.
63 twitter.com/youtopos/status/1299528787470815232.

Chapter 9.0

1 AirPowerAsia.com/2020/08/27/VIMANA-the-Ancient-Indian-Aerospace-c\Craft-TIME-FOR-INDIGENISATION.
2 ScientificAmerican.com/article/according-to-current-phys + ScientificAmerican.com/article/borrowed-time-interview-w; (Bonus Link: Academia.edu/45096393).
3 The Origami Code: Youtube.com/watch?v=iESI4o8M-pM.
4 PBS.org/wgbh/nova/article/endogenous-retroviruses.
5 MoralMachine.net; MindMatters.AI/2018/10/there-is-no-universal-moral-machine; TechnologyReview.com/2018/10/24/139313/a-global-ethics-study-aims-to-help-ai-solve-the-self-driving-trolley-problem.
6 HBR.org/2017/01/the-truth-about-blockchain; Link.Springer.com/article/10.1007/s11625-020-00786-x#Sec3.
7 PunctumBooks.com/titles/Digital-Dionysus.
8 Dan Mellamphy and Nandita Biswas Mellamphy, "Nietzsche and Networks, Nietzschean Networks: *The Digital Dionysus*," in *The Digital Dionysus: Nietzsche & the Network-Centric Condition*, edited by D. Mellamphy and N. Biswas Mellamphy (Santa Barbara: Punctum Books, 2016).
9 PunctumBooks.com/titles/Leper-Creativity-Cyclonopedia-Symposium.
10 Dan Mellamphy and Nandita Biswas Mellamphy, "*Phileas Fog*ᵍ, *or the Cyclonic Passepartout:* On the Alchemical Elements of War," in *Leper Creativity: The Cyclonopedia Symposium*, edited by Keller, Nicola Masciandaro and Eugene Thacker (New York: Punctum Books, 2012).
11 RefikAnadol.com/works/machine-hallucination.
12 BBC.com/future/article/20181204-why-we-should-worry-when-machines-hallucinate.
13 Bahar Noorizadeh, *Governance-Machines and The Future of Futures*, (2018). MercerUnion.org/exhibitions/Bahar-Noorizadeh-Governance-Machines-and-The-Future-of-Futures.

14 BBC.com/future/article/20190513-it-only-takes-35-of-people-to-change-the-world.
15 ResearchGate.net/publication/326048883_Gender_bias_in_artificial_intelligence_the_need_for_diversity_and_gender_theory_in_machine_learning.
16 KCL.AC.UK/news/artificial-intelligence-is-demonstrating-gender-bias-and-its-our-fault.
17 BBC.com/culture/article/20201209-the-street-art-that-expressed-the-worlds-pain.
18 NCBI.NLM.NIH.gov/pmc/articles/PMC7644989.
    SpringerNature.com/gp/researchers/the-source/blog/blogposts-communicating-research/research-in-the-time-of-a-pandemic--coronavirus-class-mutual-aid/18179898.
19 OpenDemocracy.net/en/digitaliberties/politics-of-artificial-intelligence-interview-with-l.
20 NetworkCultures.org/unlikeus/2013/03/26/Bernard-Stiegler-from-Neuropower-to-Noopolitics.
21 BBC.com/earth/story/20141111-plants-have-a-hidden-internet.
22 BerghahnJournals.com/view/journals/nature-and-culture/16/1/nature-and-culture.16.issue-1.xml.
23 CITAP.UNC.edu/research/critical-disinfo.
24 Arts.MIT.edu/Orbiting-Thom-Kubli; Orbiting.ThomKubli.net.
25 ScienceDaily.com/releases/2017/12/171221143114.htm; Cell.com/current-biology/comments/S0960-9822(00)00628-X.
26 Archive.org/details/introductionvirus2nechvatal/mode/2up.
27 AaronsHome.com/aaron/gallery/index.html.
28 TheWire.CO.UK/img/scale/460/307/2013/02/07/Documenta_5-01.jpg.
29 Cambridge.org/core/journals/organised-sound/article/abs/sound-objects-and-spatial-morphologies/3F20D79AAB66D8E1059F8D27778D7632.
30 DavidRokeby.com/sorting.html.
31 OJS.Library.QueensU.CA/index.php/surveillance-and-society/issue/view/876.
32 TowardsDataScience.com/deep-learning-across-mesh-on-the-fly-part-1-the-drones-8bf3d7c9b4f.
33 TheGuardian.com/news/2020/oct/15/dangerous-rise-of-military-ai-drone-swarm-autonomous-weapons.
34 Undark.org/2021/04/30/BOOK-REVIEW-this-is-how-they-tell-me-the-world-ends.
35 TheGuardian.com/film/2017/jan/05/ZERO-DAYS-REVIEW-Alex-Gibney-cyberwar-documentary.
36 OpenAccess.TheCVF.com/content_ECCVW_2018/papers/11130/Goeting_Seeing_the_World_Through_Machinic_Eyes_Reflections_on_Computer_Vision_ECCVW_2018_paper.pdf.
37 OJS.Library.QueensU.CA/index.php/surveillance-and-society/article/view/13410/9346.
38 NewPhilosopher.com/videos/The-Century-of-the-Self.
39 Wired.com/story/how-a-flock-of-drones-developed-collective-intelligence.

40 StudioDrift.com/work#/franchise-freedom.
41 Rand.org/content/dam/rand/pubs/papers/2005/P3544.pdf.
42 Books.Google.com/books/about/Figuring_Space.html?id=qpzWAAAAMAAJ&redir_esc=y.
43 Imaginations.Glendon.YorkU.CA/?p=12483.
44 Journals.SagePub.com/doi/10.1177/0263775818812084.
45 TwentyFive.FibreCultureJournal.org/FCJ-185-AN-ALGORITHMIC-AGARTHA-Post-App-Approaches-to-Synarchic-Regulation.
46 WNYCStudios.org/podcasts/notetoself/episodes/bored-brilliant-project-part-1.
47 LAReviewOfBooks.org/article/DARING-TO-HOPE-FOR-THE-IMPROBABLE-On-Bernard-Stieglers-THE-AGE-OF-DISRUPTION.
48 Wired.com/insights/2014/07/DATA-NEW-OIL-Digital-Economy.
49 Wired.com/story/NO-Data-is-Not-the-New-Oil.
50 Virilio, *War and Cinema*, 4.
51 WSJ.com/articles/SB10001424127887324123004579054823225414450; jStor.org/stable/j.ctv1198x2b.
52 Academic.OUP.com/fs/article/69/1/60/2962635.
53 WideWalls.Ch/magazine/PostHumanism-Contemporary-Art.
54 WarRoom.ArmyWarCollege.edu/articles/Organized-Weaponization-of-Social-Media.
55 SuzanneTreister.net/Camouflage/Camouflage.html.
56 Kurzweilai.net/Posthuman-Politics.
57 RebeccaCatching.com/contemporary-art/foreign-bodies/FOREIGN-BODIES-exhibition-press-release.
58 e-Flux.com/journal/54/59854/HERMES-ON-THE-HUDSON-Notes-on-Media-Theory-after-Snowden.
59 e-IR.info/2015/11/14/Larval-Terror-and-the-Digital-Darkside.
60 TheIntercept.com/2014/11/13/ART-SURVEILLANCE-explored-artists.

Chapter 10.0

1 http://www.ricegallery.org/yasuaki-onishi.
2 https://www.biometricupdate.com/202101/global-biometric-data-collection-and-surveillance-grow-despite-lack-of-regulations.
3 http://danmcquillan.io/ai_and_antifascism.html.
4 https://japantoday.com/category/tech/japanese-government-proposes-cyborgs-and-robotic-avatars-for-all-by-2050.
5 Image: Takashi Kuribayashi: Imaginarium / a Voyage of Big Ideas | Art Installations, Sculpture, Contemporary Art: https://www.stirworld.com/see-features-installation-works-of-takashi-kuribayashi-imbibe-metaphysical-ideas-on-life.
6 https://africasacountry.com/2018/11/the-idea-of-a-borderless-world.

7 https://www.unhcr.org/innovation/wp-content/uploads/2020/04/Space-and-imagination-rethinking-refugees%E2%80%99-digital-access_WEB042020.pdf.
8 https://www.axios.com/anthony-levandowski-artificial-intelligence-church-611e4b39-e6c7-48f8-aaee-9ca667ec7c2d.html.
9 https://www.archdaily.mx/mx/768667/chile-y-espana-galardonados-en-los-lamp-lighting-design-2015.
10 https://www.vox.com/culture/22289454/pandemic-year-contagion-world-war-z-station-eleven-rest-relaxation.
11 https://edition.cnn.com/videos/tech/2021/01/25/singapore-coronavirus-covid-19-contact-tracing-privacy-lu-stout-pkg-intl-hnk-vpx.cnn.
12 https://entertainment.howstuffworks.com/arts/artwork/banksys-walled-off-hotel.htm.
13 https://www.aljazeera.com/features/2021/2/7/what-is-vaccine-nationalism-and-why-is-it-so-harmful.
14 JADE, "The Home of Sigh," Barranco – Lima – Peru, https://streetartnews.net/2015/05/jade-paints-striking-mural-in-barranco.html.
15 https://www.weforum.org/agenda/2021/03/global-technology-governance-can-succeed-with-cooperation-mitsubishi/.
16 https://www.thisiscolossal.com/2014/12/mechanical-drawings-and-the-human-form-merge-in-oil-paintings-by-atsushi-koyama/.
17 https://ssir.org/articles/entry/when_good_algorithms_go_sexist_why_and_how_to_advance_ai_gender_equity#.
18 https://cssh.northeastern.edu/humanities/composite-bodies-series-entangled-nuclear-colonialisms-matters-of-force-and-the-material-force-of-justice/.
19 https://www.conradmaldives.com/stay/the-muraka/.
20 https://www.nature.com/articles/s43247-020-00018-1.
21 https://www.thisiscolossal.com/2018/02/suspended-ocean-wave-installations-by-miguel-rothschild/.
22 https://www.nscai.gov/.
23 https://theintercept.com/2021/04/02/ice-database-surveillance-lexisnexis/.
24 https://www.uclalawreview.org/injustice-ex-machina-predictive-algorithms-in-criminal-sentencing/.
25 https://www.buzzfeednews.com/article/hayesbrown/23-pictures-that-capture-just-how-huge-the-arab-spring-reall.
26 https://thebulletin.org/2021/04/meet-the-future-weapon-of-mass-destruction-the-drone-swarm/.
27 https://arthur.io/art/adam-martinakis/lightbreak-03.
28 https://indianexpress.com/article/technology/tech-news-technology/apple-ios-14-5-update-facebook-instagram-notice-says-tracking-helps-keeps-apps-free-7301610/.
29 https://thenextweb.com/news/how-politicians-manipulate-the-masses-with-simple-ai.

30 Arshin Adib-Moghaddam, "Artificial Intelligence Must Not Be Allowed to Replace the Imperfection of Human Empathy," *Business Reporter*, May 2021, https://business-reporter.co.uk/2021/04/29/artificial-intelligence-must-not-be-allowed-to-replace-the-imperfection-of-human-empathy/.

31 https://www.forbes.com/sites/davidhambling/2021/05/14/hamas-throws-kamikaze-drones-into-attacks-on-israel-claims-hit-on-chemical-plant/?sh=c03f5f710883.

32 https://thehackernews.com/2014/07/anonymous-group-takes-down-mossads_31.html.

33 https://homesthetics.net/45-of-the-most-famous-buildings-in-the-world-that-are-known-for-their-unconventional-architectural-structure/.

34 https://techcrunch.com/2021/05/23/british-ai-startup-faculty-raises-42-5m-growth-round-led-by-apax-digital-fund/.

35 https://www.dw.com/en/privacy-activists-challenge-clearview-ai-in-eu/a-57691756.

36 https://www.buzzfeed.com/lynzybilling/see-the-world-through-the-eyes-of-a-legally-blind-man?utm_term=.rc0YY6RK1#7496768.

37 https://www.newsweek.com/iphone-x-racist-apple-refunds-device-cant-tell-chinese-people-apart-woman-751263.

38 https://www.theatlantic.com/health/archive/2018/08/machine-learning-dermatology-skin-color/567619/.

39 https://futurism.com/the-byte/anonymous-threatening-elon-musk.

40 https://warontherocks.com/2022/04/new-tech-new-concepts-chinas-plans-for-ai-and-cognitive-warfare/.

41 https://www.deepmind.com/blog/agent57-outperforming-the-human-atari-benchmark.

42 https://www.ignant.com/2019/03/05/this-installation-in-japan-mimics-the-tumultuous-nature-of-ocean-waves/.

43 https://thenextweb.com/news/inside-anonymous-former-topiary-jake-davis.

44 https://www.theguardian.com/news/2021/jul/18/what-is-pegasus-spyware-and-how-does-it-hack-phones.

45 https://casavogue.globo.com/MostrasExpos/Arte/noticia/2013/09/faena-art-center-light-art-borges-anthony-mccall-mischa-kuball.html.

46 https://buenosairesstreetart.com/2021/07/covid-street-art-and-graffiti-in-buenos-aires-and-argentina/.

47 Omar Khayyam, *Rubaiyat*, trans. Edward Fitzgerald (Oxford: Oxford University Press, 2010).

48 https://fouladiprojects.com/portfolio-item/babak-kazemi/.

49 https://time.com/6104844/uber-facial-recognition-racist/.

Chapter 11.0

1. https://formfollowsfashion.gr/.
2. https://www.anothermag.com/fashion-beauty/7791/a-history-of-female-afrofuturist-fashion.
3. https://www.dezeen.com/2020/07/27/risd-graduate-violet-zhou-fashion-collection/.
4. https://mymodernmet.com/tim-walkers-wonderland-12-pics/.
5. https://www.kotaku.com.au/2017/04/fine-art-the-incredible-art-of-the-ghost-in-the-shell-movie/.
6. https://www.wmagazine.com/gallery/tilda-swinton-tim-walker-photographs.
7. https://awake-smile.blogspot.com/2016/04/wangy-xin-yu-others-in-harpers-bazaar.html#.VyiVTzArKUl.
8. https://www.fashiongonerogue.com/editorial/mame-camara-vogue-arabia-alvaro-beamud-cortes/.
9. https://damascusapparel.tumblr.com/.
10. https://litmind.com/photo/2304564.
11. https://www.thisiscolossal.com/2020/10/mono-giraud-photographs-design/.
12. https://www.yatzer.com/global-warming-effect-art-design-because-world-melting.
13. https://www.indiewire.com/2021/04/stellan-skarsgard-spent-80-hours-in-makeup-dune-villain-1234630269/.
14. https://www.dezeen.com/2016/11/02/tear-gun-yi-fei-chen-design-academy-eindhoven-dutch-design-week-2016/.
15. Fine Fettle: Fashion Photography: Android Chic (finefettleguide.blogspot.com).
16. https://www.dezeen.com/2014/11/02/anne-van-galen-warriors-of-downpour-city-silicone-accessories-endless-rainfall-dutch-design-week-2014/amp/.
17. https://www.thisiscolossal.com/2016/08/salt-bride-sigalit-landau/.
18. https://www.shinichimaruyama.com/.
19. https://www.designboom.com/art/tobias-gremmler-kung-fu-motion-05-03-2016/.
20. https://thelastfashionbible.com/2019/10/08/lady-warrior-wow-winner-2019/.
21. http://earthtoiris.com/sheguang-hu-china-fashion-week-ss-2014/.
22. https://www.prestigeonline.com/hk/style/fashion/dancing-in-the-dark-silhouettes-inspired-by-japanese-butoh-dance/.
23. https://www.foam.org/events/mous-lamrabat.
24. https://www.behance.net/x-presion.
25. https://www.pinterest.com/pin/214202526016948734/.
26. https://www.pinterest.es/pin/394065036142382962/.

Chapter 12.0

1. Excerpt from sci-fi author J.G Ballard: "Civilised life, you know, is based on a huge number of illusions in which we all collaborate willingly. The trouble is we forget after a while that they are illusions and we are deeply shocked when reality is torn down around us" ; https://www.theguardian.com/books/2003/sep/06/fiction.jgballard.
2. https://www.1news.co.nz/2021/01/25/gabe-newell-says-brain-computer-interface-tech-will-allow-video-games-far-beyond-what-human-meat-peripherals-can-comprehend/.
3. https://www.dropbox.com/s/2tz6244jimzyzm8/Eclipse%20Promotiom%20-%20LENA%20Shards%202.mp4?dl=0.
4. https://www.unrealengine.com/en-US/blog/a-first-look-at-unreal-engine-5.
5. https://blogs.nvidia.com/blog/2021/04/13/nvidia-bmw-factory-future/.
6. https://tech.fb.com/inside-facebook-reality-labs-wrist-based-interaction-for-the-next-computing-platform/.
7. https://twitter.com/_naam/status/1387872036601671685.
8. https://www.youtube.com/watch?v=P1IcaBn3ej0.
9. https://www.youtube.com/watch?v=9ViF0GBt6fQ.
10. https://www.youtube.com/watch?v=L4C2AZU3oco.
11. https://youtu.be/5V4c2_HmQwc.
12. https://www.theverge.com/2021/6/17/22537349/facebook-vr-oculus-quest-ads-privacy-questions-analysis.
13. https://www.bbc.com/news/business-54232563.
14. https://www.youtube.com/watch?v=rFcbVrQWJSU.
15. https://twitter.com/DennysKuhnert ; https://www.youtube.com/watch?v=w-w7omxJuOk.
16. https://www.uploadvr.com/facebooks-reverse-passthrough/.

Chapter 13.0

1. https://en.wikipedia.org/wiki/Ibn_Wahshiyya.

Chapter 14.0

1. https://www.timeout.com/tokyo/news/shibuya-sky-now-hosts-open-air-rooftop-yoga-classes-on-weekends-051022.
2. https://www.outlookindia.com/international/brazil-devotees-place-offerings-for-sea-goddess-yemanja-in-rio-de-janeiro-photos-259080.

3. https://jameelartscentre.org/whats-on/talk-sufi-tombs-and-sea-burials-performing-preservation-by-moad-musbahi/.
4. https://occult-world.com/pomba-gira/.

Chapter 15.0

1. https://www.britannica.com/biography/Nostradamus.
2. https://www.youtube.com/watch?v=y3RlHnK0_NE.
3. https://www.berfrois.com/2018/02/ed-simon-when-books-read-you/.
4. https://www.jstor.org/stable/24517831?seq=1.
5. https://www.jstor.org/stable/4609267?seq=1.
6. https://www.persee.fr/doc/rhs_0151-4105_2004_num_57_2_2218.
7. https://www.thoughtco.com/aztec-religion-main-aspects-169343.
8. https://www.thoughtco.com/quetzalcoatl-feathered-serpent-god-169342.
9. Illustration of the end of the world that was expected in May 1910 at the passage of the Halley's comet: https://www.wired.com/2015/01/fantastically-wrong-halleys-comet/.
10. https://en.wikipedia.org/wiki/File:Animation_of_1P%EF%BC%8FHalley_orbit_-_2061_apparition.gif.
11. Cassandra in Aeschylus, *Agamemnon*, 1194, http://www.maicar.com/GML/Cassandra.html.
12. https://er.jsc.nasa.gov/seh/chapter23.htm.
13. https://www.youtube.com/watch?v=eVF4kebiks4&ab_channel=BrilandFamily.
14. Kahlil Gibran, *The Prophet* (New York: Alfred A. Knopf, 1923).
15. https://www.poetryfoundation.org/poets/kahlil-gibran.
16. Osho: https://www.youtube.com/watch?v=hBLS_OM6Puk&ab_channel=Netflix.

Chapter 16.0

1. https://www.treehugger.com/boston-dynamics-family-strange-amazing-robots-4862756.
2. https://www.washingtonpost.com/world/2021/06/05/greece-denmark-migrants/.
3. https://www.bbc.com/news/world-us-canada-56409924.
4. https://www.bleepingcomputer.com/news/security/ukraine-arrests-clop-ransomware-gang-members-seizes-servers/.
5. https://ai.xprize.org/prizes/artificial-intelligence/teams/aifred_health.
6. https://spectrum.ieee.org/the-human-os/biomedical/ethics/with-this-cad-for-genomes-you-can-design-new-organisms.

7 https://www.bbc.com/news/world-asia-55837160.
8 https://www.cnet.com/home/services/boxabl-aims-to-build-foldable-homes-that-cut-costs-go-up-fast/.
9 https://web.archive.org/web/20210416045307/https://www.quantamagazine.org/cells-form-into-xenobots-on-their-own-20210331/.
10 https://singularityhub.com/2021/08/01/deepminds-vibrant-new-virtual-world-trains-flexible-ai-with-endless-play/.
11 https://futurism.com/neoscope/robot-skin-bruised-punched.
12 https://theconversation.com/can-consciousness-be-explained-by-quantum-physics-my-research-takes-us-a-step-closer-to-finding-out-164582.
13 https://k-punk.org/emotional-engineering/.
14 Literature: Filin, P. A., M. A. Emelina, and Mikhail Savinov, *Arktika za graniu fantastiki: budushchee severa glazami sovetskikh inzhenerov, izobretateleĭ i pisateleĭ* (Moskva: Paulsen: Arkticheskiĭ muzeĭno-vystavochnyĭ tsentr, 2018).
15 Yusoff, Kathryn and Jennifer Gabrys, «Climate Change and the Imagination: Climate Change and the Imagination», *Wiley Interdisciplinary Reviews: Climate Change* 2, no. 4 (July 2011 г.): 516–34.
16 Assuming Distance: Speculations, Fakes, and Predictions in the Age of the Coronacene mobile guide: Media activist collective Kafe-Morozhenoe and a working group

 https://garagemca.org/en/exhibition/assuming-distance-speculations-fakes-and-predictions-in-the-age-of-the-coronacene/tour/media-activist-collective-kafe-morozhenoe-and-a-working-group.
17 Russia Lifts Veil on New Arctic Military Base, but Secrets Remain—Central administrative and residential complex of the "Arkticheskiy Trilistnik" or Arctic Trefoil base (Photo: Courtesy of Ministry of Defense of the Russian Federation) Published at: May 05, 2017 – 13:29 / Updated at: April 24, 2023 – 10:17

 https://www.highnorthnews.com/en/russia-lifts-veil-new-arctic-military-base-secrets-remain.
18 https://www.npr.org/2020/07/10/889953353/nearly-6-years-after-mh17-was-shot-down-dutch-prosecutors-say-they-will-sue-russ.
19 Image caption: Israeli forces launch tear gas with a drone to disperse protesters during a protest against US president Donald Trump's Middle East plan, near Beit El checkpoint in Ramallah, West Bank on January 30, 2020 [Issam Rimawi / Anadolu Agency]; https://www.middleeasteye.net/news/drones-over-gaza-how-israel-tested-its-latest-technology-protesters.
20 Image caption: A geofence warrant issued in 2019 looking for people within 150 meters of a bank robbery [United States v. Chatrie]; https://slate.com/technology/2022/05/google-geofence-warrants-chatrie-location-tracking.html.

Chapter 17.0

1. https://www.seedvault.no/nyheter/seeds-from-strawberries-deposited-at-the-first-seed-vault-opening-of-2021/.
2. https://www.hermitagemuseum.org/wps/portal/hermitage/what-s-on/temp_exh/2019/innovation.
3. https://mosaicrooms.org/event/homelandundermynails/.
4. https://www.escapistmagazine.com/v2/in-death-stranding-loneliness-is-more-powerful-than-connection/.
5. https://www.christies.com/features/A-collaboration-between-two-artists-one-human-one-a-machine-9332-1.aspx.
6. https://bienalsur.org/en/today/77.
7. https://blog.britishmuseum.org/ancient-egyptian-coffins-and-mystery-of-black-goo/.
8. https://www.sugimotohiroshi.com/abandoned-theater.
9. https://riyadhart.sa/en/artworks/earthseed/.
10. https://www.domusweb.it/en/art/gallery/2021/02/26/between-archaeoacoustics-and-dystopia-a-sound-story-is-a-work-of-art.html.
11. https://www.akbanksanat.com/en/exhibition/distopya-ses-sanati.
12. https://www.sciencemag.org/news/2020/12/geoengineers-inch-closer-sun-dimming-balloon-test.
13. Image: The operatic performance Scary Beauty, conceived and directed by composer and musician Keiichiro Shibuya, features a humanoid android with artificial intelligence (AI) that conducts a human orchestra and sings alongside the players. http://atak.jp/en/news/2018-06-15/.
14. https://olivierdesagazan.com/performancetransfiguration.
15. Image Caption: The Groom, 2012, Photograph, 23.5 x 14 in. Courtesy the artist and Chatterjee & Lal.
16. Image Caption: Harbinger (Detail) 2014; http://sahejrahal.com/HARBINGER. Courtesy the artist, Kochi-Muziris Biennale and Chatterjee & Lal.
17. Image Caption: Page 723, Juggernaut folio, 2018. Portfolio of illustrated manuscript painted using Mud, Kandhar Ink and carpenter chalk; http://sahejrahal.com/Juggernaut; 40 x 30 in.
    Courtesy the artist and Chatterjee & Lal.
18. Bhramana III, documentation of performance. Photography: Beatriz Santiago Munoz. Courtesy the artist and Chatterjee & Lal.
19. Antraal 2019, Installation, AI simulation and found object sculptures; Feedback Loops, ACCA Melbourne 2019; Photography: Andrew Curtis; Image courtesy the artist, ACCA Melbourne and Chatterjee & Lal.
20. Captions: Forerunner 2013, HD video, 12:13, Courtesy the artist and Chatterjee & Lal. http://sahejrahal.com/FORERUNNER.
21. https://www.google.com/amp/s/amp.theguardian.com/news/2019/dec/04/are-drone-swarms-the-future-of-aerial-warfare.

22 https://www.google.com/amp/s/singularityhub.com/2021/01/20/this-artificial-heart-will-soon-be-on-the-market-in-europe/amp/.

23 https://futurism.com/amazon-rainforest-emit-absorbing-carbon/amp?__twitter_impression=true.

24 https://cvltnation.com/torture-21st-century-new-method-pain/.

25 https://futurism.com/dozens-unknown-viruses-frozen-ice/amp?__twitter_impression=true.

26 https://twitter.com/futurism/status/1420829451030511619?s=19.

27 https://www.theguardian.com/artanddesign/gallery/2016/dec/21/europes-oldest-pagans-mari-people-ikuru-kuwajima.

28 https://www.smithsonianmag.com/history/terra-cotta-soldiers-on-the-march-30942673/.

29 https://www.businessinsider.com/telsa-bots-expected-work-mars-elon-musk-artificial-intelligence-2021-8.

30 https://twitter.com/futurism/status/1439279261194522625?s=08.

31 Asad Khan, www.theentropyproject.com.

32 Image: Homo Calculus, 2017, Entropy Project. See: Ord, T., *The Precipice: Existential Risk and the Future of Humanity* (New York: Hachette Books, 2020).

Chapter 1.0

1 Jorge Luis Borges, "The Library of Babel," in *Collected Fictions*, edited by Andrew Hurley (New York: Penguin, 1999).

2 Haruki Murakami, *Hard-Boiled Wonderland and the End of the World* (New York: Vintage, 1993).

3 *The Twilight Zone*, Episode: "The Obsolete Man" (Season 2, Episode 29, 1961).

4 Friedrich Nietzsche, *On the Use and Abuse of History*, trans. A. Collins (New York: Macmillan, 1957).

5 Stanislaw Lem, *His Master's Voice* (Cambridge: MIT Press, 2020).

6 Johanna Hedva, *Minerva: Miscarriage of the Brain* (California: Sming Sming Books, 2022).

7 Loren Eiseley, "Lecture YWHA," YouTube, https://www.youtube.com/watch?v=MldNFQUD_7E&t=55s.

8 Bruno Schulz, *The Sanatorium at the Sign of the Hourglass*, trans. John Curran Davis (website: schulzian.net.).

9 Ibid.

Epilogue

1 David Roden, *Xenophilia*, https://enemyindustry.wordpress.com/2019/05/02/x-phi-or-alienation-is-not-correlation/.

Contributors

Arshin Adib-Moghaddam is a professor and author of global political thought whose recent work explores technologies of security, surveillance, and post-human warfare. He is the author of several books, including *Psycho-Nationalism* and *Is Artificial Intelligence Racist?: The Ethics of AI and the Future of Humanity*.

Danna Albanyan is a curator, former lead member of the Saudi Arabian Ministry of Culture's Department of Cultural Assets and Centers responsible for the creation of new museums, and now a lead strategist for Diriyah Art Futures (DAF), the first education center for New Media and Digital Art in the Middle Eastern region (where digital dreams are transformed into reality).

Damon Quasravie is a process engineer and philosophical writer who focuses on elemental phenomena and mystical thought. He is a co-author of the Future Cosmos Lab and the author of a forthcoming novel based on arcane desert rituals, towers of silence, and fire-worshiping technologies.

Zahra Bonari is a sociologist and director of Media and Global Affairs for the Future Studies Program, whose writing investigates ideas of "perfection" in the realms of plastic surgery, mysticism, and women's aesthetics in the Middle East.

Andrea Cetrulo is a thinker spanning the fields of sociology, urban studies, mysticism, and philosophy who worked as the Associate of Program and Content Curation for Theatrum Mundi and as a researcher for the Global Cultural Districts Network and World Cities Culture Forum. She is the editor of the book *Interior Realms* and curates the live program of Making Cultural Infrastructure.

Una Chung is a professor and author of global media studies whose work focuses on East Asian and Asian American literature, film, and visual art, contemporary transnational cultural studies, postcolonial theory, ethnic studies, globalization, affect, and new media. She has written on subjects ranging from spectrality, horror, reincarnation, and contagion, and her past pieces include "Seeing Spectral Agencies?", "After-Sight," and "Crossing Over Horror: Reincarnation and Transformation."

Dana Dawud is a multidisciplinary artist, writer, and independent researcher based in Dubai who has contributed to multiple magazines and journals across the world. Her artistic work consists of digital paintings and sound pieces that interrogate technology and identity, including The Mirage Effect, The Gateway Activation Ritual, Monad +, and Monad 3.

Anna Engelhardt is a media artist and researcher whose main interests are the (de)colonial politics of algorithmic and logistical infrastructures in post-Soviet space. Her recent projects include Machinic Infrastructures of Truth, an inquiry into the production of verification systems, and Adversarial Infrastructure, an investigation into the Russian Crimean Bridge.

Ali Eslami is a virtual reality artist and practitioner from Iran whose experimental VR project False Mirror is an award-winning mixture of speculative design and world-building. His creative simulations in False Mirror test the experiential limits of realities, blurring fictional and non-fictional narratives and questioning the constraints of physical space, time, and bodies.

Amy Ireland is a writer, theorist, editor, and experimental poet focused on questions of agency and technology in modernity. She is an author and co-editor of *Cute Accelerationism*, *Aesthetics After Finitude*, *The Xenofeminist Manifesto*, and "Black Circuit: Code for the Numbers to Come."

Ed Keller is a designer, writer, musician, multimedia artist, and independent scholar. Co-founder of Spec.AE, a speculative design practice, and AUM Studio, an architecture and new media firm, and former Director of the Center for Transformative Media at The New School (2009–20), he is the co-editor of *Leper Creativity: Cyclonopedia Symposium* and the author of "The Cosmopolitical Gesture."

Asad Khan is a computational designer and speculative architect who directs the Entropy Project, an architectural practice that transforms existential risks (X-risks) into existential catastrophes (X-katas), using the epistemic filters of remote sensing, artificial intelligence, computer simulation, and design automation, in order to investigate intelligence as a time-bound self-exterminator.

Nora Khan is a writer, editor, technology critic, and curator of the Biennale de l'Image en Mouvement who theorizes the relationship between thought and machine, AI and artistic-literary practice. She is the author of *Seeing, Naming, Knowing* and *No Context: AI Art and the Stakes for Criticism*.

Bogna Konior is a writer/professor of interactive media arts and co-director of the Artificial Intelligence and Culture Research Centre. She is the author of *The Dark Forest Theory of the Internet* and co-editor of *Machine Decision Is Not Final:*

China and the History and Future of AI. Her current work revolves around far-reaching themes of emerging technologies, cyberfeminism, mysticism, machine erotics, long-term civilizational evolution, and speculative computation.

Carla Leitão is an architect, professor, and writer whose work traces the intersection of architecture, urban systems, technology, ubiquitous cultures, and immersive VR. She is the author of pieces titled "4 Lines," "Navigation: Anticipation and Simultaneity," and "The Future of Measurement," and has staged worldwide installations titled "Suture" and "Young Blood."

Anna Longo is a philosopher and author of five volumes, including *Le paradoxe de la finitude* (The Paradox of Finitude), *La genèse du transcendantal* (The Genesis of the Transcendental), *Breaking the Spell: Speculative Realism under Discussion*, and *Time without Becoming* (Mimesis 2014). Her forthcoming book *The Game of Induction* deals with probabilistic predictive systems, and she is developing a theory of fiction as a prophetic technique.

Dejan Lukic is an anthropologist, experimental theorist of culture and art, and writer of three books including *Phantom Territoriality: Hostage Spaces of the Contemporary World*, *The Oyster*, and *Elemental Disappearances* (with Jason Mohaghegh). His forthcoming trilogy titled *Emanations* covers themes of charisma, enchantment, nature, light and shadows, and multi-ontologies.

Michael Marder is a philosopher and author whose writings span the fields of phenomenology, political thought, and environmental philosophy. He is the author of fifteen books and over one hundred academic and scientific articles, including *Plant-Thinking: A Philosophy of Vegetal Life*; *Pyropolitics: When the World Is Ablaze*; *Dust*; *The Chernobyl Herbarium*; *Energy Dreams: Of Actuality*; *Dump Philosophy: A Phenomenology of Devastation*; and co-editor of *Contemporanea: A Glossary for the Twenty-First Century*.

Dan Mellamphy is a writer, professor, multimedia artist, and independent-scholar whose work studies deception, dissimulation, duplicity, and doublespeak in their digital and analogue articulation. His published pieces can be found in anthologies such as *Serial Killing: A Philosophical Anthology*, *The Funambulist Papers*, *Alchemical Traditions from Antiquity to the Avant-Garde*, and in his co-edited book *The Digital Dionysus: Nietzsche and the Network-Centric Condition*.

Nandita Biswas Mellamphy is a political theorist and co-founder of The Electro-Governance Group (EGG) whose writings focus on algorithmic governance, net-centricity, and the war on terror. Her published works include *The Three Stigmata of Friedrich Nietzsche: Political Physiology in the Age of Nihilism*, in addition to book chapters in anthologies such as *Critical Post-Humanism &*

Planetary Futures, *Speculations of the Other Women: New Realisms in Feminist Philosophy*, and *The Imaginary App: MIT Software Studies*.

Jason Mohaghegh is a philosopher, literary theorist, and author of ten books on chaos, illusion, violence, madness, silence, disappearance, secrecy, evil, night, and apocalypse. He is the Founding Director of the Future Studies Program, and most recently has published two volumes of the *Omnicide* project and two volumes of the *Night* project alongside a work on lost books and secret societies.

Reza Negarestani is a philosopher and writer whose work has shaped movements in speculative realism, the philosophy of intelligence, rationalism, and theory fiction. He is the author of *Cyclonopedia*, *Intelligence and Spirit*, *Abducting the Outside: Collected Wirings 2003–2018*, and the co-author of *Chronosis*.

Federico Nieto is a thinker of philosophy and visual arts from Colombia whose work focuses mainly on questions of the inhuman. He is the author of "The Nihil of Time," "Skeletal Frameworks Against Abject Rot," and "The Negative Unthought," and he is currently researching cruelty as an imperative underlying human and artificial cognition and the critique of forms of life.

Sahej Rahal is a visual artist from Mumbai who creates mythic worlds of sculptures, performances, films, paintings, installations, video games, and AI programs based on sources ranging from local legends to science fiction. He is the featured artist of a solo exhibition titled Ancestors at the CSMVS Museum in Mumbai, India, and the programmer of the game Distributed Mind Test.

Will Scarlett is an anthropologist whose work theorizes experiences of "presence" in virtual immersive realities. His current book project, *Being There and Not There*, explores interactions between the senses and their surroundings that generate imaginary, metamorphic, or inhuman experiences in environments such as the forest, the city, and the ocean.

Sasha Shestakova is a writer who explores material dimensions of non-linear time and situated approaches to envisioning otherwise. She is interested in the decolonial approach toward contemporary art in Russia, which she uses to question the colonial power play implied in homogeneous categories like "post-Soviet" and "New East."

Laura Tripaldi is a scholar of materials science and nanotechnology whose work examines speculative and philosophical aspects of science and technology, with a particular focus on the concepts of complexity, self-organization, relational ontologies, artificial life, softness, and material interfaces. She is the author of the book *Parallel Minds*.

Ghazal Zamani is an anesthetist whose scientific-creative work explores ancient substances, modern techniques, and futuristic designs related to rest, painlessness, unconsciousness, and euphoria. She is the creator of the House of Nisian product line (Oblivion Collection) fusing jewelry, fragrance, fashion, cosmetics, and artisanal objects that revolve around the experience of sleep, forgetting, or nothingness.

Index

Note: Page numbers in *italics* represent figures.

180 degrees of sea image   197–8
2001: A Space Odyssey   40
2666 (Bolaño)   169

Abidi, Safdar   55
abiotic mass   186
"A-Bomb" Ginkgo trees   224
Abrahamic monotheism   118
Abraham's Paradox   117–23
absolute time image   204
Accursed Share, The (Bataille)   58
Adams, Richard
   Watership Down   149
Adib-Moghaddam, Arshin   59, 79, 277
   on emergent phenomenon in realm of "reign   77–8
   on reign   63–4
Advanced Research Projects Agency (ARPA)   265–6
advantage games   289
advertisements in VR   310–11
aerial destiny   224
"aerohaptics"   355
aesthetics   7, 47, 106, 194, 280, 287
   and ethics   146
   preserve   47
   Renaissance   164
   of satellite imagery   340
   subcultural   121
   of wreckage   162
Against Thinking Machines (ATM)   246
Ai-Da   229
al-Buraikan, Mahmoud   121
alchemical image   206

Alfred Health   334
algorithmic art   262
algorithmic enlightenment   264–5
algorithmic governance   268–9
algorithmic opacity   260
Al-Hadid, Diana   162
alien differentiation   335–6
alien image   206
Allahyari, Morehshin
   She Who Sees the Unknown   5
AlphaTauri   162
Al-Qaeda   129
altars   349
altered consciousness image   198
Amazon   94
Amazon rainforest   353
Amenhotep the Third   54
Amoore, Louise   260
   Cloud Ethics   260
   Politics of Possibility: Risk and Security Beyond Probability, The   260
Amorous Waters   228
Ampère, André-Marie   271
Anani, Nabil   191
Anarchitectural Thinking (AT)   253–4
Ancient prophecies   324, 325
ancient wisdom of mysticism   225
Anderton, John   75
android envy   300
Android Opera   347–8
Anikina, Alexandra   213
animal eye image   199
animal movements   174
animate materials   185–6

Annihilation (film) 34–6, 146
Annihilation (VanderMeer) 146
Anthropocentric Purposes 237
anthropogenesis 184
anti-temple temple 57
Antraal 350–1
Apollo 11 327
Apollo 13 327
Apology of Socrates, The (Plato) 86, 323
Arabian Nights 68
Arachne 105
Arachnean consciousness 93
Arachne's Thread 102–5
"Arachnomancy" 93
arachnomaterialism 185
archaeology of the old world 280
Argiope lobata 93
Arias, Erika 218
    "Cherubims" 218
Armstrong, Neil 327
artifacts 51
artifice 19
artificial companion-species 267
artificial intelligence (AI) 193–4, 265, 267
    bots 355
    -enhanced realities 309
    -island headquarter 291
artificial light 179
artificial movement 175
artificial rains 163
Arya, Manan 56
ashes of sky 222
Assyrian Idol Curse, The 117–23
astrolinguistics 148
authentic self 14
automated precarity 335
Automated Prometheanism 335
axiom of verticality 224
Aztecs I 324
Aztecs II 325

Babylonian Empire 117
Babylonian tablets 326
Backrooms, The 155
Bacon, Francis 119
badlands 157
Ballard, J. G. 35
baptized Xenobots 335

Barque of Amun, The 54
Bastiaan Hooimeijer (Naam) 308
Basualdo, Eduardo 345
Bataille, George 58, 72
    The Accursed Share 58
Battle of Hastings 326
"Battle-space of Cyberspace, The" in-and-as our networked condition 254
Beatles, The 328
Bechtel Corporation 50
being as deception 218
belief systems 222
Bellingcat 340
bellum omnium contra omnes 76
Benjamin, Walter 26, 77
Bergman, Ingmar 10–11
Berns, Jeffrey 333
Berthelot, Marcellin 66
Bester, Alfred 45
    The Stars My Destination 45
Bezos, Jeff 204
"Big Be-Hide, The" (Kwade) 218
bio-impostors 355–6
bio-ink image 207
biotechnological homonculi 185
Birnbaum, Daniel 347
Birtchnell, Thomas 193
    "Listening Without Ears: Artificial Intelligence in Audio Mastering" 193
Black Ice 337
Black Lives Matter protests 14
Black Wednesday 324
blank ones 302
blockchain 258–9, 333
BMW Group 308
BMW X NVIDIA 308
body
    abiotic mass 186
    animate materials 185–6
    arachnomaterialism 185
    asteroidal touch 194–5
    biotechnological homonculi 185
    carbon-based nanotechnologies 187
    chemical blossoms 189
    cyclical body-time 191
    digital skins 186
    disembodied consciousness 184–5

Elysia marginata sea slugs   188
  facial surface   192–3
  future hearing   193
  mechanical wombs   187
  posthuman body   190
  quantum perception   189
  reality shifting   188
  viral anthropogenesis   184
  virtual simulacra   187
Bolaño, Roberto
  2666   169
Bonari, Zahra   217
Book of Images (Rilke)   246
Book of Kells   29–31, *32*
Book of Kings   67
Book of Poisons, The (Ibn Wahshiyya)   315
Book of the Law   26–9, *31*
borderless canvas   287–8
borderless world   278
Borges, Jorge Luis   8
boring machines   269–70
Borisov, Petr   337
Boston Dynamics   332
Bou, Xavi
  "Ornithographies"   218
Boxabl   335
box inhabitants   335
brain
  activity   177
  -computer interfaces   306–7
  as deception-organ   242–3
Brightburn   352
Brill, Michael   55
broken-clock universe   158
Broken Tablet, the   102–5
bruised robots   336–7
brutalist image   201
Buffon, Gigi   179
Buffy the Vampire Slayer (US television series)   68
Butler, Judith   100
Butler, Samuel   235
Butlerian Jihad   246
Byars, James Lee   221

Cadigan, Pat
  Fools   36–7
Calatrava, Santiago   201
calculative calcinations   239

California Ideology   77
camera eye image   199–200
capitalism   133, 260
carbon-based nanotechnologies   187
Carpenter, Tei   55
Carrier Bag Theory of Fiction, The (Le Guin)   18
Cassandra   326
casualties of innocence   292
cellular machines   262
Cerro Rico mine   176
Certeau, Michel de   150
Cesereanu, Ruxandra   18
Cetrulo, Andrea   82, 83
chemical blossoms   189
Chen, Yi-Fei   300
Chernobyl disaster   106
Chernobyl Herbarium (Tondeur)   105–6
Chernobyl photograms   105–9, *108*, *109*
"Cherubims" (Erika)   218
Chiang, Ted   89
chimera
  defined   4
  image/artwork   10–13
  myth   5–8, *8*, *9*
  phenomenon   13–17
chimerical design   334
Chinnamasta (transformation goddess)   71–4
Choi Minhwa   164
choreography   167
Choufi, Nadim   191–2
Christianity   101
Chun, Wendy   14
ciphers   20
  of dawn   228–9
  image/artwork   33–6
  Ireland on   24–5
  Keller on   25–6
  myth   26–31, *31*, *32*
city image   201
Clastres, Pierre   134
climate change   220
climate-forming dams   337–8
climate variations   219
Clop ransomware   333–4
Cloud Ethics (Amoore)   260
code image   200

cold existence   230–1
"cold rationalism"   337
Collection of Ancient Greek Alchemists   66
"collective hallucination"   338
Colonial fantasies   339–40
colonial jungle   279
Colonnade of Amun, The   54
color hearing image   204–5
complex time   149–50
computer interface   308
Computer Simulation, Rhetoric, and the Scientific Imagination (Roundtree)   214
constellations   178
contagious communication and network-control   273
contagious consumer objects   77
contemporary contortionism   53–4
contemporary prophets   328–9
contortionists   53–5
cosmic arcs   160
cosmic augur   219
cosmic consumption   173
cosmic dance   217
cosmic nomadism   219
cosmic pareidolia   231
cosmic portrait   229
cosmic psychology   223
cosmic vibration   230
Cosmological Archive   360–90
　aftermath   372–90
　conspiracy of librarians   372–90
　Keller on   364–6, 375–6, 380–2, 385–6, 388–90
　Khan on   366–9, 373–4, 382–3
　Leitão on   369, 376–8, 383, 385–7, 390
　Mohaghegh on   360, 361, 372–4, 376–80, 383–8, 390
　Rahal on   369–71, 374–5, 380
　Room 1   361–4
　Room 2   364–6
　Room 3   366–9
　Room 4   369
　Room 5   369–71
　Room 6   371–2
　Scarlett on   371–2, 376–8
cosmological deep time   145

cosmopolitan citizenship   75–6
cosmos
　aerial destiny   224
　ashes of sky   222
　axiom of verticality   224
　being as deception   218
　burning ice   232
　cipher of dawn   228–9
　cold existence   230–1
　cosmic augur   219
　cosmic dance   217
　cosmic nomadism   219
　cosmic pareidolia   231
　cosmic portrait   229
　cosmic psychology   223
　cosmic vibration   230
　dream of the marauder   232
　elemental conquest/downfall   219
　elemental wrath   220
　eternally bleeding   225
　extra-terrestrial colonization   221
　fifth philosophy   223
　future deity   225
　future non-space   227
　future's share   233
　inanimate society   231
　infinite ones   229–30
　infinitesimal gaze   220
　labyrinth of mind   233
　the last tree   224
　laughter of the half-breed   226
　lethal enchantment   221
　liquid secrecy   228
　orbital return   222
　pleasure/horror flight   218
　post-mortem paths   222
　rapid evolution   227
　recurring flame   226
　rustle of light   226
　secret of immortality   229
　sinking island   233
　stone of eternity   221, 230
　surviving the future   227
　toxic eclipse   228
Court of Ramses, The   54
Covered Temple, The   54
Covid-19 pandemic   311
Crawford, Techie Jason   251
Creates, Marlene   214

CRISPR   159
critical disinformation studies   261
cross-cutting complicities   238–9
Crowley, Aleister   27–8, 34
cryogenic freezing   16
cryonics   172–3
crypto-art   33–4
cryptocurrency   333
cryptographic hashes   33
Crystal World (Ballard)   35
cultural short-term transmission   51
cyber-assassins   287
cyber-beyond   278–9
Cyberiad Calendar   240
cybernetics   265–6
   and post-humanism   271–2
Cybernetics: or Control and Communication in the Animal and the Machine (Wiener)   271
cyborg   74–8
cyborg biopolitics   289–90
Cyborg Ghoul   78
cyclical body-time   191
Cyclonopedia (Negarestani)   137, 239

"Dancer, The" (L'Huillier)   217
Dancing Column: On Order in Architecture (Rykwert)   49
Dante Alighieri   105
dark dance   302
Dark Room Therapy   156–7
Dashti, Gohar   232
   "Home"   232
databases   286
data-bodies   267–8
data-hegemony   267–8
Davis, Jake   288
Dead Waters   228
Deanne, Arianna   55
Dear Esther   212–13
decay   315
deciphering   25
Dee, John   238
deep learning   265, 334
DeepMind   336
deep time   145
Defense Advanced Research Projects Agency (DARPA)   265
deity/ies   225

Delphic Oracle   84–8
destruction   343–57
deterritorializations   77, 278
Dick, Philip K.   75, 240, 267
   Three Stigmata of Palmer Eldritch, The   267
Didi-Huberman, Georges   116
digital cloning   16
Digital Dionysus: Nietzsche and the Network-Centric Condition, The   259
digital duplicity   268–9
digital eyes (digitalize)   250
digital fracking of humans   270
digital gender-gaps   260
digital skins   186
digital wormfare   264
disappearance   343–57
disembodied consciousness   184–5
dissociative identity disorder   255
distributed brain drone   283
diva-shaman   298
diversification-efforts in machine-learning   260
djinn   5–6, *8*, 19
   as a mythical creature   67
Doré, Gustav   105
doubling   167
downloaded consciousness   16
dream of the marauder   232
dream space   152
Dreams-Sandbox Virtual Worlds   310
drift space   153
drone   74–8
Drones' Delirium   340
Dune (Herbert)   266
Dune (Skarsgard)   300
Dyson, Freeman   149
Dyson Sphere   155
Dystopian Sound Art exhibition   346–7

Earth Spy, The   123–28, *128*
e-bodies *vs.* twice-born bodies   237
eco-destruction fashion-design   247
ecological gestures   40
economics   324
Egan, Greg
   Schild's Ladder   146
ego-death   156–7

egoism 73
e-governance 268
Egyptian coffins and mummy cases 345
Egyptian culture 50
Egyptian temple 47–51
Egyptian temple of Luxor 53
Electro-Knights 240–1
electronic skin (e-skin) 110–12
elemental conquest/downfall 219
elemental wrath 220
elevator shafts 153
E(M)BODIME(A)NT 237
EMDR image 207–8
emergency space 159
empathy 45
   and energy 149
   and time 149
encryption 26
endless storm 300–1
energy
   and empathy 149
   and time 149
Energy Dreams: Of Actuality 102
Energylandia, Poland 171
Enlightenment 124
enveloped 298
Environmental Protection Agency (EPA) 51
Epic Games 158
equator combat 296
Erlich, Leandro 153
escape 306–13
eternally bleeding 225
eternity 317–20
euphoria/dysphoria 315
European Union 333
exhalation 88–91, 92
Exhalation (Chiang) 89
existence trading 282
Exit of Farhad and Shirin, The (Kazemi) 293
experimental jet-set 246
extra-terrestrial colonization 221
extraterrestrial life 176

Facebook 310–12
Facebook Reality Lab 308
Face of God 102–5

facial mapping 293
facial recognition and the blind eye 286
failed utopia image 207
False Mirror virtual reality project 306
fascism 247
fashion
   android envy 300
   blank ones 302
   dark dance 302
   diva-shaman 298
   endless storm 300–1
   enveloped 298
   equator combat 296
   forever look 300
   future nakedness 301
   future seduction 297
   generational fusions 299
   impact of global warming 299
   martial animation 301
   mood silhouettes 297
   neo-camouflage 299
   neo-wonderland 297
   nocturnal spectacles 303
   salt crystal dress 301
   silk and cement 296
   spinal goggles 303
   stilt-walkers 304
   ultra-color 303
   ultra-paleness 297–8
   weaponized face 300
   weird fashion 302
   what the no one wears 298
Fatal Promises 354
feedback and feedforward loops 38–40
Fenara, Irene 187
fifth philosophy 223
finance 324
floating image 199
Florescencism (revolutionary flowers) 71–4
Flusser, Vilém 237
Focillon, Henri 35, 40
   Life of Forms in Art, The 29
food sovereignty 173–4
Fools (Cadigan) 36–7
Forensic Architecture 340
forever look 300
Forteans 241

fragmented future images 255
Francis Bacon, Pope 192–4
Frankenstein (Shelley) 78
Freud, Sigmund 264
Fröhliche Wissenschaft (Nietzsche) 244
From Earth to the Moon (Verne) 327
frontal lobe control 281
full body haptics 311
Fuller, R. Buckminster 201
funeral pyre beacons 145
fungi 171
Furious Waters 228
futuristic veiling 291

Gaestel, Mikko 106
galaxy brain image 203
Galen, Ann Van 300
Gandhi, Indira 328
Garland, Alex 34–6, 146
Gateway Experience, The 157
Gateway Foundation 154
Gender Trouble 100
general system of illumination 270
generational fusions 299
generative adversarial networks (GANs) 10–11
genetic chaos space 159
genetic engineering 17
Geofence 341
geometric image 201
gestures 40
Ghoul (Netflix series) 67
Gibran, Kahlil 328
glandular space 156
glass tower mystics 317
globe-girdling communications 240
Godlings 350–1
Goeting, Marijke 264
Google 341
Google's Calico Lab 17
governance 62–4, 66, 72, 78
    algorithmic 268–9
    global technology 281
    microgovernance of bodies 280
governance-machines 259–60
Grand Theft Auto 5 309
Grandville, J. J. 200
graph

past and future of space as 144
past and future of time as 144
Greek mythology 326
Greek philosophy 119
Gregorian Calendar 240
Guzmán, Patricio 145

Hakkaart, Meike 149
Halley's Comet 325–6
hallucination engine 259
hallucination engine(s) 245
hanging torsos 11–13
Haraway, Donna 58, 111
Hard to Be a God 124
Harold II, King 326
Harry Potter 68
Hash Gematria (Myers) 33
havoc and vulnerability 284–5
"headquarters, the" 162–3
Hegelian sense 124
Helgoland (Rovelli) 161
Herbert, Frank 266
    Dune 266
hidden movement 180
hieroglyph-covered walls 49
hikikomori 154
Hillis, Danny 204
Hindu temple 47–53. *see also* Meenakshi Temple, Madurai
Hindu Temple, The (Kramrisch) 49
Hiroshi Sugimoto 345
Hitchcock, Alfred 10
hologramic contact 355
holograms 16
"Home" (Dashti) 232
"Homeland Under My Nails" at The Mosaic Rooms, London, UK 344
Homo Calculus 356
Hong Qin 159
Horemheb 54
horizon/abyss 279
"Horizon Zero Dawn" (video game) 227
"Hospitable Moon" 339
Hull, John 309
human-computer interfaces 74
Human Interference Task Force 50
humankind 30

humanoid beings 18
Hurricane Katrina 356
hyper-reality 306–13
hyperstition 20
hypersynchronization 240
hypocrisy 45

idealistic mythologies 229
ideological tricks 281
Idol 116–39
   Abraham's Paradox 117–23
   answers 136–9
   The Assyrian Idol Curse 117–23
   The Earth Spy 123–28, *128*
   image/artwork 123–28, *128*
   interlude 133–6
   myth 117–23
   phenomenon 129–33
   The Spirit Army 129–33
   The Stratachrome Master 123–28, *128*
   The Terrorist 129–33
illusion
   mapping time 211–12
   simulations 211–14
image/artwork 53–5
   10,000-year image 204
   180 degrees of sea image 197–8
   absolute time image 204
   alchemical image 206
   alien image 206
   altered consciousness 198
   animal eye image 199
   bio-ink image 207
   brutalist image 201
   camera eye image 199–200
   Chernobyl Photographs 105–9, *108*, *109*
   chimera 10–13
   Chinnamasta (transformation goddess) 71–4
   ciphers 33–6
   code image 200
   color hearing image 204–5
   contortionists 53–5
   crypto-art 33–4
   The Earth Spy 123–28, *128*
   exhalation 88–92, *91*, *92*
   failed utopia image 207

   floating image 199
   Florescencism (revolutionary flowers) 71–4
   future city image 201
   galaxy brain image 203
   generative adversarial networks 10–11
   geometric image 201
   hanging torsos 11–13
   immaterial image 203
   immortal image 203
   indigenous image 205
   in/visible image 198–9
   Liquid Orb Droplets 105–9
   magnetized image 198
   messenger image 208
   Minakata Mandala 105–9
   monolith image 202
   nightmare image 202
   no future tense image 205
   preborn image 209
   regenerative image 200
   reign(s) 71–4
   riteless image 202
   scaling image 200
   the sea monk 88–92, *91*, *92*
   seasonless image 208–9
   spectral image 206
   The Stratachrome Master 123–28, *128*
   temple 53–5
   "Testbed" 53–5
   time-travel image 203–4
   tracking image 209
   transcendental hope image 197
   tremulous image 208
   unseen image 207
immaterial image 203
immersion 306–13
immortal image 203
immortality labs 14–17
immortality threshold 17
immortalizing spaces 154
impact of global warming 299
imperial espionage 238
imperialist domino-effect 290
inanimate society 231
Indigenous futures 166
indigenous image 205

infinitely irreproducible   284
infinite objects   308–9
infinitesimal gaze   220
inheritors   333–4
Instagram   14
Intel Labs   309
intelligentized warfare   287
intelligent machines   273–4
inter-columnal spacing   54
Internet of Things (IoT)   272
interoceptors   56–8
The Interoceptors   57–8
interstellar space-time   147–8
in/visible image   198–9
Ireland, Amy   40, 44
   Book of the Law   27–9
   on ciphers   24–5
   on crypto-art   33–4
   on deciphering   25
   on memory parlors   36–8
Irizar, Fritzia   206
Ishii, Hiroshi   262
ISIS   129
It's Winter   155

Jalal al-e Ahmad   74, 277
"JAXA satellites" Corporation   56
Johnson, Boris   290
Jordan, Chris   39
Julian Calendar   240

Kac, Eduardo   147
Kafe-Morozhenoe   338
Kali   71–2
Kama   71
Kanaeokana   166
Karkle, Amy   200
Kazemi, Babak
   Exit of Farhad and Shirin   293
Keller, Ed   21, 41
   Book of Kells   29–31, 32
   on ciphers   25–6
   feedback and feedforward loops   38–40
Kennedy, John F.   328
Khalil, Mohammad Omar   344
Khan, Nora   67
   on artifice   19
   on ciphers   20

   on djinn   5–6, *8*
   on generative adversarial networks   10–11
   on virtual influencers   13–14
Khayyam, Omar   290
   Rubaiyat   290
Khlebnikov, Velimir   168, 199
killer robots   282
Kim, Krista   156
Kindred D., Philip   252
Klein Bottle house   110–12
Konopka, Bartosz   348
Kramrisch, Stella   49, 54
   Hindu Temple, The   49
Kricheli, Roman   53
Kuball, Mischa   289
Kubli, Thom   262
Kuhnert, Dennys   312
Kuo, Ashley   55
Kwade, Alicja
   "Big Be-Hide, The"   218

labyrinth of mind   233
labyrinths   177
Lagerkvist, Pär   85
Lamrabat, Mous   303
Landau, Sigalit   301
Landscape of Thorns (Brill and Abidi)   55
larval warfare   76
larval war-machines   263
Le Guin, Ursula K.   18
Leitão, Carla   40, 44, 45, 57, 59, 62
   on religions   45
   on temple   57–8
   on temple and futurity   50
   on "Testbed"   55
Lena-Virtual Being   307
Leopold, Aldo
   Sand County Almanac   39
Leper Creativity: Cyclonopedia Symposium   259
Le Temple de L'Homme: Apet-du-Sud à Louqsor (Lubicz)   49
lethal enchantment   221
L'Huillier, Nicole   217
   "Dancer, The"   217
Liber 418. *See Book of the Law*

Liber AL vel Legis. See *Book of the Law*
Life of Forms in Art, The (Focillon)   29
light speed   166–7
Lil' Miquela   13–14
Liquid Orb Droplets   105–9
liquid secrecy   228
"Listening Without Ears: Artificial Intelligence in Audio Mastering" (Birtchnell)   193
LittleBigPlanet   310
living maps   178
Longo, Anna   82–3
Long Range Acoustic Devices (LRAD)   333
Lovelock, James   58
ludic intellect   336
Lukic, Dejan   83
Lyotard, Jean-Francois   347

machine-learning/machine-thinking   170, 235
machine readability   237
machine-readable artifacts   237
machines
   algorithmic art   262
   algorithmic enlightenment   264–5
   algorithmic governance   268–9
   algorithmic opacity   260
   artificial companion-species   267
   boring   269–70
   capitalism   260
   cellular   262
   contagious communication and network-control   273
   critical disinformation studies   261
   data-bodies and data-hegemony   267–8
   digital fracking of humans   270
   digital gender-gaps   260
   digital wormfare   264
   future of warfare   272
   hallucination engine   259
   history of cybernetics   265–6
   intelligent machines   273–4
   larval war-machines   263
   moral   258
   multi-purpose self-folding devices   258
   netcentricity   259
   from neuro-power to nöo-power   261
   political   259–60
   political technologies   258–9
   politics of human obsolescence   272–3
   post-human AI   261
   programming of desire   264–5
   re-engineering ecology   266–7
   resisting biometric gaze   270–1
   sophisticated molecular machines   258
   sound-object/objet-sonore   262–3
   speculative machines   262
   time   257
   (super)vision-machines   264
   war as   259
machine-to-machine communications   74
McQuillan, Dan   278
"magical" universe   47
magnetized image   198
Mahabharata   65
Mahavidyas   71
mapping time   211–12
Multidisciplinary Association for Psychedelic Studies (Maps)   248
Marclay, Christian   240
Marder, Michael   99
martial animation   301
Maruyama, Shinichi   301
Marx, Karl   29
massive addressability   38
Maternal Waters   228
Matrix, The   92–6
Matrix Oracle, the   82, 94–6, 327–8
Mazo, Ilia   155
Mbembe, Achille   278
mechanical wombs   187
mechanism/assemblage of mechanisms   63
Media Molecule   310
Meenakshi Temple, Madurai   52
Mellamphy, Dan   44, 59, 62
   on contemporary contortionism   53–4
   on demons   45–6

on djinn 45–6
on phenomenon relating temple to futurity 56
on temple 48
Mellamphy, Nandita Biswas 59, 79
   on artistic work of reign(s) 71
   on mythic example of reign 64–6
   on reign(s) 63
   on reign to futurity 74
memes 77, 187
memory parlors
   Ireland on 36–8
   phenomenon 36–8
Menard, David George 147
mental health design 334
Merton, Robert 324
messenger image 208
Metamorphoses (Mntambo) 11
"Metaverse, The" 158
Metropolis 348
Meyer, Gregoire A.
   "When the Drape Falls" 152
microgovernance of bodies 280
militarization of peace 76
Minakata Kumagusu 106
Minakata Mandala 105–9, *108*, *109*
Minotaur 6–7, *9*
mirror game 161–2
missing million 154
missing space 154
Miura, Kōryō 56
Miura fold 56
Mntambo, Nandipha 11–13
   Metamorphoses 11
   Snake You Left Inside Me, The 11, 12
   Warriors 11
Möbius-loop 238
Moctezuma II, Aztec King 324
Mode of Existence of Technical Objects (Simondon) 243
Mohaghegh, Jason 4, 117, 240
   on fate 18
   on hanging torsos 11–13
   on immortality labs 14–17
   on Minotaur 6–7, *9*
   prophetic imagination 17–18
   on Sphinx 7–8
monolith image 202

monotheism 118, 119, 124, 125, 133
monotheistic devotion 121
monotheistic enlightenment 119
monotheistic metaphysics 121
Montereggio, Giovanni Malfatti di 238
mood silhouettes 297
moral machines 258
Moses Breaking the Tablets of the Law (Rembrandt) 102
movement
   animal 174
   artificial 175
   artificial light 179
   constellations 178
   cosmic consumption 173
   elision of touch 167
   future territories 169
   hidden 180
   imperceptibility 169–70
   labyrinths 177
   light speed 166–7
   living maps 178
   machine learning 170
   nanobots 172
   peripheral 170
   perpetual prayer machines 173
   pulsation machines 172
   refrain machine 167
   scrolling 168
   seismic vibrations 170–1
   self-channeling flow 168
   spaceless movement 172
   space-movement 180
   stasis 169
   thought-movement 181
   tunnels 171
   and void 179–80
   voided forest 169
   wandering 168–9
   without end 181
movement signature 170
moving thought(s) 236
multiple personality disorder 255
multi-purpose self-folding devices 258
Munch, Edward 194
Musk, Elon 37, 355
"Mute, The" 348
Myers, Rhea

Hash Gematria 33
Proof of Work 34
myth 64–70
   Abraham's Paradox 117–23
   Arachne's Thread 102–5
   The Assyrian Idol Curse 117–23
   Book of the Law 26–9, *31*
   The Broken Tablet 102–5
   chimera 5–8, *8*, *9*
   ciphers 26–31, *31*, *32*
   Delphic Oracle 84–8
   djinn 5–6, *8*
   Egyptian temple 47–51
   Face of God 102–5
   ghoul 64–70
   Hindu temple 47–52
   Minotaur 6–7, *9*
   ouroboros (snake/dragon) 64–70
   the Ray-Cat project 47–52
   The Sibyl 84–8
   Socrates 84–8
   Sphinx 7–8
   temple 47–52
mythic image 65
mythic spaces 163
mythic symbol 65

Naidenov, Yana 206
nakedness 301
nanobots 172
nanotechnology 17, 100, 110
Nechvatal, Joseph 262
nefarious technics 291–2
Negarestani, Reza 117, 239
   Cyclonopedia 239
neo-camouflage 299
neoliberal machinery 265
neo-wonderland 297
netcentricity 259
Netflix 94
neural resistance 278
neutral time 149–50
Nezahualcoyotl 324
Nietzsche, Friedrich 62, 72–3, 120, 243–4, 253
nightmare image 202
nocturnal spectacles 303
no future tense image 205
non-ancient sound 346

non-android collaboration 347–8
non-atmosphere 347
non-city 344
non-extinction 343
non-figuration 348
Non-Future climatology 348
non-human collaboration 346
non-language 343–4
non-metropolis 348
Non-Player Character 213
non-seen 345
non-sound 346–7
non-space 227
non-theater 345–6
Non-Topia Series: The Porter 344
non-violent resistance-
   movements 259–60
Noorduin, Wim L. 189
normalization of information-
   surveillance technologies 75
Nostalgia for the Light 145
Nostradamus 322–3
Noys, Ben 74
Numan, Gary 243
NVIDIA Omniverse 308

objective zero 26
occult considerations 251–2
Oculus Quest apps 310–11
old transhumanism 292
Ollongren, Alexander 148
Omen (Halley's Comet, I) 325
Omen (Halley's Comet, II) 325–6
Omniverse 308
Onishi, Yasuaki 277
On the Mode of Existence of Technical
   Objects (Simondon) 46, 243
open-source intelligence (OSINT) 340
Oracle 82–96
   answers 82–4
   Delphic Oracle 84–8
   exhalation 88–92, *91*, *92*
   image/artwork 88–92, *91*, *92*
   The Matrix 92–6
   myth 84–8
   phenomenon 92–6
   questions 96
   the sea monk 88–92, *91*, *92*
   The Sibyl 84–8

Socrates 84–8
spiderweb 92–6
orbital return 222
origami 56–8
origamic tessellation 56
origami design-approach 56
origami sekkei 56
"Ornithographies" (Bou) 218
Orwell, George 277
Osamu Tezuka 348
Osho 328–9
Ottoman Empire 326
ouroboros 64–70, 252
outliers 355–6
Overs, Jeff 231

paleotempestological outliers 356–7
pandemic globality 279
Pape, Lygia 198
Paradise City project 160
"paradox of human fingers" 117
"paradox of idolatry" 117
Parallel Minds (Tripaldi) 99
parasitism 354
Parvati 71
Pegasus malware 289, 340–1
perfect memory/extinctive system 288
peripheral movement 170
perpetual prayer machines 173
Persian-Turko-Arabic culture 73
Persona 11
personality overlay 36
Phaedrus 88
phenomenon
 chimera 13–17
 cyborg 74–8
 drone 74–8
 immortality labs 14–17
 interoceptors 56–8
 memory parlors 36–8
 origami 56–8
 reign(s) 74–8
 temple 56–8
 virtual influencers 13–14
Physarum polycephalum 107
Plague communication 239–40
"planetary analogues" 355
Planet of the Other 355

Plato 86, 323
 Republic, The 77
playthings of future past 351
pleasure/horror flight 218
Podolnaya, Marina 145–6
point-cloud simulation 356
poison 315
Poli, Alessandro 194–5
political discourse-bots 285
political machines 259–60
political submergence 281–2
political technologies 258–9
politico-aesthetics 280
politics of human obsolescence 272–3
Politics of Possibility: Risk and Security Beyond Probability, The (Amoore) 260
polytheism 125
Pomba Gira 319
Possessor 46
post-human AI 261
posthuman body 190
postmodern resistance 283
post-mortem paths 222
post-mortem recycling 251
Povo da Rua (people of the street) 319
power 277
 advantage games 289
 AI-island headquarter 291
 anonymous challengers 288
 archaeology of the old world 280
 borderless canvas 287–8
 borderless world 278
 casualties of innocence 292
 colonial jungle 279
 cyber-assassins 287
 cyber-beyond 278–9
 cyborg biopolitics 289–90
 database and the blind eye 286
 distributed brain drone 283
 existence trading 282
 facial mapping 293
 facial recognition and the blind eye 286
 frontal lobe control 281
 futuristic veiling 291
 havoc and vulnerability 284–5
 horizon/abyss 279

ideological tricks   281
imperialist domino-effect   290
infinitely irreproducible   284
killer robots   282
microgovernance of bodies   280
nefarious technics   291–2
neural resistance   278
old transhumanism   292
pandemic globality   279
pegasus spyware   289
perfect memory/extinctive system   288
political discourse-bots   285
political submergence   281–2
politico-aesthetics   280
postmodern resistance   283
power of misrecognition   293–4
power of suggestion   285–6
pseudo-reality *vs.* the library   284
psycho-nationalism   280
race and algorithm   283
resistance of undecipherable   292–3
ricochet and camouflage   285
robotic perfectionism   278
serotonin sellers   284
stratospheric universality   282
supersonic governmentality   277–8
topographical object of the skin   287
transposed formula   281
vaporous control   277
power of misrecognition   293–4
power of suggestion   285–6
preborn image   209
precarious labor   338
predicting the future   251
prefabricated homes   335
Presley, Elvis   328
primitive algorithms   41, 45, 46
primitive futurity   149–50
primitive humanity   217
primordial cosmic energy   71
privileged moments   47
privileged places   47
programming of desire   264–5
Promethean fantasy   339
Prometheanism   76, 335
Promobot   16
Proof of Work (Myers)   34
Prophet, The (Gibran)   328

prophetic literature   328
Prophets I   322–3
Prophets II, The   323
proteus effect   249
proto-enlightenment   119
pseudo-reality *vs.* the library   284
psycho-nationalism   280
pulsation machines   172
Purgatorio (Dante)   105
Purusha   49–50

Qin Shi Huang   354
quantum perception   189
quantum properties   174–5
Quasravie, Damon   217
question   322–9
quindecimation/ quindecimagination   241–2

race and algorithm   283
Radford, Michael   247
Ramses the Second   54
rapid evolution   227
rapper, the   319–20
Rati   71
Ray-Cat project, the   47–52, 55
reality shifting   188
recurring flame   226
Redhawk, George   286
re-engineering ecology   266–7
regenerative image   200
reign(s)
    Adib-Moghaddam on   63–4
    cyborg   74–8
    defined   62–3
    image/artwork   71–4
    Mellamphy on   63
    myth   64–70
    phenomenon   74–8
    questions   79
    theme of   65
religiosity   47, 124
Rembrandt   102, 103, 105
remote work from VR   311
Republic, The (Plato)   77
resistance of undecipherable   292–3
resisting biometric gaze   270–1
return   322–9
Revich, Boris   145–6
revolutionary interruption   338

ricochet and camouflage 285
Rig Veda 49
riteless image 202
ritual 317–20
robotic perfectionism 278
Rokeby, David
   Sorting Daemon 263
Roundtree, Aimee
   Computer Simulation, Rhetoric, and the Scientific Imagination 214
Rovelli, Carlo
   Helgoland 161
Royal Botanical Gardens, Edinburgh 356
Rubaiyat (Khayyam) 290
Rum Jungle 229
Rushkoff, Douglas 51
Russian Orthodox Church 354
rustle of light 226
Ryan, McBride Charles 111–12
Rykwert, Joseph 49
   Dancing Column: On Order in Architecture 49

sacred enclosure/sacred space 48
sacrifice 317–20
safety-measures 247–8
Salafism 129
Salazar, Mauricio 145
Salazar, Robert 56
salt crystal dress 301
Sanctuary of The Covered Temple, The 54
Sand County Almanac (Leopold) 39
Saraceno, Tomás 93, 185, 199
Satellite Aperture Radar (SAR) technology 162
scaling image 200
Schild's Ladder (Egan) 146
Schmidt, Eric 282
Schulz, Bruno 170
Schwaller, René 53–4
science fiction 327
Scodanibbio, Stefano
   Voyage That Never Ends 174
scrolling 168
sea monk 88–92, *91*, *92*
seasonless image 208–9
Seaspiracy 188
Sebeok, Thomas 50

seclusion profiteers 335
secret of immortality 229
seduction 297
seismic vibrations 170–1
seize 242
self-channeling flow 168
self-consciousness 48
self-fulfilling prophecies 20
"Self-Fulfilling Prophecy" (Merton) 324
sense-organs for the upcoming zeitgeist 252–3
serotonin sellers 284
shadow worlds 162
Shahnameh 67
Shannon, Claude 235
Sheguang Hu 302
Shelley, Mary 78
   Frankenstein 78
She Who Sees the Unknown (Allahyari) 5
Sibyl, The (Lagerkvist) 84–8
Sidi Ahmad Shashkal tomb 318
sight machines 74–5
Silence of the Lambs, The 68
siliconceptions (the silicon brain) 248–9
Silicon ideology 77
silk and cement 296
Simondon, Gilbert 46, 243
   On the Mode of Existence of Technical Objects 46, 243
simulacra 238
simulations 211–14
sinking island 233
"Situated Knowledges: The Science Question in Feminism and the Privilege of Partial Perspective" (Haraway) 111
Skarsgard, Stellan 300
   Dune 300
The Sky Oscillates Between Eternity and Its Immediate Consequences 191–2
slaughterbots 263
sleeplessness 352
Snake You Left Inside Me, The (Mntambo) 11, 12
Snøhetta 161
Social Darwinist approach 338
social distancing 239
Socrates 84–8, 323, 327

sophisticated molecular
    machines 258
"Sorry, But I Have to Interrupt You at
    This Point" 338
Sorting Daemon (Rokeby) 263
sound-object/objet-sonore 262–3
space
    artificial rains 163
    badlands 157
    broken-clock universe 158
    cosmic arcs 160
    Dark Room Therapy 156–7
    dream 152
    drift 153
    emergency 159
    Gateway Experience, The 157
    genetic chaos 159
    glandular 156
    immortalizing 154
    mirror game 161–2
    missing 154
    mythic 163
    past and future of 144
    shadow worlds 162
    Space Hotel 154
    spherical resurrection 155–6
    thought-vault 157–8
    time turning in 148
    ultra-levitation 161
    veiled 152
    virtual drowning 163 4
    walking simulation 159–60
Space Hotel 154
space-movement 180
SpaceX 178
*Spacing Philosophy: Lyotard and the
    Idea of the Exhibition* 347
species hunters 332
speciesism 188
spectral image 206
speculation 322–9
speculative machines 262
Sphinx 7–8
spiderweb 92–6
spinal goggles 303
Spirit Army, The 129–33
Spriggs, David 126
The Stars My Destination (Bester) 45
stasis 169
Stiegler, Bernard 240

stilt-walkers 304
Stirner, Max 73
stochastic theory 175
stone of eternity 221
Stratachrome Master, The 123–28, *128*
stratospheric universality 282
*Studien über Anarchie und Hierarchie
    des Wissens* 238
Sufi Sea Burials 318
Sun-dimming balloon test 347
supernatural figures 232
supersonic governmentality 277–8
surface 99–113
    answers 99–102
    Arachne's Thread 102–5
    The Broken Tablet 102–5
    Chernobyl Photographs 105–9, *108, 109*
    electronic skin 110–12
    Face of God 102–5
    image/artwork 105–9, *108, 109*
    Klein Bottle house 110–12
    Liquid Orb Droplets 105–9, *108, 109*
    Minakata Mandala 105–9, *108, 109*
    myth 102–5
    phenomenon 110–12
    questions 112–13
Sutela, Jenna 106–7
swarming technique 352
swirlons 186

"tail-devourer" 66
"Tale of the Assyrian Statue, The" 121
Targeted Dream Incubation 152
Taut, Bruno 195
    "City Crown, The" 195
Taylor, Jason deCaires 164
Tearaway 310
technicity 47, 74, 77
technological artifacts 51
technological civilization 40, 44
temple
    anti-temple 57
    concept of 50
    defined 44
    image/artwork 53–5
    myth 47–52
    phenomenon 56–8

questions 58–9
   roots of word 48
Temple of Luxor 54
Terminator II: Judgement Day 107
Terrestrial Planet Finder mission 147
territories 169
terror 315
Tesla 355
Teslasuit 311
"tessellation" 56–7
"Testbed" 53–5
Tetractys, The 239
theatre of cruelty 244–5
Theban temple 54
Third World War 323
Thomas, W. I. 324
Thomas theorem 324
thought 235
   Anarchitectural Thinking (AT) 253–4
   Auto-Man empire 243
   "Battle-space of Cyberspace, The" in-and-as our networked condition 254
   becoming glitch 252
   brain as deception-organ 242–3
   calculative calcinations 239
   cross-cutting complicities 238–9
   digital eyes (digitalize) 250
   eco-destruction fashion-design 247
   Electro-Knights 240–1
   E⁽ᴹ⁾BODIME⁽ᴬ⁾NT 237
   experimental jet-set 246
   fragmented future images 255
   future fascism 247
   future safety-measures 247–8
   hallucination engine(s) 245
   hypersynchronization 240
   imperial espionage 238
   Maps (Multidisciplinary Association for Psychedelic Studies) 248
   moving thought(s) 236
   occult considerations 251–2
   Plague communication 239–40
   positions 236
   post-mortem recycling 251
   predicting the future 251
   proteus effect 249
   quindecimation/quindecimagination 241–2

seize 242
sense-organs for the upcoming zeitgeist 252–3
siliconceptions (the silicon brain) 248–9
simulacra and the möbius-loop 238
Tetractys, The 239
theatre of cruelty 244–5
Against Thinking Machines (ATM) 246
time to think 235–6
Universe of Technical Images (UTI) 237
US Navy-Pilot flying-object sightings 241
virtual-museum "trips" 249–50
ThoughtLab 235
thought-vault 157–8
Thousand and One Nights 67
threat 343–57
Three Stigmata of Palmer Eldritch, The (Dick) 267
Tigranes the Great 326
time 145–7
   and awareness 147
   complex 149–50
   cosmological deep 145
   design for communication with deep 145
   and energy 149
   interstellar space-time 147–8
   neutral 149–50
   past and future of 144
   turning in space 148
time machines 257
time to think 235–6
time-travel image 203–4
Tokyo Ghoul Anime series 67
Tokyo Night 69
Tomorrow's Gambit 350
Tondeur, Anaïs 105, 106
topographical object of the skin 287
torture 353–4
toxic eclipse 228
tracking image 209
transcendental hope image 197
transmutation 65
transposed formula 281
tremulous image 208

Tripaldi, Laura 99
tunnels 171
Turing Test 175
Tutankhamun 54
Twain, Mark 325
Twitter 14

ubiquitous connectivity 268
ultra-color 303
ultra-levitation 161
ultra-paleness 297–8
Universe of Technical Images (UTI) 237
Unmanned Lethal Weapons (UAVs) 263
Unreal Engine 307–8
Unreal Engine 5 307
unseen image 207
Urbanomic 99
US Department of Energy 50
US Navy-Pilot flying-object sightings 241
Utagawa Kuniyoshi 88

vaccine nationalism 280
VanderMeer, Jeff 34–5, 146
van Luik, Abe 50
vaporous control 277
vastupurusha 53
vastupurushamandala 49, 53–4
Vedic Vision 49
veiled space 152
Verne, Jules 327
vertical emptiness 353
vestigial futures 189
viral transformation 66
Virilio, Paul 74, 270
 War and Cinema: The Logistics of Perceptio 270
virtual 306–13
virtual drowning 163–4
virtual-museum "trips" 249–50
virtual reality (VR)
 advertisements in 310–11
 remote work from 311
(super)vision-machines 264
Vitruvian Man (Leonardo) 49
VMAX Card 52
Vodopianov, Yuri 339
void
 defined 180
 and movement 179–80
von Ranke, Leopold 73
Voyage That Never Ends (Scodanibbio) 174
Vujicic, Silvio 208

Wahhabism 129
walking simulation 159–60
Wallenstein, Sven-Olov 347
wandering 168–9
Wang Shui 190
War and Cinema: The Logistics of Perceptio (Virilio) 270
war as machines 259
warfare 272
Warriors (Mntambo) 11
Warwick, Kevin 78
waste isolation pilot plant (WIPP) 55
Watership Down (Adams) 149
wave-powered boat 179
weaponized face 300
Weber, Max 133
weird fashion 302
Weryk, Robert 208
Western culture 50
Western metaphysics 101
Western theo-ontology 101
what the no one wears 298
"When the Drape Falls" (Meyer) 152
Wiener, Norbert 271
 Cybernetics: or Control and Communication in the Animal and the Machine 271
William the Conqueror 326
Winds & Leaves (flora-builder game) 310
Witmore, Michael 38
Wolfram, Stephen 144, 145
World Trade Organization (WTO) 290

Xinhai Revolution 326
XLand 336

Yunardi, Rinaldy A. 302

Zanhour, Nada 193
Zedani, Ayman 346
Zhou, Violet 297
Zoom 14
Zupa, Rav 71